Pasold Studies in Textile History 2

Cloth and Clothing
in Medieval Europe

Eleanora Mary Carus-Wilson 1897–1977

Pasold Studies in Textile History 2

Cloth and Clothing
in Medieval Europe

Essays in Memory of Professor E. M. Carus-Wilson

Edited by
N. B. Harte and K. G. Ponting

Heinemann Educational Books
The Pasold Research Fund Ltd

Heinemann Educational Books Ltd
22 Bedford Square, London WC1B 3HH
LONDON EDINBURGH MELBOURNE AUCKLAND
HONG KONG SINGAPORE KUALA LUMPUR NEW DELHI
IBADAN NAIROBI JOHANNESBURG
EXETER (NH) KINGSTON PORT OF SPAIN

British Library Cataloguing in Publication Data

Cloth and clothing in medieval Europe. – (Pasold
studies in textile history; 2)
1. Textile industry – Europe – History – Addresses,
essays, lectures
2. Carus-Wilson, E. M.
I. Harte, N. B.   II. Ponting, K. G.
III. Carus-Wilson, E. M.   IV. Series
338.4′7677′0094   HD9865

ISBN 0-435-32382-2

The Pasold Research Fund Ltd
The Pasold Research Fund was founded by the late Mr Eric W.
Pasold in 1964 to further studies in the history of textiles. In addition
to giving grants for research, and organising a bi-annual conference
in conjunction with the Social Science Research Council, the Fund
publishes the journal *Textile History* each year. It has also brought out
a number of studies in the field.

Pasold Studies in Textile History

1 *European Textile Printers in the Eighteenth Century: A Study of Peel and
   Oberkampf* S. D. Chapman and S. Chassagne
2 *Cloth and Clothing in Medieval Europe: Essays in Memory of Professor
   E. M. Carus-Wilson* edited by N. B. Harte and K. G. Ponting
3 *The British Wool Textile Industry, 1770–1914* K. G. Ponting and
   D. Jenkins
4 *Medieval English Clothmaking: An Economic Survey* A. R. Bridbury

Filmset in Monophoto by Pearl Island Filmsetters (H.K.) Ltd. and
printed in Singapore by Koon Wah Printing Pte Ltd, for Imago
Publishing Ltd.

Contents

List of Figures

Preface

Since this collection of essays was planned in honour of Professor E. M. Carus-Wilson, it has unfortunately become a volume in her memory. She died in February 1977 in her eightieth year. Some six weeks previously she had been told of the plans in the course of a felicitous lunch with the editors, during which she was as lively and charming as ever. It seemed that she had already got to hear of what was afoot, but it was clear that she derived considerable pleasure from knowing about the scheme. In many ways so archetypically English a woman, she was conscious of the honour being done to her by so many overseas scholars, all from continental Europe and North America. This book in fact contains contributions representing no less than a dozen different nationalities. It is thus an unusually distinguished international commemoration of the work of an outstanding English scholar.

In putting it together, we as editors have been subjected to the vagaries of international communication in all manner of ways. We are indebted to the contributors for bearing with us, and for bearing with each other. To one of them, Professor John Munro of Toronto, our debt is indeed considerable. His assistance has been appreciable, and much appreciated; his profound knowledge of the subject has untangled many puzzles for us. In particular, he generously undertook overseeing the revision of the article by Dr Veronika Gervers, whose tragically early death took place soon after she had submitted the draft of her contribution.

We have accumulated other debts of gratitude. The advice of Olive Coleman of the London School of Economics has been most helpful throughout. So too, at various points, has been that of Dr Frank Carter, Dr David d'Avray, David Morgan and Dr Helen Clarke of University College London, Professor Joyce Youings of the University of Exeter, Professor Mark Whiting of the University of Bristol, Dr

Jordan Goodman of the University of Essex, Professor Christopher Brooke of the University of Cambridge, Dr David Wilson, Director of the British Museum and Simon Lloyd, formerly of Heinemann's, our agreeable publishers, now of the University of Newcastle. Ruby Way of the Pasold Research Fund provided skilled typing assistance with material that sometimes appeared intractable. We are indebted to them, and to a good few others. We are grateful to Westfield College for permission to reproduce the Baron photograph which appears as the frontispiece.

London   N.B.H.
Bath   K.G.P.

1 Introduction
N. B. Harte and K. G. Ponting

Most of the scholarship of the late Professor E. M. Carus-Wilson was devoted to the economic history of the European textile industry in the Middle Ages. The present volume consists of further contributions to this field made by a number of scholars who wish to mark their deep gratitude to her and to her work. It is appropriate that it should open with a record of Professor Carus-Wilson's life and work.

I

Eleanora Mary Carus-Wilson lived for nearly eighty years. She was born in Montreal on 27 December 1897, and she died in London, where she spent nearly all her life, on 1 February 1977.[1] Her forbears appositely figure both in Burke's *Landed Gentry* and in the Catalogue of the British Library. The first Carus-Wilson evolved in 1793 when by sign manual William Carus added the name and took the arms of Wilson on succeeding to the estates of his mother's family at Casterton Hall in Westmorland. William Carus-Wilson (1764–1851) served briefly as MP for Cockermouth and for over fifty years as a JP in Westmorland, Lancashire and the West Riding of Yorkshire. His son, the Revd William Carus-Wilson (1791–1859), was a religious and philanthropic writer of repute, who became Chaplain to the Duke of Sussex and founder of the school at Casterton made famous by the Brontë sisters. In turn, his second son, the Revd Charles Carus-Wilson (1825–77) was also a theological writer, serving as Vicar of Eastry in Kent and as Vicar of Ramsgate. In the next generation, one of his

[1]Obituary tributes are to be found in *The Times*, 7 February 1977 and 11 February 1977, in the *Economic History Review*, 2nd ser., XXX, 2 (May 1977), pp. iii–v (by Joyce Youings) and in *Textile History*, VIII (1977), p. 5. We have also drawn on the address given by the Principal of Westfield College at the thanksgiving service in her memory on 28 April 1977, for which we are indebted to Dr Bryan Thwaites.

sons, Charles Ashley Carus-Wilson (1860–1942), educated at Hailey-
bury and Pembroke College, Cambridge, became Professor of Electri-
cal Engineering at McGill University in Montreal for some years in
the 1890s. Soon after his daughter Eleanora was born, he produced
his book on *Electro-Dynamics* and returned to England to practise
in London as a consulting engineer. He had married Mary Louisa
Georgina Petrie (1861–1935), whose father had been one of the
founders of Westfield College and who herself had been one of the first
women students at University College London in 1878 before going to
Westfield as the College's first lecturer in English.[2] She established a
reputation as a writer on Christian and missionary subjects. Both
Eleanora Carus-Wilson's parents, like her earlier forbears, lived up
to the old Wilson motto: *Non nobis solum* – not for ourselves alone.

Nora Carus-Wilson was brought up at Hanover Lodge, her mother's
family house north of Holland Park that was to remain her own home
for the rest of her life. She was educated at St Paul's Girls' School and
then – naturally enough – at Westfield College, where she graduated
in history in 1921. At home she developed her lifelong attachment to
Christian life and practice; at St Paul's, where Gustav Holst taught,
she developed her lifelong passion for music, and at Westfield she
developed her lifelong fascination for medieval history. She was inspired there by Caroline Skeel, the first teacher at Westfield College
given the status of a professor in the University of London and who,
in 1926, was to be among the founder members of the Economic
History Society.

For some years after graduating, Carus-Wilson taught for part of
her week in a boarding school, returning to London for the rest of
the week to pursue her medieval researches. She chose Bristol, with
special reference to its overseas trade, as her subject, and in 1926 was
awarded an MA with distinction for her thesis. Her first publication,
on the merchant adventurers of Bristol in the fifteenth century,
appeared in the *Transactions of the Royal Historical Society* in 1928. It
was followed in 1929 in the second volume of the *Economic History
Review* by what she modestly called 'a criticism' of the fifteenth-century
aulnage accounts, elegantly and devastatingly exposing them as 'works
of art rather than transcripts of fact'. This subject was one suggested
to her by Eileen Power (1889–1940), then Reader in Economic
History at the London School of Economics, a much-loved woman of
enormous ability and style, who was a great influence on her. Carus-
Wilson was a member of the famous seminar that Eileen Power
conducted on medieval economic history, and she contributed two

---

[2] We are obliged to Dr Janet Sondheimer for information concerning Mary Petrie from the
Westfield College archives.

memorable articles on the overseas trade of Bristol and on the Iceland trade to the important volume produced by the seminar.[3] The article on Bristol is illustrated with her own carefully drawn maps which give an idea of her calligraphy to those not fortunate enough to have been among her many correspondents.

The award of a Leverhulme Research Fellowship in 1936–38 afforded Carus-Wilson the opportunity of extending her interests into the great cloth industry of medieval England. Her work on this, the central scholarly interest of her life, was interrupted by some years of wartime exile to Colwyn Bay as a temporary civil servant with the Ministry of Food. Despite the exigencies of that period, she produced two seminal articles for the *Economic History Review*, and at the end of the war she returned to London to take up her first full-time academic appointment at the age of 48. Eileen Power had died suddenly in 1940, and her successor in the chair of economic history at the London School of Economics was T. S. Ashton, a distinguished economic historian, but no medievalist. Ashton offered Carus-Wilson a lectureship with responsibility for the teaching of medieval economic history, and she was delighted to accept it. Promotion came rapidly; she became a Reader in 1948 and in 1953 a personal chair was created for her. The LSE became her academic home for the rest of her life.

Articles developing her established interests continued to flow – regularly if not often – from her pen, notably her characteristically lucid survey of the medieval European woollen industry in the *Cambridge Economic History of Europe*.[4] She embarked on two major projects, one of which unfortunately remained incomplete at the time of her death. The first was an exhaustive study of the complex documents which yield a detailed statistical portrait of English overseas trade in the important period between 1275 and 1547. She undertook this in co-operation with Olive Coleman, and their definitive work on this subject was published in 1963. The continuity and comprehensiveness of the figures thus made available for English wool and cloth exports are without parallel in the rest of Europe. Second, she began to prepare a full study of the English cloth industry from Roman times to the sixteenth century, and after many years of work on all the surviving sources, she gave, in 1965, the Ford lectures at Oxford on this subject, a development of the memorable lectures Eileen Power had delivered in the same series on the wool trade shortly before her premature death. The Carus-Wilson lectures were equally memorable, masterly – and

---

[3] Eileen Power and M. M. Postan (eds.), *Studies in English Trade in the Fifteenth Century* (London, 1933). A full bibliography of E. M. Carus-Wilson's writings, compiled by Olive Coleman, is to be found on pp. 7–9.

[4] This was revised shortly before her death for a new edition of the volume, publication of which is expected shortly.

masterful – in terms both of substance and of delivery. The major book which should have developed from them remained, however, unfinished. Perfection remained beyond a perfectionist's grasp.

She was true to her main interests throughout her life. Her last publication, in 1975, dealt with Bristol, as had her first, in 1928. Several of her articles were gathered together in 1954 in a book entitled *Medieval Merchant Venturers*. 'Though diverse in origin and content', she explained, 'they have in fact a common theme . . . ' She went on:

> they are all concerned with England's oversea commercial ventures in the later middle ages and with the native English woollen industry whose remarkable growth during that period so transformed those ventures that England ceased to be the Australia of the middle ages, supplying raw wool to more highly developed industrial societies on the continent, and herself became Europe's principal producer of manufactured woollens.[5]

Besides developing this critical theme in Britain's history, it is a volume which easily disproves the old jibe that economic history is full of every sort of figure except the human. Numbers there certainly are, but the realities of social life and of the lives of once-living individuals are never overlooked. Quantities, she believed, were the beginning, not the end, of historical study, posing questions as much as answering them.[6] The quality of her writing, moreover, ensured that her work was readily accessible to non-specialists, a delight for any literate person to read.

Her deep sense of the reality of the past, combined with her love for exploring the countryside by bicycle and on foot – 'mountains', after all, were coupled with 'music' as her interests in *Who's Who* – led her to be concerned with historical topography and with the developing discipline of medieval archaeology. She contributed an article on the significance in terms of textile technology of the sculptures in the Lane Chapel at Cullompton in Devon to the first number of *Medieval Archaeology* in 1957. She went on to play a leading part in organising the series of excavations in King's Lynn, as Chairman of the King's Lynn Archaeological Survey Advisory Committee from 1963 until her death.[7]

The volume of *Essays in Economic History* which she edited in 1954, followed by two more in 1962, made her even better known; her name

---

[5] E. M. Carus-Wilson, *Medieval Merchant Venturers* (2nd edn, 1967), p. ix.

[6] E. M. Carus-Wilson and Olive Coleman, *England's Export Trade, 1275–1547* (Oxford, 1963), p. 33.

[7] Her part is acknowledged in the two volumes of the King's Lynn Archaeological Survey which have been published to date – Vanessa Parker, *The Making of King's Lynn: Secular Buildings from the Eleventh to the Seventeenth Century* (Chichester, 1971) and Helen Clarke and Alan Carter, *Excavations in King's Lynn, 1963–70* (Society for Medieval Archaeology, Monograph Series, VII, 1977), the second of which is dedicated to her.

became familiar to generations of students. These three volumes were a product of her chairmanship between 1951 and 1967 of a committee of the Economic History Society which laid the foundations of its successful publishing policy. She served as a member of the Society's Council for many years, becoming its President in 1966–69 in succession to her fellow medievalist, Professor Sir Michael Postan. In the same years she served too as President of the Society for Medieval Archaeology. She filled these offices with considerable grace and distinction after her nominal retirement from the London School of Economics in 1965, after which she became an Emeritus Professor. In 1969 she was made an Honorary Fellow of the School. Other recognitions naturally came her way; she became an Associate Member of the Royal Academy of Belgium in 1961, a Fellow of the British Academy in 1963 and in 1968 Smith College, Massachusetts, made her an honorary doctor. In her last years, she was increasingly involved again in the affairs of Westfield College. Her only publication outside her chosen field was her jubilee history of the College in 1932, and in 1967 she became Vice-Chairman of the College's governing body and in 1974 President of the Westfield College Association. A hall of residence at the College has appropriately been named after her. It was on her way to preside over a meeting of the governing body at Westfield that, almost as trim and youthful as ever, she suddenly collapsed and died.

To the end, she remained committed to the young and especially to those who wanted to pursue her own interests. She offered much encouragement to the Pasold Research Fund's efforts on behalf of textile history, and was a regular attender at its conferences. Many will cherish the memory at such a meeting of Nora Carus-Wilson challenging one of the editors of this volume on a specific point concerned with dyeing, a subject with which he had had much practical experience. 'But I've done it myself', she said, with a toss of her head, 'in my kitchen sink'. It was a devastating moment. The other editor remembers her giving a graphic account of her time pulling flax during the First World War. Brought up in an era when young ladies were not expected to be domesticated, she added practical experience to her knowledge of the documents.

II

The essays that follow fall into three groups. Those in Part I deal with the technical properties of textiles or the fibres from which they were made, and with the techniques of weaving and dyeing. Several of the contributions in this group deal in various ways with aspects of the subject which attracted Carus-Wilson's especial interest. One in particular appears finally to unravel the mystery of 'scarlet'. Part II consists of essays dealing with the textile industries or the textile trades on a regional basis, from the earliest cloth guild in Brabant in the thirteenth century to Fugger enterprise in sixteenth-century Germany. Part III deals with some of the uses to which textiles were put, especially as clothing of various types. It includes a survey of the earliest form of 'ready-made' clothing, that produced by the rise of knitting. Some of the contributions are thus more particular, some more general; but all bear upon a theme of major significance in the economic development of Europe.

2 A List of the Published Writings of E. M. Carus-Wilson
Compiled by Olive Coleman

'The merchant adventurers of Bristol in the fifteenth century', *Transactions of the Royal Historical Society*, 4th ser. IX (1928); revised and reprinted as a pamphlet by the Historical Association, Bristol branch (University of Bristol, 1962).

'The aulnage accounts: a criticism', *Economic History Review*, II, i (1929); reprinted in *Medieval Merchant Venturers*, q.v.

(Ed.), *Westfield College, University of London 1882–1932* (London, Favil Press for Westfield College, 1932).

'The origins and early development of the merchant adventurers' organization in London as shown in their own medieval records', *Economic History Review*, IV, ii (1933); reprinted in *Medieval Merchant Venturers*, q.v.

'The overseas trade of Bristol in the fifteenth century' in E. Power and M. M. Postan (eds.), *Studies in English Trade in the Fifteenth Century* (London, Routledge & Kegan Paul, 1933; reprinted, 1951 and New York, Barnes & Noble, 1967); reprinted in *Medieval Merchant Venturers*, q.v.

'The Iceland venture' in E. Power and M. M. Postan (eds.), *Studies in English Trade in the Fifteenth Century*, ut supra; reprinted in *Medieval Merchant Venturers*, q.v.

(Ed.), *The Overseas Trade of Bristol in the Later Middle Ages* (Bristol Record Society Publications, VII, 1936); reprinted, with a new preface and additional bibliography (London, Merlin Press, 1967; New York, Barnes & Noble, 1968).

'An industrial revolution of the thirteenth century', *Economic History Review*, XI, i (1941); reprinted in *Medieval Merchant Venturers*, q.v. and in *Essays in Economic History*, q.v., vol. I.

'The English cloth industry in the late twelfth and early thirteenth centuries', *Economic History Review*, XIV, i (1944); reprinted in *Medieval Merchant Venturers*, q.v.

'The effects of the acquisition and of the loss of Gascony on the English wine trade', *Bulletin of the Institute of Historical Research*, XXI, 63 (1947); reprinted in *Medieval Merchant Venturers*, q.v.

'Trends in the export of English woollens in the fourteenth century', *Economic History Review*, 2nd ser., III, ii (1950); reprinted in *Medieval Merchant Venturers*, q.v.

'The woollen industry' in M. M. Postan and E. E. Rich (eds.), *The Cambridge Economic History of Europe*, II (Cambridge, CUP, 1952).

'La guède française en Angleterre: un grand commerce du moyen âge', *Revue du Nord*, XXXV, 138 (1953).

Medieval Merchant Venturers (London, Methuen, 1954; 2nd edn., London, Methuen, and New York, Barnes & Noble, 1967).

(Ed.), *Essays in Economic History*; reprints edited for the Economic History Society, 3 volumes (Vol. I, London, Edward Arnold and New York, St Martin's Press, 1954; Vols. II and III, London, Edward Arnold, 1962 and New York, St Martin's Press, 1963; Vols. I, II and III, New York, St Martin's Press, 1966).

'The significance of the secular sculptures in the Lane Chapel, Cullompton', *Medieval Archaeology*, I (1957).

'Towns and trade' in A. L. Poole (ed.), *Medieval England* (Oxford, Clarendon Press, 1958).

'Evidences of industrial growth on some fifteenth-century manors', *Economic History Review*, 2nd ser., XII, ii (1959); reprinted in *Essays in Economic History*, q.v., vol. II.

'The woollen industry before 1550' in *The Victoria History of the Counties of England: Wiltshire*, IV (London, Institute of Historical Research, 1959).

'Études faites depuis 1945, sur les "Customs Accounts" Anglais au moyen âge' in *Actes du Quatrième Colloque Internationale d'Histoire Maritime* (1959) (Paris, 1962).

'The medieval trade of the ports of the Wash', *Medieval Archaeology*, VI–VII (1962–63).

The Expansion of Exeter at the Close of the Middle Ages, Harte Memorial Lecture in Local History, 1961 (Exeter, University of Exeter, 1963).

(With Olive Coleman), *England's Export Trade 1275–1547* (Oxford, Clarendon Press, 1963).

'The first half-century of the Borough of Stratford-upon-Avon, *Economic History Review*, 2nd ser., XVIII, i (1965).

'Haberget: a medieval textile conundrum', *Medieval Archaeology*, XIII (1969).

'The oversea trade of late medieval Coventry' in *Économies et Sociétés au Moyen Age: Mélanges offerts à Edouard Perroy* (Paris, Publications de la Sorbonne, Série: Etudes, t. 5, 1973).

'Die Hanse und England' in *Hanse in Europe: Brucke Zwischen den Märkten 12. – 17. Jahrhundert*, Ausstellung des Kölnischen Stadtmuseums, 9. Juni – 9 September, 1973 (Cologne, 1973).

(With M. D. Lobel), 'Bristol' in M. D. Lobel (ed.), *Historic Towns*, II (London, Scolar Press, and Baltimore, Johns Hopkins University, in association with the Historic Towns Trust, 1975).

Part One

3 The Medieval Scarlet and the Economics of Sartorial Splendour[1]
John H. Munro

Introduction

The origins and nature of the medieval scarlet, a term originally applied to a textile and only later to the colour, are an historical enigma that has intrigued scholars for generations. In this century, the debate has focused on two rival theories. According to the first and much older theory, the European scarlet was originally an imitation of a highly luxurious garment (composition unknown) from the Islamic East, probably Persia. According to the second, it was instead a woollen of Flemish origin, whose luxury qualities and exceptionally high price were determined essentially by the shearing and complementary finishing processes. Proponents of both theories would agree, however, that dyeing was initially not a prime consideration, since scarlets were originally produced in a wide range of colours.

The burden of this essay is that both theories are defective; and that, whatever the ultimate etymological origin of the term, medieval scarlets owed their splendour, fame, and high cost to the dyeing processes. The first part of this complex topic deals with scarlet and purple, as two closely related colour spectrums, in the ancient and medieval worlds; the second, with the rival 'Persian' and 'Flemish' etymologies; the third, with the textile itself, in particular the weaving, shearing, and dyeing processes; the fourth, with post-medieval innovations in dyeing that produced the colour we now know as scarlet; and the final section, with a summary analysis of production costs and relative values of scarlets as medieval garments of sartorial splendour.

[1] I wish to thank the following scholars for their most valuable advice and assistance: Marta Hoffmann (Oslo), Liliane Masschelein-Kleiner (Brussels), Max Saltzman (Los Angeles), Nobuko Kajitani (New York), Kenneth Ponting (Bath); and from Toronto, the late Veronika Gervers, Michael Gervers, Hartwig Mayer, Harry Roe, Michael Herren, George Rigg, Andrew Watson, Richard Taylor and Edward Heinemann.

I

The woollen scarlet was incontestably the most renowned luxury textile manufactured in medieval Europe, even if rivalled and often surpassed in value by oriental and Italian silks.[2] Scarlets, worn by popes, emperors, kings, and princes, were indeed the medieval European successor to the famed 'royal purples' of the classical and Byzantine worlds.[3] Both terms, purple and scarlet, developed dual meanings in their own eras: the most aristocratic of textiles, and the rich lustrous colours associated with them. The two colours, or spectrums of colour, were in fact closely related; and both were produced from costly animal dyestuffs.[4]

To the Classical and Byzantine worlds, 'purple' ($\pi o \rho \phi \upsilon \rho \alpha$, *purpura*, *purpureus*) designated not a unique purple, but several colours and shades produced from the glandular mucus of various related Mediterranean and Atlantic molluscs of the whelk family: principally the *Murex brandaris*, *Murex trunculus* and *Purpura haemastoma*. By selecting various combinations of dyestuffs from these molluscs, by varying their exposure to sunlight, by using several additives (salt, honey, urine, orchil), dyers could achieve a wide range of colours: light to dark purples, violets, heliotropes, deep-red blacks, reddish browns, sanguine, crimson, rose-reds, blues and even shades of green. The famous Tyrian purple, known as *blatta* ($\beta \lambda \alpha \tau \tau \alpha$) – literally 'congealed blood' – was a mélange of deep violet and scarlet-hued purple dyes, produced from the *Murex brandaris* and *Purpura haemastoma* respectively. Indeed, the majority of 'royal purples' seem to have been rather more red than blue in appearance. Although such purples might vary considerably in price, according to their composition, even the cheapest was far more costly than any other dyestuffs, because so many of these rare, perishable molluscs were required to produce the dyestuff. Thus, for example, 1200 murexes (*Murex brandaris*) would yield only 1.4 grams of 6–6′

---

[2] For a comparison of textile prices, see Table 13.3 in John H. Munro, 'Industrial protectionism in medieval Flanders: urban or national?' in Harry Miskimin, David Herlihy and Abraham Udovitch (eds.), *The Medieval City* (New Haven, 1977), pp. 257–63; and Tables 3.14–3.15 in this book.

[3] See in particular Christopher Rowe, 'Conceptions of colour and colour symbolism in the ancient world' in Adolf Portmann and Rudolf Ritsema (eds.), *The Realms of Colour* (*Eranos Yearbook 1972*, vol. 42), (Leiden, 1974), pp. 359–60; Jacques André, *Étude sur les termes de couleur dans la langue latine* (*Études et commentaires* no. 7), (Paris, 1949), pp. 88–102; Lucien Gerschel, 'Couleur et teinture chez divers peuples indo-européens', *Annales: E.S.C.*, XXI (1966), pp. 608–30.

[4] Often no great distinction was made between the two colour terms in the ancient world. Thus two of the gospels state that soldiers dressed Christ in 'purple' robes before His crucifixion: Mark 15: 17 and John 19: 2; the other two, in 'scarlet' robes: Matthew 27: 28 and Luke 23: 11. Cf. *Holy Bible: King James Version* (1611) and *The New Testament According to the Eastern Text*, G. M. Lamsa, (ed.) (Philadelphia, 1940), from the original Aramaic. The argument will be substantiated in the course of this essay; but see also the sources cited in nn. 3 above and 5 below.

dibromindigo dye.[5] According to Diocletian's Edict of Maximum Prices of AD 301, one pound (327.5 g) of wool dyed in μεταξαβλαττης, the best purple, was worth the same as one pound of refined gold: 50 000 denarii.[6] In Diocletian's edict, and throughout the Classical world, both the colour now called scarlet and the textile so dyed were then known as *coccum* or *coccina* (adjectival forms: *coccinus*, *coccineus*, *coccinatus*), from the Greek κοκκος, meaning a berry.[7] Indeed the substance that produced this rich red colour appeared to be a small bluish berry; but in fact it was an insect, a pregnant one. Just as with 'royal purple', not one but several related species produced this dyestuff. By far the most important for ancient and medieval Europe were two scale-insects or shield-lice of the Coccidae family (genus *Coccus*), each of which was parasitic upon a particular species of evergreen Mediterranean oak: the *Kermococcus vermilio*, living on the so-called kermes oak *Quercus coccifera* (πρινος to the Greeks); and the *Coccus ilicis*, infesting the holm oak *Quercus ilex* (σμιλαξ to the Greeks).[8] According to Pliny

[5] See Robert Forbes, 'Dyes and dyeing' in *Studies in Ancient Technology*, 2nd rev. edn, 9 vols. (Leiden, 1964), IV, pp. 114–22; L. B. Jensen, 'Royal purple of Tyre', *Journal of Near Eastern Studies*, XXII (1963), pp. 104–18; Wolfgang Born, 'Purple', *Ciba Review*, no. 4 (December 1937), pp. 106–29; R. A. Donkin, 'Spanish red: An ethnogeographical study of cochineal and the opuntia cactus', *Transactions of the American Philosophical Society*, vol. 67: part 5 (Philadelphia, 1977), pp. 7–8; André, *Termes de couleur* (n. 3 above), pp. 90–102. For contemporary accounts, see Pliny the Elder (AD 23–79), *Natural History*, edited and translated (Latin and English texts) by Harris Rackham, W. H. S. Jones, D. E. Eicholz, 10 vols. (London, Loeb Classical Library, 1938–62), III, pp. 246–59 (Book IX.125–41); IX, pp. 292–5 (Book XXXV.44); Isidore of Seville (AD 570–636), *Isidori Hispalensis episcopi etymologiarum sive originum, libri XX* [hereafter Isidore, *Etymologiarum*], W. M. Lindsay (ed.), 2 vols. (Oxford, 1911), II, Book XIX.xxviii.1–7, xxiv.8.

[6] For comparison, some other prices from Diocletian's edict: 1 lb of wool (12 oz = 327.5 g) dyed in other Tyrian purples: 32 000 and 16 000 denarii; 1 lb wool dyed in scarlet with Nicene kermes (κοκκηρας – see below): only 1500 den.; 1 lb of 'washed wool from Tarentum', the best listed: just 175 den.; a stone mason's daily wage: 50 den. Tenney Frank (ed.), *An Economic Survey of Ancient Rome*, 5 vols. (Baltimore, 1933–40), V, pp. 338, 382–4, 412. I owe this reference to the late Veronika Gervers.

[7] The colour was also called *puniceus*, *punicus*, *poeniceus*, *phoenicus*, *phoeniceam*, because the ancient Phoenicians were reputed to have originated dyeing in scarlet. For contemporary descriptions, see: Theophrastus (BC 371–287), *Enquiry into Plants and Minor Works on Odours*, edited and translated (Greek and English texts) by Arthur Hort, 2 vols. (London and New York, 1916), I, pp. 198–201 (Book III.vii.3–5: 'και η πρινος τον φοινικουν [Latin *phoenicus*] κοκκον'); I, pp. 208–9 (Book III.viii.6); I, pp. 258–9 (Book III.xvi.1–2: 'κοκκον τινα φοινικουν'); Pliny, *Natural History*, III, pp. 258–9 (Book IX.lxv.140–1); IV, pp. 398–9 (Book XVI.viii.19–21); IV, pp. 408–9 (Book XVI.xii.32); VI, pp. 294–6 (Book XXII.iii.3–5); VII, pp. 8–9 (Book XXIV, iv, 8); Isidore, *Etymologiarum*, II, Book XIX.xxii.10, XIX.xxviii.1 ('Russata, quam Graeci phoeniceam vocant, nos coccinam'); André, *Termes de couleur* (n. 3 above), pp. 88–90, 116–17; H. Michel, 'κοκκος or kermes', *The Classical Review*, new ser., V (1955), p. 246; Charleton Lewis and Charles Short, *A Latin Dictionary* (Oxford, 1879; reissued 1966), p. 357. See also n. 8 below.

[8] See n. 7 above and J. and Charles Cotte, 'Le kermès dans l'Antiquité', *Revue archéologique*, 5th ser., VII (1918), pp. 92–112; Wolfgang Born, 'Scarlet', *Ciba Review*, no. 7 (March 1938), pp. 206–27; Stuart Robinson, *A History of Dyed Textiles* (Cambridge, Mass., 1969), pp. 23–5; Guy de Poerck, *La draperie médiévale en Flandre et en Artois: technique et terminologie*, 3 vols. (Bruges, 1951), I, pp. 181–2, II, p. 100; III, p. 51; Maurice Lombard, *Les textiles dans le monde musulman, VIIe–XIIe siècles* (*Etudes d'économie médiévale*, vol. III), (Paris, 1978), pp. 119–22; Forbes, 'Dyes' (n. 5 above), IV, pp. 102–6; Donkin, *Spanish Red* (n. 5 above), pp. 9–10. See also nn. 10 and 13 below.

the Elder (AD 23–79), the best varieties of these *cocci* were to be found in Portugal and adjacent parts of Spain (*Lusitania*), Tunisia (*Africa*), and parts of Asia Minor (*Galatia, Pisidia, Cilicea*); the worst, from Sardinia.[9] In medieval times, they were also cultivated in Provence and Languedoc, Valencia and Andalusia, Morocco and the Maghreb, Greece, the Aegean islands and Crete.

Medieval Europe also obtained some very similar scarlet dyestuffs, though in far smaller amounts, from two other members of the Coccidae family, one Asian and the other east European. The Asian insect, now called *Porphyrophora hameli*, was found principally in the Caucasus lands of Armenia, Georgia and Azerbaijan, and also in adjacent parts of Anatolia and Iran. Arabic and other eastern writers confused it with the two Mediterranean *Cocci*, even though it fed not upon oaks but a species of wild grass, *Dactylis litoralis*, also called Piminella and Poa-Punges. It was reputedly unexcelled for its scarlet dyes, and was certainly very expensive.[10] Its close cousin in eastern Europe, however, produced the least-esteemed scarlet dyestuff. Known in the medieval era as 'St John's Blood' (from the 24 June harvest), it came from a shield-louse living on the roots of the knawel or scleranth plant, *Scleranthus perennis*, cultivated in Poland, Prussia, Saxony, Lithuania and the Ukraine. The more modern names for this scale-insect are *Coccus polonicus, Margarodes polonicus, Porphyrophora polonica* and, most popularly, Polish cochineal.[11] That last term, of course, came to be applied in apposition to the much more renowned, closely related coccid, Mexican cochineal, introduced into European textile dyeing only from the sixteenth century.[12] The scarlet dye of this cochineal is produced by carminic acid; this same chemical, according to some authorities, was also found in *Coccus polonicus* and *Porphyrophora hameli*.

---

[9] Pliny, *Natural History* (n. 5 above), III, pp. 258–9 (Book ix.lxv.140–1: 'Coccum Galatiae rubens granum ... aut Emeritam Lusitaniae in maxima laude est'); IV, pp. 408–9 (Book xvi.xii.32); VI, pp. 294–6 (Book xxii.iii.305). According to the Venetian dyer-author of *Plictho de l'arte de tentori* (1548), the best varieties of this dyestuff came from southern Italy (Puglia to Calabria), Valencia, and 'Spain', respectively; but elsewhere he ranks those from Armenia first, those from Syria second, and those from Spain third. Gioanventura Rosetti, *The Plictho*, trans. and ed. S. M. Edelstein and H. C. Borghetty (Cambridge, Mass. 1969), no. 46, pp. 108–9, 94 respectively. See also n. 10.

[10] H. Kurdian, 'Ḳirmiz', *Journal of the American Oriental Society*, LXI (1941), pp. 105–7; G. Levi della Vida, 'On Ḳirmiz', ibid., LXI (1941), pp. 287–8; Forbes 'Dyes' (n. 5 above), IV, pp. 102–4; Donkin, *Spanish Red* (n. 5 above), pp. 8–10; Lombard, *Les textiles* (n. 8 above), pp. 119–22. See also nn. 9, 12, and 76.

[11] Born, 'Scarlet' (n. 8 above), pp. 208–9; Lombard, *Les textiles*, (n. 8), pp. 119–22; Donkin, *Spanish Red* (n. 5 above), p. 10; Forbes, 'Dyes' (n. 5 above), IV, p. 102. Similar dye-bearing insects of Russia are the *Coccus fragariae* and *Coccus uvae ursi*, inhabiting the strawberry and bearberry bushes, respectively. See also nn. 8, 10, 12 and 13.

[12] See below p. 63 and nn. 117–18.

The other two Mediterranean *cocci*, however, contained a somewhat different dyeing agent: kermesic acid.[13]

The female Mediterranean *Cocci*, the *Cocci polonici*, and presumably also the Armenian *Cocci*, were harvested in May and June, just before their eggs were laid. They were then killed by vinegar vapours and dried in the sun until turning a dark brownish red. Their dessicated bodies, with the eggs, were crushed and mixed with water to produce the scarlet dye (which was 'fixed' with alum, the standard mordant). Once dessicated, this dyestuff could be stored for long periods and be transported over great distances without any impairment in quality. In that respect scarlet dyes enjoyed a great advantage over the 'royal purple', which could be produced only from freshly caught shellfish of the afore-mentioned types.[14] That severe limitation undoubtedly assisted the Roman and then Byzantine governments in making purple-dyeing a highly restricted state monopoly from the reign of Emperor Alexander Severus (AD 225–35).[15] The very nature of the scarlet dyestuffs, with their widely dispersed sources and high portability, did not permit such a royal monopoly, not even in the days of the centralised Roman Empire. In the medieval era, scarlet dyeing flourished in almost all major textile towns across Europe that had ready commercial access to these *Cocci*.

The term *coccum* itself, however, died out in later Roman or early medieval times. Because this dyestuff resembled small seeds or grains when dessicated, it acquired that very name in various medieval European languages: *granum* in Latin; *grana* in Italian, Spanish and Portuguese; *graine* in French; *grein* in German and Dutch; *grain* in

[13] According to Judith Hofenk-De Graaff and Wilma Roelofs, *On the Occurrence of Red Dyestuffs in Textile Materials from the Period 1450–1600* (International Council of Museums, Madrid, 1972), pp. 6–9, the formulae for carminic acid is $C_{22}H_{20}O_{13}$; and for kermesic acid, $C_{18}H_{12}O_9$. The same formulae for kermesic acid but a slightly different one for carminic acid, $C_{22}H_{22}O_{13}$, is given in M. Edouard Justin-Mueller, 'Cochenille et kermès', *Bulletin de la société chimique de France*, 4th ser., vol. XXXIX (1926), pp. 791–2, no. 77, Subsequently, in her essay, 'The chemistry of red dyestuffs in medieval and early modern Europe', published in this volume (pp. 71–9. Mme Hofenk-De Graaff has given a revised formula for kermesic acid: $C_{16}H_{10}O_3$. She also maintains, in *Red Dyestuffs*, p. 8, that the chemical composition of Polish cochineal 'is a mixture of carminic acid and kermesic acid'; but she notes the contention of other authorities that it contains carminic acid alone. For this latter view (re *Coccus polonicus*, *Porphyrophora hameli*), see also Walter Endrei and L. Hajnal, 'Analyse de colorants pour textiles', *Bulletin de liaison du centre international d'étude des textiles anciens*, no. 13 (January 1961), p. 38; Kurdian, 'Ḳirmiz' (n. 10 above), pp. 105–7; Forbes, 'Dyes' (n. 5 above), IV, p. 102.

[14] See sources cited in nn. 5, 8, 10 and 13 above.

[15] In AD 369, the Roman imperial government made the monopoly even more restrictive by reserving for its exclusive use all purple-dyed products. After the fall of the western Empire, purple-manufacturing came to be concentrated largely at Constantinople. See F. W. Walbank, 'Trade and industry under the later Roman Empire', *Cambridge Economic History of Europe*, II (Cambridge, 1952), pp. 72–4; Steven Runciman, 'Byzantine trade and industry', ibid., II, pp. 103–15; E. M. Carus-Wilson, 'The woollen industry', ibid., II, pp. 359–62; Etienne Sabbe, 'L'importation des tissus orientaux en Europe occidentale au haut moyen âge, IXe et Xe siècles', *Revue belge de philologie et d'histoire*, XIV (1935), pp. 811–48, 1261–88; Born, 'Purple' (n. 5 above), pp. 121–4.

English. Pliny himself had called it 'rubens granum'.[16] In the medieval Arabic world, however, both the coccid insects and their dyestuff were called *ḳirmiz*, meaning a worm (derived from the Persian and Armenian *karmir*, from the Sanskrit *kirmir, kirmidja*). Such a description is to be found in numerous medieval Arabic and Persian texts (which almost invariably assumed that *Kermococcus vermilio, Coccus ilicis* and *Porphyrophora hameli* were all the same 'worm').[17] Indeed even Pliny had also described *coccum* (berry) as a 'little worm': *scolecium* and *vermiculum*. Then St Jerome, in compiling the *Vulgate* Bible *c.* AD 390, also used *vermiculus* to mean 'scarlet' in Exodus 35 : 25. From that time, if not before, this word gradually displaced *coccum, coccina* in popular usage; and certainly in Carolingian times, at the latest, a scarlet-dyed garment was usually called *vermiculatus* rather than the older *coccina, coccinea*.[18] Our word vermilion, a scarlet shade, comes of course from *vermiculus* via the French *vermeil*. But all the modern European names for the Mediterranean *cocci* and their scarlet dyestuff are based not on the Latin but the Arabic: *kermes* in English, German, Portuguese and Dutch; *kermès* in French; *chermes* in Italian; and *carmes* in Spanish. Crimson is also derived from the same Arabic word, in its adjectival form *ḳirmizi*, via the French *cramoisi*.

II

Obviously none of these textile and dyestuff terms has any evident linguistic relationship with 'scarlet'. In fact no such word or root exists in any of the Classical or other ancient languages; and in medieval European languages scarlet makes its first documented appearance

---

[16] Pliny, *Natural History* (n. 5 above), III, pp. 258–9 (Book IX.lxv.140); IV, pp. 408–9 (Book XVI.xii.32); VI, pp. 294–6 (Book XXII.iii.3–5).

[17] R. B. Serjeant, *Islamic Textiles: Material for a History up to the Islamic Conquest* (Beirut, 1972), pp. 64–5, 206 (al-Djaḥīẓ, *c.* AD 850); 64, 67 (al-Iṣṭaḳhrī, *c.* AD 950; Ibn Ḥawḳal, *c.* AD 957–88); 68, 73 (Mustawfi Ḳazwīnī, AD 1281–1340); 220 (al-Gharnāṭī, *c.* AD 1160) and also pp. 36, 55, 156, 171, 206, 220. See also Lombard, *Les textiles* (n. 8 above), pp. 119–22; Born, 'Scarlet' (n. 8 above), p. 206; Kurdian, 'Ḳirmiz' (n. 10 above), pp. 105–7; Donkin, *Spanish Red* (n. 5 above), pp. 9–10; della Vida, 'On Ḳirmiz' (n. 10 above), pp. 287–8.

[18] On *vermiculus-i*, see Pliny, *Natural History* (n. 5 above), IV, pp. 408–9 (Book XVI.xii.32); VII, pp. 8–9 (Book XXIV.iv.8: 'in vermiculum se mutans, quod ideo scolecium vocant improbantque'); *Vulgate*, Exodus 35 : 25: 'dederunt hyacinthum, purpuram, et vermiculum'; Isidore, *Etymologiarum*, II, Book XIX.xxviii.1: 'κόκκον Graeci nos rubrum seu vermiculum dicimus; est enim vermiculus ex silvestribus frondibus'; Alfred Boretz (ed.), *Capitularia regum francorum*, 2 vols. (*Monumenta Germaniae Historica: Legum sectio* II, Hannover, 1883), I, pp. 83–7, no. 32: 43, *capitulare de villis, c.* AD 800: 'lanam, waisdo, vermiculo, warentia, pectines laninas'; L. A. Muratori (ed.), *Antiquitates italicae medii aevi sive dissertationes*, II, (Milan, 1739; reissued 1965), p. 379: 'Alia compositio vermiculi' (before AD 900); Reiner Hildebrandt (ed.), *Summarium Heinrici*, I: *Textkritische Ausgabe der ersten Fassung, Buch I–X* (Berlin, 1974), p. 320 (Book IX.ii), 328 (Book IX.ix: 'Coccum Greci, nos rubrum seu vermiculum dicimus *rotphellol*'), written *c.* AD 1007–32; Charles du Frèsne (Du Cange) (ed.), *Glossarium mediae et infimae latinitatis*, new edn, Léopold Favre, 10 vols. (Paris, 1883–7), VIII, p. 282; Sabbe, 'Tissus orientaux' (n. 15 above), pp. 832–3. Sabbe was incorrect in stating that 'le coccineus et le vermiculatus étaient donc deux espèces d'étoffes distincts'. He was evidently confusing *coccinea* with the eastern *purpurae* textiles.

only in the eleventh century, as a specific textile term in Old High German and late Latin.[19] The term(s) then quickly spread to other Romance and Germanic languages with very similar forms. In late Latin, in was variously spelled *scarlata, scarlatum, scarletum, scarlaccum, scarlateus, scarletus, squalata, escallata, escarlata, escarletum, esquarletum.* In medieval (and modern) Italian it is *scarlatto*; in Spanish and Portuguese, *escarlat*; in Old French, variously *escarlate, escarlatte, escarlet, escallate, esquerlat, esquallate, escrelate* (in modern French, *écarlate*)." In late Old High German, the various forms found are *scarlachen, sharlachen, scorlachen, scorlachin* and *scarlahhan*, which produced the Middle High German forms *scharlachen, scharlachin, scharlach, scharlat* and *scharlatin* (modern German, *scharlach*). In Middle Low German and Middle Dutch (Flemish), it appears as *scharlaken, scarlaken, scaerlaken, scherlaken* and *scharlaten* (modern Dutch, *scharlaken*), producing the Old Norse *skarlat, skarlak* and *skarlakkan*, and Old Swedish *skarlet* (modern Swedish, *scharlakan*; modern Danish, *skarlagen*). Middle English texts, influenced by a combination of Germanic and Romance forms, variously spelled it *skarlet, scarlet, scharlette, scarlatte, scarlat, scarleit* and *skarlote.*

The enigma posed by the sudden eleventh-century appearances of scarlet is equally matched by the mystery of the word's specific meaning. The popular notion of so long ago that the medieval scarlet was necessarily a textile having this unique brilliant red colour was effectively refuted by nineteenth-century historical, literary and especially philological scholarship. A multitude of texts in many

[19] For the following, I consulted four historical dictionaries in medieval Latin, fifteen in the Romance languages, fourteen in Germanic languages, and nine in English. The more important ones are cited below in notes 20, 22, 27–8, 35–6, 42, 44, 49–50, and in this note. J.-B. Weckerlin, in his *Le drap 'escarlate' au moyen âge* (Lyons, 1905), pp. 22 n. 1 and p. 75, asserted that the earliest appearance of 'scarlet' was in a charter of *c.*1050 by which Emperor Heinrich III granted the Count of Cleves 'tres pannos scarlitinos anglicanos'. But he provided no source, and I could not find such a charter in the *Monumenta Germaniae Historica*. He also noted a reference to 'pannos albos et nigros ... virides et scarlaticos' in Jean de Garlande's *Dictionarius* as edited by Hercule Géraud, *Paris sous Philippe le Bel d'après des documents originaux* (Paris, 1837), p. 595. Géraud and Weckerlin attributed this dictionary to the middle or late eleventh century; but in fact Johannes de Garlandia (*c.*1195–1272) composed it at the Sorbonne between 1218 and 1229. See Thomas Wright (ed.), *A Volume of Vocabularies from the Tenth Century to the Fifteenth*, II (2nd edn, Liverpool, 1882), pp. 120–38; L. J. Paetow (ed.), *Morale Scolarium of John of Garlande* (Berkeley, 1927), pp. 128–31. Gustav Schmoller also asserted, in *Die Strassburger Tucher- und Weberzunft* (Strasbourg, 1879), p. 426, that 'der Name Scharlach, scarlatum, kommt seit den 11. Jahrhundert vor.' But the earliest references given in his source, Muratori, *Antiquitates* (n. 18 above), II, pp. 417–18, are works of Gervaise of Tillbury (grandson of Henry II) and Ricobaldi, written *c.* AD 1190–1215. The earliest text cited in Du Cange, *Glossarium* (n. 18 above), VII, p. 340, is also by Gervaise. The earliest text in medieval Latin that I can verify is 'de scarlata rubea tunicam' in a charter of Humbert of Bourbon to Cluny Abbey, *c.*1100 (possibly 23 April 1105), in August Bernard and A. Bruel (eds.), *Recueil des chartes de l'abbaye de Cluny*, V: *1091–1210* (Paris, 1894), p. 154, no. 3906. See also J. F. Niermeyer and C. van de Kieft (eds.), *Mediae latinitatis lexicon minus* (Leiden, 1976), p. 944. For eleventh-century appearances of 'scarlachen' in Old High German, see pp. 27–8 and n. 49 below.

European languages can be cited to demonstrate that the colours attributed to medieval scarlets were frequently black, purple, violet, murrey (mulberry: purple-red), brown, grey, blue, perse (dark greyish-blue), green – or even white.[20] Consequently one must explain not only the origins and evolution of the word scarlet, but also the nature and mode of manufacturing this medieval textile, and the reasons for its ultimate association with that particular red colour.

Two rival, quite conflicting theories have long been advanced to elucidate the puzzling etymology and nature of the medieval scarlet. The first had long been current when it received the imprimatur of the renowned Du Cange (Charles du Frèsne, 1610–88). His *Glossarium* stated that the word scarlet was generally thought to be derived from 'the Arabic Yxquerlat, because it sounds the same'.[21] The word is, in fact, Persian, and it is *sakirlāt* (سَقِرْلاط), with the variants, over several centuries, of *sakirlāt* (سَقِرْلاط), *sakarlāt*, *saghirlāt*, *sakillāt*, *sakilāt*, *sakallāt*, *sikillāt*, *saklātā*, *saklātūn*, *saklātin*, *siklātūn*. Subsequently, especially during the flowering of linguistic sciences in the nineteenth century, most philologists came to accept this Persian origin for the word scarlet. Indeed the vast majority of current dictionaries in all Romance and Germanic languages still present this Persian etymology as established fact, as does the most recent history of Islamic textiles, by the eminent Maurice Lombard.[22] Support for this etymology can

[20]See Weckerlin, *Drap escarlate*, pp. 11–20, 75–90; Niermeyer, *Lexicon*, p. 944; R. E. Latham, *Revised Medieval Latin Word List from British and Irish Sources*, rev. edn (London, 1965), p. 422; Muratori, *Antiquitates*, (n. 18), II, pp. 416–17; Miguel Gual Camarena, *Vocabulario del comercio medieval: Colección de aranceles de la corona de Aragon, siglos XIII y XIV* (Tarragona, 1968), pp. 302–3; Jesusa Alfau de Solalinde, *Nomenclatura de los tejidos españoles del siglo XIII* (Madrid, 1969), pp. 95–8; Jean Baptiste la Curne de Sainte-Palaye, *Dictionnaire historique de l'ancien langage françois*, 10 vols. (Paris, 1875–82), V, pp. 463–4; Fréderic Godefroy, *Dictionnaire de l'ancienne langue française et de tous ses dialectes du IXe au XVe siècle*, 9 vols. (Paris, 1881–93), III, p. 354; R. Grandsaignes d'Hauterive, *Dictionnaire d'ancien français* (Paris, 1947), p. 234; Adolf Tobler and Erhard Lommatsche (eds.), *Altfranzösisches Wörterbuch*, 9 vols. (Berlin–Wiesbaden, 1925–71), III, pp. 816–17; Jacob and Wilhelm Grimm, *Deutsche Wörterbuch*, 17 vols. (Leipzig, 1854–1971), VIII, pp. 2200–2; Georg Benecke and Wilhelm Müller (eds.), *Mittelhochdeutsches Wörterbuch*, 3 vols. (Leipzig, 1854–61), II.ii, p. 87; Mathias Lexer, *Mittelhochdeutsches Handwörterbuch*, 3 vols. (Leipzig, 1872–78), II, p. 663; Oskar Schade, *Altdeutsches Wörterbuch*, 2 vols. (Halle, 1882), II, p. 781; Eeclo Verwijs and Jacob Verdam (eds.), *Middelnederlandsch Woordenboek*, 11 vols. (The Hague, 1885–1952), VII, col. 325–6; *A New English Dictionary on Historical Principles (Oxford English Dictionary)*, 10 vols. (Oxford, 1888–1928), VIII, p. 189.

[21]*Glossarium* (n. 18 above), p. 340. For the following see n. 23 below.

[22]Lombard, *Les textiles* (n. 8 above), pp. 242–3; Niermeyer, *Lexicon* (n. 19 above), p. 944; F. D. Diez, *Etymologisches Wörterbuch der romanischen Sprachen*, 5th edn (Bonn, 1887), p. 284; Carlo Battisti and Giovanni Alessio, *Dizionario etimologico italiano*, V (Florence, 1968), p. 3376; G. B. Pellegrini, *Gli arabismi nelle lingue neolatine con speciale riguardo all'Italia*, II (Brescia, 1972), p. 114; D. Leopoldo de Eguilaz y Yanguas, *Glosario etimológico de la palabras españolas de origen oriental* (Granada, 1886), p. 391; Joan Coromines, *Diccionario crítico de la lengua castellana*, II (Bern, 1954), p. 337; Grandsaignes d'Hauterive, *Dictionnaire* (n. 20 above), p. 234; Grimm, *Wörterbuch* (n. 20 above), VIII, pp. 2200–2; Lexer, *Handwörterbuch* (n. 20 above), II, p. 663; Schade, *Wörterbuch* (n. 20 above), II, p. 781; Friedrich Kluge and Walther Mitzka (eds.), *Etymologisches Wörterbuch der deutschen Sprache*, 18th edn (Berlin, 1960), p. 636; N. van Wijk (ed.), *Franck's etymologische woordenboek der Nederlandsche taal*, II (The Hague, 1912), pp. 575–6; Jan de Vries, *Nederlands etymologische*

be found, moreover, in some Persian dictionaries, which explicitly define *saḵirlāt* and all the above-listed variants as 'a warm woollen broadcloth' and as 'a scarlet-coloured cloth' especially.[23] This attractive etymology has, however, several grave defects. First and foremost, there is no evidence that the word *saḵirlāt* or any other Persian variant, including *saḵalāṭ*, the one now favoured by the *Oxford* and *Webster's* dictionaries, was used (as scarlet cloth) before the late thirteenth century, long after the various forms of scarlet had become firmly established in west European languages.[24] The earliest documented Persian usage is found in a letter from the *ṣadr* or grand vizier Rashīd al-Dīn, *c.* 1290–1318, ordering his son to have a *saghirlāt* from Rūm (Byzantine or other Christian lands) sent to Tabriz.[25] Since the Italians had by this time long established a substantial export trade in luxury woollens to the Islamic Middle East, including even Persia, this *saghirlāt* was almost certainly European, and most probably a scarlet. Many Persian dictionaries, furthermore, define *saḵirlāt*, *saḵalāṭ*, and the other variants as woollens, scarlet-coloured woollens, manufactured in Europe; and they agree that the word itself is not Persian in origin.[26] Undoubtedly some European word for scarlet, probably the Italian *scarlatto*, determined the final form of *saḵirlāt*, and its particular association with scarlet woollens.

woordenboek (Leiden, 1963), p. 609; Jan de Vries, *Altnordisches etymologisches Wörterbuch* (Leiden, 1961), p. 485; *Oxford English Dictionary*, VIII (1914), p. 189 (1933 edn, IX, pp. 189–90); *Webster's New International Dictionary of the English Language*, 2nd edn (1961), p. 2231 ('siqillat' given as Arabic); *Webster's New Collegiate Dictionary*, 8th edn (1976), p. 1031 ('saqalat' as Persian); Eric Partridge, *Origins: A Short Etymological Dictionary of Modern English*, II (Amsterdam, 1967), p. 1393; William Morris (ed.), *The American Heritage Dictionary of the English Language* (Boston, 1971), p. 1169: *Concise Oxford Dictionary*, 4th edn (1951), p. 1104. But for the 5th edition of 1964 (p. 1124), see below p. 26 and n. 44.

[23] See A. Hontum-Schindler, 'The word "scarlet"', *Journal and Proceedings of the Asiatic Society of Bengal*, new ser., VI (1910), pp. 263–6 (citing 'saḵirlāt, saḵilāṭ, saḵillāt, saḵallāṭ, saḵlāṭin, siḵlāṭūn = woollen cloth, cloth made in Europe', from dictionaries dating from the seventeenth century); J. A. Vullers, *Lexicon persico-latinum etymologicum*, II (Bonn, 1864), pp. 303–4 ('saḵirlāt, saḵirlāt: vestis lanea,quam in regno Francorum texunt; pannus cocco tinctus; siḵilat, saḵalāt, saḵalāt: stragulum laneum'); Francis Johnson, *A Dictionary: Persian, Arabic, and English* (London, 1852), p. 705 ('saḵallāṭ, saḵlāṭūn, saḵlāṭin, saḵlāṭā: scarlet cloth'); A. N. Wollaston, *A Complete English–Persian Dictionary* (London, 1889), p. 1131 ('saḵarlāt: scarlet cloth, European'); F. Steinglass, *A Comprehensive Persian–English Dictionary*, 5th edn (London, 1963), p. 686–7 ('saḵirlāt: warm woollen cloth; saḵirlāt, saḵallāṭ, saḵallāṭ, saḵlāṭā, saḵlāṭūn, saḵlāṭin: scarlet cloth or dress'; also: 'saḵlāṭūn: city in Rūm where scarlet cloth is made'). Note: ḵ = q = ḳaf.

[24] See R. P. A. Dozy and W. H. Engelmann, *Glossaire des mots espagnols et portugais dérivés de l'arabe*, 2nd edn (Leiden, 1869), pp. 379–80; R. P. A. Dozy, *Dictionnaire détaillé des noms des vêtements chez les Arabes* (Amsterdam, 1845), p. 111; Hontum-Schindler, 'Scarlet' (n. 23 above), pp. 263–5; and nn. 25, 44 below. Hontum-Schindler also maintains that 'of all the forms given I consider saḵirlāt, or better saghirlāt, to be the original and fundamental one'; and further, that this word was derived from the Chinese sa-ha-la' – a contention I find unsupportable. See also *Oxford English Dictionary*, IX, p. 189; *Webster's New Collegiate Dictionary* (1976 edn), p. 1031; n. 44 below.

[25] Hontum-Schindler, 'Scarlet' (n. 23 above), p. 264; H. A. R. Gibbs, J. H. Kramers *et al.* (eds.), *Encyclopaedia of Islam*, III.ii, pp. 1124–5. It should be noted, however, that because of the earlier predominance of Arabic we have very few genuinely Persian texts before the thirteenth century.

[26] See nn. 23–4 above.

The true or more important ancestor of the Persian terms *saḳirlāt* – *saḳalāṭ* – *siḳillāṭ* was, however, almost certainly a much older Arabic word: *siḳlāṭ* (ﺳﻘﻼﻁ) or more commonly *siḳlāṭūn* (ﺳﻘﻼﻃﻮﻥ). Indeed the latter is one of the variants of *saḳirlāt* given in some Persian dictionaries, which also indicate that either popular etymology or some lexicographers confused the spelling and meaning of the Arabic and Italian terms, attributing attributes of each to *saḳirlāt*. Some scholars have suggested that the Arabic *siḳlāṭ* may even be the direct source of the European terms for scarlet.[27] But it cannot be the ultimate origin; for *siḳlāṭ* is clearly a loan word itself, borrowed from a Graeco-Roman term. The majority of philologists believe that it is derived from the Greek κυκλας, Latinised as *cyclas*: a circular mantle with a border of royal purple or gold embroidery, serving as a female robe of state; and several Arabic and Persian dictionaries do give 'female robe', and a 'gold embroidered fabric' as meanings for *siḳlāṭ* – *siḳlāṭūn* – *siḳillāṭ*.[28] A minority of scholars, however, including most recently Maurice Lombard, accept Georges Colin's thesis that *siḳlāṭ* comes instead from the Latin *sigillatus* via the Byzantine Greek σιγιλλατος-ον , originally meaning a woollen or linen textile decorated with seals or rings.[29] Colin himself supported this etymology by citing a text to that effect by the ninth-century Arab philologist al-Asma'ī (d. AD 828).[30] Lombard maintained that the technique of manufacturing these textiles spread from Byzantine Syria to Mesopotamia and Arabic lands by at least the sixth century, though the nature and composition of the textile at that time are uncertain.[31] In any event, from

---

[27] *Webster's New International Dictionary*, 2nd edn (1961), p. 2231; Karl Lokotsch, *Etymologisches Wörterbuch der europäischen (germanischen, romanischen, und slavischen) Wörter orientalischen Ursprung* (Heidelberg, 1927), p. 142; Wilhelm Meyer-Lübke, *Romanischen etymologisches Wörterbuch*, 3rd edn (Heidelberg, 1935), p. 634, no. 7661. The following editors of dictionaries and etymologies cited in n. 22 above, while contending that the European forms of scarlet are derived from the Persian *saḳirlāt*, etc. acknowledge that the Persian forms themselves are derived in turn from the Arabic *siḳlāṭ*: Battisti, Pellegrini, Eguilaz y Yanguas, Corominas, Grandsaignes d'Hauterive, Kluge and Mitzka, de Vries, Partridge, Klein, and Morris. For the Arabic, see R. P. A. Dozy, *Supplément aux dictionnaires arabes*, 3rd edn, I (Leiden, 1881), p. 663. I am greatly indebted to Professor Andrew Watson and Mr Richard Taylor for their assistance with Arabic and Arabic sources.
[28] Wilhelm Heyd, *Histoire du commerce du Levant au moyen âge*, 2 vols. (Leipzig, 1885–6), II, p. 700; *Oxford English Dictionary*, vol. II, p. 414; *Webster's New International Dictionary*, 2nd edn (1961), p. 2231; and, in nn. 22 and 27 above, the dictionaries edited by Lokotsch (p. 142), Battisti (V, p. 3376), Eguilaz y Yanguas (pp. 378–9, 391), Kluge and Mitzka (p. 636), de Vries (p. 609). See also Dozy, *Supplément* (n. 27), I, p. 663; Vullers, *Lexicon persico-latinum* (n. 23), II, p. 304 (*siḳilāṭ*); Steinglass, *Persian–English Dictionary* (n. 23), p. 687 (*siḳlāṭ, siḳillāṭ*); Johnson, *Dictionary* (n. 23), p. 705 (*siḳlāṭ*); Lewis and Short, *Latin Dictionary* (n. 7), p. 1696; Isidore, *Etymologiarum*, Book XIX.xxiv.10–11.
[29] Georges Colin, 'Latin sigillatus > roman siglaton et escarlat', *Romania*, LVI (1930), pp. 178–90, 418. Colin also contends that 'saqirlāt, dérivé lointain du sigillatus latin' is the immediate ancestor of the European words for scarlet (pp. 189–90). See further Lombard, *Les textiles* (n. 8), pp. 242–3. Also supporting Colin are those dictionaries in n. 22 above edited by Pellegrini, Corominas, Partridge, Klein, and Morris. See also Solalinde, *Tejidos españoles* (n. 20 above), pp. 78–82, 98–9. She evidently favours *cyclas* over *sigillatus*, but admits that the question remains moot.
[30] Colin, 'Sigillatus', p. 179.
[31] Lombard, *Les textiles* (n. 8), pp. 242–3; Colin, 'Sigillatus', pp. 178–80.

the'ninth and tenth centuries, long before 'scarlet' can be documented in any European language, the word *siklāṭūn* figures prominently in Arabic documents and literature on textiles, from Spain to Persia.[32] Thus such an Arabic origin for the European scarlet would seem most logical: as yet another Arabic commercial term transmitted to European languages by Italian trade or the Christian conquests of Muslim Sicily and Spain.

Tracing the origins of scarlet to *siklāṭūn*, however, also presents several severe difficulties. In the first place, even though this Arabic textile was certainly as luxurious, costly and princely as the European scarlets, it was not a woollen – despite its supposed Byzantine origins. From the earliest Arabic descriptions available, the *siklāṭūn* was indisputably a silk: a rich, heavy damask silk, usually ornately brocaded and often embroidered in gold. Furthermore, its traditional colour had long been blue, at least in the eastern Mediterranean regions.[33] The *siklāṭūn* of Muslim Spain, however, came to be frequently dyed a scarlet colour, especially those produced at Almería, in the rich kermes-producing region of Andalusia, from at least the eleventh century.[34] Nevertheless those such as Colin, who ascribe the various

---

[32] Serjeant, *Islamic Textiles* (n. 17 above), pp. 21, 23–4, 29, 68, 78, 84, 92, 144, 158, 164–5, 168–70, 202, 213. The earliest references given here are in Spain, *c.* AD 957–88 (Ibn Ḥawkal, p. 164); in Tabaristan, *c.* AD 976–1012 (al-Yazdādi, p. 78); at Baghdad, *c.* AD 975–83 (Tha'ālibī, p. 29); and at Isfahan, AD 982 (Ḥudud al-'Alam, p. 84). See also Lombard, *Textiles* (n. 8), pp. 242–3; Colin, 'Sigillatus' (n. 29), pp. 178–86; S. D. Goitein, *Letters of Medieval Jewish Traders* (Princeton, 1973), p. 77 (document *c.* 1010: Kairouan); S. D. Goitein, *A Mediterranean Society: The Jewish Communities of the Arab World as Portrayed in the Documents of the Cairo Geniza*, 2 vols. (Los Angeles, 1967), I, pp. 102–3, 419. In none of the documents given or quoted above do the forms *sakirlāt, sakalāt, siklillāt*, etc. appear; *siklāṭūn* is invariably the one used (even if transcribed by some as 'siglaton').

[33] Heyd, *Commerce* (n. 28 above), II, p. 700; Colin, 'Sigillatus' (n. 29), pp. 180–1, 183; Corominas, *Diccionario* (n. 22 above), II, p. 337; Solalinde, *Tejidos españoles* (n. 20 above), pp. 78–82; Eguilaz y Yanguas, *Glosario*, (n. 22), pp. 378–9; and the sources cited in n. 32 above. The documents published by Goitein, however, indicate that *siklāṭūn* could also be blue and white, light green, blue–black, white and red, white and black (*Jewish Traders*, p. 77; *Mediterranean Society*, I, p. 419). Cf. also al-Idrisi, *Sifat al-Maghrib wa-ard al-Sudan* (*Description de l'Afrique et de l'Espagne par Edrisi*), R. P. A. Dozy and J. de Goeje (eds.) (Leiden, 1866), pp. 240, 316.

[34] Colin, 'Sigillatus' (n. 29), pp. 181–3, 188–90, 418; Heyd, *Commerce* (n. 28), II, p. 700; Solalinde, *Tejidos españoles* (n. 20), pp. 81–2; Lombard, *Les textiles* (n. 8), p. 243. Colin in fact still attributes the term scarlet to 'un doublet de sigillāt: saqirlāt, dont le lieu de naissance est encore incertain. Sa couleur, non fixée au début, finit par être le rouge' (p. 190). See also Frithiof Rundgren 'Sillagdun = al-aḥāmira = al-Rūm', *Orientalia Suecana*, III (1954), pp. 135–43; and Agnes Geijer, *A History of Textile Art* (London, 1979), p. 279, n. 9. Rundgren, supported by Geijer, has modified Colin's thesis by suggesting that scarlet, also derived in his view from *sakirlāt*, acquired its red connotation from a cognate Arabic word *sillaġdun* or *silġaddun*, a loan word he also believes to be derived from *sigillatus* or more likely *kyklas-kyklados*, via the forms *sikillat, sigillat, siklad, sikkad, silġadd*. He argues that this word could have had the meaning al-aḥāmira = al-Rūm = red; and that al-Rūm was derived from (a) the description of Esau–Edom as 'red' in Genesis 25: 25; and (b) the later Jewish tradition that Edom was the founder of the Roman nation. But even though Rundgren's theory would support my own thesis that scarlet meant grain-dyed, I find it quite unconvincing, for these reasons: (a) al-Rūm surely refers to Christian lands, that is, Western red; (b) *sillaġdun* was an extremely rare word in Arabic, not found in most dictionaries, that also had several other meanings; (c) the linguistic connection between *sillaġdun, sikillat* and scarlet – hardly self-evident – remains unproved; (d) his textual references are too few and meagre. If there is a connection to give these words the meaning of red, the origin could as well be the European term for scarlet.

European terms for scarlet directly to *siklāṭūn*, especially the Spanish variety, ignore a crucial question: why was the noun scarlet applied to woollens alone in Europe, never to the costly silks dyed in kermes? In medieval Latin, such silks were instead usually called *examitum* or *samitum* from the Byzantine Greek εξαμιτον (six-warp threads); in Spanish, *xamete* or *jamete*; in Italian, *sciameto*; in French, Portuguese and Middle High German, *samit*; in Middle English, *samite*, *samyt*, *samit*.[35] Furthermore, the name given to another very costly silk, one usually brocaded or interwoven with gold, was virtually identical in form to the Arabic *siklāṭūn* in various European languages. It appears as early as AD 922 in Spanish as *siclaton*, *ciclaton*; in Old French it is similarly *ciclaton*, *ciglaton*, *siglaton*; in Middle High German, *siglat*, *ciclat*, *siklatun*; in Middle Dutch, *siglatoen*; in Old Norse, *siklat*, *siklatun*; and in Middle English, *ciclatoun*, *ciclatun*, *siklatoun*, *siglatoun*.[36] Surely, therefore, when these terms are so close in form and meaning to *siklāṭūn*, it is even more difficult to argue that this same Arabic word was also the source of a totally different textile term, scarlet, and one with such striking phonetic differences.

The rival and much younger theory ascribes a purely European origin to scarlet, both as a word and as a textile. The Belgian historian Henri Pirenne first suggested the theory to his French colleague J.-B. Weckerlin, who developed it in his famed monograph, *Le drap 'escarlate' au moyen âge: essai sur l'étymologie et la signification du mot écarlate*, published in 1905. Just as Pirenne later argued that the early medieval *pallia fresonica*, Frisian cloths, were Flemish made, so he believed that his Flemish homeland was the birthplace of the scarlet and that the word itself originated in the Flemish *scarlaken*, *schaerlaken*, *scaerlaken*.[37] That word appears to consist of the two substantives 'shear' (*schaer*) and 'cloth' (*laken*); and thus Pirenne suggested that the word meant 'shorn cloth'. Weckerlin modified this view by contending that the meaning was more 'a cloth to be shorn, or re-shorn'. In their view, the most luxurious of all fine woollens were those that were napped, shorn and re-shorn three times or more, in order to obliterate the weave and produce a texture as fine as silk. Such *scarlaken* would have been made, of course, only from the very finest wools: in medieval times, indisputably English wools. Other scholars have also maintained that only

---

[35] Du Cange, *Glossarium* (n. 18), VII, p. 340; *OED*, VIIii, p. 77. See also below p. 59 and n. 99.
[36] Corominas, *Diccionario* (n. 22), II, p. 337; Victor Oelschlager, *A Medieval Spanish Word List* (Madison, Wisc., 1940), p. 43; *OED*, II, p. 414; de Vries, *Wörterbuch* (n. 22), p. 475; Tobler and Lommatsche, *Wörterbuch* (n. 20), III, p. 817; Eguilaz y Yanguas, *Glosario* (n. 22), pp. 378–9; S. William Beck, *The Draper's Dictionary: A Manual of Textile Fabrics* (London, n.d.), p. 62.
[37] See Weckerlin, *Drap escarlate* (n. 19 above), pp. 12–13; Henri Pirenne, 'Draps de Frise ou draps de Flandre?', *Vierteljahrschrift für Sozial und Wirtschaftsgeschichte*, VII (1909), republished in *Histoire économique de l'occident médiéval*, E. Coornaert (ed.) (Bruges. 1951), pp. 54–61; also pp. 189–91. Pirenne had suggested 'drap-tondu' as the meaning.

fine English wools could have sustained so many repeated shearings.[38] Thus, stated Weckerlin, 'par suite de ces apprêts et spécialement de ces tondes nombreuses données à cette catégorie de draps fins, le nom de "scarlaken" était encore bien approprié'. He suggests that this term first arose during the early days of the world-renowned Flemish cloth industry, when many of the finest woollens were sent to Italy for final shearing, dyeing and finishing, especially to Florence's Arte di Calimala. In his view, Flemish cloth merchants at the fairs of Flanders and Champagne designated all such woollens destined for Italy simply as 'cloths to be shorn' – as *scarlaken*; and in that fashion this Flemish word passed, more or less transformed, into Low Latin, the Romance and Germanic languages as 'scarlet'.[39]

According to Weckerlin, the actual colour of a scarlet was originally quite immaterial, since the essential feature of the textile was the extensive shearing. Hence his explanation for the many colours and shades attributed to scarlets in medieval texts. He then argued that the aristocracy, the chief consumers, came to prefer vivid, dazzling colours, above all that rich, bright vermilion red produced by kermes, the colour that best symbolised regal and military power, indeed divine power, to the medieval mind. Consequently, as later medieval drapers responded to the dictates of fashion by having their finest, multi-sheared woollens dyed exclusively in kermes, and only those woollens, the word scarlet developed a new, ultimately predominant meaning: the colour of that textile.[40]

Weckerlin's thesis has proved to be such an attractive, all-encompassing explanation, so neatly resolving both the etymological mysteries and the paradox of colours associated with the scarlet, that it has clearly dominated the historical literature on medieval textiles for the past seventy-five years. Undoubtedly Pirenne's strong advocacy of this thesis, indeed co-authorship, helps to explain its very widespread acceptance by historians.[41] Philologists, however, so long loyal to the

---

[38] Weckerlin, *Drap escarlate* (n. 19), pp. 22 n. 1, 25–55; see also Marta Hoffman's invaluable study *The Warp-Weighted Loom: Studies in the History and Technology of an Ancient Implement* (Oslo, 1964), pp. 266–7.

[39] Weckerlin, *Drap escarlate*, pp. 21, 73.

[40] Weckerlin, *Drap escarlate*, pp. 21–2, 84–90.

[41] See especially Georges Espinas, *La draperie dans la Flandre française au moyen âge*, 2 vols. (Paris, 1923), II, pp. 292–4; Henri Laurent, *La draperie des Pays Bas en France et dans les pays méditerranéens, XII–XVe siècle* (Paris, 1935), pp. 209–20; Renée Doehaerd, *Les relations commerciales entre Gênes, la Belgique, et l'Outremont d'après les archives notariales génoises aux XIIIe et XIVe siècles*, 3 vols. (Brussels, 1941), I, p. 197; III, p. 1293; Jacques Heers, 'La mode et les marchés des draps de laine: Gênes et la Montagne à la fin du moyen âge', *Annales: ESC*, XXVI (1971), p. 1111; Françoise Piponnier, 'À propos de textiles anciens, principalement médiévaux', *Annales: ESC*, XXII (1967), pp. 864–6; Gerschel, 'Couleur et teinture' (n. 3 above), pp. 621–33; Agnes Geijer, 'The pallium fresonicum of the Viking Age: was it manufactured in Syria?', *Fornvännen*, IV (1965), pp. 130–2; Hoffmann, *Warp-Weighted Loom* (n. 38 above), pp. 265–9; E. M. Carus-Wilson, 'The English cloth industry in the late twelfth and early thirteenth centuries', *Economic History Review*, 1st ser., XIV (1944), reprinted in her *Medieval Merchant Venturers* (London, 1954), pp. 218–20; E. M. Carus-Wilson and Olive Coleman, *England's Export Trade, 1275–1547* (Oxford, 1963), pp. 14–15.

far older 'Persian' theory, have been slow to succumb to its lures. Only in recent years have a few philologists, all quite conversant with the historical literature on textiles, dared to plump for *scarlaken* over *sakirlār* or *sakalāt*, as the origin of 'scarlet': chiefly the Belgian Guy de Poerck and the Spaniards Miguel Gual Camarena and Jesusa Alfau de Solalinde.[42] Both Maurice Lombard in *Les textiles dans le monde musulman* (1978) and J. F. Niermeyer in *Mediae latinitatis lexicon minus* (1976) still prefer the Persian source; but at least they do cite the Weckerlin thesis as a possible alternative.[43] The editors of the *Oxford English Dictionary*, however, have made no mention of Weckerlin; but possibly the controversy over the etymology of scarlet has succeeded in undermining their faith in the old 'Persian' theory. For in the 1964 edition of the *Concise Oxford Dictionary*, they finally abandoned the *sakalāt* etymology by tersely stating: 'ultimate origin [of scarlet] unknown'.[44]

The *OED* editors, and many others, may have been reluctant to accept the Weckerlin thesis as the alternative because in fact it presents as many etymological difficulties as the rival 'Persian' theory. The basic premise of Weckerlin's arguments is that the Flemish cloth industry was of such paramount importance from at least the eleventh century that its merchants could impose the Flemish word *scarlaken*, in the sense just defined, upon medieval Latin and the other west European languages. The Flemish towns were, to be sure, becoming industrially prominent by that time; but they were far from being pre-eminent in textiles. Even within the county of Flanders itself, which then included an important francophone region, the French-speaking towns of Lille and Douai at least rivalled, possibly surpassed, any of the Flemish-speaking towns in cloth-making. Indeed, until about 1300, the francophone towns of southern Flanders and neighbouring Artois, Picardy, Hainaut, the bishoprics of Tournai and Cambrai remained collectively more important in the cloth trade. Francophones dominated the famous Hanse of the Seventeen Towns governing that trade at the Flemish and Champagne fairs, where so

---

[42] Guy de Poerck, *Draperie médiévale* (n. 8 above), I, pp. 213–14; II, pp. 70–1; III, p. 125; Gual Camarena, *Commercio medieval* (n. 20 above), pp. 302–3; Solalinde, *Tejidos españoles* (n. 20 above), pp. 94–8; see also, Kurt Zangger, *Contribution à la terminologie des tissus en ancien français attestés dans les textes français, provençaux, italiens, espagnols, allemands et latins* (Bern, mimeo, 1945), pp. 50–1, also supporting Weckerlin.

[43] Lombard, *Les textiles* (n. 8 above), p. 243; Niermeyer, *Lexicon* (see n. 19), p. 944.

[44] E. M. McIntosh and G. W. S. Friedrichsen, *Concise Oxford Dictionary*, 5th edn (1964), p. 1124; see also C. T. Onions, G. W. S. Friedrichsen and R. W. Burchfield (eds.), *The Oxford Dictionary of English Etymology* (Oxford, 1966), p. 795. Much earlier, in 1911, Wilhelm Meyer-Lübke had stated, under the entry 'Scharlach': 'Ursprung unbekannt; pers. *saquirlāth* ... kann nicht die Grundlage der rom. Wörter sein, sondern ist selber entlehnt'; in *Romanisches etymologisches Wörterbuch*, 1st edn (Heidelberg, 1911), p. 577, no. 7661. The same is argued by the chief proponent of the alternative etymology: Weckerlin, *Drap escarlate* (n. 19 above), p. 19 n. 3.

many of those *draps à tondre* were sold.[45] Even in Flemish Ieper (Ypres) most of the records were kept in Latin and French until the anti-French revolt and Flemish victory at Kortrijk (Courtrai) in 1302.[46] After the French kings had annexed francophone Flanders in the early fourteenth century, and contributed to the final ruin of the cloth industry there and in Artois, the *Vlaamse* textile towns in Flanders, then Brabant and Holland did become industrially dominant. But that dominance – short-lived in the face of growing English competition – comes far too late to explain the much earlier appearances of scarlet in Latin, French, Spanish and Italian. Furthermore, the earliest text cited by Weckerlin, c. AD 1050 – 'tres pannos scarlitinos anglicanos' – certainly indicates English, not Flemish cloths.[47]

Nor can one readily accept Weckerlin's hypothesis to explain the transmission of *scarlaken* to other European languages. It seems quite unlikely that the Italians would have adopted this Flemish word when they called cloths purchased from the northern fairs *panni franceschi, panni francigeni, panni Francie*.[48] Nor, as a Romance-speaking people, would they have readily borrowed a word from such a difficult language as Flemish. Surely French, so closely cognate to Italian and so much more dominant than Flemish, would have been the far likelier source for a word to describe these *draps à tondre* at the northern, especially Champagne, fairs.

There is, however, an alternative Germanic etymology, evidently unknown to Weckerlin, that poses fewer historical problems. In fact the earliest documented appearance of 'scarlet' in Europe is to be found in the Old High German commentary known as the *Summarium Heinrici*, composed at Worms between AD 1007 and 1032. The word appears in the section 'De diversitate vestimentorum' as a gloss upon a corrupt text from the *Etymologiarum* of Isidore of Seville (*c.* AD

[45] In the thirteenth century, only four of the twenty-two towns of the so-called 'XVII viles' were Flemish-speaking (in italics): Arras, Amiens, Abbeville, Montrueil-sur-Mer, Reims, St Quentin, St Omer, Cambrai, Tournai, Aubenton, Valenciennes, *Ghent, Bruges, Ieper (Ypres), Diksmuide,* Lille, Douai, Chalons, Beauvais, Huy, Bailleul, Péronne. See M. G. Fagniez (ed.), *Documents relatifs à l'histoire de l'industrie et du commerce en France*, 2 vols. (Paris, 1898–1900), I, pp. 205–6, no. 190 (*c.* 1250). Of the thirty-one towns recorded in the Genoese notarial accounts as furnishing woollens to Genoese merchants from northern Europe in the thirteenth century, only six were Flemish-speaking. Doehaerd, *Gênes* (n. 41 above), I, pp. 189–92; III, p. 1291.

[46] See Georges Espinas and Henri Pirenne (eds.), *Recueil de documents relatifs à l'histoire de l'industrie drapière en Flandre: 1re partie*, 4 vols. (Brussels, 1906–20), III, 437–834; I. L. A. Diegerick (ed.), *Inventaire analytique et chronologique des chartes et documents appartenant aux archives de la ville d'Ypres*, 5 vols. (Bruges, 1853–60).

[47] Weckerlin, *Drap escarlate*, p. 22 n. 1; p. 75. He is quite unjustified, in my view, in translating this as 'trois draps écarlates de laine anglaise' to defend his theory of the Flemish origins of scarlets.

[48] Doehaerd, *Gênes* (n. 41 above), I, pp. 192–5; II–III, nos. 537–8, 557, 918, 1069, 1354, 1372, 1374, 1414, 1420, 1543, 1753, 1820, 1839 in particular. See also Pirenne, *Histoire économique* (n. 37 above), pp. 190–1.

570–636): 'Ralla vel rullo que vulgo rasilis dictur – *scarlachen*'.[49] Both Classical and medieval Latin *rasilis* (from *radere*) meant 'scraped, rubbed, polished, smoothed, or shaved'; and in a later medieval English list of Latin words (*c.* 1440) the word *ralla* was defined as a 'shaving cloth'.[50] Thus, whatever Isidore himself had meant by these two words, they have at least some relationship to shearing. Certainly the later *Heinrici* gloss of his etymology permits only one logical interpretation: shear[ed], shorn cloth. For the Old High German forms *scar* (*schar*) and *lachen*, like their Flemish cognates, have precisely these meanings.

Quite possibly the *Heinrici* glossator regarded this shorn woollen cloth as a novelty. Dr Marta Hoffmann has rightly called the shorn woollen 'the most important innovation of the medieval [textile] industry' and has argued that it first appeared (or reappeared) in northern European manufacturing in the late tenth or early eleventh century, the very era of the *Summarium Heinrici*. She further suggests that the appearances of the shorn woollen may be related to the contemporary introduction of the horizontal (broad) loom, which Walter Endrei and E. M. Carus-Wilson have also dated to this very period.[51] This loom evidently displaced the ancient vertical or warp-weighted loom, whose chief product had been a narrow worsted or possibly woollen fabric noted especially for its striking lozenge-twill weaves. Such cloths were evidently unfulled and certainly unshorn. Thus the feature that most distinguished the new, true woollens from the previous fabrics was the obliteration of any visible weave, as a result

---

[49] Hildebrandt, *Summarium Heinrici* (n. 18 above), I, pp. xxi–xxiv, 321 (Liber IX.ii). Some of the extant twelfth-century manuscripts are also cited in E. G. Graff, *Althochdeutscher Sprachschatz*, 7 vols. (Berlin, 1834), II, pp. 156–9; Elias Steinmeyer and Eduard Sievers, *Die althochdeutschen Glossen*, 5 vols. (Berlin, 1879–1922), III, p. 147; Jacob Grimm, *Deutsche Grammatik*, 4 vols. (Berlin, 1878), II, p. 598; *OED*, VIII, p. 189. See also Hoffmann, *Warp-Weighted Loom* (n. 38 above), pp. 266, 377; Moriz Heyne, *Funf Bücher deutschen Hausaltertumer von den altesten geschichtlichen Zeiten bis zum 16. Jahrhundert*, III (Leipzig, 1930), pp. 219–20. The actual text in Isidore, *Etymologiarum*, II, Book XIX.xxii.23 is: 'Ralla, quae vulgo rasilis dicitur'. I am indebted to my colleague Professor Hartiwg Meyer for locating and assisting me with the *Summarium Heinrici*.

[50] Latham, *Medieval Latin Word List* (n. 20 above), p. 391. But see Lorenz Diefenbach (ed.), *Novum glossarium latino-germanicum mediae et infimae aetatis* (Frankfurt, 1867), pp. 312–13: defining *ralla*, *rasilis* as 'scharlach Kleit', evidently on the basis of *Summarium Heinrici* manuscripts. My colleague Professor Michael Herren advises me that '*Ralla* is from the adj, *rallus a um*, which is derived through syncope and assimilation from *rarulus*: hence "thin". Its association with *rasilis* can be attributed to a false etymology. There is a noun *rallum* – "instrument for scraping the earth from the ploughshare" – [which] is apparently correctly derived from *rado*. Isidore, however, confused *rallus a um* with *rallum i* (noun) and incorrectly assigned the first word with the definition *rasilis* from *rado*.' (Letter of 12 December 1977.)

[51] Dr Hoffmann does not go so far as to state the following argument explicitly; but I do not believe that it does any violence to her views. See her *Warp-Weighted Loom* (n. 38 above), pp. 266–80 in particular and also pp. 183–93, 229–57, 258–65. On the new horizontal treadle loom, see also E. M. Carus-Wilson, 'Haberget: a medieval textile conundrum', *Medieval Archaeology*, XIII (1969), pp. 148–66; Walter Endrei, 'L'apparition en Europe du métier à marche', *Bulletin de liaison du centre international d'étude des textiles anciens*, no. 8 (July 1958), pp. 22–7.

of the fulling, napping and especially the shearing processes. The shorn surface of the woollen, furthermore, was much finer and softer than that of any other contemporary fabric, except the silk, then a most rare commodity in northern Europe.

Hence these new, fine woollens may originally have been called 'shear-cloths', shorn cloths, a term that undoubtedly connoted a costly luxury as well. Nevertheless, it seems unlikely that the Germanic *scarlachen* is the sole source of the term scarlet. One may conjecture, if not prove, that scarlet has both Arabic and Germanic roots; that popular etymology transformed both the construction and meaning of the word in the various European languages by association with both the new, shorn woollens and the luxurious *siklātūn*, indeed the scarlet, kermes-dyed Spanish *siklātūn*. Evidently the Arabic word had its greatest influence on the neighbouring Mediterranean Romance forms, which invariably ended with a 't', usually 'lat', construction. Conversely, *scarlachen* exercised a much stronger influence on the northern, Germanic languages, which all retained the 'ch' or 'k' endings; it may also be responsible for the first syllable 'ar' construction in most medieval and all modern forms of scarlet. As the manufacture of shorn woollens became far more commonplace, with a wide variety of fabrics by the twelfth century, the term scarlet probably came to be reserved for just the most luxurious, most resplendent woollens.[52]

III

In view of this discussion, are we therefore compelled to accept Weckerlin's other contention, his major thesis, that extensive shearing was the essential, crucially distinguishing feature of those medieval woollens called scarlets; and that such shearing was chiefly responsible for their very high costs and exalted status as the luxury textile *par excellence*? In order to test the Weckerlin thesis, and to discover the exact nature of the medieval scarlet, I have investigated two sets of sources in its supposed homeland and adjacent lands, from the thirteenth to late sixteenth centuries. The first set comprises guild codes (*keures*), industrial regulations and commercial ordinances issued in Douai, Ieper (Ypres), Bruges, Ghent, Estaires, Armentières, Valenciennes, Arras, St Omer, Rouen, Paris, Lyons, Brussels, Leuven, Malines (Mechelen), Leiden and London, from *c.* 1225 to *c.* 1585. The second set consists of prices of scarlets, various other woollens

---

[52] Note the wide range of Artesian and Fleinish woollen products (and worsteds) documented for the twelfth and thirteenth centuries in Doehaerd, *Gênes* (n. 41 above), I–III; Espinas and Pirenne, *Recueil* (n. 46), I–IV; de Poerck, *Draperie* (n. 8), I, pp. 199–300; R. L. Reynolds, 'The market for northern textiles in Genoa, 1179–1200', *Revue belge de philologie et d'histoire*, VIII (1929), pp. 831–51.

and worsteds listed in the municipal treasurer's accounts of Flemish, Brabantine and Dutch towns and in the English customs and royal wardrobe accounts, variously from c. 1300 to c. 1520. Many of these cloth price series also contained the fees for dyeing, shearing and finishing; and occasionally also total production costs.[53]

Weckerlin himself found virtually no information on the actual production of scarlets, apart from a few (and misleading) finishing fees. But to Weckerlin the very lack of such information, in particular of any guild *keures* whatsoever on the manufacture of scarlets, was itself proof of this thesis that the scarlet 'was not a single type of woollen but a whole series of fine cloths that became scarlets only after undergoing a series of finishing processes of which repeated shearing formed the base'.[54] The term scarlet was therefore a purely commercial one, not industrial; and one can readily agree that the finishing processes were indeed more commercial than industrial, since they usually took place at the behest of cloth merchants, who had bought the woollens from the industrial drapers, and who had them finished according to their knowledge of current fashion and market demands.[55]

Weckerlin's survey of industrial regulations was, however, both incomplete and inaccurate. He missed a large number of archival records, many of them still unpublished. They show that at least five towns did issue ordinances specifying to some degree the dimensions of scarlets and their mode of production: St Omer (c. 1280, c. 1350–75); Brussels (1282, 1376, 1380, 1444, 1466, 1497); Leuven (1298); Malines (1331–32); and Ghent (c. 1360). The most complete regulations are to be found in Brussels, whose scarlets were amongst the most renowned in Europe. These *scaerlakens* were to be made from only the very finest English wools: in the fifteenth century, specifically Herefordshire or Shropshire March, or the best Cotswolds, or the best Lincolnshire Lindsey, indeed listed as the costliest English staple wools in Table 3.1.[56] As Table 3.2 shows, the Brussels scarlets were originally much larger and always more densely woven than any other high-quality

---

[53] The cloth prices have been extracted from unpublished accounts of semi-annual or annual cloth purchases for garbing the civic officials, as given in the annual civic treasurer's reports in the municipal archives of Bruges, Franc de Bruges, Ghent, Ieper, Kortrijk, Malines and Leuven (some now deposited in the Algemeen Rijksarchief of Belgium). Most of the guild keures have now been published by Espinas and Pirenne, Espinas, de Sagher, Joossen, Delepierre, Willemsen and Posthumus. But I have also utilised unpublished keures in the municipal archives of Brussels, Leuven and Malines (Mechelen).

[54] Weckerlin, *Drap escarlate*, pp. 77, 21, respectively.

[55] See Hans van Werveke, *De koopman-ondernemer en de ondernemer in de Vlaamsche lakennijverheid van de middeleeuwen* (*Mededelingen van de koninklijke Vlaamse Academie voor Wetenschappen, Letteren, en Schone Kunsten van België, Klasse der Letteren*, vol. VIII: 4, Antwerp, 1946).

[56] Stadsarchief te Brussel, het Wit Correctieboek no. XVI, fol. 193ʳ (20 March 1444: 'van Maertscher wolle of vander bester Cudzewoutscher wolle, of vander bester Linderzee wolle'); no. 1435,

woollen produced in that city. Fourteenth-century ordinances of St Omer, Ghent and Malines similarly indicate that the scarlet was the largest cloth that each then manufactured.[57] In the late thirteenth century, furthermore, fullers' keures in St Omer, Brussels and Leuven set the highest fees for *scaerlakenen*; and fulling was indisputably a major industrial process preceding any finishing.[58] Those fees obviously accorded with the greater dimensions of *scaerlakenen*; but fullers' and dyers' fee schedules in several late medieval towns indicate that 'white, blue, grey, medley' and variously coloured cloths could also have the same 'scarlet length' (*scarlakens lingde*).[59] Fifteenth-century price lists for Flemish and English cloths also demonstrate that other high-quality woollens also had precisely the same large dimensions and contained the same high-quality English wools.[60] If dimensions, weaves and wool contents were once distinguishing features of the medieval scarlet, clearly some other process was also necessary to make a cloth exclusively a scarlet.

The drapery regulations, however, lend no support to Weckerlin's thesis that this process was multiple shearing. Whether one wishes to argue that shearing was a commercial or industrial process, it was regulated with copious guild keures and civic ordinances in the Low Countries from a very early period – indeed from a time when Weckerlin supposed that most Flemish *draps à tondre* were being sent to Italy for finishing. These shearing keures, some running to 95 articles, discuss in detail the finishing of woollens, from the cheaper to the costliest woollens. But not a single keure that I have examined, from Douai's in 1225 to those of sixteenth-century Leuven (1556) and Leiden

fol. 30ᵛ. (16 November 1467). See also John Munro, 'Wool-price schedules and the qualities of English wools in the later Middle Ages, 1270–1499', *Textile History*, IX (1978), pp. 118–69; and Munro, 'The 1357 wool price schedule and the decline of Yorkshire wool values', *Textile History*, X (1979), pp. 211–19.

[57] Espinas and Pirenne, *Recueil* (n. 46), III, p. 329, no. 704 (St Omer, *c.*1350–75: 'les milleurs de 13 quartiers, excepté les escarlates, qui doivent estre de plus grant largheur et valeur'); ibid., II, p. 492 (Ghent, *c.* 1360: 'dat men gheen lanc laken breden en mach langer dan 13 vierendele, uteghesteken scaerlaken, die sal men breden 14 vierendeele breed'); Stadsarchief te Mechelen, SDI: 3, fol. 9ᵛ (September 1331: 'wat langher lakene scarlaken lingde ten ramen comt moet 50 ellen lanc staen op die ramen'); précis in Henri Joossen, 'Recueil de documents relatifs à l'histoire de l'industrie drapière à Malines, des origines à 1384', *Bulletin de la commission royale d'histoire*, XCIX (1935), p. 510, no. 56.

[58] See Espinas and Pirenne, *Recueil* (n. 46), III, p. 247, no. 651 (St Omer, *c.* 1280); Felicien Favresse (ed.), 'Actes intéressant la ville de Bruxelles, 1154 – 2 décembre 1302', *Bulletin de la commission royale d'histoire*, CIII (1938), pp. 454–61, no. 33 (June 1282); Floris Prims, 'De eerste eeuw van de lakennijverheid te Antwerpen, 1226–1328', *Antwerpsch archievenblad*, 2nd ser., III (1928), pp. 133–4, 147–8, no. 8 (Leuven, September 1298). See also de Poerck, *Draperie* (n. 8), I, pp. 90–112.

[59] See Espinas and Pirenne, *Recueil* (n. 46), II, pp. 588–9, no. 533 (Ghent, 1350–1); and the sources cited above in nn. 57–8 (for Malines, Brussels, Leuven); and Table 3.3.

[60] See Tables 3.2, 3.6 and 3.11; and Munro, 'Industrial protectionism' (n. 2 above), pp. 257–63 (Table 13.3).

Table 3.1   Prices of twenty English wools at the Calais Staple, in pounds groot
Flemish per sack of English weight^a (364 lb = 165.11 kg), c. 1475 and 1499

Name of the wool/county of origin	c.1475 £ gr.^{b}	1499 £ gr.^{c}	1499 Index
Leominster (Herefordshire)		37.498	100.0
Shropshire and Herefordshire March	18.134	28.543	76.1
Fine Cotswold	16.321	21.827	58.2
Berkshire	14.961	19.588	52.2
Middle March		18.469	49.3
High Lindsey, Lincolnshire	14.961	15.671	41.8
Middle Cotswold		15.111	40.3
Low Lindsey, Lincs.		15.111	40.3
Kesteven, Lincs.	14.055	14.552	38.8
Holland, Lincs.	13.374	13.992	37.3
Middle Berkshire		13.992	37.3
Rutland	13.147	13.992	37.3
Kent	10.880	12.872	34.3
Surrey	12.014	12.313	32.8
Norfolk	10.427	12.313	32.8
Middle Young Cotswold		11.753	31.3
Middle Lindsey		10.635	28.4
Middle Kesteven		10.074	26.9
Middle Holland		9.514	25.4
Middle Rutland		9.514	25.4

Notes: ^{a} Converted from the Calais sack weight of 315 lb.
^{b} Converted from pounds sterling: £1 sterling = £1.177 groot.
^{c} Converted from pounds sterling: £1 sterling = £1.453 groot.
Throughout this essay I have calculated exchange rates on the basis of the relative (pure) silver contents of the coinages concerned, as detailed in Table 3.16. In May 1499, the exchange rate, if based on the two gold coinages (English noble and Burgundian florin) would have been: £1 sterling = £1.462 groot or 29s 3d gr. The coinage rates in the 1499 schedule indicate that the current exchange rate at Calais was then about 28s gr., closer to the silver-based rate of 29s than to the gold-based rate.
Sources: British Library, Cotton Vespasian, E. IX, fols. 106^r–7^r ('Noumbre of Weyghtes', c.1475). Algemeen Rijksarchief (België), Rekenkamer reg. no. 1158, fols. 226–7 (1499). Some wools from both schedules have been omitted.

(1568–85), prescribes any specific mode of shearing scarlets.[61] Nor does Weckerlin himself cite any text or regulation to prove that scarlets had to receive more shearings than other woollens. Surely

[61] See in particular Espinas and Pirenne, *Recueil* (n. 46), II, pp. 19–21, no. 217 (Douai, July 1229); nos. 218, 240, 316, 386 (Douai, 1245–1403); ibid., III, pp. 454–6, no. 751 (Ieper, September 1280); nos. 757, 784–7 (Ieper, 1300–93); ibid., III, pp. 580–7, no. 532 (Ghent, 1349–50); pp. 589–94, no. 534 (Ghent, 1350); ibid., I, pp. 436–42, no. 141 (Bruges, 1284); pp. 542–52, no. 150, (Bruges, 1303); Octave Delepierre and M. F. Willems (eds.), *Collection des keuren ou statuts de tous les métiers de Bruges* (Ghent, 1842), pp. 60–81 (1408–70); Standsarchief te Brussel, no. 1436, fol. 114–16 (Brussels, 1481); M. G. Willemsen, 'Le règlement général de la draperie malinoise de 1544', *Bulletin du cercle archéologique de Malines*, XX (1910), pp. 1–115; Stadsarchief te Leuven, nos. 718, 722–3, 1526, 2712 (1481–1556); Nicolaas Posthumus (ed.), *Bronnen tot de geschiedenis van de Leidsche textielnijverheid*, 3 vols. (The Hague, 1910–12), I, pp. 84–6, no. 74 (1415); pp. 164–5, no. 132 (1436); pp. 548–54, no. 440: viii (1472–1541); II, pp. 489–94, no. 1034 (1541–64); pp. 556–9, no. 1119 (1552); pp. 691–4, no. 1214: vii (1568–85). See also de Poerck, *Draperie* (n. 8), I, pp. 108–49; Espinas, *Draperie* (n. 41 above), II, pp. 221–46, 751–5.

that omission is significant – especially in view of other regulations for making scarlets.

The one text that Weckerlin does cite to demonstrate that multiple shearing of scarlets is an entry from the Comptes de l'Argenterie of Philip V the Long of France (1316) : 'une escarllate de 24 aunes tondue 3 fois pour Noël'.[62] But many of the shearers' *keures* show clearly that such triple shearing was commonplace for other much lower-quality woollens, which could never be considered scarlets. Thus even the little rural Flemish *nouvelle draperie* of Estaires on the Lys, in a *keure* dated 1428, required the *retondeur* to apply 'trois tours de forces' to its 'plains draps', listed here in Table 3.2.[63] The most detailed, explicit shearer's *keures* extant are those of late-fifteenth- and sixteenth-century Leuven, which then manufactured a wide variety of cloths from domestic and foreign wools – but no scarlets by that time. According to size and quality, these Leuven woollens were to be given one, two or three shearings each, with four to seven 'trecken' or nappings per shearing. Three types of cloth, also listed in Table 3.2, were each to receive three shearings: (1) *Vier Bellen*, made from domestic wools, with a total of fourteen nappings over 14 hours; (2) *Laken van Vijf Loyen*, of 'good' English, Spanish or mixed such wools, with eighteen nappings over 18 hours; and (3) *Raemlaken van Vijf Looden* (five seals), of 'fine' English wools, with fifteen nappings over $22\frac{1}{2}$ hours. The 'fine' wools so specified were Middle Cotswolds, Lindseys, Kestevens and Middle Berkshires, which were in fact, as Table 3.1 shows, middle-grade English wools, priced at only 37–40 per cent of the amount charged for Leominster (Herefordshire) wools, the most expensive at the Calais Staple.[64] Such Leominster wools were prescribed for Malines's *gulden aeren* cloths, in Table 3.2, and, as noted, for Brussels' *scaerlakenen*.

Seemingly stronger support for the Weckerlin thesis can be found, however, in several schedules of shearing fees. Weckerlin, in fact, regarded the two French schedules, presented in Table 3.3 for Paris and Lyons, as essential evidence for his thesis.[65] For comparison, two Flemish shearing schedules, for Ghent and Bruges, have also been given in this table. These four schedules indeed do show that the highest shearing fees were for scarlets. But that is in itself hardly surprising, since the Leuven shearing regulations just discussed, and many others

[62] Louis Douet-d'Arcq (ed.), *Comptes de l'Argenterie des rois de France au XIVe siècle* (Paris, 1851), p. 29; Weckerlin, *Drap escarlate*, p. 50.

[63] Henri de Sagher (ed.), *Recueil de documents relatifs à l'histoire de l'industrie drapière en Flandre*, 2me *partie*, 3 vols. (Brussels, 1951–66), II, pp. 276–7, no. 265 (18 September 1428); pp. 280–1, no. 266 (27 April 1430). The shearer was to receive 8s 0d *par.* a cloth (1430: 7s 6d), while the fuller's fee was 9s 0d *par.* (1430: 13s 6d).

[64] Stadsarchief te Leuven, no. 722, fols. 46r–59r, 127r–9r (1481, 1528, 1556); no. 718, fols. 21v–38v (30 October 1556). See also n. 56 above.

[65] Weckerlin, *Drap escarlate*, pp. 42 n. 2, 43 n. 2. See also sources cited in Table 3.3 and esp. n. 111.

Table 3.2   Warp counts and dimensions of scarlets and other woollens produced in the Low Countries and England, 1282–1554

| Cloth and place of manufacture | Warp count | Dimensions in ells (length) and quarter-ells (width)[a] | | | | | |
| | | On Loom | | Fulled | | Tentered | |
		Length ells	Width qtrs	Length ells	Width qtrs	Length ells	Width qtrs
Brussels (1282–1467)							
Scaerlaken							
1282		48				42*	12
1444–67[b]	3300	42*				35	
Langhe Laken[b]	3000	42				35*	
Corte Laken[b]							
1444	2700	37½				32*	
1467	2400		15		8		
	2100		14		8		
Bellaerts (1467)[c]							
short	2250	28	15	20	8		
	1500	28	13½	20	8		
long	2250	42	15	30	8		
	1500	42	13½	30	8		
Malines (1331–1554)							
Scaerlaken (1331)			16*			48	
Langhe Pleine (1331)			16			39	
Corte Laken (1331–43)							
whites, blues	2400		14	32		36	11
medley	1800		13	32		36	11
Gulden Aeren (1554) [d]	3120	48	16*	30*	10*	32	11½
Leuven (1481–1556)							
Vier Bellen[e]	1984		14	30	8½	32	
Raemlaken: 5 Looden[f]	2232		14	30	9	32	
First seal (proposed in 1519 only)[g]	2400	43	16	30	10	32*	12*
Bruges (c. 1390–1458)							
Scaerlaken							
to 1408				42½	10		
1408–58				36	10		
Langhe Breede Laken							
to 1408				42½	10		
1408–58				36	10		
Cuerlaken	2010	43	15	30	9	32	11
Bellaerts (1458)[h]	2160	43	16	30	10	32*	12
Ghent (1544)							
Dickedinnen of 5 Seals[i]	2066	42½	14½	30	9½		
Estaires (1428)							
Plain Drap[j]	1392	40	12			36	9½

Cloth and place of manufacture	Warp count	Dimensions in ells (length) and quarter-ells (width)[a]					
		On Loom		Fulled		Tentered	
		Length ells	Width qtrs	Length ells	Width qtrs	Length ells	Width qtrs
Armentières (1510–29)							
Oultreffins[k]	1800	42	12	30	8		
England (15th century)							
Scarlet: 30 yards				40.3	9.4		
Long cloth: 30 yards				40.3	9.4		
Short cloth: 24 yards[l]				32.2	9.4		

Notes: [*] Estimated dimension.

[a] 1 Brussels ell = 27.36 in = 0.695 m; 1 Mechelen ell = 27.13 in = 0.689 m; 1 Flemish ell = 27.56 in = 0.700 m; 1 English cloth yard = 37 in = 0.940 m.

[b] 'Laken van de drie staten' to be made from fine March, best Cotswold, or best Lindsey (Lincs.) wool only (1443, 1444, 1467).

[c] To be made from English, Spanish, Scottish, domestic 'and other good wools' (produced from March 1444).

[d] From Leominster (Herefordshire), wools only; to weigh 58 lb of Mechelen (27.22 kg) when finished.

[e] Made from domestic wools ('bester schaerwollen').

[f] Made from Fine Kesteven, Fine Lindsey, Middle Cotswold, Middle Berkshire.

[g] To be made from Fine Cotswold, Middle March, Fine Berkshire, Young Cotswold, Middle Cotswold, and Refuse of March 'op de maniere vander drappieren van Ghent ende elders in Vlaenderen'; to weigh 90 lb on the loom (proposal only).

[h] Made from fine English wools only: 'omme te *greyne* of zwart te makene of anders wit of blaeu te latene'.

[i] Made from Fine March, Fine Cotswold, Fine Berkshire, and Middle March; to weigh 51 Ghent lb (22.13 kg) when finished.

[j] Made from good English wools; second-quality cloth from English, Spanish, Scottish and Flemish wools (with 1296 warp count).

[k] Made from two-thirds Spanish wools and one-third fine English wools: Fine Cotswold, Fine Lindsey, Fine Berkshire, Fine Young Cotswold only. To weigh 88 lb on the loom and 52 lb Flem. (24.12 kg) finished.

[l] To weigh 64 lb when finished (29.03 kg).

Sources: *Brussels*: Stadsarchief te Brussel, no. 1435, fols. 1–21, 30–4; no. 1436, fols. 13–25; Het Wit Correctieboek, no. XVI, fols. 190–3.

Malines: Stadsarchief te Mechelen, SDL:3; M. G. Willemsen (ed.), 'Le règlement général de la draperie malinoise de 1544', *Bulletin du cercle archéologique de Malines*, XX (1910), pp. 156–90.

Leuven: Stadsarchief te Leuven, nos. 718, fols. 21–38; no. 722, fols. 46–59, 127–9; no. 723, fols. 1–5; no. 1526, fols. 203–10; no. 2712, fols. 56–67.

Bruges: Stadsarchief te Brugge, Stadsrekeningen 1390–1406; Algemeen Rijksarchief, Rekenkamer, reg. nos. 32 461–76; Octave Delepierre and M. F. Willems (eds.), *Collection des keuren ou statuts de tous les métiers de Bruges* (Ghent, 1842), pp. 20–2.

Ghent: M. J. Lameere and H. Simont (eds.), *Recueil des ordonnances des Pays-Bas: 2me série, 1506–1700* (Brussels, 1910), V, pp. 272–83.

Armentières and Estaires: Henri De Sagher (ed.), *Recueil de documents relatifs à l'histoire de l'industrie drapière en Flandre: 2me partie*, 3 vols. (Brussels, 1951–66), I, pp. 102–17, no. 36; pp. 144–9, nos. 40–1; II, pp. 277–81, nos. 265–7.

England: *Statutes of the Realm*, I–IV, *passim* (and especially IV:1, 136–7, 5–6 Ed. VI, c. 6).

Table 3.3   Costs of shearing woollen cloths in Flanders and France during the fourteenth and fifteenth centuries

Cloth type and place of manufacture	Width in quarter-ells	Shearing cost Per ell in deniers	Cloth of 35 ells in shillings	Cost of shearing 35-ell cloth in shillings groot Flemish Current value	1350 value
Flanders		parisis*	parisis*	groot	groot
Ghent, 1350–51					
Plain Scaerlaken	14	12d	35s 0d	2.92s	2.92s
	10	10d	29s 2d	2.43s	2.43s
	9	8d	23s 4d	1.94s	1.94s
Dark-blue and	13–14	12d	35s 0d	2.92s	2.92s
murrey cloths	10	10d	29s 2d	2.43s	2.43s
	9	8d	23s 4d	1.94s	1.94s
Medley (Ghemingden)	12–13	6d	17s 6d	1.46s	1.46s
	9	4d	11s 8d	0.97s	0.97s
	8	2d	5s 10d	0.49s	0.49s
Dickedinnen (medley)	7	2d	5s 10d	0.49s	0.49s
Small Driedadden (med)	6	$\frac{1}{4}$d	9d	0.06s	0.06s
White (Witte)	12–13	6d	17s 6d	1.46s	1.46s
	10	4d	11s 8d	0.97s	0.97s
	9	3d	8s 9d	0.73s	0.73s
	8	2d	5s 10d	0.49s	0.49s
Gorsemen (white)	5–7	1d	2s 11d	0.24s	0.24s
Tiretaine of wool		1d	2s 11d	0.24s	0.24s
Scaerlaken Strijpt		4d	11s 8d	0.97s	0.97s
Other Good Strijpten		2d	5s 10d	0.49s	0.49s
Slichten Strijpten		$\frac{1}{4}$d	9d	0.06s	0.06s
Bruges, c.1408					
Scaerlaken		24d	70s 0d	5.83s	2.90s
Broad Ghent Cloth		18d	52s 6d	4.38s	2.18s
Broadcloths of Ypres, Brussels, Malines		12d	35s 0d	2.92s	1.45s
Bruges Cuerlaken		8d	23s 4d	1.94s	0.97s
Small Cloths of Ypres, Wervik, Kortrijk, Roesselare		8d	23s 4d	1.94s	0.97s
Other small cloths		6d	17s 6d	1.44s	0.72s
France		tournois	tournois	groot	groot
Paris, January 1351					
escarlate		12d	35s 0d	1.84s	1.84s
drap of 24 ells		5d	14s 7d	0.77s	0.77s
drap marbré and other drap of 20 ells		4d	11s 8d	0.61s	0.61s

| Cloth type and place of manufacture | Width in quarter-ells | Shearing cost | | Cost of shearing 35-ell cloth in shillings groot Flemish | |
		Per ell in deniers	Cloth of 35 ells in shillings	Current value	1350 value
drap rayé	4d	11s 8d		0.61s	0.61s
'gros drap' for journeymen, etc.	3d	8s 9d		0.46s	0.46s
Lyons, May 1482					
escarlate	40d	116s 8d		18.30s	5.41s
Rouen cloth	20d	58s 4d		9.15s	2.70s
Bourges cloth	10d	29s 2d		4.58s	1.35s
Languedoc cloth	8d	23s 4d		3.66s	1.08s
Autres draps de moindre pris	5d	14s 7d		2.29s	0.68s

Notes: * 12d parisis Flemish = 1d groot Flemish. After *c.* 1320, the Flemish parisis monetary system, tied to the pound groot, no longer bore any direct relationship with the French parisis system.

For the monetary conversions, 1 kg of pure silver = £2.016 gr. in 1350–1, £4.050 in 1408, and £6.821 gr. in May 1482, in Flanders; in France, 1 kg pure silver = £38.371 tournois in January 1351 and £43.487 in 1482.

Source: Georges Espinas and Henri Pirenne (eds.), *Recueil de documents relatifs à l'industrie drapière en Flandre, Ire partie*, 4 vols. (Brussels, 1906–20), II, pp. 588–9, no. 533; Octave Delepierre and M. F. Willems (eds.), *Collection des keuren ou statuts de tous les métiers de Bruges* (Ghent, 1842), p. 72; René de Lespinasse (ed.), *Les métiers et corporations de la ville de Paris*, 3 vols. (Paris, 1886–97), I, p. 34, no. II.xxxvi; M. Gustave Fagniez (ed.), *Documents relatifs de l'industrie et du commerce en France*, 2 vols. (Paris, 1898–1900), II, pp. 284–7, no. 159:11 (p. 286).

as well, indicate that the number of shearings depended upon the grade of cloth. Furthermore, just as the previously discussed fullers' schedules set fees according to the size of the cloth, so do these four schedules: or rather these schedules set them according to a combination of the size, weave and value of the cloth. Thus the lowest fee in the Bruges schedule was for 'other small cloths'; and in the Lyons schedule, for 'other cloths of lesser value'. As the various tables demonstrate, scarlets were indisputably the most costly of all woollens, and usually the largest; presumably they were also the most extensively finished. Even so, the fees for shearing scarlets were not exclusively the highest in the Ghent schedule, at least, which set precisely the same fees per width, for 'murrey [*moreitenen*] and good deep-blue [*zadblauwen*] cloths'. Furthermore, the fee for shearing *scaerlaken strijpt* (striped or rayed) was only one-third the fee for shearing *scaerlaken plein*, *zadblauwen* and *moreitenen* cloths. The context of this schedule, it must be noted, was largely of size and colour.

But the most important and hitherto unobserved feature of these schedules in Table 3.3 is the fact that the shearing fees represent only a very small, insignificant proportion of the wholesale value of the finished scarlets. Thus, in the 1350–51 Ghent schedule, the fee for shearing the largest scarlet (14 quarters) was only 2.22 per cent of the price of red and brown Ghent *scarlakenen* purchased about that time (£6 11s 9d *groot* Flemish); and that same year, the Parisian fee for shearing a scarlet of equivalent value was considerably lower, at 1.40 per cent of the price.[66] Much earlier, in 1316, the fee for shearing that 'escarlatte de 24 aunes tondue 3 fois', cited by Weckerlin, cost the French queen even less: 8s *parisis* (worth 6s 5d *tournois*), only 0.83 per cent of the purchase price of £48 *par.*[67] In 1340, Count Eudes of Artois paid a higher fee of 40s *par.* for the shearing of two *escallates* worth £70 *par.*; but that cost of 2.86 per cent was still within the range of current Flemish fees.[68] Table 3.3 may suggest that by the late fifteenth century the real (deflated) cost of shearing had increased; and historians generally agree that the real wages of organised skilled labour rose strongly in the late Middle Ages, in response to the sharp decline in population, in the supply of skilled labour especially.[69] Nevertheless, in *constant* silver values, the fee stipulated in Bruges's 1408 shearing schedule is virtually the same (2.9s) as the Ghent fee of 1350; and in current 1408 values that fee was again just 2.53 per cent of the price of a perse-brown Bruges *scaerlaken* purchased that year for £11 10s 0d *groot.*[70] The last and latest fee listed in this table, for shearing scarlets at Lyons in May 1482, is, on the other hand, by far the highest that I have encountered. Even so, at 40d *tournois* or 6.275d *groot* Flemish per ell, that represented just 4.23 per cent of the price paid that same month in Bruges for a *rozeide scaerlaken* of 30 ells: £18 11s 1d *groot.*[71] As Tables 3.4–3.12 also indicate, the costs of finishing scarlets and other woollens in Malines, Leuven, Ghent, Ieper (Ypres) and Bruges in the late fourteenth and fifteenth centuries account for no more than 4 per cent of the total price, and typically just 2.5 per cent. These tables also support the contention that shearing charges were generally proportional to cloth values.

[66] Ghent cloth purchases recorded in stadsrekening 1349–50, Stadsarchief te Gent, no. 400: 7(4), fol. 134^r.

[67] Douet-d'Arcq, *Comptes* (n. 62 above), p. 29.

[68] Espinas and Pirenne, *Recueil* (n. 46), III, 297, no. 679. See also ibid., pp. 321–2, no. 701 (shearing costs in Artois, January 1381).

[69] See E. H. Phelps Brown and Sheila Hopkins, 'Seven centuries of the prices of consumables compared with builders' wage-rates', *Economica*, new ser., XXIII (1956), republished in E. M. Carus-Wilson (ed.), *Essays in Economic History*, II (London, 1962), pp. 179–96; Harry Miskimin, *Economy of Early Renaissance Europe, 1300–1460* (Cambridge, 1975), pp. 25–31, 73–111 (on the supply of and demand for skilled labour).

[70] Bruges cloth purchases recorded in stadsrekening 1407–8, in Algemeen Rijksarchief van België [hereafter ARA Belg.], Rekenkamer reg. no. 32 462, fol. 35^v.

[71] ARA Belg., Rek. no. 32 534, fol. 54^r (Bruges stadsrekening). See Table 3.11.

Finally, all these tables show that, in striking contrast to the shearing fees, fees for dyeing were often a very large proportion of the final cloth price, sometimes the largest single component of total production costs. Of these dyeing costs, moreover, the raw material itself could account for 75–98 per cent.[72] Indisputably, in medieval Europe, the most expensive of all dyestuffs used was kermes (grain). As Tables 3.5 and 3.9 indicate, the kermes used in mid-fifteenth-century Flanders cost up to twenty-nine times as much as madder, the most commonly used red dyestuff: $38\frac{1}{2}$d *groot* per lb as against $1\frac{1}{3}$d per lb.[73] Thus, while the material and labour costs together of dyeing in various colours other than scarlet ranged from 3.7 to 21.6 per cent of cloth prices in Tables 3.6–3.8, the kermes alone was responsible for over 60 per cent of the total cost of some scarlets.[74] As Table 3.4 shows, kermes accounted for an average of approximately 40 per cent of the total costs of cloth production at Malines, from 1361 to 1416; at Ieper (Ypres), for an average of 36 per cent of such costs in the eleven surviving accounts of the fifteenth century, listed in Table 3.5. Certainly no other production input, except occasionally the very finest English wools, was responsible for such a large share of the cost of scarlets, to explain their extremely high price. Some further proof of that assertion can be found in Tables 3.5–3.12. These demonstrate first that, in the late medieval draperies of Malines, Ghent, Ieper and Bruges, the basic manufacturing costs before dyeing and finishing were roughly the same for both scarlets and other high-quality woollens; and that the *labour* costs of shearing, dyeing and other processes of production accounted for quite small proportions of the final price. Furthermore, Table 3.11 shows that in fifteenth-century Bruges the prices of scarlets (*scaerlakenen*) ranged from 25 to 107 per cent, and averaged 56 per cent, more than the prices of the next most expensive dyed woollens: *langhe breede lakenen*, having precisely the same large dimensions but containing no kermes (nor necessarily the same wools).[75] The rather wide variations in the prices of the scarlets themselves usually reflect differences in the quantities of kermes used and in the several varieties

---

[72] See in particular Tables 3.5, 3.9 and 3.12; Munro, 'Industrial protectionism' (n. 2 above), p. 257, Table 13.2; de Poerck, *Draperie* (n. 8), I, pp. 150–98.

[73] At Ieper, in 1453, Provençal grain cost $38\frac{1}{2}$d per lb (463.9 g). The price given in Table 3.5 (35.9d) is an average (ARA Belg., Rek. no. 38 677, fol. 32ʳ). Weckerlin makes a false distinction between kermes and grain, describing the former as a 'drogue venant de l'Orient', 'un produit de qualité supérieure et différent de la graine ... qui venait de l'Europe occidentale', *Drap escarlate*, pp. 63–4. See pp. 16 and n. 10 above and n. 76 below.

[74] In Malines at Christmas 1378 (60.4 per cent, of £7.12); Easter 1379 (62.3 per cent of £6.72); Easter 1380 (58.7 per cent of £6.95). Stadsarchief te Mechelen, SI nos. 57–8.

[75] The average price of Bruges *scaerlakenen* and of the next most expensive fine woollens in Table 3.11 were £12.226 *groot* and £7.833 respectively; the average prices of Ieper *scaerlakenen* and of the next most costly woollens purchased at the Franc de Bruges, in Table 3.10, were £10.258 gr and £5.379, respectively. See also Tables 3.13–3.15 for the price ranges of English scarlets and of other English woollens.

Table 3.4 Costs of dyeing in grain (kermes) and of finishing fine woollen cloths at Malines, in pounds oude groot (old gros) and pounds groot Flemish, in five-year averages, from 1360–64 to 1415–19

Years	Cost of unfinished white or blue cloth[a] (£ oude groot)	Percentage of total	Pounds of grain per cloth	Price of grain in d. per pound[b] (£ oude groot)	Cost of grain per cloth in £ oude groot	Percentage of total	Labour cost of dyeing and finishing (£ oude groot)	Percentage of total	Final price of the dyed and finished cloth (£ oude groot)[c]	(£ groot Flemish)[d]
1360–4	1.729	64.4	22.5	9.5d	0.888	33.1	0.068	2.5	2.685	
1365–9	2.100	50.1	25.6	18.8d	2.008	48.0	0.079	1.9	4.187	
1370–4	2.366	54.6	30.4	14.7d	1.857	42.9	0.107	2.5	4.330	10.719
1375–9	2.556	50.1	34.1	16.8d	2.392	46.9	0.149	2.9	5.097	13.123
1380–4	2.521	50.6	35.6	15.5d	2.297	46.2	0.160	3.2	4.978	12.994
1385–9	2.447	52.8	31.1	15.6d	2.018	43.6	0.168	3.6	4.633	13.881
1390–4	2.787	61.8	23.7	16.2d	1.601	35.5	0.121	2.7	4.509	10.146
1395–9	2.921	63.5	24.1	15.6d	1.569	34.1	0.112	2.4	4.602	10.354
1400–4	3.547	65.2	28.2	15.1d	1.771	32.6	0.119	2.2	5.437	12.234
1405–9	3.935	63.2	31.6	16.1d	2.123	34.1	0.168	2.7	6.226	14.008
1410–4[e]	4.218	55.7	34.2	22.1d	3.145	41.5	0.212	2.8	7.575	17.044
1415–9[f]	3.721	57.0	36.4	17.0d	2.575	39.5	0.230	3.5	6.526	14.684

Notes:
[a] From the 1390s the cloths are indicated as being 40 ells in length [27.56 m = 30.14 yds].
[b] The Malines pound = 469.25 g.
[c] A Malines money-of-account originally based on the silver gros of St Louis (1266–1303 = 4.044 g pure silver). Thus theoretically it once contained 970.56 g pure silver; but by 1390 it was worth only 555.525 g pure silver.
[d] From the monetary reform of December 1389 to the debasement of 1416 (the 1407 and 1409 alterations being abortive), the Flemish pound groot contained 246.90 g pure silver. In that period, £1 oude groot = £2.250 groot Flemish.
[e] Average of 1412–14 only. When converted from prices in £ groot Brabant at official rates, the average price would be £17.487 groot Flemish.
[f] Average of 1415–16 (Easter) only. When converted from prices in £ groot Brabant at official rates, the average price would be £16.783 groot Flemish.

Source: Stadsarchief te Mechelen, Stadsrekeningen SI: nos. 38–92; Algemeen Rijksarchief (België), Rekenkamer, reg. nos. 41, 204–223.

Table 3.5 Costs of dyeing and finishing fine woollen cloths of 30–32 ells in grain (kermes) at Ieper (Ypres), in pounds groot Flemish, in the fifteenth century

Year	Cost of the unfinished cloth	Percentage of total	Pounds of grain per cloth	Price of grain per lb^a in d	Cost of grain per cloth	Percentage of total	Labour cost of dyeing	Percentage of total	Cost of finishing	Percentage of total	Final price of the finished cloth
1406	£5 10s 0d	65.2	25.0	24 d	£2 10s 0 d	29.6	5s 7d	3.3	3s 2d	1.9	£8 8s 9 d
1408	£5 10s 0d^b	64.0	28.0	24 d	£2 16s 0 d	32.6	4s 4d	2.5	1s 6d	0.9	£8 11s 10 d
1408	£5 11s 0d	69.2	20.0	26 d	£2 3s 4 d	27.0	4s 3d	2.7	1s 10d	1.1	£8 0s 5 d
1409	£5 10s 0d	58.4	32.0	27 d	£3 12s 0 d	38.2	4s 5d	2.4	1s 10d	1.0	£9 8s 3 d
1410	£5 0s 0d	53.0	34.0	29 d	£4 2s 2 d	43.6	4s 6d	2.4	1s 11d	1.0	£9 8s 7 d
1419	£5 1s 8d	51.4	[33.2]^c	[36 d]^c	£4 8s 6 d	44.7	[4s 6d]^c	2.3	3s 1d	1.6	£9 17s 9 d
1427	£4 18s 0d^d	43.3	33.9	41.2d^e	£5 16s 5 d	51.5	7s 9d	3.4	3s 8d	1.6	£11 5s 10 d
1436	£6 0s 0d	58.1	35.0	26.7d	£3 17s 10½d	37.2	8s 7d	4.1	(^f)	(^f)	£10 6s 5½d
1453	£7 0s 0d^g	60.1	27.0	35.9d^e	£4 0s 9 d	34.6	12s 4d	5.3	(^g)	(^g)	£11 13s 1 d
1454	£6 10s 0d^g	56.5	30.4	35.7	£4 10s 6 d	39.4	9s 5d	4.1	(^g)	(^g)	£11 9s 11 d
1486	£9 10s 0d^b	74.2	—	—	£2 5s 0 d	17.6	13s 6d	5.3	7s 6d	2.9	£12 16s 0 d

Notes: ^a Probably the pound of Bruges = 463.9 g.
^b Cloth dyed blue in the wool.
^c Estimated share of total dyeing (or dyeing and finishing) cost from costs given.
^d At the end of this account: 'elken root scaerlakene ghecocht te £4 4s par [7s 0d groot] d'elne'. Thus this scarlet had 32.3 ells.
^e Average price of Valencian, Provençal and Georgian grain used together, in 1427 and 1453; of three lots of Provençal grain used in 1454.
^f Finishing costs included with dyeing costs.
^g Finishing costs not given; possibly included in the basic cost of the cloth. Length of cloth specified as 30 ells in both years.

Source: Algemeen Rijksarchief (België), Rekenkamer, reg. nos. 38636, fol. 12^r; no. 38637, fols. 34–5^v; no. 38638, fols. 35^v–7; no. 38639, fols. 41^r–3^v; no. 38644, fols. 38–9^r; no. 38652, fol. 27^r; no. 38660, fols. 44^r–^v; no. 38677, fol. 32^r; no. 38678, fol. 30^v; no. 38710, fol. 57^r.

Table 3.6 Costs of dyeing and finishing fine white and blue cloths of Ghent for garbing the civic aldermen: in pounds groot Flemish, in five-year averages, from 1410–14 to 1470–75

Years	Costs of unfinished blue or white cloth	Percentage of the total	Cost of dyeing in the piece	Percentage of total	Cost of shearing and finishing	Percentage of the total	Final price of the cloth	Colours:[a] B = blue (various) P = perse M = murrey V = violet R = red (madder)
1410–4[c]	£5.667	93.3	£0.369	6.1	£0.040	0.7	£6.076	B, M, P–B
1415–9[d]	£5.500	96.1	£0.225	3.9	(b)	(b)	£5.725	B, B
1420–4[e]	£6.600	95.3	£0.325	4.7	(b)	(b)	£6.925	P
1425–9[f]	£5.900	91.4	£0.552	8.6	(b)	(b)	£6.452	V, M
1430–4[g]	£6.675	90.3	£0.613	8.3	£0.102	1.4	£7.390	B, M, R, P
1435–9[h]	£7.000	86.1	£1.100	13.5	£0.033	0.4	£8.133	B, M
1440–4[i]	£6.900	83.6	£1.258	15.3	£0.088	1.1	£8.246	M,M
1445–9[j]	£6.650	83.9	£1.189	15.0	£0.086	1.1	£7.925	M, M, M, M
1450–4[k]	£6.125	89.1	£0.750	10.9	(b)	(b)	£6.875	M, M
1455–9[l]	£6.000	82.2	£1.100	15.1	£0.196	2.7	£7.296	M, M
1465–9[m]	£7.000	84.8	£1.050	12.7	£0.200	2.4	£8.250	M, M
1470–4[n]	£7.375	85.5	£1.050	12.2	£0.200	2.3	£8.625	M

Notes: [a] Cloths dyed in grain have been excluded.
[b] Finishing costs included with dyeing costs.
[c] 1411, 1414 only.   [d] 1417, 1419 only.   [e] 1420 only.   [f] 1425, 1429 only.
[g] 1431–34.   [h] 1438 only.   [i] 1443–44 only.   [j] 1445, 1447–49.
[k] 1450, 1452 only.   [l] 1455–56 only.   [m] 1460–67 missing; 1468–69 only.   [n] 1471 only.

Source: Stadsarchief te Gent, Stadsrekeningen nos. 400:11–26.

Table 3.7 Costs of dyeing and finishing fine cloths (of English wools) at Leuven, in pounds groot Flemish, in five-year averages, from 1410–14 to 1415–19 and from 1440–44 to 1490–94

Years	Costs of unfinished blue or white cloth	Percentage of the total	Cost of dyeing	Percentage of the total	Cost of finishing	Percentage of the total	Final price of the cloth	Colours[+]
1410–14[a]	£3.305	94.8	£0.180	5.2	£*		£3.485	R, S, G, Rs
1415–19[b]	£3.117	84.4	£0.577	15.6	£*		£3.694	Bk, Bk
1420–39	—		—				—	
1440–44[c]	£3.288	78.4	£0.907	21.6	£*		£4.195	Bk, Bk
1445–49	£3.250	82.2	£0.703	17.8	£*		£3.953	Bk, Bk, Bk, S, B
1450–54[d]	£2.864	80.6	£0.691	19.4	£*		£3.555	Bk, S, R, R
1455–59[e]	£3.464	82.8	£0.625	14.9	£0.093	2.2	£4.182	S, Bk, B, R
1460–64[f]	£4.235	82.6	£0.800	15.6	£0.095	1.9	£5.130	S, B, Bk, S
1465–69	£4.791	84.3	£0.795	14.0	£0.095	1.7	£5.681	R, G, Bk, B, Bk
1470–74	£4.433	80.5	£0.967	17.6	£0.105	1.9	£5.505	S, G, Bk, B, Bk
1475–79[g]	£4.593	79.2	£1.125	19.4	£0.083	1.4	£5.801	SBr, B
1480–84[h]	£5.197	79.6	£1.250	19.1	£0.083	1.3	£6.530	Bk
1485–89[i]	£6.938	81.0	£1.625	19.0	£*		£8.563	Bk
1490–94[j]	£6.179	83.1	£1.083	14.6	£0.177	2.3	£7.439	Bk, Bk, M, Bk

Notes: [+] Colour code: R = red; Rs = rose; S = sanguine; B = blue; Bk = black; M = murrey; G = green; SBr = sanguine-brown.

* Finishing costs included in the amount under Cost of Dyeing.
[a] Mean of 1410–11 only.
[b] Mean of 1415, 1417 only.
[c] Mean of 1442, 1444 only.
[d] Mean of 1450–52 only.
[e] Mean of 1455, 1457–59 only.
[f] Mean of 1460, 1462–64 only.
[g] Mean of 1475–76, 1479 only.
[h] 1481 only.
[i] 1487 only.
[j] Mean of 1490–91, 1494 only.

Source: Stadsarchief te Leuven, Stadsrekeningen nos. 5011–31, 5072–117.

Table 3.8 Costs of dyeing and finishing fine white and blue cloths at Malines, in pounds groot Flemish, in selected years from 1417 to 1469

Year	Cost of unfinished white or blue cloth	Percentage of the total	Cost of dyeing	Percentage of the total	Cost of finishing	Percentage of the total	Final price of the cloth	Colour
1417[a]	£12.954	89.7	£1.419	9.8	£0.071	0.5	£14.444	Black
1438[b]	£ 6.300	86.6	£0.925	12.7	£0.050	0.7	£ 7.275	Blue, Green
1443	£ 6.333	94.9	£0.271	4.1	£0.067	1.0	£ 6.671	Green
1444	£ 5.675	87.9	£0.711	11.0	£0.067	1.0	£ 6.453	Red (madder)
1446	£ 5.700	82.6	£1.130	16.4	£0.067	1.0	£ 6.897	Blue
1447	£ 5.067	85.5	£0.792	13.4	£0.067	1.1	£ 5.925	Blue
1448[c]	£ 5.700	92.1	£0.390	6.3	£0.100	1.6	£ 6.190	Red (madder)
1450	£ 5.700	82.0	£0.983	14.1	£0.267	3.8	£ 6.950	Murrey
1451	£ 5.383	90.3	£0.450	7.6	£0.125	2.1	£ 5.958	Red, Violet
1452	£ 5.542	85.8	£0.792	12.3	£0.125	1.9	£ 6.458	Black
1453	£ 6.967	90.6	£0.600	7.8	£0.126	1.6	£ 7.693	Violet
1468	£ 4.275	87.1	£0.500	10.2	£0.133	2.7	£ 4.908	Red (madder)
1469	£ 5.811	92.4	£0.333	5.3	£0.142	2.3	£ 6.286	Violet

Notes: [a] 1.0 pond groot Brabant = 0.8888 pond groot of Flanders.

[b] From December 1435, 1.0 pond groot Brabant = 0.6667 pond groot of Flanders.

[c] See Table 3.9 on the costs of dyeing and finishing this cloth.

Source: Stadsarchief te Mechelen, Stadsrekeningen SI: nos. 93, 119–23, 125–8, 144–5; Algemeen Rijksarchief (België), Rekenkamer, reg. nos. 41 233–34, 41 236–42, 41 258–9.

Table 3.9 Cost of dyeing and finishing one red woollen cloth at Malines, Easter 1448, in pounds groot of Brabant and Flanders

	Pounds groot of Brabant	Pounds groot of Flanders		Percentage
Cost of one unfinished 'white' cloth: 1 'witte gecarde laken' priced at 36 Rhenish florins, at 57d groot Brabant each	£8 11s 0d £8.550	£5 14s 0d	£5.700	92.1
Cost of dyeing red in madder:				
(a) 38 lb. of fine Bruges madder ('crappemede') at 2d groot per lb.	(6s 4d)	(4s 2½d)		(3.4)
(b) 6 lb. of alum at 4d 18 mites groot per lb.	(2s 4½d)	(1s 7d)		(1.3)
(c) labour in dyeing	(3s 0d)	(2s 0d)		(1.6)
Total dyeing charges	11s 8½d £0.585	7s 9½d	£0.390	6.3
Cost of finishing: 'te scheerene ende te strickene'	3s 0d £0.150	2s 0d	£0.100	1.6
Final price	£9 5s 8½d £9.285	£6 3s 9½d	£6.190	100.0

Source: Stadsarchief te Mechelen, Stadsrekening SI: no. 123, fol. 137ʳ.

Table 3.10 *Prices of Scaerlakens (scarlets) and of other dyed woollens purchased by the government of the Franc de Bruges (Het Brugse Vrije), in pounds groot Flemish, in selected years, from 1396 to 1446**

Year	Price of the scaerlaken (in pounds groot Flemish)	Description of the scaerlaken	Price of the cloth (in pounds groot Flemish)	Description and colour of the cloth
1396	9.525	scaerlaken	4.950	broad green cloth
1401	7.000	broad 'rode scaerlaken'	6.000	broad medley cloth ('gheminghede')
1404	6.600	rode breede scaerlaken	5.800	broad green cloth
1407	7.600	roode breede ghegreinde scaerlaken	3.625	black cloth of Kortrijk (30 ells)
1408	9.150	breede sanguine vulle ghegreinde scaerlakene	6.500	broad brown murrey cloth ('moreit')
1409	9.000	breede peersche scaerlakene	6.000	blue cloth ('zeghel blaeuwe')
1411	8.300	roode breede scaerlaken de twee-deel greynde	3.625	light blue cloths of Diest (Brabant) (30 ells)
1412	9.500	breede sanguine scaerlaken	3.438	dark green cloths of Diest (30 ells)
1414	9.850	roode breede scaerlaken al up ghegreint	3.750	red cloths of Kortrijk (30 ells)

1417	breede vulle ghegreinde scaerlaken	11.000	6.500	broad black cloths
1418	breede rode vulle ghegreinde scaerlaken	11.000	3.375	red and black cloths of **Kortrijk** (30 ells)
1419	breede rode vulle ghegreinde scaerlaken	10.000	3.875	black cloths of **Kortrijk** (30 ells)
1421	breede sancwine vulle ghegreinde scaerlaken	10.000	4.000	red cloths of **Kortrijk** (30 ells)
1422	breede roode vulle ghegreinde scaerlaken	10.000	5.250	broad blue cloth of 30 ells
1425	brede rode vulle ghegreinde scaerlaken	11.600	5.250	broad sanguine cloth of 30 ells
1426	brede sanguine vulle ghegreinde scaerlaken	10.500	5.250	broad red cloth of 30 ells
1427	brede rode vulle ghegreinde scaerlaken	11.000	8.000	broad black cloth
1428	rode brede vulle ghegreinde scaerlakene	12.400	5.500 / 5.625	broad red cloth / broad black cloth

continued overleaf

Table 3.10 continued

Year	Price of the scaerlaken (in pounds groot Flemish)	Description of the scaerlaken	Price of the cloth (in pounds groot Flemish)	Description and colour of the cloth
1430	14.600	brede fine rode vulle ghegreynde scaerlaken	5.750	broad blue cloth
1434	13.000	brede roseide vulle ghegreinde scaerlaken	9.000	broad white-grey medley ('mynxele') cloth
1436/8	11.250	brede vulle ghegreinde sanguyne scaerlaken	6.913	fine broad black cloth
1441	12.567	brede fine witte Yperssche lakenen te vaerwene root scaerlakene met vulle greine[a]	6.000	fine broad black cloth of Menen
1446	7.000[b] 10.500[c] 14.000[d]	fine vulle ghegreinde scaerlakene of Wervik	3.500 5.250	fine blue cloths of Wervik (20 ells) fine blue cloths of Wervik (30 ells)

Notes: * The cloths were manufactured in Ieper (Ypres), unless otherwise stated.
[a] £8 0s 0d for the 'white' cloth; £4 10s 0d for the grain and dyeing costs; 1s 4d groot for the finishing costs.
[b] Wervik scaerlaken of 20 ells: 46 purchased instead of usual 23 cloths.
[c] Equivalent price for 30 ells.
[d] Equivalent price for 40 ells: if 46 Wervik scarlets = 23 Ieper scarlets.

Source: Algemeen Rijksarchief (België), Rekenkamer, Stadsrekeningen van het Brugse Vrije, reg. nos. 42 521–57.

Table 3.11 Prices of Bruges woollens as purchased by the civic government : scaerlaken, langhe breede laken and cuerlaken, in pounds groot Flemish, in various years, 1401–82

Year	Scaerlaken (scarlet) $42\frac{1}{2}$ ells by 10 quarter-ells[a] Colour	Price (in pounds groot Flemish)	Cost of ell[a] (in shillings)	Breede laken $42\frac{1}{2}$ ells by 10 quarters Price (in pounds groot Flemish)	Cost of ell (in shillings)	Cuerlaken 32 ells by 9 quarters Price (in pounds groot Flemish)	Cost of ell (in shillings)
1401	Rose	14.800	7.05*	10.000	4.76*	—	—
1402	Red	14.000	6.67*	9.500	4.52*	6.000	3.75
1403	Brown	15.250	7.18	10.000	4.71	6.250	3.91
1404	Red	16.600	7.81	10.000	4.71	6.250	3.91
1405	Brown	16.500	7.76	9.500	4.47	6.250	3.91
1406	Red	14.000	6.59	9.500	4.47	6.250	3.91
1407	Rose	14.500	6.82	7.000	3.29	6.250	3.91
1408	Brown–Perse	13.413	6.31	—	—	—	—

* 42 ells.

Notes: [a] One ell of Bruges = 0.700 metre = 27.56 inches.

Table 3.11 continued

Year	Scaerlaken (scarlet) 33 ells by 10 quarters	Price (in pounds groot Flemish)	Cost of ell[a] (in shillings)	Breede laken 33 ells by 10 quarters		Cuerlaken 32 ells by 9 quarters	
1408	Brown–Perse	11.500	6.97	7.600	4.61	6.000	3.75
1409	Red	9.000	5.45	6.000	3.63	5.000	3.13
1410	Rose[b]	9.000	5.45	5.800	3.52	5.000	3.13
1411	Brown–Perse[b]	9.250	5.61	5.500[b]	3.33	—	—
1413	Red	10.000	6.06	6.500	3.94	5.000	3.13
1414	Perse[c]	10.000	6.06	7.000	4.24	5.100	3.19
1416	Red[d]	10.500	6.36	7.000	4.24	5.100	3.19
1417	Red[d]	11.250	6.82	6.500	3.94	5.300	3.31
1419	Unspecified[e]	10.475	6.35	6.750	4.09	5.000	3.13
1420	Red[b]	9.000	5.45	7.000	4.24	5.400	3.38
1421	Perse	9.500	5.76	7.000	4.24	5.850	3.66
1422	Red[b]	8.750	5.30	7.000	4.24	5.000	3.13
1427	Brown[b]	9.250	5.61	6.000	3.63	5.050	3.16
1429	Green–Perse[f]	11.200	6.79	—	—	5.200	3.25
1430	Red[b]	13.000	7.88	6.800	4.12	5.800	3.63
1432	Red[g]	12.704	7.70	7.000	4.24	6.000	3.75
1434	Red[h]	13.400	8.12	7.250	4.39	6.300	3.94
1435	Red[h]	13.238	8.02	7.000	4.24	6.400	4.00
1441	Red, Perse[i]	11.000	6.67	8.100	4.91	7.500	4.69
1442	Red[j]	10.800	6.55	8.300	5.03	7.450	4.66
1447	Perse[k]	12.250	7.42	7.500	4.55	—	—
1448	Red	12.500	7.58	8.000	4.85	6.800	4.25
1449	Perse[k]	12.767	7.74	8.250	5.00	7.250	4.53
1450	Red[l]	13.813	8.37	8.000	4.85	6.800	4.25
1482	Rose[m]	[18.554]	12.37[n]	[14.054]	9.37[n]	—	—
		20.409	12.37	15.459	9.37	—	—

of this dyestuff. In the Ieper and Malines cloth accounts, the amounts of kermes specified ranged from 17.7 lb to 55 lb per cloth (about 25.7 kg), with an average of 30 lb (14 kg) in both draperies. According to these accounts, Provençal kermes was usually the most expensive, followed by Valencian or Georgian kermes (or *Porphyrophora hameli*), while the prices of all fluctuated widely.[76]

Nevertheless, the view that the medieval scarlet was a fine woollen containing a kermes dye still seems to be contradicted by all those contemporary texts attributing a wide range of colours to the scarlet.

[76] See ARA Belg., Rek. nos. 38 652, fol. 27^r (1427: Provençal grain at 48d per lb; Valencian grain at 40.8d per lb; Georgian–Armenian grain at 36d per lb); no. 38 677, fol. 32^r (1453: Provençal grain at 38½d per lb; Georgian grain at 34d per lb; Valencian grain at 32d per lb); no. 38 678, fol. 30^v (1454: Provençal grain at 38d, 36d, and 34d per lb). See also n. 9 and Table 3.5. The Venetian dyer-author Gioanventura Rosetti (1548) similarly prescribed 30 lb of grain per cloth in scarlet dyeing (20 lb of Provençal grain and 10 lb of Valencian grain). *Plictho* (n. 9), no. 88, pp. 33, 124; also no. 46, pp. 108–9. See also the less detailed fifteenth-century Venetian dyeing manual *Un manuale di tintoria del quattrocento*, Giovanni Rebora (ed.) (Milan, 1970), pp. 121–2, nos. cxx–cxxv ('A far uno belo pano de scarlatto; a granar questo pano').

Notes:
^{b} Cloth made in Ypres.
^{c} 'Persche ghegrynde scaerlakene'.
^{d} 'Witte fine Brussche lakene omme te greynene ende roode scaerlakene daeraf ghemaect' (white cloth £6.000 + £4.500 for grain, in 1416).
^{e} Colour not specified: blue cloth £6.750 + £3.725 for the grain.
^{f} 'Fine Brugsche lakene de welke waren ghedaen groene persche ... ghegreynt zynde al up bereet, coste elc de voorseide persch scaerlakene, £11 4s 0d.'
^{g} 'Fine witte lakene ... omme scaerlakene daer af te makene' (white £7.000 + 'van greynene ende van varwene' £5.704 = £12.704).
^{h} 'Fine witte Brugsche lakene, de welke waren ghedaen greynen ... de voorseide scaerlakene.'
^{i} 'Greynen persch' (cloth £7.500 + £3.500 for the grain = £11.000).
^{j} White cloth £8.300 + £2.500 for the grain = £10.800.
^{k} 'Fine peersche lakenen Brughsche ... mids dat zij vul ghegreint waren.'
^{l} 'Roode Brucghsche scaerlakene, die vul ghegreint waren.'
^{m} 'Fijn witte Bruchsche laken (£11.000) ... te roozeydene ende te greynene (£7.500) ... uter wulle te scheerne ende te verziene, 1s 1d.'
^{n} The 'scaerlakene' was 30 ells long. The original price is in square brackets, with the value of 33 ells given underneath. Price per ell was given in the account.

Source: Stadsarchief te Brugge, Stadsrekeningen, 1401–82; Algemeen Rijksarchief, Rekenkamer, reg. nos. 32 461–534.

Table 3.12 Costs of manufacturing five black cloths from a sack of fine Cotswold wool at Ieper (Ypres) in 1501, in pounds groot Flemish and English sterling

Input or stage of manufacturing five cloths	Subtotals (in pounds groot)	Total of input or stage for five cloths (in pounds groot)	Cost per cloth (in pounds groot)	Cost per cloth (in pounds sterling)[a]	Percentage of total costs
Wool: one sack fine Cotswold[b]	32.856				51.9
tax	0.150	33.006	6.601	4.543	2.7
Wool preparation		1.721	0.344	0.237	
Draper's cost in spinning, weaving fulling, tentering		16.667	3.333	2.294	26.2
(Pre-finishing manufacturing)		(51.394)	(10.278)	(7.074)	(80.8)
Dyeing in Black:					
alum	1.667				
blue-dyeing in woad (wool)	5.500				
red-dyeing in madder (cloth)	4.000				
dyers' assistants	0.067	11.234	2.247	1.546	17.7
Shearing and finishing		1.000	0.200	0.138	1.5
Totals		63.628	12.725	8.758	100.0

Notes: [a] 1 pound groot = 0.688 pound sterling; 1 pound sterling = 1.453 pound groot.
         [b] 1 woolsack Flemish weight = 360 Flem. lb = 168.387 kg = 371.23 lb avoir. = 1.02 English sack.

Source: Algemeen Rijksarchief, Rekenkamer, reg. no. 38 723, fol. 40ᵛ.

The most difficult to reconcile, the most contradictory, is the term 'white scarlet'. Its meaning, however, was a simple one that in no way precluded some application of the kermes dye. For in medieval textile terminology, 'white' meant not an applied colour but undyed, or not yet dyed. In the former and less usual sense, a white scarlet was one with a 'white' undyed background for some scarlet-coloured, grain-dyed design. Thus, for example, Froissart described the king of Portugal in 1386 as 'vestu de blance escarlatte à une *vermeille* croix de Saint Jeorge'; and accounts of Joanna II of Artois in 1335 record the purchase of two 'esquallates blanches *goutées de vermoil'* – flecked with vermilion, grain.[77] The much more common meaning was the latter sense: a fine woollen of scarlet dimensions that was going to be dyed in grain. Thus an account of some woollens confiscated from a St Omer merchant at Calais in 1306 states: '6 blankes sortes dont on fait escarlates; item, 2 escarlates sanguines; une escarlate cleire sanguine; une escarlate de vermeille coleur' (all vivid shades of red).[78]

This particular sense of 'white scarlet' was undoubtedly derived from the almost universal tripartite designation of woollens in European drapery ordinances according to the colour of their wools before being woven on the loom: as bluc, medley (*mellé, ghemingde, gheminghede, strijpte*), or white. 'White cloths' were those that were woven from undyed wools and that were subsequently dyed 'in the piece', after the fulling and initial finishing processes, usually with a mordant dyestuff. By far the most important mordant dyes were reds: madder, from the European herb *Rubia tinctorum*, producing alizarin; Brazil-wood, from the tropical trees genus *Caesalpinia*; and – of course – kermes. Such dyes were 'fixed', made fast, to the cloth by the chemical properties of the mordant, chiefly alum or cream of tartar, whose hydroxides formed a firm union with both the wool fibres and the dye chemicals. At the same time, such mordants also assisted in fixing the dye by cleansing the cloth of any remaining oils and grease not removed by scouring and fulling – oils necessarily added to the wools to facilitate combing/carding, spinning, weaving and felting.[79] William Partridge, in his *Practical Treatise on Dying* [*sic*] (1823), suggests another reason why mordant-dyeing more often took place 'in the piece' than 'in the wools': 'for if the same quantity [of mordant] were used on the wool,

[77] Froissart, *Chroniques*, Kervyn de Lettenhove, (ed.), 25 vols. (Brussels, 1876–7), XI, p. 405 (2–3 November 1386); Espinas and Pirenne, *Recueil* (n. 46), III, pp. 290–1, no. 673; and also p. 296, no. 677 (May 1340).

[78] Espinas and Pirenne, *Recueil* (n. 46), III, p. 278, no. 658.

[79] See, for example, Espinas and Pirenne, *Recueil* (n. 46), III, p. 464, no. 733: 54, at Ieper, October 1291: 'ke nus faiseur ki fait draes bleus ou blans ou melleis'. For dyeing and other technical matters, see de Poerck, *Draperie médiévale* (n. 8), I, pp. 45–7, 90–112, 150–87, esp. 169; Espinas, *Draperie* (n. 41), II, pp. 221–46; J. W. Radcliffe, *Manufacture of Woollen and Worsted Yarns* (Manchester, 1913), pp. 160–5.

it would, in the greater number of colours, render it unfit for spinning, weaving, and fulling'.[80] The indigo blue extracted from the European woad plant *Isatis tinctoria* and (subsequently) from the Indian indigo plant genus *Indigofera* was, however, one of the very few medieval dyes not requiring such mordants. Partly for this reason, many cloths, the so-called 'blue cloths', were woven from wools that had already been dyed this colour, before or after being spun.[81] The third class of cloths, the 'medleys', were those whose yarns were spun from a mélange of different or differently-coloured wools, or those whose warp and weft yarns were differently coloured, as in striped or ray cloths.

An example of this tripartite designation that also includes the 'white scarlet', undyed and pre-finished, can be found in a Brussels drapery ordinance of 1376 specifying the number and colour of selvage threads to be added in weaving 'langhe witte scaerlakene, langhe blaeuwe lakene, langhe ghemingde lakene' and other smaller cloths.[82] A St Omer ordinance of 1280 similarly used the term 'white scarlet' in forbidding fullers to sell outside the town any 'flokons d'escarlates blankes ne blewes' – wool residues from the fulling processes.[83] These two texts, furthermore, certainly do not support Weckerlin's fundamental contention that the term scarlet was applied to fine woollens only after they had been shorn and fully finished. The final text to be cited for 'white scarlets' is a later St Omer drapery ordinance of 1320: it set brokerage fees of 6s 0d *parisis* for all cloths called 'dickedinne, mellé en graine et entre pers [deep blue or bluish grey], et tout drap omple que on dist blanque escarlate'. The word 'omple' here means plain, uniform, of just one colour, as when dyed grain-scarlet 'in the piece' only.[84]

This last text in fact also reveals the most significant feature of those so-called 'blue cloths': a capacity for a striking metamorphosis that fully explains all the other colours quite correctly attributed to medieval scarlets. For in medieval draperies, woad-indigo served as the

[80] William Partridge, *A Practical Treatise on Dying* [sic] *of Woollen, Cotton, and Skein Silk* (New York, 1823; republished as *Pasold Occasional Papers*, vol. I, J. de L. Mann and K. G. Ponting (eds.); Edington, Wilts, 1973), p. 100. Partridge notes, however, on p. 177 that weld-yellow dyes mordanted with alum were an exception. See also Ponting's notes 91 (p. 239) and 174 (p. 252).

[81] de Poerck, *Draperie médiévale* (n. 8), I, pp. 150–69; Espinas, *Draperie*, (n. 41), II, pp. 221–46; Partridge, *Practical Treatise*, (n. 80), pp. 95–101, 112–21, 152–63; and also Ponting's notes nn. 103–11 (pp. 240–2), for additional, most useful information on vegetable dyes. Although woad and indigo dyeing did indeed require the addition of wood ashes or potash, this additive did not serve as a mordant but as a chemical agent to make the woad or indigo soluble in water. De Poerck, I, 162–4.

[82] Félicien Favresse, 'Règlements inédits sur la vente des laines et des draps et sur les métiers de la draperie bruxelloise, 1363–94', *Bulletin de la commission royale d'histoire*, CXI (1946), pp. 153–4.

[83] Espinas and Pirenne, *Receuil* (n. 46), III, p. 247, no. 651: 111 (*c.*1280).

[84] Ibid., (n. 46), III, p. 286, no. 668 (*c.*1320). See also Espinas, *Draperie* (n. 41), II, p. 151, n. 9: 'plain drap omple . . . taint en graine', purchased by the countess of Artois in November 1337; and p. 153; and also Laurent, *Draperie* (n. 41), pp. 211–21; de Poerck, *Draperie médiévale* (n. 8), II, pp. 137–8.

essential foundation – what the Flemish called *moeder blaeu* – for creating a wide range of other colours. Thus a blue-dyed cloth, often dyed first 'in the wools', was redyed in the piece with red and/or weld-yellow, sometimes with more woad, to produce, for example: browns, reddish-browns, greys, blacks, purples, violets, murreys [mulberry], perse, perse–browns, perse–greens, other greens – and also the blood-red yet blue-based *sanguines*.[85] In many medieval lands, woollens so dyed in any of these red- and blue-based colours were called 'scarlets' when, and only when, the red component was kermes. That all such colours contained some red may not be so readily obvious. But drapery regulations from Bruges and Leiden explicitly confirm that red dyes were used in producing blacks, greys – a black-related shade – and the dark, greyish to blackish perse blues;[86] and Table 3.12 demonstrates the production of a black woollen from wools dyed first in the woad and then redyed in the piece with red–madder. Understandably, it is far more difficult to believe that any red could be found in green shades. Nevertheless, late medieval dyers' keures for Ieper, Malines and Leiden all permitted the use of madder in green-dyeing, stipulating only that the blue cloths must be made thoroughly green before the madder could be added.[87] Furthermore, the previously cited nineteenth-century dyer William Partridge states that 'for all greens intended to have a red here, take any of the foregoing receipts [green-dye recipes], leave out one-third of the yellow dyes, and add from one to three pounds of barwood or camwood [or] as much madder'.[88] Certainly

[85] See de Poerck, *Draperie médiévale* (n. 8), I, pp. 150–68, and esp. 189–90, 193–8. For sanguines, see the fourteenth-century Béthune dyers' keure in Espinas and Pirenne, *Recueil* (n. 46), I, p. 320, no. 129: 16: 'toutes sanguines ou violettes cleres ... soient taintes le waide premièrement ... et aprez waranchiés sur le waide'; and the St Omer dyers' ordinance of *c*. 1350–75 in ibid., III, p. 329, no. 704: 'cler bleu pour faire sanguines; ce tout de pure waides [woad]'. See also Table 3.10.

[86] For black-dyeing see also the Leiden dyers' keure of 1541: 'dat die blaeuverwers gheen laeckenen zwart verwen noch doen verwen en sullen dan mit guet gebrant weedt [woad], berenclaeu, hertshoeren ende bliexer assche [potash] ... mit zemel, aluyn, die men hiet folie of glas, mede, die men hiet crap [madder called crap]' in Posthumus, *Bronnen* (n. 61), II, p. 478, no. 1034: VI: 1. For perse-dyeing, see the Leiden dyers' keure of 1472: 'dat die meester verwers van den rootsieders [red-dyers] elc enen eedt doen, dat zy gheen roden noch pairtsen [reds nor perse] meden en sullen dan fynen crappe [crappemede = madder], in ibid., I, p. 537, no. 440: 22; also ibid., II, p. 482, no. 1034: VI: 15: 1 (1541). For greys, see the Bruges dyers keure for *nouveux gris* of 1458, requiring the best *crappemede*, in Delepierre and Willems, *Keuren* (n. 61), pp. 100–2. For these colours, see also de Poerck, *Draperie médiévale* (n. 8), I, pp. 190, 195–6.

[87] For Malines, see the dyers' keure of *c*.1331: 'wat blawer lakene lichte ofte sat dat moet wel gegroent sijn eer men se *meden* mach' in Joossen, 'Recueil de documents', *BCRH* (n. 57), p. 493, no. 48: 3. For Ieper, see the red-dyers' keure of *c*.1350–1400: 'wat lakene dat men verloren groene vaerwen wille, moet eerst zijn wel jegroent eer dat ment *meed* [add madder]'. Espinas and Pirenne, *Recueil* (n. 46), III, p. 619, no. 789: 20. For Leiden, see the dyers' keure on green and perse dyeing of 1453: 'soe wat blaeuverwer enige groenen anneemt te verwen, die sel se oic mit anders gheen stof maken dan mit fynen alluyn ende mit fynen crappe [mede = madder]' in Posthumus, *Bronnen*, (n. 61), I, p. 325, no. 263: VI: 22; also ibid., I, p. 536, no. 440: VII: 18 (1472); ibid., II, p. 482, no. 1034: VI: 15: 1 (1541).

[88] Partridge, *Practical Treatise* (n. 80), p. 181.

for all these colours kermes could be used instead of madder or Brazil-wood.

The contention that medieval scarlets were necessarily dyed in kermes but frequently in other, blue-based colours as well is not entirely novel. As long ago as 1887, the French art historian Victor Gay, in his *Glossaire archéologique du moyen âge*, had given this definition of the medieval term scarlet: 'dyeing in any bright colour or shade to which an immersion in a kermes bath added a particular brilliance [*éclat*]'.[89] Weckerlin, however, scornfully dismissed this interpretation:[90]

> This opinion concerning a supplementary bath of kermes, in order to provide a special lustre, is obviously quite false. Practically speaking, this type of [mixed] dyeing would be completely impossible, for it would result in dull, blackish shades, without any lustre. Gay's opinion, moreover, is not based on any text nor any dyeing regulation that could imply any such technique.

In my view, Gay was indeed incorrect in two important respects: that the initial dyeing was in 'any bright colour or shade', and that the final colour was necessarily brilliant. Clearly the base was always a woad–indigo blue; and the end result, except for sanguines, would have been darker hues: browns, blacks and purples, especially. But Weckerlin himself failed to produce any texts to support his rebuttal. Although he could not possibly deny that a red dye was used in these common colours, he evidently thought that to mix and 'adulterate' such a costly, luxurious dye as kermes with other colours would have been preposterous. Indeed, he then proceeded to stress his previously outlined thesis that late medieval drapers came to have their woollen scarlets dyed exclusively in grain. A great many scarlets, to be sure, were so dyed to receive 'unadulterated' that rich lustrous red we call scarlet. But Weckerlin was mistaken in believing that late medieval fashion prized this colour for the finest woollens to the exclusion of other, darker colours. In fact, in the later fifteenth century, blacks and deep blues became the leading colours for the woollens that Flemish towns purchased for their aldermen and princely guests (see Tables 3.6–3.8).[91] Furthermore, Weckerlin was simply wrong in denying that grain-dyeing could be mixed with other colours. References abound,

---

[89] Victor Gay, *Glossaire archéologique du moyen âge et de la Renaissance*, 2 vols. (Paris, 1887–1928), I, p. 593.

[90] *Drap escarlate*, p. 17; see also pp. 22–3, 84–90.

[91] As indicated by the records of cloth purchase for aldermen and princely guests in the urban treasurers' accounts of Ieper, Bruges, Ghent, Malines and Leuven in the Algemeen Rijksarchief (Belgium) and the *stadsarchieven* of the above towns, except Ieper. At Malines, virtually all cloths purchased from the mid-1490s to the end of the series in 1550 were black. Stadsarchief te Mechelen, Stadsrekeningen SI nos. 169–225. At Leiden, however, black was not so prominent.

for example, to 'violetes et sanguines de graine'; and, it should be noted, a grain-dyed violet or murrey would have been the closest feasible imitation of the still highly esteemed royal purple.[92] The only dyestuffs known to me that were forbidden to be mixed with grain-dyeing were madder and Brazil-wood; and that ban was clearly intended to prevent fraud, counterfeiting, in producing 'red' scarlets.[93]

On the contrary, many ancient, medieval and early modern texts can be cited to refute Weckerlin's singular arguments on grain-dyeing. Thus in the Classical era, *Hysgine* purple was produced by dyeing the wool or cloth in kermes and then in two baths of Tyrian purple.[94] Later, a third-century Greek dye recipe in the *Papyrus Holmiensis* states:[95]

> Dress the wool with blue ... wash and dry the wool; then dissolve the kermes in water, mix with common orchil, and boil. Immerse the wool and it will become scarlet. [*sic*: probably sanguine or purple]

Similarly, in early modern England, a state paper of 1614 notes that a third of the Suffolk cloths exported were first dyed blue in the wool with indigo and then redyed in the piece with cochineal, the successor to kermes, to produce 'violets, murreys, silver colour, peach colour'.[96] In late medieval Flanders and Brabant, the municipal accounts contain hundreds of entries demonstrating the same mode of dyeing *scaerlakenen*:[97]

> van den selve [blaeuwe] lakene bruyn scaerlakene te makene; bruynscaer-lakene met grein
>
> satblauwe lakene die men greynde [als] persche gheghrynde scaerlakene

---

[92] See, for example, Espinas and Pirenne, *Recueil* (n. 46), III, p. 295, no. 676 (1338); p. 299, no. 681 (1340); p. 300, no. 683 (1340).

[93] See ibid., I, p. 467, no. 144: 14 (Bruges, 1294); III, p. 468, no. 754: 17 (Ieper, *c*.1300); 521, no. 768: 66 (Ieper, fourteenth century); 621, no. 789: 29 (Ieper, 1363–1416); Joossen, 'Recueil de documents' (n. 57), pp. 528–33, no. 62. But see also n. 105.

[94] Pliny, *Natural History* (n. 5), III, pp. 258–9 (Book ix.lxv.141: 'quin et terrena miscere coccoque tindum Tyrio tinguere ut fieret hysginum'); Isidore, *Etymologiarum* (n. 5), II (Book xix.xxiv.8); Born, 'Purple' (n. 5), pp. 113–15.

[95] G. A. Faber, 'Dyeing in Greece', *Ciba Review*, no. 9 (May 1938), p. 290, evidently from K. Reinking, 'Ueber die älteste Beschreibung der Küpenfärberei im Papyrus Graecus Holmiensis', *Melliand Textilberichten*, I (1925), no. 5, pp. 349–51; or his *Wollfärbevorschriften aus den griechischen Papyri* (Leipzig, 1938), both unavailable to me.

[96] Cited in George Unwin, 'Industries' in William Page (ed.), *Victoria County History: Suffolk*, II (1907), pp. 261–2; and R. L. Lee, 'American cochineal in European commerce, 1526–1625', *Journal of Modern History*, XXIII (1951), pp. 251–2.

[97] Stadsarchief te Mechelen, SI nos. 45, fol. 70[r] (1366); 58, fol. 85[r] (1379); 64, fol. 23[r] (1386); 84, fol. 168[v] (1408); ARA Belg., Rek. no. 32483, fol. 31[r] (Bruges, 1429). See also examples cited in Rosetti's Venetian dyeing manual of 1548, *The Plictho* (n. 9): for 'peacock blues', in nos. 70, p. 115; no. 75, p. 116; no. 92, p. 125; and also for quince shades, no. 67, p. 115 (3 lb of grain, 8 lb of weld, 15 lb of young fustic, and 20 lb of alum).

fine Brugsche lakene de welke waren ghedaen groene persche, ende ghegrynt zynde al up bereet . . . coste elc de voors. persche scaerlakene, £11 4s 0d.

(to produce brown scarlets from the same blue cloths; brown scarlets with grain

deep-blue cloths, which are made perse grain-dyed scarlets

fine Bruges cloths, which were made green–perse; and having been dyed in grain and completely finished, each of the aforesaid perse–scarlets cost £11 4s 0d [groot Flemish])

In Table 3.4, moreover, 38 per cent of the cloths purchased for garbing the Malines alderman at Christmas and Easter (1361–1417) had been first dyed blue in the wool and then redyed in grain 'in the piece' to become variously coloured *scaerlakenen*.

Finally, all these accounts and records indicate that the term *scaerlaken* referred only to grain-dyed woollens, with or without other dyes. The following are more sample entries from the treasurers' accounts:[98]

brede fine witte Ypersche lakenen omme te vaerwene root scaerlakene met vulle greine

fine witte Brugsche lakenen omme te greinene ende rood scaerlakene *daer af ghemaect*

(fine white broadcloths of Ieper (Ypres) to be dyed red scarlets with full grain

fine white cloths of Bruges to be dyed in grain and *thereby* to be made red scarlets [to be made red scarlets by dyeing in grain])

Other examples are given, without translations, in Tables 3.10 and 3.11. The prices of Bruges and Ieper *scaerlakenen* in those two tables are, it must be noted, very closely comparable to the total costs of producing grain-dyed woollens at Ieper, as detailed in Table 3.5 (1406–86). Clearly that comparability at these high price levels would have been quite impossible without grain-dyeing.

Certainly from a very early date, much earlier than Weckerlin would admit, medieval writers very explicitly associated scarlets with kermes dyestuffs. About AD 1200 or before, Gervaise of Tilbury (Tilleberiensis), grandson of Henry II, provided this definition of *vermiculus*:[99]

---

[98] ARA Belg., Rek. no. 42554, fol. 43ᵛ (Bruges Vrij, 1440–41); no. 32471, fol. 48ᵛ (Bruges, May 1417). See also no. 32470, fol. 26ᵛ (Bruges, May 1416); 32502, fol. 22ʳ (Bruges, May 1450); 41221, fol. 182ᵛ (Malines, Easter, 1409); and Tables 3.10–3.11.

[99] Du Cange, *Glossarium* (n. 18), VII, p. 340. Weckerlin, *Drap escarlate* (n. 19), pp. 78–9, gives a different interpretation.

Vermiculus hic est, quo tinguntur pretiosissimi Regum panni, sive serici ut *examiti*; sive lanei, ut *Scarlata*

(Vermiculum is that [this thing] by which the most costly of the King's cloths are dyed, whether silks, namely as samites; or woollens, as Scarlets)

Thus only woollens dyed in kermes and no other fabrics could be called scarlets; but silks dyed that colour were certainly compared directly to scarlets, as in this description from the thirteenth-century French romance *Merlin*: 'une nef couverte de drap de soie aussi *vermeil* coume une *escrelate*'.[100] An even more explicitly exclusive association between kermes and scarlets can be found in this definition by Matteo Silvaticus, *c.* 1297:[101]

Coccus vel kermes, Arab. karmas: Latine vero grana tinctorum, unde tinguntur Scarlatum; veste coccinea in tincta cocco, scilicet granis de Scarleto

(Coccus or kermes, Arabic karmas: in Latin indeed dyers' grains, from which Scarlets are dyed; scarlet-coloured clothing, dyed in kermes, namely grains of Scarlet)

An equally exclusive association, direct from the horse's mouth, so to speak, can be found in this proposed fee schedule of the Ghent dyers, issued in 1374:[102]

van eene scaerlakene, te ziedene ende te greinene, 5s

(for one scarlet, to boil [in the dyer's solution in the vat] and to dye in grain, 5s groot.)

The quantity of grain that had to be applied to dye scarlets, and justify the term, varied from place to place. The Douai dyers' keure of *c.* 1250 stipulated a minimum of 22 lb 'de boine graine' per cloth.[103] Fourteenth-century Ghent was evidently satisfied with much less grain. Thus the Ghent *Lakenhalle*, in setting cloth brokerage fees in 1335, specified 4s 0d *parisis* for each 'courte escarlate, ou il a wyt [8] livres de graine ou deseure'.[104] While all the draperies of the medieval Low Countries were quite content to call variously coloured woollens *scaerlakenen* so long as they contained the requisite amount of grain, some French towns and the English in general, however, came to

---

[100] Tobler and Lommatsche, *Wörterbuch* (n. 20), III, p. 816, citing *Merlin, roman en prose du XIIIe siècle* (Paris, 1886 edn), p. 175.

[101] Du Cange, *Glossarium* (n. 18), VII, p. 340.

[102] Espinas and Pirenne, *Recueil* (n. 16), II, p. 541, no. 496.

[103] Ibid., II, p. 57, no. 229: 77.

[104] Ibid., II, p. 418, no. 423: 1–2.

restrict the term scarlet to just those woollens wholly and solely dyed in grain. Thus an article of the Paris drapery statutes, reconfirmed in July 1362, forbade anyone to sell any cloth 'pour escarlate se il n'est tout pur de graine, sans autre mistion de teinture quelconque'; the next article also forbade merchants to sell cloths called 'mi-graine, se il n'y a la moitié grainne'.[105] That same classification of woollens evidently also prevailed in the Rouen drapery, the most important in Normandy; for an ordinance dated 1424 set brokerage fees at 3d *tournois* per ell of cloth, except for 'la demi-graine, dont ils auront six deniers pour aulne, et d'escarlate pour douze deniers'. The same ordinance's subsequent reference to kermes as 'graine d'escarlattes', Silvaticus's term, further suggests that 'escarlate' meant uniquely a full-grained cloth.[106]

In England, a more explicit tripartite classification of dyed woollens was consistently applied in royal accounts from at least Edward I's *Carta Mercatoria* and 'New Custom' of February 1303. These edicts required aliens importing or exporting woollens to pay the following taxes: 2s 0d sterling for each 'scarleta et panno tincto in grano' (article 16); 1s 6d for each 'panno in quo pars grani fuerit intermixta' (article 17); and 1s 0d for each 'panno alio sine grano' (article 18).[107] Quite obviously the extent of this graduated tax was determined by the kermes content: whole grain, partial grain or no grain. Nevertheless Weckerlin and others have insisted that article 16 makes a further distinction between two superior yet different woollens: Weckerlin's true, highly shorn 'scarlet', and cloths dyed in grain.[108] But surely, according to this logic, any such 'scarlet' that was also dyed fully in grain should have been taxed at an even higher rate, indeed double the amount. In any event, the medieval English customs accounts use the terms 'scarleta', the favoured term, and 'panno tincto in grano' quite indifferently, evidently as synonyms.[109] Furthermore, a late

[105] René de Lespinasse (ed.), *Les métiers et corporations de la ville de Paris*, 3 vols. (Paris, 1886–97), III, p. 148, no. xi.iii.25–6 (statutes authorised by Philip IV in April 1310). These articles were reconfirmed on 23 December 1407 (p. 157). Dye recipes in Rosetti's *Plictho* (n. 9) of 1548 employ the term *scarlattino* for cloths of half-grain: with for example 3 lb grain, 25 lb madder, 1½ lb brazil, and 24 lb alum per cloth, in pp. 17, 24; no. 45, p. 107; no. 63, p. 114. See also n. 93, 115.

[106] Charles Ouin-Lacroix, *Histoire des anciens corporations d'arts et métiers et des confréries religieuses de la capitale de la Normandie* (Rouen, 1850), pp. 616–21.

[107] Full text in N. S. B. Gras, *The Early English Customs System* (Cambridge, Mass., 1918), pp. 259–64, no. 29. See also Thomas Ryder (ed.), *Foedera, conventiones, litterae*, Rec. Com. edn (London, 1821), ii.ii, pp. 747–8. By the cloth custom of 3 March 1347, the export tax on a scarlet was raised to 3s 6d for aliens and 2s 4d for denizens; on a cloth of half-grain, to 2s 7d for aliens and 1s 9d for denizens; and on a cloth without grain, to 1s 9d for aliens and 1s 2d for denizens. Hanse merchants refused to pay more than the 1303 rates (Gras, p. 72).

[108] See Weckerlin, *Drap escarlate*, p. 84 n. 1; Carus-Wilson and Coleman, *England's Export Trade* (n. 41 above), p. 15.

[109] I have examined all of the English enrolled customs accounts from 1303 to 1520 in the Public Record Office, LTR Exchequer, series E 356/1–25; and also many of the 'particulars' accounts in the KR Exchequer series E 122.

fifteenth-century survey of the 'Kynges Custum and Subsidie' made no distinction at all in tax classifications between these two terms, listing simply 'Cloth wythout greyn', 'Cloth in greyn' and 'Cloth half-grayned'.[110] If indeed a clear distinction was meant in occasional joint entries of 'scarleta et panno tincto in grano' in the customs accounts, it was unlikely the one meant by Weckerlin. For other evidence indicates that it would have been the same distinction suggested in the 1362 Paris drapery statutes: between pure 'whole grain' and 'whole grain' supplemented by other colours. Thus a parliamentary petition of 1410 accused certain aliens of secretly using their own kermes in their London hostels to dye woollens 'en scarlet, en sangwyn [blood-red, containing blue], et *en autres colours d'entier grayn'* and of disguising them in barrels to evade the customs on scarlets and 'autre Drap d'entier grayn'.[111] Similarly a Yarmouth customs account (March–Mich. 1432) refers to 'pannis de scarleta, de sange-weyn, et de *alia coloribus de integro grano*, vel de dimidio grano'.[112] Finally, the royal wardrobe accounts also reserve the term scarlet exclusively for those woollens dyed this colour wholly and solely in grain. At the same time, they demonstrate that English drapers produced about as many fine woollens variously coloured with both kermes and other dyestuffs, generally having a blue base, at prices comparable to those of at least the cheaper scarlets. A few sample entries are given in Table 3.13.[113]

Weckerlin had also contended, to be sure, that by the fourteenth century the term scarlet had taken on its modern meaning of the grain-dyed red colour, at least within the textile trades themselves, if not necessarily in popular or literary usage, which 'preserved the old meaning of fine [shorn] cloth', divorced from a specific colour, 'up to the early sixteenth century'.[114] But all the English and Flemish–Brabantine evidence presented here flatly contradicts Weckerlin's seemingly corollary conclusions: that *all* fine shorn woollens came to be dyed solely in grain; that any mixed dyeing with kermes and other dyestuffs was 'completely impossible'. Furthermore, even though French and English official records do reserve the term scarlet for

---

[110] Gras, *Customs* (n. 107), pp. 690–3, Appendix B (between 1473 and 1503).

[111] *Rotuli Parliamentorum*, 6 vols. (London, 1767–77), III, p. 626: no. 26. See also the London shearers' fee schedule of 1452 in *London and Middlesex Archaeological Society*, IV, p. 42: 'for shearing of scarlet and all other engrained cloth, every yard, two pence': as cited in Ephraim Lipson, *Economic History of England*, I: *Middle Ages*, 7th edn (London, 1937), pp. 337–8.

[112] PRO, LTR Exchequer E 356/18, m. 37.

[113] The accounts in the PRO Exchequer that I have examined are: (a) particulars of the royal wardrobe for various years, 1304–1483 in E 101 series: 308/6, 360/12, 371/10, 405/14, 405/22, 406/9, 407/1, 407/13, 409/2, 409/6, 409/12; and LC 9/50 (an edition of which was most kindly made available to me by Dr Anne Sutton); (b) enrolled wardrobe accounts, for virtually consecutive years, 1326–1463, in E 361 series nos. 3–6.

[114] Weckerlin, *Drap escarlate*, pp. 11, 22–3, 85–90.

Table 3.13   Purchases of grain-dyed woollens for the royal wardrobes of Edward III, Henry IV, Henry VI and Richard III, selected years

Year of account	Description of the grain-dyed cloth	Price of the woollen 30 ells	1 ell
1328–29	4 pannis longis in grano diversis coloris		
1361–62	1 ulna demi panni scarletti 12 ulnis violettis longis in grano 4 ulnis pannis nigris longis in grano		
1412–13	71 pannis 12 ulnis pannis scarlettis 2 pannis 6 ulnis pannis sanguinis in grano		
1438–39	pannis scarletis [cheapest]	£14 2s 6d	9s 5d
	pannis scarletis [dearest]	£28 10s 0d	19s 0d
	pannis murris in grano	£17 4s 0d	11s 6d
	pannis violet [is] in grano	£13 10s 0d	9s 0d
	pannis violet et sanguine in grano	£16 10s 0d	11s 0d
1443–44	pannis scarletis [cheapest]	£14 5s 0d	9s 6d
	pannis scarletis [dearest]	£28 10s 0d	19s 0d
	pannis violetis in grano	£14 5s 0d	9s 6d
	pannis sanguine in grano	£18 0s 0d	12s 0d
1483–84	scarlet [cheapest]	£12 0s 0d	8s 0d
	scarlet [dearest]	£25 0s 0d	16s 8d
	murrey clothe engrayned	£15 0s 0d	10s 0d
	violet clothe engrayned	£19 10s 0d	13s 0d

Sources: PRO, Exchequer, E 361/3 m. 11 (1328–29); E 361/4 m. 6 (1361–62); E 361/6 m. 7 (1413); E 101/409/2 (1438–39); E 101/409/12 (1443–44); LC 9/50, fol. 20–1 (1483–84) from MS edited A. F. Sutton and P. W. Hammond.

those woollens dyed in grain alone, the draperies of the Low Countries – and not just popular usage – continued to designate all woollens containing sufficient grain as *scaerlakenen*, scarlets, no matter what colour, until a much later era, certainly until the late fifteenth century.[115] By that time the Flemish and Brabantine woollen industries

[115] In the municipal treasurers' accounts of the Low Countries, the last recorded sale of a scarlet that I have found is for 1486: at Ieper (Ypres), a *breeden scaerblaeuwen Ypersschen laken*, dyed in blue and grain, for £12 18s 0d *groot*, in ARA Belg., Rek. reg. no. 38 710, fol. 57ᵛ. See n. 105 for references to grain and madder-dyed *scarlattini* in the 1548 *Plictho*. Venice became a leading producer of scarlets (*panni in scarlatti*) in the sixteenth century.

were suffering a serious, irredeemable decay, and had ceased to be significant producers of scarlets.[116]

IV

If, at various times in different places, in most by the thirteenth century, the adjective scarlet had come to mean specifically the grain-dyed colour, since all scarlets contained this dye, the colour itself underwent two subtle but significant changes in the early modern era. The first resulted from the introduction of a new scarlet dyestuff: the previously mentioned cochineal, which the Spanish discovered during their conquest of Mexico in the early sixteenth century. So closely did this scale insect resemble the Mediterranean kermes *Cocci* that they named it *Grana cochinilla*. Its modern scientific name is *Coccus cacti* or more properly *Dactylopius coccus*. The former term is derived from the parasite's hosts, two closely related species of Mexican cactus plants, commonly known as nopals: principally the *Opuntia ficus indica*, whose fruit resembles large figs; and secondarily the *Nopalea cochenillifera*. The natural wild variety of cochineal, called *Grana silvestre*, was harvested when pregnant not once but six times a year. The domesticated, refined *Grana fina* is twice the size and produces a much richer dye; but it yields fewer harvests, usually three a year (May, July and October), with about 250 kg per hectare (about 225 lb per acre, averaging 70,000 insects per lb) of nopals. The harvested cochineals were either killed directly by hot water and then dried (red–brown), or were baked slowly in the hot sun (silver), or were baked in hot pans or ovens (black).[117]

From about the 1560s, perhaps forty years after the first shipments reached Spain (1523–26), cochineal began displacing kermes in the textile-dyeing of most European countries.[118] It was certainly far more abundant in supply; and furthermore it yielded a richer, more powerful dye, so that far smaller quantities were required per cloth. Later dye recipes specified only 3–5 lb (1.36–2.27 kg) 'for dyeing a Cloth into Scarlet or other Grain Colours': about 10 to 17 per cent of

[116] For the sharp decline in Flemish–Brabantine cloth production during the fifteenth century, see John Munro, 'Monetary contraction and industrial change in the late medieval Low Countries, 1335–1500' in Nicholas Mayhew (ed.), *Coinage in the Low Countries, 880–1500* (*British Archaeological Reports*, International series no. 54, Oxford, 1979), pp. 95–161; and Munro, 'Industrial protectionism' (n. 2 above), pp. 247–53.

[117] Donkin, *Spanish Red* (n. 5 above), pp. 11–18, 24–38; Born, 'Scarlet' (n. 8), pp. 214–20; Forbes, 'Dyes' (n. 5), IV, pp. 102–4; R. L. Lee, 'Cochineal production and trade in New Spain', *The Americas*, IV (1947–8), pp. 458–63; Lee, 'American cochineal' (n. 96), pp. 205–24; Susan Fairlie, 'Dyestuffs in the eighteenth century', *Economic History Review*, 2nd ser., XVII (1965), pp. 489–92, 498–9.

[118] Scientific analyses of dyes in early modern textiles prove that this displacement occurred rapidly in the sixteenth century. See Hofenk-De Graaff and Roelofs, *Red Dyestuffs* (n. 13 above), pp. 1–5, 6–9, 24–35; Judith Hofenk-De Graaff, 'L'analyse des matières colorantes dans les textiles anciens', *Bulletin de liaison du centre international d'étude des textiles anciens*, no. 35 (1972), pp. 12–21; Endrei and Hajnal, 'Analyse de colorants' (n. 13 above), p. 32; and n. 122 below.

the average amount of kermes per cloth used in the medieval Flemish draperies.[119] Presumably cochineal was originally cheaper to use than kermes. But from 1589 to 1642, the price of cochineal on the Amsterdam market rose fourfold (in grams of silver); and in 1715 a House of Commons report complained that after recent sharp increases in cochineal prices, dyeing a £9 white broadcloth in scarlet cost more than the cloth itself: £10 15s 0d sterling.[120] Obviously such high prices reflect a strong demand for cochineal as a dyestuff producing an impressive scarlet – in fact, with the standard alum mordant, a carmine red (from carminic acid). The chemist Edouard Justin-Mueller has contended, however, that cochineal dyes were much less fast and solid, 'à la transpiration particulièrement', than kermes, which thus continued to enjoy some advantage in humid tropical climates.[121]

The other innovation that transformed early modern scarlet dyeing was the discovery or invention of a new mordant, *c.* 1607, based on tin chloride. It is generally attributed to the Dutch-born London dyer Cornelius Drebbel (1572–1634), though it may have resulted from earlier experiments in the Low Countries.[122] According to a later dye recipe, for two broadcloths measuring 74 yards, the process required 16 oz granulated tin dissolved in 8 pints *aqua fortis* (nitric acid) or *aqua regia* (nitro-hydrochloric acid), salt and 4 pints water. When this tin liquor was brought to a boil, the dyer added $3\frac{1}{2}$ lb alum, 5 lb cream of tartar and $6\frac{1}{4}$ lb of cochineal.[123] The resulting scarlet was a distinc-

[119]Parliament, *Journals of the House of Commons*, XVIII: *1714–18* (London, 1803), pp. 382–3; Partridge, *Treatise* (n. 80 above), pp. 184–6 (also notes by K. G. Ponting, pp. 240, 258); Lee, 'American cochineal' (n. 96), p. 221; Fairlie, 'Dyestuffs' (n. 117), p. 489; Donkin, *Spanish Red* (n. 5), p. 23, stating 'cochineal proved to be ten or twelve times more powerful [than kermes] pound for pound'. For kermes, see Tables 3.4–3.5.

[120]Lee, 'American cochineal' (n. 96), pp. 220–2, tables I–II; *Journals of the House of Commons*, XVIII, pp. 382–3.

[121]'Cochenille et kermès' (n. 13 above), p. 791. He maintains that kermes reacts far less to alkalis than cochineal; and that cochineal dyes, when stained by perspiration (containing ammonia), turn bluish, blackish.

[122]H. G. Smith, 'Cornelius Drebbel and English Scarlet Dyeing', *Ciba Review*, no. 7 (March 1938), pp. 231–2; Born, 'Scarlet' (n. 8), pp. 220–1; Lee, 'American cochineal' (n. 96), pp. 222–4; Fairlie, 'Dyestuffs' (n. 117), pp. 492, 506. For a technical analysis of dyeing in kermes, cochineal, and other red dyestuffs in early modern Antwerp, and the victory of cochineal dyeing with tin chloride ('écarlate de Hollande'), see Liliane Masschelein-Kleiner and Luc Maes, 'Etude technique de la tapisserie des Pays Bas méridionaux: les tapisseries anversoises des XVIe et XVIIe siècles, les teintures et le textile', *Bulletin de l'institut royal du patrimoine artistique*, XVI (1976–77), pp. 143–53. They suggest that a German chemist in the Low Countries may have been the first to develop the tin-chloride technique, *c.*1563 (p. 145).

[123]Partridge, *Treatise* (n. 80 above), pp. 101–4, 184–6 (and notes by K. G. Ponting, pp. 239–40, 252). A later dye recipe, published in 1890, prescribed the following 'single-bath' method for Cochineal Scarlet: 'Fill the dye-bath half full of water, add 6–8 per cent of oxalic acid [$H_2C_2O_4$], 6 per cent of stannous chloride [$SnCl_2$], and 5–12 per cent of ground Cochineal; boil up 5–10 minutes, then fill up the dye-bath with cold water. Introduce the woollen material, heat up the bath to the boiling point in the course of $\frac{3}{4}$–1 hour, and boil $\frac{1}{2}$ hour ... One may use with advantage [a] mixture of stannous and stannic chloride [$SnCl_2 + SnCl_4$] with tartar' to produce the most brilliant scarlets. John J. Hummel, *The Dyeing of Textile Fabrics* (London, 1890), p. 350; and see also pp. 348–53.

tively vivid, lustrous, organish-hued red rather than the crimson of natural cochineal. It was also definitely a much more brilliant colour than that produced by kermes and at least equally fast. The modern scarlet is not essentially different; but it is now produced vastly more cheaply from several synthetic aniline dyes derived from coal tars: chiefly 'ponceaux' and polyazo compounds, which supplanted cochineal from the 1880s. Similarly other synthetic dyes can be made to achieve a 'royal purple' identical to ancient Tyre's *Murex brandaris* dye, 6–6′ dibromindigo. But demand for it is 'so small that no factory manufactures it'.[124] Scarlet still reigns supreme.

V

While dyestuffs provided the essential ingredient of scarlet cloths, the wools were certainly the next most important input, sometimes rivalling the kermes or cochineal in cost. From Table 3.1, on late-fifteenth-century wool prices at the Calais Staple, one can roughly gauge the relative costs of wools in cloths of various qualities, by reckoning 4 to 6 cloths to a woolsack of 364 lb (165.1 kg). Since the highest price in Table 3.1 is virtually four times the lowest, much of the variation in medieval textile prices in general can be attributed to the wide range of wool costs, as well as to those of dyestuffs.[125] In the very fine *non*-scarlet cloths produced in the late medieval Low Countries, as noted earlier, English wool was clearly the single most expensive input. Sometimes it was responsible for as much as 75 per cent of the pre-dyeing and finishing costs.[126] In the example of Ieper's cloth manufactures given in Table 3.12, the fine Cotswold wool (priced 16 per cent higher than at Calais) accounted for 64.2 per cent of pre-finishing costs, and 51.9 per cent of the dyed cloth's total cost. Note that the total manufacturing costs in wool preparation, combing, spinning, weaving, fulling and tentering amounted to only 28.9 per cent of total costs. Even that proportion was as high as it was because of the very large amounts of labour, some highly skilled, to perform all these tasks.

---

[124] M. C. Neuberger, 'Modern scarlet dyes', *Ciba Review*, no. 7 (March 1938), p. 228; Hummel, *Dyeing* (n. 118), pp. 348, 417–24: 'Many of the [oxyazo] scarlets have largely displaced Cochineal in wool-dyeing [as of 1885]. For plain scarlet dyes . . . they are even preferable to Cochineal, since the colour does not become dull and bluish on washing with soap.' (See n. 121 above). For polyazo compounds of scarlet, see Hummel, pp. 420–4, nos. 388–90, 393–7.

[125] See Munro, 'Wool Price Schedules', pp. 118–69 and '1357 Wool Price Schedule', pp. 211–19 (both in n. 5C), Munro, 'Industrial Protectionism' (n. 2), pp. 251–67, Tables 13.1, 13.2 and 13.5; R. H. Tawney and Eileen Power (eds.), *Tudor Economic Documents*, 3 vols. (London, 1924), I, pp. 178–84.

[126] Munro, 'Industrial Protectionism' (n. 2), pp. 232, 256, Table 13.2.

Thus, even though this medieval luxury industry was indeed labour-intensive, in terms of 'value added', raw materials nevertheless were still responsible for the preponderant share of total production costs and of the incomes so generated. Those who grew rich in this woollens trade were those merchants and drapers who had the necessarily large capitals to invest in costly inventories of wools and dyestuffs and finished textiles, and to undertake the risks produced by sudden fluctuations in prices and trading volumes. To be sure, the dyers and shearers, professional guild-organised artisans earning fees from many client merchants, did receive the quite decent incomes that even 3 to 5 per cent of such high cloth prices could produce. But the archival records indicate that the host of other cloth workers and artisans, from wool sorters to fullers and weavers (except those that became drapers), received very meagre incomes indeed.[127]

At the same time, clearly not even the best paid skilled artisans of this era could have hoped to buy the finer woollens, and certainly not scarlets. For example, in Henry VI's wardrobe account of 1438–39, the cheapest scarlet cost £14 2s 6d sterling. A master mason, then earning 6d a day, would have had to spend his full wages for 565 workdays (about 2 years 9 months) to buy one; or, to buy the $7\frac{1}{2}$ yards in an alderman's livery, about 141 days' wages. The highest priced scarlet, at £28 10s 0d, would have cost 1140 days' wages ($5\frac{1}{2}$ years).[128] In Flanders, a master mason earning $6\frac{2}{3}$d groot per day in 1440–41 would have had to spend 452 days' wages (2 years 2 months) to buy an Ieper scarlet priced that year at £12 11s 4d groot (£11 7s 8d sterling).[129] For that same amount of money in 1440, the following goods could have been purchased at the Antwerp market: approximately 2720 kg Flemish cheese (5996 lb); or 850 kg butter (1873 lb); or 22 000 smoked red herrings; or 1100 litres of good quality Rhine wine; or 780 metres of coarse linen.[130] Because productivity, wages, and prices have altered so radically since then, modern comparisons are difficult to make. Today the most costly luxury garment is the Russian sable fur coat, priced from US$20 000 to $45 000 or more (1982); but the less expensive ones would still not cost more than the annual income of many skilled, unionised North American workers.

---

[127] See Hans Van Werveke, De koopman-ondernemer (n. 55); Van Werveke, 'De economische en sociale gevolgen van de muntpolitiek der graven van Vlaanderen (1337–1433)' in his Miscellanea Mediaevalia (Ghent, 1968), pp. 243–54. See also n. 53.

[128] PRO, Exchequer E 101/409/2, fol. 6ʳ–11ᵛ; Munro, 'Industrial protectionism' (n. 2), pp. 257–60, Table 13.3; Phelps Brown and Hopkins, 'Seven centuries' (n. 70 above), pp. 177, 184; Herman Van der Wee, Growth of the Antwerp Market and the European Economy, Fourteenth to Sixteenth Centuries, 3 vols. (The Hague, 1963), I, p. 540, Appendix 48 (208 workdays per year).

[129] ARA Belg., Rek. reg. no. 42 554, fol. 43ᵛ (Brugse Vrij); Munro, 'Industrial Protectionism' (n. 2), pp. 261–3, Table 13.3.

[130] From Van der Wee, Antwerp Market (n. 128), I, pp. 212, 219, 259, 275, 284, 297, 458–9, 540.

Table 3.14 Prices of scarlets and of other English dyed woollens purchased in various years for the royal wardrobes of Henry IV, V and VI and Richard III in pounds sterling, and shillings per yard*

Dyed woollen	1407–08 Piece (pounds)	Yard (shillings)	1408–09 Piece (pounds)	Yard (shillings)	1419–20 Piece (pounds)	Yard (shillings)	1422–23 Piece (pounds)	Yard (shillings)
Scarlets: 30 by 1.75 yards								
highest price	20.000	13.33	20.000	13.33	21.500	14.33	20.000	13.33
mean price	20.000	13.33	19.617	13.08	20.357	13.57	16.018	10.68
lowest price	20.000	13.33	15.000	12.00	18.750	12.50	12.500	8.33
Cloths dyed in grain with other colours: 30 by 1.75 yards								
highest price	15.000	10.00	14.250	9.50	13.755	9.17	12.250	8.17
mean price	14.077	9.38	13.889	9.26	13.755	9.17	11.817	7.88
lowest price	13.500	9.00	12.750	8.50	13.755	9.17	11.000	7.33
Dyed long broad cloths: 30 by 1.75 yards								
highest price	10.000	6.67	10.500	7.00	14.250	9.50	10.000	6.67
mean price	9.008	6.01	8.185	5.46	7.628	5.09	7.520	5.01
lowest price	7.500	5.00	6.000	4.00	6.000	4.00	6.000	4.00
Dyed short broad cloths: 24 by 1.75 yards								
highest price	3.600	3.00	4.000	3.33	4.600	3.83	2.600	2.17
mean price	3.073	2.56	2.705	2.25	2.437	2.03	2.080	1.73
lowest price	3.000	2.50	2.450	2.04	1.400	1.17	1.000	0.83

continued overleaf

Table 3.14 continued

Dyed woollen	1438–39 Piece (pounds)	Yard* (shillings)	1440–41 Piece (pounds)	Yard (shillings)	1443–44 Piece (pounds)	Yard (shillings)	1483–84 Piece (pounds)	Yard (shillings)
Scarlets: 30 by 1.75 yards								
highest price	28.500	19.00			28.500	19.00	25.000	16.67
mean price	18.034	12.02			14.915	9.94	15.187	10.12
lowest price	14.125	9.42			13.500	9.00	12.000	8.00
Cloths dyed in grain with other colours: 30 by 1.75 yards								
highest price	17.250	11.50	17.250	11.50	27.000	18.00	20.000	13.33
mean price	15.211	10.14	14.952	9.97	14.481	9.65	19.210	12.81
lowest price	12.000	8.00	13.500	9.00	12.000	8.00	15.000	10.00
Dyed long broadcloths: 30 by 1.75 yards								
highest price	14.000	9.33	14.000	9.33	12.000	8.00	10.000	6.67
mean price	7.466	4.98	8.049	5.37	7.501	5.00	7.503	5.00
lowest price	6.000	4.00	6.000	4.00	6.000	4.00	5.500	3.67
Dyed short broadcloths: 24 by 1.75 yards								
highest price	4.000	3.33	4.700	3.92	4.600	3.83	3.000	2.50
mean price	2.545	2.12	2.990	2.49	3.036	2.53	2.818	2.35
lowest price	1.400	1.17	1.400	1.17	1.100	0.92	1.000	0.83

Note: * 1 yard of the cloth assize = 37 inches = 93.98 cm.
Source: Public Record Office, KR Exchequer, E 101/405/14, 405/22, 406/9, 407/1, 407/13, 409/2, 409/6, 409/12; LC 9/50 (from MS edited by Anne F. Sutton and P. W. Hammond).

Table 3.15 Prices of velvet, damask and satin silks purchased in various years for the royal wardrobes of Henry IV, V and VI, in shillings sterling per yard*

Silk fabric	1407–08 (shillings)	1408–09 (shillings)	1419–20 (shillings)	1422–23 (shillings)	1438–39 (shillings)	1440–41 (shillings)	1443–44 (shillings)
Velvets							
highest price	16.67	22.50	20.00	17.50	23.33	36.80	30.00
mean price	15.91	20.74	15.04	13.14	15.09	20.97	17.25
lowest price	13.33	16.00	8.33	10.50	12.50	12.50	12.50
Damasks							
highest price	13.00		12.25	10.00	12.08		13.33
mean price	11.45		11.29	10.00	12.03		12.78
lowest price	11.11		11.10	10.00	12.00		11.00
Satins							
highest price	11.67	18.75		5.25	9.00		8.33
mean price	8.21	8.21		5.25	8.83		8.33
lowest price	5.00	5.00		5.25	8.75		8.33

Note: * 1 yard of the cloth assize = 37 inches = 93.98 cm.
Source: Public Record Office, KR Exchequer, E 101/405/14, 405/22, 406/9, 407/1, 407/13, 409/2, 409/6, 409/12.

Table 3.16   Values of one kilogram of pure silver in English pounds sterling and in Flemish pounds groot, and relative moneys-of-account values, 1393 to 1499

Date	Value of one kilogram pure silver in: Pounds sterling	Pounds groot	Value of one pound groot Flemish in pounds sterling English	Value of one pound sterling in pounds groot Flemish
June 1393	3.862	4.050	0.954	1.049
August 1409	3.862	3.482	1.109	0.902
November 1411	4.634	3.482	1.331	0.751
December 1416	4.634	4.263	1.087	0.920
June 1418	4.634	4.832	0.959	1.043
November 1428	4.634	5.474	0.847	1.181
October 1433	4.634	5.116	0.906	1.104
August 1464	5.793	5.116	1.132	0.883
May 1466	5.793	5.862	0.988	1.012
October 1467	5.793	6.004	0.965	1.036
December 1474	5.793	6.821	0.849	1.177
November 1477	5.793	7.674	0.755	1.325
July 1482	5.793	8.527	0.679	1.472
March 1484	5.793	6.821	0.849	1.177
April 1485	5.793	10.232	0.566	1.766
December 1485	5.793	8.527	0.679	1.472
August 1486	5.793	9.379	0.618	1.619
July 1487	5.793	11.750	0.493	2.028
June 1488	5.793	14.244	0.407	2.459
November 1488	5.793	17.480	0.331	3.017
July 1489	5.793	15.348	0.377	2.649
January 1490	5.793	5.685	1.019	0.981
March 1492	5.793	7.248	0.799	1.251
September 1493	5.793	8.154	0.710	1.408
May 1496	5.793	8.420	0.688	1.453
May 1499	5.793	8.527*		

* Both the Antwerp and Bruges mints retained the former valuation of pure silver in double *pattards* at £8.420 groot per kg, but they slightly debased the single *pattard*, so raising the value of pure silver in *this* coinage to £8.527 groot per kg.

Sources: Burgundian mint accounts; see John H. Munro, 'Bullion Flows and Monetary Contraction in Late Medieval England and the Low Countries', in John Richards (ed.), *Precious Metals in the Medieval and Early-Modern Worlds* (Durham, N.C., 1982), Table 10. Temporary fluctuations recorded at only one mint have been eliminated from this Table 3.16.

Of course such extravagance in dress, such sartorial splendour, medieval or modern, is far beyond the average person's notion of luxury. The world of the scarlet was for the few, the very few indeed: a world of popes, emperors, archbishops, princes – and also of Flemish civic aldermen, to whom we owe so many medieval cloth prices.

4 The Chemistry of Red Dyestuffs in Medieval and Early Modern Europe
Judith H. Hofenk-De Graaff

The textile dyers of medieval and early modern Europe were exceptionally well equipped with red dyestuffs, having at least seven at
their disposal. Professor Munro's companion essay in this volume has
already discussed the historical application of the three that were
animal in origin, derived from related Coccidal insects: kermes,
Polish cochineal and the true cochineal from Mexico. This essay
may thus commence directly with a chemical analysis of these three,
which all belong to the group of antraquinones. The dyeing component
of kermes is *kermesic* acid, present as a salt with the following structure
formula (after Fairbairn):[1]

kermesic acid, $C_{16}H_{10}O_3$

The cochineal from Mexico, *Coccus cacti* or *Grana cochinilla*, contains
carminic acid as its dyeing component, with the following structure
formula (after Mühlemann):[2]

carminic acid, $C_{22}H_{20}O_{13}$

[1] R. H. Thomson, *Naturally Occurring Quinones* (London and New York, 1971), p. 457, citing J. W.
Fairbairn and A. B. Shresta in *Journal of Pharmacology*, XVIII (1966), p. 467. A somewhat different
formula for kermesic acid was given by M. Edouard Justin-Mueller, 'Cochenille et kermes',
Bulletin de la société chimique de France, 4th ser., XXXIX (1926), pp. 791 ?· $C_{16}H_{12}O_9$
[2] Thomson, *Quinones*, p. 459, citing H. Mühlemann in *Pharm. Acta Helv.*, XXVII (1952), p. 17.
Justin-Mueller (n. 1 above) again gives a slightly different formula for carminic acid: $C_{22}H_{22}O_{13}$.

According to our chemical analyses, the Polish cochineal obtained from *Magarodes polonicus* contains a combination of both kermesic and carminic acids, with the above structure formulae.[3]

The other related animal dyestuff was Lac-dye, which is derived from *Coccus lacca*, a Coccidal insect living on the *Ficus religiosa* and other similar trees native to India, Burma and South-East Asia. There is no evidence, however, that European textile dyers made any significant use of Lac-dye before the late eighteenth century, when the East India Company began importing this dyestuff into England.[4] But its chemical composition deserves to be noted to complete this analysis of animal red-dyestuffs. According to Thomson, Lac-dye contains a mixture of various antraquinones, which can be separated chromatographically. One of the most important constituents is *laccaic acid A*, with the structure formula:[5]

laccaic acid A, $C_{26}H_{19}O_{12}$

Recent investigations of Schofield and Venkataraman have led them to give the names laccaic acid A, B, C, D and E for various other related compounds found in Lac-dyes.[6]

Since kermes, Polish cochineal, Mexican cochineal and the Lac-dyes are all chemically similar, the methods of dyeing with them are all more or less similar. Indeed, as antraquinones, they are all mordant dyes, dyes that can be applied to the textile only after the fabric has been first treated with a metallic salt.[7] After dyeing with the appropriate organic red dyestuff, an insoluble metal-complex is formed and 'fixed' to the fibre. The colour or shade so produced depends in fact upon the type of metallic salt used. Thus aluminium (alum) gives a crimson shade; tin, a scarlet colour; chrome, purple; and copper,

---

[3] See also O. Dimroth, 'Ueber den Farbstoff der Kermes', *Ber. deutschen chemischen Gesellschaft*, XLIII (1910), pp. 1387–401. Some authorities have stated that the chemical composition of Polish cochineal is the same as that of Mexican cochineal. See F. Brunello, *L'arte della tenturia nella storia dell'umarita* (Vincenza, 1968).

[4] See R. E. Schmidt, 'Ueber den Farbstoff des Lac-dye', *Ber. deutschen chemischen Gesellschaft*, II (1887), pp. 1285–303; E. H. Schafer, 'Rosewood, dragon's blood, and lac', *Journal of the American Oriental Society*, LXXVII (1957), pp. 129–36; R. J. Forbes, 'Dyes and dyeing', *Studies in Ancient Technology*, 2nd edn, 9 vols. (Leiden, 1964), IV, pp. 114–30.

[5] Thomson, *Quinones* (see n. 1), p. 463.

[6] Ibid., citing works of Schofield and Venkataraman.

[7] Judith Hofenk-De Graaff, *Natural Dyestuffs: Origin, Chemical Composition, and Identification* (International Council of Museums, Amsterdam, 1969).

claret. In ancient and medieval times, only a few metal salts were available for mordanting wool and silk.[8] By far the most common of these was alum, producing bright crimson shades, as noted, when used with kermes and cochineal; some iron compounds were also used to create violet shades. In medieval scarlet-dyeing, the dyebath that followed upon mordanting with alum was prepared from kermes, winestone, arsenic and edible mushroom; the last was utilised for its large tannin content and its abilities to produce fermentation.[9] In early modern times, as already noted in Munro's essay, the use of tin-chloride mordants produced the modern scarlet colour as we know it now: a brilliant fiery red shade.

Because the chemical compositions and colours of the four insect dyestuffs are similar, and because the colours may vary in shade according to the mordant used, detection and identification of these dyestuffs in ancient and medieval textiles are no easy tasks. One of the first to develop chemical analyses of these insect-based dyestuffs in ancient textiles was the French chemist R. Pfister in a series of celebrated articles published in the 1930s. His chief method of analysis was to boil the sample of dyed textile in hydrochloric acid and then to mix and shake the acidic solution with various organic solvents, recording the different colour reactions.[10] The purpose of the initial hydrochloric acid bath was to decompose the metal-complex, to hydrolyse its composition and separate the organic dyestuff from the metallic salt (alum or tin) serving as the mordant. Otherwise the dyestuff would remain insoluble on the fibre. Pfister has provided the accompanying table of results, with the various colour reactions, shown in Table 4.1.[11]

This chemical method can be quite successful, but it is rather too subjective, since it depends upon the visual interpretation of the colour reactions. It also requires relatively large samples, which can only rarely be obtained from ancient textiles.

The simplest and most certain form of this method is to employ ethyl ether. After the metal complex of the dyestuff has been decomposed in hydrochloric or sulphuric acid, the acidic solution is shaken with the ethyl ether. With this mixture, kermes is completely extracted,

---

[8] In those eras, it was not possible to dye linen and cotton fabrics effectively with these dyestuffs; but in early modern times they were dyed successfully with madder and known as 'Turkish reds'. See G. Schaeffer and R. Haller, 'Krapp und Turkischrot', *Ciba Rundschau*, 47 (1940).

[9] See Gioaventura Rosetti, *The Plichto* (1st edn, 1548), translated and edited by S. M. Edelstein and H. G. Borghetty (London, 1969), pp. 134–9; Dimroth, 'Kermes' (n. 3 above); F. Mayer, *Chemie der organische Farbstoffe*, II: *Naturliche organische Farbstoffe* (Berlin, 1935).

[10] R. Pfister, 'Teinture et alchemie dans l'Orient hellénistique', *Seminarium Kondakovianum*, VII (Prague, 1935), pp. 1 59; Pfister, 'Matériaux pour servir au classement des textiles égyptiens posterieures à la conquête arabe', *Revue des arts asiatiques*, X (1936), pp. 1–15, 73–85.

[11] See sources cited in n. 10 above.

Table 4.1   Pfister's table of chemical and colour reactions of insect-based red dyestuffs to hydrochloric acid and various organic solvents

Treatment	Kermes	Cochineal	Lac-dye	Polish cochineal
Hydrochloric acid	light pink	light pink	orange–red	orange
Petroleum ether (30–50)	nothing	nothing	nothing	nothing
Ethyl ether	extract is completely orange	nothing	extract is partially visible after dilution with HCl	nothing
Benzene	solvent is slightly coloured; the acid is a little bit clearer	nothing	nothing	nothing
Chloroform	solvent is slightly coloured	nothing	nothing	nothing
Ethyl acetate	complete extraction	partial extraction	extract is pink; the acid keeps its original colour	partial extraction
Amyl alcohol	extract is orange	extract is orange	extract is completely pink–orange	extract is completely pink–orange

cochineal not at all, and lac-dye only partially; that is, both the ethyl ether and the acidic solution are coloured.[12]

Currently, however, more sophisticated analytical methods can be used to detect natural dyestuffs in ancient textiles: first, chromatographic methods, including paper chromatography, thin-layer chromatography and, as the latest development, high-performance liquid chromatography; and secondly, spectrophotometric methods, including infra-red spectrophotometry, ultraviolet spectrophotometry and mass spectrometry. These methods require only a small quantity of textile material and can provide very exact results, with very detailed information about the ancient dyestuffs, especially when these methods are employed in combination. But with these methods there

[12] Personal communication to the author from Professor Mark Whiting, Department of Chemistry, University of Bristol.

still remains the problem of unknown impurities, which may create considerable difficulties in interpreting the results.

Perhaps the most effective of these methods is thin-layer chromatography, which requires only a very simple preparation of the sample, takes little time, and is relatively inexpensive.[13] The textile sample required is just a small thread of 0.5 cm, or even less, perhaps extracted from the back of the textile without causing any damage. The sample is first boiled for a few minutes with 10 per cent hydrochloric acid, again in order to decompose the metal-complex, to hydrolyse its composition, separating the dyestuff from the fibre. After hydrolysis the fibre is moved together with the hydrochloric acid to a micro-extraction apparatus, constructed according to this author's own design. The acid is evaporated and the hydrolysed sample is dissolved in 2 ml methylalcohol (or amyl alcohol). Over approximately one hour, the sample is extracted in this apparatus, resulting in a concentrated dyestuff solution of about 1 ml, to be used in the thin-layer chromatographic analysis. That analysis requires as a carrier material 10 per cent acetylated cellulose, pre-coated sheets of Cel 300 Ac-10 supplied by Mackerey Nagel. The plates are pre-washed with the required eluent in order to remove all impurities; and the eluent used is tetrahydrofurane/ethylacetate/water/35:6:45 (according to Stahl).[14] A so-called Pasteur capillary, whose tip has an internal diameter of 100 micron, is used to apply the extracted dyestuff solution to the plate. After elution, the 'spots' that arise are sprayed with a 0.5 normal solution of KOH, observed in ultraviolet light having a wavelength of 350 mu, and are then identified. Positive colour photographs are immediately taken with a Polaroid technical camera MP_3, with a type RO orange filter.

The present author and her colleagues have used this method to analyse hundreds of samples of ancient, medieval and early modern dyed textiles.[15] One major result of this research programme has been concrete evidence to substantiate the historical assertion that Mexican cochineal within fifty years of its introduction into Europe (*c*. 1520–30) fully displaced kermes in scarlet textile dyeing.

The other four red dyestuffs of the medieval and early modern European textile industries were all vegetable in origin: madder,

---

[13] See Judith Hofenk-De Graaff and Wilma G. Roelofs, *On the Occurrence of Red Dyestuffs in Textile Materials from the Period 1450–1600: Origin, Chemical Constitution, and Identification* (International Council of Museums, Madrid, 1972), pp. 1–5, 24–33; K. Randerath, *Dümschicht Chromatografie* (Verlag Chemie GMBH Weinheim/Bergsu. 1965), p. 258. See also n. 15 below.

[14] Randerath, *Chromatografie*, p. 258.

[15] Hofenk-De Graaff, *Natural Dyestuffs* (n. 7 above); Hofenk-De Graaff and Roelofs, *Red Dyestuffs* (n. 13 above), pp. 11–33; Judith Hofenk-De Graaff, 'Comments on comments', *Bulletin de liaison du centre international d'étude des textiles anciens*, 43–4 (1976), pp. 101–12.

Brazil-wood, orchil (archil) and henna. By far the most important, the most frequently and widely used, was madder. It was obtained from the roots of two related herbaceous climbing plants with yellowish flowers: the *Rubia tinctoria*, originally indigenous to the Middle East; and the *Rubia peregrina*, a plant of Persian origin introduced into Spain by the Arabs.[16] During the Middle Ages, madder plants were widely cultivated in western Europe, especially in France and the Low Countries. But the quality of the oriental madder is superior to that of the European varieties because the roots of the eastern plant contain a higher percentage of the madder dyestuff.

The red dyestuffs contained in the roots of *Rubia tinctoria* are various glucosides of *alizarin* and *purpurin*. The chemical compositions of the two dyeing materials are:[17]

alizarin, $C_{14}H_8O_4$ purpurin, $C_{14}H_8O_5$

Purpurin is inferior to alizarin; and dyed textiles of high quality would contain less purpurin. The colour produced by madder ranges from moderate to strong red. These colours become fast only when the yarn or cloth has been mordanted before dyeing with a metal salt. In ancient and medieval times, alum was almost exclusively used, though iron salts were evidently also employed on occasion. From the early-seventeenth century, following upon Drebbel's afore-mentioned discovery of the tin-chloride method of scarlet dyeing, stannic salts came to be widely used in mordanting with madder.[18]

The other well-known but much less used red dyestuff was Brazil-wood, extracted from tropical trees of the genus *Caesalpinia*. Although Brazil-wood appears to have been quite highly prized in medieval times, the somewhat different varieties used in early modern times had a rather poor light fastness, much inferior to that of madder. The original Brazil-wood came from *Caesalpinia sappan* trees grown in eastern Asia. Long before the discovery of the New World and of the

[16] G. Schaeffer and R. Haller, 'Krapp und Turkischrot' (see n. 8).

[17] Thomson, *Quinones* (n. 1 above), pp. 373, 407; F. Mayer, *Organische Farbstoffe* (n. 9 above), pp. 72–6; A. G. Perkin and A. E. Everest, *The Natural Organic Colouring Matters* (London, 1918), pp. 22ff.

[18] H. G. Smith, 'Cornelius Drebbel and English scarlet dyeing', *Ciba Review*, 7 (March 1938), pp. 231–2; Susan Fairlie, 'Dyestuffs in the eighteenth century', *Economic History Review*, 2nd ser., XVII (1965), pp. 489–99; L. A. Driessen, 'Cochenille' (unpublished MS, Amsterdam, 1930).

land that later came to be named Brazil, Brazil-wood was imported into Europe via the famous Asian silk-routes or via the Red Sea route.[19] Its use can be traced as far back as the tenth century when it is discussed in German dye recipes of that era (Preiselig); and *c.* 1190, a 'Spaniard named Kimichi wrote about dyewoods called 'bresil' or 'brasil'.[20] From the time of Marco Polo's famous journeys to the Far East (1271–90), Brazil-wood from Ceylon was introduced into Europe; and after *c.* 1350 so were various similar redwoods from Java and the neighbouring Indonesian islands.[21]

Brazil-wood was imported in the form of large blocks that had to be rasped into smaller pieces, for two reasons: first, so that the dyestuff present as *brassillin* might be oxidised by the air into *Brasilein*; and second, so that the developed Brasilein might be extracted from the wood with water. The chemical composition of the *Brasilein* extracted from Brazil-wood is:[22]

Brasilein, $C_{16}H_{12}O_5$

Various other botanically related species of the genus *Caesalpinia* also produced similar 'soluble' redwood dyestuffs that came to be used in early modern European textile dyeing, all under the general name of 'Brazil-woods'.[23] About nine varieties are known, of which four were especially important. Of these *Fernambuco* or *Pernambuco* wood is the richest in colouring matter; it is extracted from the

[19] Hofenk-De Graaff, *Natural Dyestuffs* (n. 7 above); G. Schaeffer, 'Die Färbehölzer', *Ciba Rundschau*, 47 (1940): Hofenk-De Graaff and Roelofs, *Red Dyestuffs* (n. 13 above), p. 89. See n. 23 below.

[20] Schaeffer, 'Die Färbehölzer' (n. 19 above); see also H. G. T. Frencken, *'t Bouck va Wondre* (1513), H. Timmermans, (ed.) (Roermond, 1934); Rosetti, *Plichto* (n. 9 above). Indeed about half of the extant medieval recipes for red-dyeing required some Brazil-wood; and of the red textile fabrics dating from *c.*1100–1450, about 80 per cent have been found to contain Brazil-woods. Hofenk-De Graaff and Roelofs, *Red Dyestuffs* (n. 13 above).

[21] From about 1450 the presence of eastern Brazil-woods in European textile fabric samples suddenly disappears; that probably reflects the Turkish disruptions of traditional eastern trade routes. Then, from the later sixteenth century, redwood dyes unexpectedly reappear in the European textile samples. These are undoubtedly Latin American redwood dyes. After a short time, these new redwood dyestuffs also disappear from European textile samples, for reasons suggested in n. 23 below. See also sources cited in n. 19 above.

[22] F. Mayer, *Organische Farbstoffe* (n. 9 above); Perkin and Everest, *Organic Colouring Matters* (n. 17 above).

[23] Whatever the quality of medieval Brazil-woods, those that were imported from the various Latin American areas listed proved to have a rather poor light fastness, and these Brazil-woods came to be forbidden as red dyestuffs for higher-quality textiles in many countries of early modern Europe. Hofenk-De Graaff and Roelofs, *Red Dyestuffs* (n. 13 above), p. 89.

Caesalpinia crista trees of Jamaica and Brazil. The *Brazil-wood* derived from the *Caesalpinia brasiliensis* of Brazil contains only about one-half of the dyestuff found in *Fernambuco* wood. *Peachwood* is the product of *Caesalpinia echinta* trees, found in much of Central America and the northern parts of South America. Finally, the so-called *Limawood*, extracted from a variety of the *Caesalpinia sappan* trees growing in the Philippine Islands, was also imported into Europe; but its quality was much inferior to that of *Sappanwood*, the original 'Brazil-wood' of medieval Europe, which continued to be employed in textile dyeing.

Although it has been said that the chemical composition of these *Caesalpinia* redwood dyestuffs is the same, a chemical analysis gives different results for all of them. The original *Caesalpinia sappan* in particular differs markedly from the *Caesalpinia brasiliensis*. But the particular causes of these differences have yet to be fully explained.

Nevertheless, their dyeing properties are very similar in producing bright red shades. They are all also mordant dyestuffs; and again in medieval Europe the dominant mordant was alum. In early modern Europe, sumach, tin and iron salts also came to be used as mordants.

The remaining two organic red dyestuffs, archil and henna, had such a very limited application in European textile dyeing that similar chemical analyses of their colouring properties are not warranted. Archil, a corruption of the older 'orchil' (Middle English *orchell*), is a red–violet dyestuff with a very low light fastness. It was extracted from various lichens of the genera *Roccella* and *Lecanora*, thallophytic plants consisting of algae and fungi growing together symbiotically on rocks. This dyestuff was generally used in combination with other red dyes to darken the shade, and to produce violets (even if only temporarily).[24] Henna is produced from the leaves of the henna plant, the Egyptian privet, a tropical shrub of the loosestrife family whose scientific name is *Lawsonia inermis*. The dyestuff so obtained is a dark reddish-brown; and historically it is far more famous as the dye used by ancient Egyptian women (and more modern women as well) to tint their hair this colour.

---

[24] In ancient times, archil was occasionally used to imitate real purple, according to the *Papyrus Graecus Holmiensis*. Even in seventeenth-century Holland it was used by the famous family of tapestry weavers, the Spierings; but in all their tapestries, the once brilliant violet parts have almost completely faded away. See in particular, A. Kok, 'A short history of the orchil dyes', *The Lichenologists*, III (1966), pp. 248–72.

Appendix: Recipe for Dyeing Silk Scarlet, attributed to Dirc Willemszzon van der Heyden, c. 1614–28

To dye your silk a beautiful scarlet you must boil the raw silk well before dyeing. Rinse the silk well in river water, rinse it again in hot water, and then again in the river. Repeat this several times. The final rinsing bath must be in rain-water. When dyeing with carmine [cochineal], you may use only rain-water.

Take a kettle of yellow copper, put rain-water in it, and then heat the water. For every pound of silk, put eight ounces of good quality alum into the warm water; and for every pound of silk, two ounces of rock-salt. Heat the kettle, stir well until everything is dissolved, and continue heating until the liquid boils. Then, for every pound of silk, put in one ounce of arsenic and stir well until the arsenic can no longer be seen. Boil the liquid for a while and dampen down the fire. Leave the kettle for a while; then stir again and put your silk into the kettle, on the wooden bars. Repeat this twelve times. During this time, the kettle will become cold. When it is fully cold, place the silk into the kettle and leave it there for twenty-four hours. To dye the silk crimson take the silk out and wring it out by hand. Rinse it first in cold river-water and then in rain-water; it is best to do so in warm rain-water. Take the same kettle, after it has been well cleaned, and fill it with rain-water. If you want a dark colour, the kettle must not be much larger than the quantity of silk to be dyed. Heat the kettle and when it becomes hot put in three ounces of gum arabic for every pound of silk. Stir well until it is dissolved and when it is not quite boiling put in this bath three ounces of well-crushed gall nuts for every pound of silk. Boil well; and for every pound of silk put in four ounces of well-crushed and sifted cochineal. Stir well and if desired put a little root of turmeric into the dye-bath. Boil the kettle for two hours, then add cold rain-water to the kettle and lower the fire. Then put your silk into the kettle and draw the silk through the kettle four times. Wring out the silk carefully by hand and cool the silk on the wooden bars. Now the silk has acquired its ground shade. Boil the kettle again, and when the dye liquid starts to boil, hang your silk in the kettle and boil for two hours. During this time you must stir your silk well but carefully. After two hours, take the silk out carefully and wring it out with your hands. Put the silk into a clean sack for two or three hours. Then rinse it very thoroughly, let it dry, and your silk will become a beautiful crimson.

Source: W. L. J. de Nie, *De ontwikkeling der Noord-Nederlandsche textielververwij van de 14e tot de 18e eeuw* (unpublished doctoral dissertation, Leiden, 1937).

5   The Textile Finds from Birka
Agnes Geijer

During the Viking era, Birka was the principal trade emporium of
the Nordic countries, closely linked with Haitabu, the famous commercial town on the estuary of the River Sli in what is now Schleswig.
Haitabu was the gateway to Friesland and the trade routes further
south. Birka also commanded several routes to the south-east towards
Byzantium and the eastern interior by way of the Russian rivers.
Owing to its position on the island of Björkö in Lake Mälar, Birka
commanded the waterways further inland while affording free access
to the Baltic and the Gulf of Finland, whence various routes lead on to
the Black Sea and, via the Volga, on to the Caspian sea.

It was to Birka that Ansgar, the Apostle of the North, was sent to
convert the heathen Swedes in 829 or 830 and again in 850. The town
was destroyed around the year 1000. Its international fame rests upon
the abundant burial finds which bear witness to its conspicuous role
in the trade between east and west. Archaeological research began
there by chance in 1871 when Hjalmar Stolpe (1841–1905) com-
menced excavations expecting to find amber. Subsequently between
1874 and 1881 he explored the burial grounds found in the so-called
Svarta jorden (black earth). Some 1100 graves were excavated and many
remarkable discoveries were made. Studies based on part of the
material were published by Stolpe himself and later by other scholars.[1]
The massive task of publishing a full report on the discoveries as a
whole was eventually entrusted to Holger Arbman in 1931, and his
two-volume catalogue was published in 1943.[2]

When Arbman started on the inventory of the extensive material,
a great deal was still packed exactly as Stolpe had left it. Arbman had
not expected it to include many textiles; in fact, it proved to contain

[1] T. J. Arne, *La Suède et l'Orient* (Uppsala, 1914).
[2] H. Arbman, *Birka: Untersuchungen und Studien, I: Die Gräber* (Uppsala, 1940–43).

the largest and most diversified archaeological finds in this field in the whole of Europe. Immediately recognisable as textile remains were lumps of earth containing textile fragments which were barely visible, but which were all left exactly as they had been found during the excavation. In addition, some very small and delicate items had been tucked down in small boxes immediately after discovery and were consequently preserved. Further textiles of various kinds were found adhering to metal objects, corrosive salts from which had impregnated the textile fibres and consequently preserved them.

The growing volume of finds involving textile materials led to the present writer being called in and to the decision that a whole volume of the published report should be devoted to the textiles. This volume appeared in German in 1938.[3] After more than forty years, I welcome the opportunity of reviewing the results of my researches, and of offering some revised opinions based both on my own work and that of other scholars.

My first task was to free the textile remains from soil and dirt, and, as far as possible, to soften the fibres so that the textiles could be unfolded. This was mainly done by using distilled water which was applied drop by drop to the fragments laid out on sheets of glass, where soft brushes and various pegs could be used and where filter paper could absorb the dirt. The detailed attention this work required afforded excellent opportunities for further examination and technical analysis, the results of which were directly recorded by means of crayon drawings.

Woollen fabrics

Woollen fabrics constituted the largest and most variegated category of textiles among the finds. They were divided into four groups. The first group (W 1–9) comprised coarse and loose fabrics of uneven and rough yarn, which were apparently never intended for use as clothing. Without doubt they were local products. Another group included some specimens of an ordinary woven type which were listed as W 34–45. They resemble the ordinary tweeds of our own time, being made in plain 2/2 twill of woolly yarn, usually Z-spun for the warp and loosely S-spun for the weft. These specimens all showed to a greater or lesser extent some sign of having been fulled. I am not prepared at present to speculate about the origin of these textiles.

[3] A. Geijer, *Birka, III: Die Textilfunde aus den Gräbern* (Uppsala, 1938). The book contains 191 pages of text, with 50 figures and 40 plates, each containing several items. The system of notation for the various specimens perhaps calls for an explanation. The initial letter refers to the German word for the type or technical category – W for wool, woollen fabrics, FH for flax/hemp, L for linen fabrics, S for silk fabrics, B for bands, braids, P for *passementerie*, lace trimmings, St for *Stickerei*, embroidery, and the numeral refers to the specimen described.

The overwhelming majority of the Birka woollens were classifiable as worsted fabrics, that is, they were woven with yarn made from combed wool which produces a glossy surface without any sign of woolliness. The yarn is very fine and even, always Z-spun and the same in both warp and weft. A small number of these fabrics (W 22–4, 28–30) are in tabby weave with a ribbed effect (Figure 5.1), while the others are all twills.

5.1 Plain worsted fabrics, 'tabby weave'. Actual size

Most interest attaches to the patterned worsteds described either as broken 2/2 lozenge twill or diamond twill, the 4-end type definitely being the most common kind, and to the extremely fine 3-end type (W 14–20). In addition there are two examples of 'herringbone twill' (W 12–13). The standard weave, denoted W 10, occurred in at least sixty cases (see Figure 5.2).

The fine quality of these worsteds is best described by the tightness of threads per centimetre in the warp and weft being respectively 28/14, 32/12, 38/14 and 46/15 in the 4-end twills and 50/17, 52/14, and 60/17 in the 3-end specimens. The relationship of warp and weft can be proved by several still extant selvages – two sideway selvages and some starting borders (see Figure 5.3). Examination of these small remains suggest that the warp-weighted loom was used; the schematic diagram in Figure 5.4 demonstrates the principle of warping generally occurring in connection with this type of loom.

5.2 *Various kinds of worsted twill, 'diamond' (lozenge) and 'herring-bone'.
Enlarged to twice actual size. Below, pieces of type W10 showing starting
border and sideways selvage*

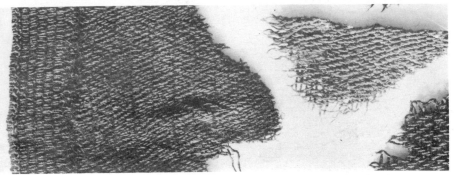

5.3 *Diagram of the W10 type, 'sharp cut lozenge twill', with starting
border.*

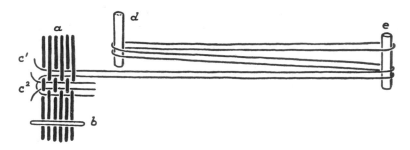

5.4   Diagram showing the system of warping used for weaves in Figures 5.2 and 5.3 a warp of the border; b shedding device used for the band warp; c threads first used as weft in the band and secondly serving as warp in the fabric; d and e are pegs for stretching the warp

We turn now to the probable origin of the woollen fabrics. It was obvious that apart from the coarse, no doubt home-made fabrics first mentioned, all the woollens probably came from one or other specialised manufacturing centre. This seems particularly likely in the case of the fine worsteds, since their production must have depended on a constant supply of high-quality wool, together with well-organised spinners and workers experienced in the skilled form of weaving which they embodied.

But where might these areas have been situated? In the 1930s, when my book was in preparation, there was still no historical research in this field of technology and nothing had been published to enable any relevant comparison to be made. On the other hand, some written documents from this period had generated an erudite discussion between certain scholars, headed by the Belgian historian Henri Pirenne, dealing especially with the Frisian trade. The facts emerging from these discussions led me to broach the idea that the fine fabrics from Birka could be identical with the famous *pallia fresonica*, which was presumed to have been made in the Frisian area. My hypothesis first met with approval, but later objections were raised by Dr Marta Hoffmann in her survey of early medieval weaving in north-western Europe.[4] Partly because some of the historical sources quoted by me in 1938 later proved to be unreliable, and partly on technological grounds, Dr Hoffmann queried the likelihood of the high-class worsteds having been manufactured on the North Sea coast at that time. In her opinion the textiles exported by the Frisians were only coarse, home-made products. She put forward the alternative suggestion that

[4] M. Hoffmann, *The Warp-Weighted Loom. Studies in the History and Technology of an Ancient Implement* (Oslo, 1964).

the worsteds which were found in Birka, Oseberg and other Viking sites could have come from Syria. The immediate reason for this hypothesis arose from a publication by the French scholar, R. Pfister, stating that a fabric apparently identical with the fine W10 type at Birka was among the finds made at Palmyra, the Syrian trading town destroyed in AD 273.[5] In a paper I wrote in 1965 reviewing Dr Hoffmann's work I expressed my agreement.[6] However, I am still inclined to believe that the term *pallium fresonicum* may be justifiable. We know that the word *pallium*, which is of Greek origin, usually meant a precious garment. In this connection I would call attention to a paper by E. Sabbe showing that Frisian merchants took over the importation of oriental luxuries by way of Marseilles, a trade which, under the Merovingians, had been in the hands of Syrian merchants.[7]

As the lozenge-twill worsted preserved at Birka was clearly a much appreciated luxury article during the Viking era, proof of its Syrian origin would be of great interest for north European archaeology. There are, however, wider implications arising from the identification of the Palmyra specimen with its equivalents in the north European finds which seem to prove that this kind of textile production persisted for over seven centuries. On the other hand, recent excavations have revealed new specimens of lozenge twills resembling those from Birka but coarser and of slightly later date. All this raises problems which have yet to be satisfactorily solved. Further investigation is needed to discover if more than one production area was involved.

Another matter to consider in this connection is the enigmatic term *haberget, haubergie*, etc., which was investigaged by Professor Carus-Wilson herself.[8] The word occurs frequently in English and French records and poetry of the twelfth and thirteenth centuries and seems often to have been used as material for distinguished garments. Carus-Wilson described the *haberget* as a 'diamond-twill worsted' and compared it to the Nordic material – which, however, mainly dates from an earlier period than her texts. All this raises problems. Consideration needs to be given to the points raised in another contribution to this volume by Margareta Nockert describing a rather well-preserved burial from Leksand in Sweden.[9]

---

[5] R. Pfister, *Nouveau textiles de Palmyre* (Paris, 1937), types L 43 and 44, pl. VI, pp. 24f; and 'Le rôle de l'Iran dans les textiles d'Antinoë', *Ars Islamica*, XIII (1948), Figure 59.

[6] A. Geijer, 'Var järnålderns "frisiska kläde" tillverkat i Syrien?' [The *pallium fresonicum* of the Viking Age, was it manufactured in Syria?], *Fornvännen*, LX (Stockholm, 1965), pp. 112–32.

[7] E. Sabbe, 'L'importation des tissus orientaux en Europe occidental au haut moyen age, IXe et X^e siecles', *Revue Belge de Philologie et d'Histoire* (1935).

[8] E. M. Carus Wilson, 'Haberget: A medieval tex ile conundrum', *Medieval Archaeology*, XIII (1969).

[9] M. Nockert, 'A Scandinavian haberget?', below pp. 100–107.

My own inclination is to stress the difference in appearance between the earlier and the later group of diamond twills; as far as I can see, not all of the latter are real worsteds. On the one hand, there is the extremely fine quality of the items from Palmyra, Birka and Oseberg, all characterised by their very dense warp of even and glossy yarn, which practically covers the weft, thus producing a smooth and shiny fabric – a weave which, because of the dense warp, seems bound to be the product of the warp-weighted loom. In this kind of loom the weft is packed or beaten *within* the shed with a sword beater, a method which allows the warp to be very dense. In the ordinary treadle loom, on the other hand, the weft is packed with a beater fitted with a reed. Clearly, a dense and fragile warp would have been worn out by the batting reed. Furthermore, we have to consider the more recent specimens of diamond twills, mostly made of coarser yarn varying in warp and weft – some of them shown in Carus-Wilson's article and rightly described as resembling a ring-mail, or *Hauberk*. Such woollens could also have been woven on a treadle loom in either England or in France.

Silk fabrics

Silk fabrics were found in about forty-five graves. Mostly they were of the well-known kind commonly occurring in Iran and the eastern Mediterranean, namely the multi-coloured weft-faced compound twill, also known as *samitum*. Beside this rather ordinary type of silk, there were a few fragments of taffeta (that is, silk tabby weave) and one specimen of a self-patterned weave similar to what is known as 'Han damask' and quite probably of Chinese origin (see Figure 5.5). This exceedingly fine fabric (54/46 threads/cm) formed a seam which had been hidden by a silver lace, corrosion salts from which had had the effect of preserving the precious silk. Under a magnifying glass it was possible to distinguish traces of gold paint, possibly printed. The grave in question, No. 944, belonged to a man and contained elaborate items of oriental character, including seven bullet-shaped bronze buttons which may have belonged to an oriental caftan.

Linen fabrics

Linen would seem to be the collective designation for plain fabrics in tabby weave where the yarn consists of either flax or hemp, closely related bast fibres which are, to some extent, customarily interchangeable the world over. Like all vegetable fibres, they decay rapidly when exposed to damp. In archaeological finds it is only in the immediate vicinity of metal objects that traces of such material can be preserved – generally after a more or less complete destruction of the actual fibres – either in the form of hardened remnants or of impressions in the patina of the metal. It was the difficulty involved in firmly distinguishing

5.5   Self-patterned silk of Chinese origin. Enlarged to twice actual size, photographed under translucence

between the two bast species that led me to employ the cryptic designation FH (*Flachs Hanf*, that is, flax, hemp) in the original classification. Such finds were made in about forty-five graves.

Some of these remains revealed the result of a treatment not previously observed in archaeological finds, but known from folk costumes, particularly in Finland and south-eastern Europe. The technique is a form of pleating, or *plissé*, achieved by gathering the fabric with a needle and thread, and subsequently drawing the thread straight (see Figure 5.6). After removing the thread, the fabric was soaked in water and stretched in the direction of the pleats, and then left to dry. When fully dried the fabric remains tightly pleated. This technique is especially suitable for linen fabrics, but if again exposed to wet or washing the treatment easily becomes undone. As can be illustrated by Swedish ethnological material the method could also be applied to woollens, but this requires more protracted treatment, including the application of heat.

My first assumption was that all the linen products were of native origin. This was based on the fact that Hälsingland and other coastal provinces along the Bothnian Gulf were famous for their extensive flax cultivation and their linen industry in recorded history from the twelfth century. However, recent research by various authors has led me to doubt whether this industry could so early have attained the capacity reflected by the Birka finds. I have, in fact, propounded the hypothesis that the linen industry of Hälsingland resulted from Baltic

5.6   *Reverse of a bronze buckle containing linen fabric hardened by the metallic corrosion. The* plissé *pleating executed by the 'needle and thread' technique. Actual size*

trade and thus from Slavonic influence.[10] We know that southern Russia developed an extensive linen industry at an early stage. This surmise tallies perfectly with a recent suggestion by Inga Hägg – based on ethnological material from Slovakian territory – to the effect that the pleated shirts worn by the women of Birka were imported from Kiev.[11] My only objection to this suggestion is that all the linen remains

[10] A. Geijer, *Ur textilkonstens historia* (Lund, 1972), p. 90; *A History of Textile Art* (London, 1979), p. 64.

[11] I Hägg, *Kvinnodräkten i Birka. Livplaggens rekonstruktion* (Uppsala, 1974).

– not only the pleated ones – were probably imported in the same condition, pleated and ready to wear, and that in the cases where the fabric is smooth, the garment may simply have been washed or exposed to rain, thereby losing its pleating.

Costume trimmings of gold and silver

There is plenty of written evidence from ancient times and the early Middle Ages indicating that prominent people wore clothes which were interwoven or otherwise decorated with gold. Extant specimens of gold thread, however, are rare. As far as I have been able to ascertain, the very few specimens known from western European finds are usually done in a technique which is different from the gold thread predominantly found at Birka. The type of gold thread which I venture to designate as 'western' corresponds to the technique described by Theophilus as *aurum battutum*, whereby the gold is hammered out into a thin sheet which is then cut into narrow strips, termed 'lamella' (German *Lahn*).[12] This lamella could be woven in flat, but mostly it was spun and wound around a core of linen, wool or silk.

The gold and silver thread found in Birka is a solid wire (German *Draht*, Latin *aurum tractiticum*). It is round in cross-section and is produced by drawing a metal rod through progressively smaller holes, a technique also employed by goldsmiths. In the Birka finds the wire of gold or silver has been adapted for three different uses: as additional effects in woven braids, as plaited '*passements*' of various shapes, and to produce variously worked ornaments which may be called embroideries (see Figure 5.7).

For the *passementerie* a special kind of metal thread has sometimes been used which is extremely rare in textile work, namely the spiral wire – a very fine wire which has been wound tightly around a core (see, for instance, Figure 5.8). The art of making the same kind of wire in pewter was developed long ago by the Lapps of northern Sweden, who used it in their dress trimmings embroidered in 'couched work'. This unusual technique aroused attention early. The remarkable affinity of the technique to the Birka gold works has led to the conclusion that it was developed through the contacts between Lapps and merchants from Birka.[13] In the Birka items P 1–27 both kinds of gold and silver wire occur, that is, both the simple solid type and the spiral type. These *passementerie* trimmings shaped either into c na-

---

[12] W. Theobald, *Technik des Kunsthandwerks im zehnten Jahrhundert. Des Theophilus presbyter Diversarum artium schedula. Im Auswahl neu ausgegoben, übersetzt und erläutert* (Berlin, 1933)

[13] The art of drawing pewter into a 'wire', as met with among the Lapps in northern Sweden, was observed by Johannes Schefferus (*Lapponia*, 1673) and subsequently discussed by various Scandinavian scholars; see Geijer, *Birka III* (see n. 3), pp. 68–74.

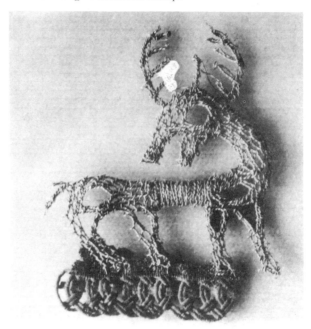

*5.7   The Golden Stag worked in solid gold wire in the twined wire technique
with inlay of mica. Embroidered on a piece of silk fabric trimmed with a silver
passement. Enlarged to twice actual size*

mental knots or into long plaited laces had been attached to silk
materials, in some cases apparently belonging to the headgear.

The miniature figures and ornaments which I hesitantly termed
Stickerei (St 1–33) form a rather odd and heterogeneous group of
embroidery which, however, may sometimes have been done without
the use of a needle. The very few counterparts which I was able to
detect elsewhere had not been described or written about at the time,
and I was therefore obliged to invent the terms to be used. The
specimens St 5–15 *Ösenstich* might perhaps be called 'reverse chain-
stitch' in English.[14] With all its variations, it is an ingenious and
versatile technique. Sometimes such stitches, like normal needlework,
were worked upon a silk fabric and sometimes they were used for joining
together two pieces of fabric, while sometimes they appear without
any woven ground or are combined with plaiting, in which case the
result is reminiscent of goldsmith's work. One of the most beautiful

[14] M. Thomas, *Dictionary of Embroidery Stitches* (London, 1934) uses the term 'reverse chain-stitch'
for a similarly constructed stitch. I am indebted to Mrs Elsa Guðjonsson of Reykjavik for this
reference and for valuable advice concerning embroidery terms.

achievements of this technique is a set of four pendants – or, perhaps, standing ornaments – from a kind of headgear (St 10). Each pendant is constructed of four squares of silk fabric which are embroidered with this kind of stitch, the silk pieces being joined along the edges with the same stitches. Besides the ten examples of this genre (St 5–14) found at Birka, five more items of a more complex variety were found, mostly in Gotland, the famous island where the ground is extraordinarily rich in Oriental finds.

Another kind of stitch was termed *Slingenstich*, perhaps translatable as 'twined wire technique'. This is unique to the best of my belief. It was executed with two wire ends, one of which is 'passive' while the other is 'active', that is to say, attaching itself either to a ground fabric or to the previous stitches. This technique is used by itself or

5.8   *Lumps of earth still containing silver passements formed by knots of spiral wire. This silver trimming was applied upon a strip of 'samitum' silk, which by means of silk stitches was sewn onto a very thin fabric, probably linen. Enlarged*

together with plaiting to make a kind of 'fold' – reminiscent of the setting of a jewel – for mounting pieces of thin mica, foliated glass, sheets of gold or gilded leather (see Figures 5.9–5.11). The result of this technique is sometimes extremely refined, as in the case of the gold stag (Figure 5.7), but in other instances it looks primitive and has the appearance of being improvised by a non-professional.

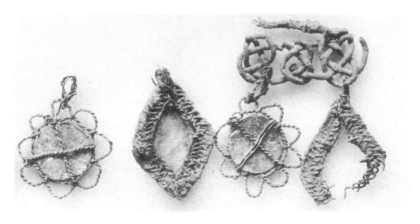

5.9   *Trimming border of spiral wire with pendants containing pieces of mica mounted in a 'setting' of solid wire. Enlarged to twice actual size*

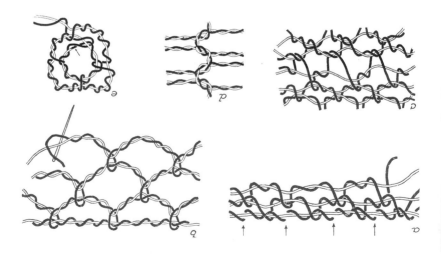

5.10   *Diagrams of the twined wire technique (as used in Figure 5.7). The 'active' wire is shown in full black*

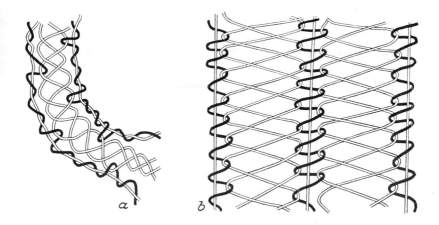

5.11   Diagram of the 'setting' used for mounting glittering pieces of mica or gilded leather on a woven ground

Apart from these two techniques which are undoubtedly oriental in origin, there are two cases of gold embroidery of a Western type (St 1–2) where the gold, sometimes combined with silver, is a true spun thread, consisting of a lamella wound around a silk core. It was used for embroidery in stem-stitch on a textile ground, now decayed – and entirely a Western style of work.

Tablet-woven bands

The most extensive group of gold or silver items found at Birka were the tablet-woven bands or braids, of which specimens were found in almost sixty graves, often with several variants occurring together. The entire group is of uniform technique and quality and displays consistent types of geometrical patterns covering the centre of the braid between a few continuous strings, though there are some striking variations (see Figures 5.12–5.15). This suggests a very large volume of output, of which the entire Birka collection may constitute only a fraction.

The warp is either entirely or predominantly of silk, now brownish all over but originally apparently multi-coloured. A tablet weave normally consists of parallel strings, each string comprising four threads twisted together by means of a square tablet with holes in the corners. If all the threads are of the same colour and if all the tablets are turned in the same way, a regular surface visible on the back of the braid will be produced. This is sometimes the case here, but often the reverse of the patterned area is irregular and the twists are uneven, which must indicate that the threads were of different colours and that the tablets were twisted individually according to the requirement of a multi-coloured pattern. In other cases, the reverse surface is porous because certain threads (no doubt originally linen) have rotted away. This indicates a method which saves the precious silk material, though obviously its main purpose was to create rich patterns by turning the tablets individually. It is a very exacting technique and the execution is strikingly even and uniform.

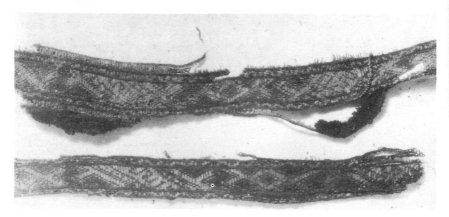

5.12   Tablet-woven bands of silk and silver wire. Actual size. Photographed in water to make the coroded silver stand out light

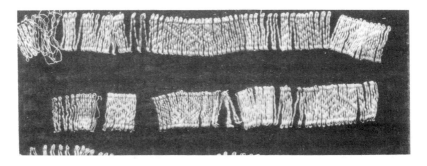

5.13   Solid gold wire from a tablet-woven band of which the silk has decayed. Note the impression of the pattern

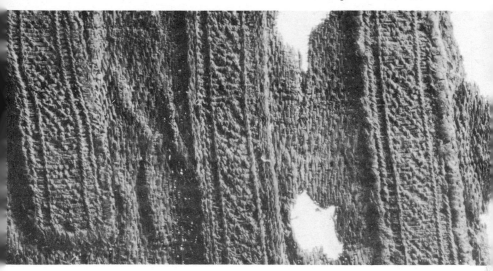

5.14 *Portion of 'samitum' silk with a trimming of tablet-woven bands, probably from a caftan. Enlarged to twice actual size*

5.15 *Patterns of tablet-woven bands. The vertical lines signify the silk strings standing out against the ground of gold or silver*

All bands have two kinds of weft: the metal weft visible on the obverse and the ordinary weft which is hidden within the evenly twisted side strings. With one or two exceptions the surface weft consists of an actual wire of gold or silver, in most cases two paired, extremely fine wires following each other – also a method of achieving most effect with the least possible material. A further method of increasing the effect of brilliant metal was to rub or press the surface of the finishing band with some hard tool; this method is attested by the remaining gold wire from braids.

The existence of advanced tablet-weaving in the Nordic countries, even before the Viking era, at first led me to believe that most of the bands found in Birka were of native origin. However, I have since abandoned this idea and I am now convinced that the entire group was imported, probably via Russia, from Byzantium and that other consignments from more or less the same source later reached the West by other routes. Eventually this art took root in the West and gave rise to many different forms of band weaving, including perhaps the 'red gold bands' often mentioned in Nordic folksong.

My increasing belief that all of the Birka tablet bands were oriental products rather than Swedish ones was corroborated by the two important complexes of related gold items (embroideries and bands) preserved in Durham in England and in Maeseyck in Belgium and which are datable quite precisely to AD 905–16 and about 850 respectively, the latter also being attributed to an English workshop.[15] The gold thread in them is throughout of the Western type, spun around a core which, in one of the Maeseyck braids, proved to be of horsehair. Here the thread is always introduced single, and not paired as in the Birka bands, a method which would testify to a higher standard of craftsmanship than found in most bands that are to be considered as Western products.[16]

Miscellaneous fabrics

All the categories which have been mentioned so far appear to have

---

[15] G. M. Crowfoot, 'The braids' in C. F. Battiscombe (ed.), *The Relics of Saint Cuthbert, Durham Cathedral* (Durham, 1956); Marguerite Calberg, 'Tissus et broderies attribués aux Saintes Harlinde et Relinde', *Bulletin de la Societée Royale d'archéologie de Bruxelles* (1951).

[16] The few finds of gold thread outside Birka were accounted for in *Birka III*, p. 70. Besides the publications by Crowfoot and Calberg mentioned in the previous note, the following instances are to be mentioned. Concerning France, see M. Fleury and A. France-Lanord, 'Les bijoux mérovingiens d'Arnegonde', *Arts de France*, I (Paris, 1961); idem, 'Das Grab des Arnegundis in Saint-Denis', *Germania*, XL (1962); A. France-Lanord, 'Les textiles brodés d'or dans les tombes princières d'époque mérovingiennes à Saint-Denis', *Contribution to the 1965 Congress of the International Institute for Conservation* (Stockholm, 1975). Concerning Scandinavia see M. Hald, *Olddanske textiler* (Copenhagen, 1950), p. 203 (treating the tablet bands with spun gold weft from the Mammen find) and B. Hougen, 'Gulltråd fra Goksta', *Honos Ella Kivikoski, Eripainos* (Helsinki, 1975) accounting for two small finds of gold wire in Norway.

been imported from far away. The reader is therefore bound to ask whether any native textiles have been found, comparable to those known from other Nordic finds. No doubt native textiles also existed in Birka, though the surviving specimens are few and far between owing to the difficult conditions in which they would have had to survive. The reason for this was that they did not form part of clothing, which by reason of its metal accessories was more likely to be preserved. Eight specimens of decorative textiles are of domestic origin, probably used as covers placed over corpses. Two of these must have been splendid examples of the complicated soumak-tapestry technique (Figure 5.16) which is abundantly represented in the Oseberg finds, while some of the other remains indicate somewhat simpler weaves with brocaded patterns. Mention should also be made of some very fragmentary remains of a kind of *rya* (pile rug) and traces of squirrel, marten and beaver furs, as well as plumage and down, which belonged to some rich burials.

5.16   Specimen of a tapestry-soumak weave. Multi-coloured woollens originally standing out against a linen (?) ground

Costume

The primary focus of my investigations, for obvious reasons, had to be on the textile materials as such, that is, on analyses of the various items and technical categories. So far as possible, too, by means of comparison, I dealt with the attribution of the products to their origin. However, most of the textiles clearly formed parts of clothing, and so the problem of what the costumes had looked like could not be totally neglected. My observations and explanatory suggestions were presented in the last chapter of the book.

In spite of the minute quantity of textile fragments preserved, thanks to their position adjacent to metal objects, their original function could in many cases be deduced from the excellent plan drawings made by Stolpe during his excavation work. In addition, some help in explaining puzzling features could be gathered from various ethnographical sources. However, serious publications on this matter were still rare in the 1930s when *Birka III* was being written.

The pair of bronze buckles belonging to the woman's costume had protected some valuable details. The fine linen fabric – sometimes pleated by the special method described above – formed a long shirt worn next to the body. Outside the shirt, the women used to wear a kind of skirt, the appearance of which could be reconstructed from analogous garments from the Baltic area. It consists of a square cloth wrapped around the body and supported by straps over the shoulders. Remarkably enough, women's burials in Birka provide no trace of any kind of belt, a circumstance which is paralleled by the figures represented on the big stone monuments at Gotland and by a number of miniature silver figures from Viking times.

From the burial remains of male costume at Birka, it is difficult to judge how men dressed. Some garments seem to have been of foreign origin, or maybe the buried man was a foreigner himself. In five or six cases the deceased had worn sleeved coats buttoned in front with small ball-shaped buttons of solid bronze; in three cases seven or eight such buttons were found *in situ*, in one no less than eighteen buttons. Around the waist, three of these well-dressed gentlemen had worn leather belts with applied bronze ornaments of Khazarian origin, as well as variously decorated money boxes, one containing an Arabian coin (*dirhem*). We do not know the basic material of these coats, but the model is likely to have been like the utility garment of the Iranian and other Central Asian riding people, that is, the riding caftan which eventually developed to become the courtiers' attire in Byzantium, the *scaramagnon*, described by Kondakov and also discussed by the present writer.[17] It seems probable that the numerous strips of *samitum*

[17] N. P. Kondakov, 'Les costumes orientaux à la cour byzantine', *Byzantion* (1927); A. Geijer, 'A silk from Antinoë and the Sasanian textile art', *Orientalia suecana*, XII (Uppsala, 1964).

(silk) found in the Birka graves might have served as trimming of such coats. This view is based on the analogy with numerous caftans found in Egyptian Antinoë. The relatively large pieces of silk fabric with applied tablet-woven bands which were preserved in a double grave might have belonged to a caftan of this kind.

A large and extremely variegated collection of trimmings with gold and silver ingredients – tablet bands, *passementerie*, laces and embroideries – may have belonged to various types of headgear, many of which are possible to identify with the aid of Stolpe's plan drawings. But the task of reconstructing these headgears is not an easy one.

6   A Scandinavian Haberget?
Margareta Nockert

In the spring of 1971 the excavation for the arranging of a bridal
chamber beneath the porch of the church of Leksand, Dalecarlia,
Sweden, was started. Almost immediately parts of a skeleton were
found. The archaeological examination showed that part of a grave-
field had been discovered which extended outside the church as well.
The graves were lying very closely together and in five layers beneath
each other. Judging from the number of skulls, or fragments of skulls,
approximately 160 individuals were buried beneath the present porch.
The graves were east–west oriented according to the Christian tradition, but were equipped with often costly burial gifts. Among the finds
there were about thirty coins. The oldest coin is from the tenth century
and the most recent from the fourteenth century.

In the bottom layer of the excavation a grave was found containing
remarkably well-preserved textiles. The part of the grave containing
these textiles was taken to the textile department of the Central
Office and Museum of National Antiquities in Stockholm for further
excavation.

The skeleton had mouldered away except for the skull. The age
of the person was estimated to be between forty and sixty years. It was
not possible to determine the sex, but it appeared from the surrounding
finds that the buried person was a woman. Over the top of the head a
roll of wool was lying and along the left side of the skull lay a lock of
hair around which were wound threads of wool which had originally
been yellow and red. There were no marks of any woven material
either on the roll or in the hair. From the shoulders and *c.* 12 cm down
over the chest lay a folded piece of diamond twill (broken 2/2 lozenge
twill) which continued down along the two long sides of the grave.
From the right shoulder down the right side lay a tablet-woven band
of 4.5 cm width, which was sewn along the piece of diamond twill as
a completed edging. From the left shoulder ran a similar band which
crossed over the chest and continued down the right side of the grave.

All the textile fragments originate from one and the same garment, that is, the cloak or mantle in which the woman's body was swathed. The front edgings of the cloak were decorated with a tablet-woven band with a richly varied geometrical pattern. The band was woven in yellow, red, orange and green wool. A green piece of string was sewn on the outer edging of the band. The inside of the cloak was edged with a piece of red ribbed woollen fabric striped in yellow and green.

6.1 (left) *Fragment of tablet-woven band. The pattern is in yellow, orange and green against a red ground*

6.2 (right) *Reconstruction of the pattern in Figure 6.1*

6.3   The edging on the inside of the cloak. A piece of red ribbed woollen fabric striped in yellow and green is sewn on along the diamond twill

A loop of string was sewn on to the edging of the cloak at the right shoulder. A similar unattached loop was lying close by. A little further down the right side lay a string, possibly intended to hold the cloak together. Two fragments of diamond twill which were found on the right side beneath the pelvis were cut off obliquely and edged with a ribbed band of the same colour as the cloth itself. The angle between the warp threads of the twill and the band is about 45 degrees. These fragments indicate that the cloak was originally half-circular, which can be proved by calculating the original size of the cloak. The largest fragment of diamond twill, 75 by 52 cm, was taken as a basis for the calculation of the height of the back of the cloak. This fragment has a selvage and the largest preserved piece of cloth is 70 cm wide; 68.5 cm from the selvage there is, on a stretch of 2 cm, remnants of the selvage of the red ribbed fabric. Since other fragments show that the ribbed piece of fabric has been sewn on 5 cm away from the selvage of the diamond twill, the twill's loom-width can be calculated to be 73.5 cm. Along the selvage of the fragment there was another piece of fabric sewn on, which also had a selvage. This latter fragment is only preserved in a width of 5 cm. It must be thought unlikely that such a narrow strip of fabric would have been considered necessary to sew on. It is more probable that two pieces of fabric with the same width would have been sewn together from the beginning.[1]

The height of the back of the cloak should in that case be 150 cm. The length of the body is calculated to be 165–70 cm, which would mean that the back of the cloak reached down to the woman's feet.

About one metre of the patterned tablet-woven band, which decorates the front-edging of the cloak, is preserved. Judging from the place of the band fragments in the grave, their length must have been at least two metres. Judging from the proportions the length of the cloak was probably originally something between two and **three** metres. This cloak is probably a so-called '*Schnurmantel*', a half-circular cloak reaching down to the feet with the front kept together by **a band** or a string.[2] This type of cloak was fashionable during the later **part** of the twelfth and the thirteenth centuries.

[1] A Swedish moss-find dating from the 1350s or 1360s, the Bocksten find, contains a half-circular cloak which is sewn together out of two whole loom-widths. A. Sandklef, 'The Bocksten find', *Acta Ethnologica* (1937), pp. 1–64.
[2] P. Post, 'Von mittelalterlichen Schnurmantel', *Zeitschrift für Waffen und Kostümkunde*, XIII (1932–34), pp. 123–8.

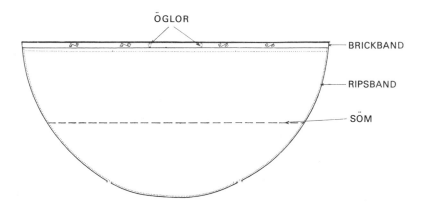

6.4   *Reconstruction-drawing of the cloak*

It is difficult to determine the age of the grave. There are no datable finds like clasps or similar items. It lies beneath two completely empty graves. It was only possible to do one C14 analysis, so it has not been possible to confirm the obtained date of 1210 ± 120.[3] Dating the grave on the basis of the textile finds is difficult since almost no comparative finds exist. There are also no parallels to the special technical workmanship of the tablet-woven bands. Some of the ornamental designs still exist on the bands woven in Leksand today, but it is also the common Roman decorative style found throughout Europe between the eleventh and thirteenth centuries. Nor has the roll around the hair any archaeological parallels in other European finds. In any case, the type of cloak suggests a date in the early Middle Ages, probably not later than the end of the thirteenth century, a date which agrees with the results of the C14 analysis.

The cloak is made of worsted which was yellow when it was taken out of the grave. After a short while in the air it was transformed into a grey–yellow colour. The binding of the weave is, as mentioned earlier, a broken 2/2 lozenge twill, that is, a kind of lozenge twill with '*sharp cut*' in both the warp and the weft (see Figure 6.5). The diagonal is broken after thirty threads in the warp and eleven threads in the weft. Only one selvage is preserved and the largest known loom-width is 70 cm. (The original loom-width, 73.5 cm, was possible to reconstruct as mentioned). The warp consists of one thread of finely and evenly Z-spun wool yarn with a thread-count of twenty-two threads per centimetre. The weft is thicker than the warp and S-spun with a thread-count of ten to eleven threads per centimetre. Two picks have been used alternately. This method is used partly to give the fabric an even and smooth surface and partly to stop the selvages from contracting.

In Scandinavia there are finds of diamond twill between about 700 and the late Viking Age. The greatest collection of finds is from Birka where diamond twill was found in forty-five graves.[4] In these cloths the yarn for both warp and weft is consistently fine and evenly Z-spun. The warp is two or three times closer than the weft. The diagonal-line of the twill always turns with a '*sharp cut*' which is characteristic for fabrics woven in a warp-weighted loom and is connected with the kind of warping-method typical for this kind of loom.[5]

As mentioned by Agnes Geijer in her revised summary of her work on the Birka textiles, she identified the diamond worsteds in Birka as the renowned '*pallia fresonica*', a textile which earlier scholars had

[3] The laboratory for radiocarbon dating, Stockholm St 3668.

[4] A. Geijer, *Birka III, Die Textilfunde aus den Gräbern* (Uppsala, 1938).

[5] A. Geijer, *Birka III*, p. 31; M. Hoffmann, *The Warp-Weighted Loom* (Oslo, 1964).

6.5   *Diagram of the broken 2/2 lozenge twill*

6.6   *Diagram of the selvage of the broken 2/2 lozenge twill*

thought to be manufactured somewhere along the shores of the English Channel. Hoffman has opposed this hypothesis and suggested (with the support of finds from Palmyra, which was destroyed in 273) that they were produced in the eastern part of the Mediterranean area and in Syria.[6] Geijer has given support to this suggestion concerning Syria but considers it likely that *pallia fresonica* might have represented various kinds of fine imported textiles offered for sale by Friesian merchants.[7]

All the fragments of diamond twill found in Birka are of a much finer quality – 32 × 12 – 55 × 20 threads per centimetre – than the piece of fabric found in Leksand. However, there are other finds from the Viking period whose quality resembles this piece of fabric from Leksand. As examples, two finds from Norway can be mentioned, from Kaupang and Hamaröy, which have a thread-count of 22 × 11 respectively, 20–22 × 9–10 threads per centimetre, and two finds from Sweden, from Spånga and Valbo, which have a thread-count of 22 × 12 respectively, 20 × 10 threads per centimetre. So far it has not proved possible to say where these rougher pieces of fabric might have been produced. The difference between the pieces of fabric found in Leksand and the finds of diamond twill from the Viking period is that the Leksand fabric has different directions of spinning in warp and weft, which is a phenomenon not known in Viking times.

Since the earliest finds of diamond twill are not of a later date than the tenth century, it has been assumed that the technique disappeared when the loom with the horizontal warp was introduced into Europe. This new kind of loom seems to have spread to western Europe in the eleventh century. At the same time the machinery method for fulling arose and a new kind of fabric came into fashion. The binding of the weave no longer mattered so much, while the treatment of the surface of the fabric was of great consequence. It is possible to study this development from the large body of finds from medieval city excavations where most of the fragments are fulled. Only a small number of worsted fragments has been found. The majority of these fragments were woven in a common 2/1 twill and a smaller number of lozenge twill in different designs. There is no consistency concerning the spinning direction of the warp respective to the weft in the medieval worsteds. Most of the previously examined pieces of fabric have a Z-spun warp and a S-spun weft, but it was not unusual for both directions of thread to be Z-spun.

---

[6] M. Hoffmann, *The Warp-Weighted Loom*, p. 229.

[7] A. Geijer, 'Var järnålderns "frisiska˙ kläde" tillverkat i. Syrien?' [The *pallium fresonicum* of the Viking Age: was it manufactured in Syria?], *Fornvännen*, (Stockholm, 1965), pp. 112–32.

The high quality of the diamond twill found in Leksand points to its being professionally produced and it was probably imported. Where could this fabric have been produced? Professor Carus-Wilson has investigated the meaning of the word 'haberget' which is found as a name for a kind of fabric in English and French sources from the middle of the twelfth century to the end of the thirteenth century.[8] This fabric could be of different qualities and colours so the characteristics of them ought to be found in the texture. The word 'haberget' is the same word as 'hauberk' which means ringmail. In pictorial reproductions of ringmail – see, for instance, the Bayeux tapestry – a diagonal checked pattern resembling diamond twill is used. In an Icelandic source the name for lozenge twill is used, as a 'kenning' for a coat of ringmail; *hringofinn serkr*, a shirt woven with rings. In Iceland lozenge twill is called *hringavaðmál* and in Norway the word *ringvend* is used parallel with *gåsöye*.[9]

It is clear that diamond twill is a typical product of the warp-weighted loom. Since the design was very popular during the Viking period, it was probably still produced for some time on the new horizontal loom until it was gradually replaced by other products typical of this kind of loom. This might be the explanation of why the word 'haberget' disappears towards the end of the thirteenth century. 'Haberget' seems to have been a common product of the English town of Stamford, but might have been produced in other places as well. Stamford was a city of Danish origin and it had lively trade relations with Scandinavia. Professor Carus-Wilson knew of no find of diamond twill to verify her hypothesis about 'haberget' being the same as diamond twill. The fabric found in Leksand might be of English origin and might well have been called 'haberget', though we still know too little to draw any firm conclusions.[10]

---

[8] E. M. Carus-Wilson, 'Haberget: A medieval textile conundrum', *Medieval Archaeology*, XIII (1969), pp. 148–66.

[9] Strömberg, Geijer, Hald and Hoffmann, *Nordisk textilteknisk terminologi* [Scandinavian terminology of textile term], 2nd edn (Oslo, 1974).

[10] The author is now working on a larger group of material probably of English origin with the intention of classifying this matter further.

7 The Productivity of Weaving in Late Medieval Flanders
Walter Endrei

The economic and political events which brought about the crisis of the Flemish cloth industry in the sixteenth century were merely the conclusion of a long course of decline.[1] The cause lay in the tenacious clinging to traditional manufacturing processes, which again could be ascribed to the rigid social structure following the failure of fourteenth-century social movements. Cloth-makers of Flanders and the Brabant would, in fact, reject the new ways of spinning and finishing, as most strikingly proved by their having banned fulling mills.[2] We also have reasonable grounds for believing that they adhered to the medieval weaving processes in the same manner. This supposition is supported by the fact that, in spite of several additions and improvements made to the Flemish *keures* (guild rules) between the thirteenth and sixteenth centuries, the technical requirements remained largely unchanged.

Therefore, when attempting to establish the productivity of weaving, we may safely refer to sixteenth-century data along with the rather scant information available from the fourteenth and fifteenth centuries. For our starting point, we chose Guilleaume d'Enghien's investigation of the Flemish cloth industry in 1592–93, undoubtedly commanded by Philip II. Enghien's report was discussed by de Sagher in 1937,[3] but a much better evaluation of it can be derived from the more recently published edition of the documents themselves.[4]

---

[1] The number of looms in Ieper (Ypres) in 1406 may still be put at 3000–4000 of which there were but 100 left by 1545. H. Pirenne: *Histoire économique de l'Occident médiéval* (Bruges, 1951), p. 463. T. Wittman, *A flamand posztóipar tőkés lehetőségei a manufaktura-korszak küszöbén* (Századok, 1961), pp. 2–3, 236–80.

[2] R. van Uytven, 'The fulling mill', *Acta Historiae Neerlandica*, DIV (1971)

[3] H. de Sagher: 'Une enquête sur la situation de l'industrie drapière en Flandre à la fin du XVIe siècle' in *Etudes d'Histoire dédiées à la Mémoire de Henri Pirenne* (Bruxelles, 1937).

[4] Sagher, Werveke and Wyffels, *Recueil de documents relatifs à l'histoire de l'industrie drapière en Flandre, Deuxième Partie*, I–III (Bruxelles, 1951–66), hereinafter *Recueil*.

One of the fullest records has been preserved in the archives of Armentières. In the 1590s, 401 looms were to be found there, and another 12 in the environs. The number of masters was 350. In view of the normal use of two-men, wide-treadle looms, this number implies the existence of at least another 450–500 hands.[5] The majority of the masters owned one or two looms, but some shops had as many as four.

The collectors of data for Enghien's investigation noted down exactly where and how many pieces were found, indicating also their condition: that is, on the loom, in the dye house, in fulling or under control. They listed the following products in different stages.

bay (baye)   522 pieces
estamet(te)[6]   2216 pieces
woollen cloth   766 pieces

This is a true reflection of the changing fashion, for the woollen cloth trade had by then seriously declined. Nevertheless, in view of its labour intensity, it still played an important part in the town's industry as demonstrated to some extent by the measurements.

Table 7.1

	Piece length ells (27 in)	Width	Price: patards (2d) per ell
Cloth	28–30	$2\frac{1}{8}$	53–57
Estamet	18–23	$2\frac{1}{8}$	41–54
Bay	35	$1\frac{3}{4}$	16

According to the data in Table 7.1, as well as to the warp-count, an average piece of woollen cloth was equal to 1.1 estamet or 2.5 bays respectively. In other words, the equivalent of about 3000 pieces of cloth was registered.

This was the stage the investigation had reached on 7 April 1593, when it became necessary to determine how long the cloth manufacture took. Fortunately a 'certain notebook' has been discovered from which the number of pieces presented for the inspection of raw cloths (*perche crue*) in the years 1592–93 can be determined:[7]

[5] *Recueil*, I, p. 435.
[6] Concerning the quality of bay see W. Endrei, *Középkori angol textilimportunk gyapjuszövetei* (Századok, 1970), p. 294. The estamet is a finer but also twill-woven, fulled pile cloth. A regulation issued in 1567 concerns 'des cherges, carizees, estamettes et aultres' articles, that is, a product similar to kersey.
[7] *Recueil*, I, pp. 1, 452–3. These figures may be somewhat amended by those of the statement on p. 466, but there the quantity is given in demi-draps.

Table 7.2

	Estamet	Cloth	Bay
4 May–4 August 1592	2152	582	829
3 August–30 October 1592	2068	574	817
4 November–5 February 1593	1900	599	823
8 February–7 April 1593	1459	496	668
Unexamined	58	10	10
Total	7637	2261	3147

This amounts to the equivalent of 10 463 pieces of cloth for eleven months, corresponding to an annual production of 11 414 pieces. We get similar results from the data of a notebook in which the collection of duties was registered between 1588 and 1594:[8]

	Estamet	Cloth	Bay
9 May 1592 – 8 May 1593	8190	1693	3506

This is equivalent to 10 811 pieces of cloth, giving a maximum of 26–8 pieces a year for one loom, which barely exceeds half of the often mentioned one piece a week.[9]

The weekly time required for weaving is confirmed by a statement recorded in the course of an assessment in Haubourdin made in 1593. Three cloth-makers and the quality-control officer made the following statement: 'one piece of cloth requires 10–12 days of handling for proper beating, carding and spinning; 6–7 days for weaving; some seven for fulling'.[10] Let us approach the productivity of cloth-weaving with more technical accuracy. In the case of Armentières, for instance, the only objective index is the length of weft yarn used at a unit time.[11] This is usually expressed in metres per hour;[12] in the present case this cannot be established without a thorough reconstruction of parameters for the cloth at issue.

[8] I must point out that the text quoted from p. 468 of *Recueil* is misleading. The infliction of the 12d duty concerned both half and whole pieces of cloth. Compare with p. 463 where, according to the original text of the regulation the infliction of 'douze deniers par. sur chascun drap ou demy drap' was decided on account of the town's fortification. Consequently the summary on p. 466 is not correct.

[9] C. Cipolla, *The Fontana Economic History of Europe: The Middle Ages* (London, 1972), p. 255.

[10] 'ung drap depuis que la laine se tire de la balle jusque'a ce qu'elle soit preste d'estre mise es mains de tondeur ... leur convient employer 10 a 12 jours, tant pour battre, triller que filler la laisne en quantité souffisante; six a 7 jours pour le tistre; environ une sepmaine pour le fouller', *Recueil*, II, p. 323.

[11] 75 loom owners made statements, 46 declaring eight pieces, 12 seven pieces monthly production. *Recueil*, I, p. 643. It is very likely that so-called demi draps, half pieces of 15–22 ells were meant here.

[12] W. Endrei, *A fonás és szövés termelékenységének alakulása. Technikatörténeti Szemle* (1966), pp. 1–2, 134–41.

Our starting point will be the *keures* whose texts were modified six times between 1510 and 1538.[13] In Armentières the 'ultrafine' and 'fine' types of cloth were predominant[14] and here the data are fairly consistent. The finished measurements are

length 28.5–30 ells
width 2.125 ells

The two types differ in weight:

ultrafine 50–2 lb
fine 44–6 lb

This latter has to be ascribed to the different use of yarns.

Table 7.3

	Number of warp ends	*Warp weight (in lb)*	*Weft weight (in lb)*	*Total weight*
Ultrafine	1800	36	56	92
Fine	1536	36	48	84

It is a known fact that fulling, napping and shearing produced radical changes in weight and measurement, as demonstrated here by the comparison between the 92 (84) lb weight of the yarns and that of the finished goods. The loss during winding, warping and weaving is but 4–9 per cent and 10–13 per cent respectively, but there is a further loss of about 40 per cent during the finishing processes. The decrease of substance again involves a considerable loss of surface. The length shrinks to 28–30 ells, that is, by 25–30 per cent equivalent to a 55 per cent decrease in surface. Thus the loss in weight (wool-grease and shearings) is comparatively less than that of the dimension. This is why thickening of the cloth, compactness and increase of the specific weight can be observed.

Because of these facts we are confronted with difficulties in our task of establishing the basic density and weft length. Unfortunately no precise data are available concerning the raw dimensions of the Armentières fine cloths; but using the analogy of the Estaires regulations, which do indicate these dimensions, we can assume a width of

---

[13] *Recueil*, I, pp. 102–91.
[14] There existed also a middling quality, while in 1565 Count Egmont granted production of a cloth wider and more expensive even than the ultrafine quality. *Recueil*, I, p. 192.

3.25–3.5 ells for Armentières' raw cloth.[15] The rate of shrinking observed during the fulling is rather diverse. According to Espinas, it varied in Flanders between 5–12.5 per cent in length and 12.5–50 per cent in width.[16] English sources mention one-third in length and half of the width.[17]

In this way we can now determine the warp-count. Reckoning 0.700 m for the Flemish ell, we can make the following calculations for 'ultrafine' cloth.

$$D_{wa\,1} = \frac{1800}{3.25 \times 70.0} = 7.91/cm$$

The warp-count of 'fine cloth' would be

$$D_{wa\,2} = \frac{1536}{3.25 \times 70.0} = 6.75/cm$$

The weight of the weft exceeds that of the warp by 56 per cent and 33 per cent respectively in the two cloths. Thus $D_{wa} = D_{we}$ is a reasonable value for getting the length of weft used for a piece:

$$l_{we} = D_{wa} \times l_c \times w_c \times 0.700^2 \times C$$

l_c and w_c meaning the length and width of the cloth in ells. C the crimp coefficient; that is,

$$l_{we\,1} = 7.91 \times 40 \times 3.25 \times 0.490 \times 108 = 54\,418 \text{ m}$$
$$l_{we\,2} = 6.75 \times 40 \times 3.25 \times 0.490 \times 108 = 46\,437 \text{ m}$$

Now comes the determination of the production time. Our conclusion having been half a piece of cloth a week, we must still consider the number of working days and hours. From a 1575 notebook, bearing the title 'Régistre des aunes des draps d'Armentièrs', we learn that in the ninety days between 7 February and 7 May 1575 there were nine holidays kept besides the thirteen Sundays, leaving but sixty-eight working days.[18] This tallies with the picture of the contemporary England of the Tudors: a statute of 1552 reduced the forty-six holidays of the tradesmen to twenty-seven and grants half a day free before the 15th.[19] Thus we may hardly reckon with more than 280 working

---

[15] Measurements of the raw cloth can seldom be found in the regulations. According to the *keure* of Estaires, one copy was destroyed by fire in the Middle Ages, the other one during the Second World War, 'le dit plain drap sera sur l'ostille (loom) de 40 aulnes de lonc et de 3 aulnes de large . . . lequel drap prest a taillier ruenir a (deux) aunes de large tant seullement et non plus', *Recueil*, II, p. 276.

[16] G. Espinas, *La draperie dans la Flandre Française au Moyen Age*, II (Paris, 1923), p. 227.

[17] J. de L. Mann, *The Cloth Industry in the West of England from 1640 to 1880* (Oxford, 1971), p. 295.

[18] *Recueil*, I, pp. 459–60.

[19] M. A. Bienefeld: *Working Hours in British Industry* (London, 1972), p. 19.

days a year. That brings down the average number of weekly working days to 5.2; after deduction of the free Saturday afternoons, to less than 5.

The working day, on the other hand, was fairly well utilised when the market was favourable, for how else could the frequent punishments for night work be explained?[20] On average, however, weavers might have spent not more than 10–12 hours at the loom,[21] less one or two hours lunch break. Thus we may assume that there were actually 50–60 working hours a week. Now, if we wish to determine on a yearly average the per-capita wefting length per hour, counting half a piece a week, we get the following results:

$$Pa_1 = \frac{54\,418}{55 \times 2 \times 2} = 247.4 \text{ m/h}$$

$$Pa_2 = \frac{46\,437}{55 \times 2 \times 2} = 211.1 \text{ m/h}$$

This is far below an earlier productivity estimate, based on eighteenth-century Hungarian data concerning two-men looms, which indicated 800 m/h.[22] This could still be ascribed to technical developments, but at the same time, this estimate of 211 m/h is exceedingly moderate compared to estimates of Flemish production limits in earlier centuries, determined evidently by the pressures of a slack market. To this we will revert later.

What is the possible explanation? For one thing, the investigations from which these data originate may have been made in a critical period of the Flemish industry. On the other hand, we probably calculated with the average of a very fluctuating production dependent on demand and season. If we wish to approach the potential productivity of the looms the best results achieved should be taken as a standard.

---

[20] Generally speaking work is forbidden 'par nuyt apres l'eure de noef heures du soir ne devant quatre heures du matin', *Recueil*, I, p. 110. Work by candlelight would be punished 'Accusation: avoir travaillé a la chandeille . . .' 1573, nevertheless daily 12–13 working hours on an average seem to be too much. Many towns do not allow 'werke voor de zonne no achter de zonne', ibid., p. 524. The prohibition of work by candlelight was actually forced by fire-protection. The sentences above were pronounced of course, in January when one needed candlelight for weaving already in the afternoon hours. At the same time there was an interesting experiment in Poperinge in 1603, according to which 'van Baemesse tot half maerte' work at candlelight is allowed 'zoude moghen weifven bijder keersse . . . van's morghens ten vijf heuren tot den taeghe, ende des avondts tot den acht heuren ende nijt langher', *Recueil*, III, pp. 356–7.

[21] In an earlier paper I reckoned 150 weaving hours for the cloth-weaver of the period taking for a basis pieces of about the same length. This indicated 75 hours' work for one person. 'Changements dans la productivité lainière du Moyen Age', *Annales* (1971), no. 6, p. 1298.

[22] W. Endrei, *L'évolution des techniques du filage et du tissage* (Paris, 1968), p. 89.

The diagram (Figure 7.1) of cloth production in Armentières between 1588 and 1594 shows that the three months from the 9 November to the 8 February, when days were the shortest, marks a distinct period.[23] The working intensity becomes even more perceivable by breaking down a year's production into months. For this purpose a report of the fiscal year 1516/17 is available.[24]

Table 7.4

Month	Output
16 August–1 October 1516 (6 weeks)	1444 pieces
October 1516	631 pieces
November 1516	623 pieces
December 1516	$364\frac{1}{2}$ pieces
January 1517	329 pieces
February 1517	161 pieces
March 1517	783 pieces
April 1517	1233 pieces
May 1517	473 pieces
June 1517	1044 pieces
1 July–16 August (6 weeks)	$603\frac{1}{2}$ pieces

It is most important to note the seasonal variations. As can be seen in the table for 1516/17 of Neuve Église, monthly production was at its lowest level in the winter months of December to February, averaging just 284.8 pieces a month, when working days were shortest. Production was also quite low in the six weeks from 1 July to 16 August (averaging 402.3 pieces a month), when summer field work was required. But the level of production in April, 1233 pieces, was more than four times the winter average and three times the early summer average. A similar case can be found later in the century at Armentières: 162 pieces produced during the winter of 1588/89, but some 870 pieces in the summer of 1593.

The potential productivity should thus be calculated on the basis of the production achieved under optimal market conditions and in the most favourable season. In the case of Neuve Église this would be April 1517, while the best results of Armentières ensue from the quarter following the Enghien investigations (9 May – 8 August 1593).

Limiting our calculation to the 843 pieces of cloth coming off 68 looms (out of the 413 in the Armentières district), an average of 12.4

[23] *Recueil*, I, p. 466.
[24] *Recueil*, II, pp. 207–9.

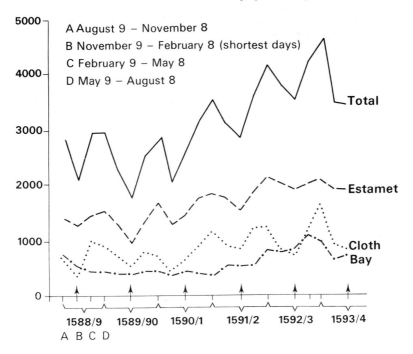

7.1 *Cloth production in Armentières, 1588–94*

pieces per loom was woven during the thirteen-week period, which brings us near to one piece a week. On the basis of the average weft length calculated above for fine and ultrafine cloths, marked $(l_{we\,1} + l_{we\,2})/2$ we get for one day (averaging the weft lengths of the ultrafine and the fine):

$$P_{qd} = \frac{52\,566 \times 843}{68 \times 70 \times 2} = 4654.7 \text{ m/day}$$

Converting it to the supposed 12–13 summer working hours, we get a production value of

$$P_{qh} = 358\text{–}388 \text{ m/h}$$

Although this is twice as much as the value arrived at on the basis of the examination, it is still far below the hypothetical capacity. Of course, it tallies with the 6–7 days of the Haubourdin cloth-makers; but then we counted an average for 136 hands working for 68 masters and there must have been also considerable differences between lazy and industrious workers, beginners and experts, not to mention that agricultural work from May to July took many off from their work. There must have been several masters who spent much of their time in their field or vegetable garden.

We get a better approach to the hypothetical capacity by analysing the above-mentioned fourteenth- and fifteenth-century maximum ratings. These *keure* regulations derive from the autumnal years of the Flemish cloth industry and were issued with the intention of not letting the immense volume of production bring about a decline of prices. Numerous restrictions on production were imposed: limitations on the number of masters and hands; relentless liquidation of cloth-making in the country; burning of equipment on the master's death, etc. In some Flemish towns even the maximum output per day was regulated.

The oldest *keure* containing restrictions is the one from Wervek that commanded no one to produce more than 38 ells in a three-day period, 33 ells in two days or 17 ells a day.[25] A later version, issued between 1466–80, reconfirms these limitations.[26] At the same time an Estaires wage tariff indicates, for cloths made of English wool, a limitation of only 8 ells in winter and 6 ells in summer, while for cloths of Scottish and Spanish wool one of 10 ells in summer and 7 ells in winter.[27]

The above figures contradict not only the values we have calculated for Armentières but are distinctly inconsistent. While the production limit of Estaires seems to be more or less in keeping with the 400 m/h, that is, 3.5 ells per day, considered as a fair summer average for Armentières, Wervek's maximum is almost five times as high.

This contradiction can be attributed to the different types of cloth only to a certain extent. Undeniably the cloth produced in the Wervek was of a lower warp-count (1296 and later on 144) and also narrower (1.75 ells),[28] but this fact only provides an index number of 1.35 approximately; accordingly the maximum of 17 ells per day would correspond to 12.6 ells of cloth at Armentières. So the resolution to this problem must be found elsewhere.

In the first edition of the Wervek *keure* there is a clause dealing with the delivery terms of cloth-weavers. The regulation declares that the clothier must not require more than the average production, counting 4 ells per day in the winter months and 8 ells per day in the summer

[25] 'Item wie meer dade te werke dan 38 ellen stickwer in 3 daghen of 33 ellen in 2 daghen of 17 ellen up eenen dach, dat's de boete [penalty] van 10 s. par', *Recueil*, III, p. 469.

[26] Ibid., p. 579.

[27] 'Que un tissheran ne pourra tischer luy 2 e [he and another person] de laine engleisse chascun jour que 8 aunnes ... parmi l'iver sans candeille, 6 aunnes et neant plus ... [1434]', *Recueil*, II, p. 281.

[28] *Recueil*, III, pp. 463, 543 and 574.

months.[29] Consequently 4 ells per loom in winter and 8 ells per loom in summer was considered in Wervek a high but reasonable output. The explanation of the discrepancy is the supposition that the regulations were designed to restrict a whole workshop: the total output by length from the two to four looms of the average clothier.

Orders limiting the number of looms were a general phenomena all over Europe in the late fourteenth and the fifteenth centuries. In Arras, for instance, only four and later two looms were permitted for any clothier.[30] At the same time other regulations limited the yearly or daily production.[31] Presumably Wervek's restriction of 17 ells per day indicates that clothiers normally possessed three or four looms each.

The Estaires regulations are, however, quite different. Since they clearly concern one master plus one hand, that is, the capacity of one loom, it is worthwhile defining exactly the production and correlating it with the Armentières data. The index number of the local cloth is 1.1 approximately; consequently the limits of 10 and 8 ells respectively correspond to 9.2 or 7.3 Armentières cloth. This certainly means that two cloth-weavers must have woven a weft length of

$$P_1 = \frac{52\,566 \times 9.1}{40 \times 12 \times 2} = 498 \text{ m/h}$$

per capita in 12 summer hours.[32]

From this point of view we can compare the hypothetical productivity values of 68 looms during the boom period in the summer of 1593, reckoned on the basis of the average production of 413 looms in Armentières during the fiscal year of 1592/93.

Table 7.5

	Period	m/h	$P_t = 100$
P_a 1592/93 (cloth, estamet, bay)	1 year	209–69	50
P summer 1593 (cloth)	3 months	358–88	78
P_t theoretical performance	—	460–98	100

[29] *Recueil*, III, p. 464. 'Item wat manne die enich laken gheconvent heift, hik eis't sculdich of the wevene omne't selve dat hij't gheconvent heift, up datti weven nach tuschen Sinte Bamesse ende alf maerle 4 ellen's daechs ende vort 8 ellen's daechs.'

[30] J. Kulischer, *Allgemeine Wirtschaftsgeschichte des Mittelalters und der Neuzeit I* (München, 1928), pp. 210–17.

[31] Ibid., p. 222. In Jihlava the yearly production limit was subject to the civil standing. K. Werner, *Urkundliche Geschichte der Iglauer Tuchmacher Zunft* (Leipzig, 1861), p. 50.

[32] We are justified in assuming 16 working hours in summer (as, for example, the 10–12 hours yearly average for Armentières), since in Flanders the shortest winter day lasts 7 hours and 45 minutes, the longest one 16 hours and 30 minutes.

If we convert this theoretical capacity to an average of 280 ten-hour working days, from 49 to 53 pieces of Armentières cloth would come off one loom. The production would have reached 78 per cent of this amount (38–41 pieces) had the boom of the summer in 1593 lasted longer (during the three months the output was 12.4 per loom). The output of the fiscal year, 50 per cent of the maximum indicated, demonstrates a poor performance of 25–6 pieces, as discussed above, equivalent to half a piece per week.

The above productivity values of medieval cloth-weaving are supported by other authors. Van Uytven mentions a case of complaint lodged by St Omer weavers in the late fourteenth century: its settlement increased the minimum weaving time allowed for a piece of 42 ells from 5 days to 8 without changing the piece-price.[33] In another place the same author considers 1200 ells (4–4.5 ells per day) to be the average yearly output, adding that 'la production réelle était de loin inférieur à ce chiffre'.

Melis established the time needed for cloth-making from the books of the Datini business-house in Prato. From there we learn that, although the production of a piece may have taken as much as 150 days, a fortnight should be considered the average weaving period.[34] On the other hand, there are data indicating that a weaver had received the warp yarn on 15 May 1396, the weft yarn, in parts, between the 18th and 24th, but still managed to supply the finished piece by 26 May. If we deduct but one and a half days for the intervening weekend, we get a production value of 3.56 m per day, reckoning the standard dimensions for the Florentine cloth at the time as reported by Doren. By projecting the same data on to 10 or 12 working hours per day, we obtain a result of 455 or 379 m/h picks respectively. This comes close to both the above hypothetical production and to data from a Florentine source of the fifteenth century published by de Roover.[35]

Mann reports data from the year 1544 according to which a cloth-weaver 'for ten years past hath always occupied within his house two brode looms where yerly he and his have weaved three score clothes at the least'.[36] This output of 30 pieces per year per weaver (that is, 60:2) though low, closely corresponds to the 36 pieces per year[37] estimated from the 1579–80 accounts of the Brasov cloth-makers.[38]

[33] R. van Uytven, 'Technique, productivité et production au moyen age', manuscript (1971).

[34] F. Melis, *Aspetti della vita economica medievale*, I (Siena, 1692), p. 633.

[35] R. de Roover, 'Labour conditions in Florence around 1400', in N. Rubinstein (ed.), *Florentine Studies* (1968), p. 303.

[36] J. de L. Mann, *Cloth Industry in the West of England*, p. 323 (see n. 17).

[37] F. Edler de Roover, 'Andrea Banchi', *Studies in Medieval and Renaissance History*, III (Lincoln, Nebraska, 1966), pp. 233–85.

[38] Goldenberg-Belu, 'Registrul productici si comertului cu postav de la Brasov din 1576–82', *Acta Musei Napocensis*, VI (Cluj, 1969), pp. 127–51.

All this confirms our supposition that in the optimal case the production of a two-man loom expressed in the inserted weft length per hour ranged from 450 to 500 m/h (50 pieces) in the Middle Ages. But under good average market conditions the output of 350–400 m/h (40 pieces) may be considered as normal. At times when the production data are reported to have been below this level, the weavers could not possibly maintain themselves without supplementary employment.

8 Three Samples of English Fifteenth-Century Cloth
Philippe Wolff

The registers of the mid-fifteenth-century notary John Leysac are among the best preserved in Toulouse. About thirty of them are still extant in the Departmental Archives of the Haute-Garonne, and inside one of them remains a sheet of paper recording the transaction which is discussed here.[1]

I

In itself, this contract presents nothing extraordinary. Ramonet de Guyssendut, a merchant of Limendous – a village situated some ten miles east of Pau (now in Pyrénées-Atlantiques, *arrondissement* of Pau, canton of Soumoulou) – sold on credit four pieces of English cloth to a merchant of Toulouse, Peter Tolut. He was to receive the money corresponding to the price, some 64 écus, on 17 April 1458, the day on which the contract was agreed. The four pieces of cloth were to be delivered in Toulouse within the following two months. Of these four pieces, three were said to be *rosatz*, which can be translated as pink, but technically *bordeaux* would be more correct. The other one is said to be red, which is less problematical. A merchant from Morlaas, a town seven miles north-west of Limendous, witnessed the contract.

Transactions such as this were common in the mid-fifteenth century. Owing to the numerous tolls that were exacted in the Garonne valley, and the military operations which took place there, the route from Toulouse to Bayonne via Pau and the Bearn became an important one in the trade between England and the Toulouse region in the later fourteenth and early fifteenth centuries.[2] It was an overland route,

[1] Archives départmentales de la Haute-Garonne (Toulouse), 3 E 5097, fol. 46.
[2] P. Wolff, *Commerces et marchands de Toulouse (vers 1350–vers 1450)* (Paris, 1954), pp. 119–29 and map II; and idem, 'English cloth in Toulouse, 1380–1450', *Economic History Review*, 2nd ser., II, 3 (1950), pp. 290–4.

more expensive than the way by the river. But the Bearnese were neutral in the war between the English and French monarchies, and they well knew how to use this advantage. They became the main transporters – by four-wheel ox-cart – and the main dealers on this route.[3] To England were sent casks of woad, a dyestuff much cultivated east and north-east of Toulouse, in the Lauragais and Albigeois. From England there came cloth of a good middle quality, such as was often stipulated for the bride in numerous marriage treaties among the typical citizens or the well-to-do peasants.[4]

Nor were the individuals involved in this contract especially noteworthy. Limendous was situated on the direct way from Toulouse to Bayonne; but we do not possess any other evidence concerning Ramonet de Guyssendut. We do have a little more information concerning Peter Tolut, but it does not show him to be a very important merchant in Toulouse.[5]

The document is thus an unexceptional one, except that some samples of English cloth remained affixed to the sheet, and they have been kept inside a notarial register, sheltered from light and from moisture, and are thus preserved in good condition. It is not so common today to handle fragments of the great English medieval broadcloth, the material to which Professor Carus-Wilson devoted so much of her work. It is a pity that we cannot know to which category of English cloth these samples belonged; it could well be that it is just the sort of cloth, made in Castle Combe, of which she wrote.[6] In any case I feel sure that this surviving evidence would have been of interest to Professor Carus-Wilson.

The method of sale needs to be noticed. It was made with the help of samples, and it has to be kept in mind that in this case the samples were provided by the buyer. They were a relatively common type of cloth, and the seller, who knew the quality well, let the notary fix them to the sheet of paper on which the transaction was recorded.

The document itself is published below, first in the original *langue d'oc*, and then translated into English. A technical analysis of the samples follows.[7]

[3] *Commerces et marchands de Toulouse*, pp. 449–50 and 458–9.

[4] Ibid., pp. 238–40.

[5] Ibid., pp. 494–5; he was a member of a company of which Guihem de Lavit was the head.

[6] E. M. Carus-Wilson, 'Evidences of industrial growth on some fifteenth-century manors', *Economic History Review*, 2nd ser., XII (1959).

[7] For their help with this, I am indebted to the Institut Royal du Patrimoine Artistique in Brussels, and for which I would like to thank R. Sneyers, the Director, as well as Dr L. Masschelein, J. Vinckier and L. Maes, his collaborating technologists.

II

Sapian totz que lo present cartel veyran ny lygeran, que Ramonet de Guyssendut merchan del loc de Lumendos en Bearn confesse a dever a senher Peyre Tholut merchan de Tholoza quatre draps d' A[n]glat[er]ra, so es assaver tres rozatz et 1 roge, losquals draps deven estre ta bos e ta vels coma son las mostras que lod[it] Peyre Tholut m'a baylad[as], dels quals draps jeu Ramonet de Guyssendut ly promete de baylar dasi a dos mezes p[ro]tdanament venent en Th[oloz]a. Et meystre Joh[an] Lezat not[ari] de Tholoza n'a mitat de lasd[itas] most[ras].

[autre main:] et losd[its] quatre draptz confessi a deure ald[it] Peyre Tolut per causa de compra d'aquels p[er] lo pres pessa de setze escutz, que monta tout sexanta e quatre escutz, losquals LXIIII jo confessi aver agutz realment e d'aquels som content e lod[it] Tolut en quiti.

Item es conventuat entre lod[it] Peyre Tholut he my Ramonet de Quyssendut que, se losd[itz] draps non eran ta vos ny tavels coma son lasd[itas] mostras que lod[it] Peyre Tholut m'a baylad[as], jeu Ramonet de Guissendut ly devy star al interesse desd[itz] draps a la d[ita]de dos merchans en cas que jeu ny el no nos poguessem acordar. Et ly deve fa portar losd[itz] draps en la p[rese]nt vila de Tholoza a mo[n] propy cost [et] a mo[n] propy despe[n]s.

Et per so Arnaut Guilhem d'Andons mercha[n] de Morlas se met fermanss[a] per mi Ramonet de Guissendut et principal paguado coma de son deute propy en cas que jeu Ramonet de Guissendut no fessa so desus scriut, et promet[en] lod[it] Arnaut G[uilhe]m et jeu Ramonet de Guissendut de tenir so desus scriut, et asosus la pena de quatre marcz d'argen applicadors la mytat al Rey n[ost]re s[enh]er et l'autra mytat ald[it] P[eyr]e Tolut.

Et per mayor afermetat Me Johan Lezat not[ari] de Tholoza n'a p[re]za carta et ny te las mostras desd[itz] draps, et jeu Ramonet de Guyssendut he Arnaut Guilhem d'Andons avem prometut de tenir so desus scriut, et nost hem senhat de dejos de nostra propia ma. Scriut a Th[oloz]a lo XVII jor d'avriel M IIII^c LVIII.

> Ramonet de Gui[ss]andut. Ita est
> Ar. Guilhe[m] d'Andonhs suy fermanss[a] p[er]
> lod[it] R[amon]et et p[ri]ncipal pagador

This can be translated as follows:

Be it known to all seeing or reading the present contract, that Ramonet de Guyssendut merchant of Limendous in Bearn declares that he owes four pieces of English cloth, i.e. three pink and one red, to Peyre Tholut merchant of Toulouse, which pieces have to be as good and as fair as are the samples that the aforesaid Peyre Tholut gave to me, and which I Ramonet de Guyssendut promise to deliver within the next two months in Toulouse. And Master Johan Lezat, notary of Toulouse, delivered the said samples to me.

[In another hand:] and I confess that I owe these four pieces of cloth to the aforesaid Peyre Tolut, because he bought them at the price of sexteen ecus the piece, that is, a total of sixty-four ecus, which LXIIII ecus I confess to have received actually, so that I am satisfied with them, and discharge Tolut.

Item it is understood between the aforesaid Peyre Tholut and me Ramonet de Quyssendut that, if these pieces were not as good and as fair as are the samples that the aforesaid Peyre Tholut gave to me, I Ramonet de Quyssendut am to stand for the value of the said pieces, according to the judgement of two merchants if I and he could not agree together. And I must have the said pieces conveyed to the present city of Toulouse at my own cost and expense.

And for this Arnaut Guilhem d'Andons merchant of Morlaas answers for me Ramonet de Guissendut and will be the main payer, as if it was his own debt, in case I Ramonet de Guissendut did not act according to what is written above, and the aforesaid Arnaut Guilhem and I Ramonet de Guissendut promise to comply with what is written above, under the penalty of four silver marks applicable half to our Lord the King and the other half to the aforesaid Peyre Tolut.

And for greater security Master Johan Lezat notary of Toulouse made a deed of it, and affixed the samples of the said pieces to it, and I Ramonet de Guyssendut and Arnaut Guilhem d'Andons promised to comply with what is written above, and we undersigned with our own hand. Written in Toulouse the 17th day of April 1458.

Ramonet de Guissendut. Thus it is

Ar. Guilhem d'Andons am surety for the said

Ramon and main payer

8.1   Three of the earliest surviving pieces of English cloth, attached to the Toulouse contract dated 17 April, 1458

III

The three samples attached to this document are fastened with a blue string to a piece of paper (about 8.3 by 12 cm) which in turn is attached to the manuscript itself with a white string (see Figure 8.1). The samples of cloth are here numbered from the top downward.

Sample	1	2	3
Maximum dimensions (cm)	1.75 by 4.8	0.8 by 4.7	2.3 by 4.7
Colour	bordeaux (light)	red	bordeaux (dark)

All three samples are pieces of broadcloth. The approximate thickness is 1.5 mm for samples 1 and 2, and 2 mm for sample 3. Each sample is made from wool fibres; the wefts are spun in S-twist, while the warps are spun in Z-twist.

The weave pattern is normally not visible in broadcloth; nevertheless it can be seen on a small place in sample 3, where some fibres near the surface have disappeared. The pattern is that of plain tabby weave; it counts about four warp yarns and about three weft yarns per three mm. The weave pattern is completely covered in the other samples; nevertheless it seems that the pattern of these samples is plain weave too. The three samples are teaseled on both sides. The cloth of each sample was dyed after weaving. The blue and white strings are made from flax fibres; each string is a 2-ply yarn, made by twisting in S-twist two single yarns spun in Z-twist.

Analysis of the mordant was carried out by X-ray fluorescence. The usual mordants of the Middle Ages were iron and alum. Iron was not detected, but alum could be present.

The dyestuffs were identified by a method described elsewhere.[8] Sample 1 was dyed with madder (*Rubia tinctorum*) and traces of indigo. The latter came probably from woad (*Isatis tinctoria*) which was widely cultivated in Europe at that time. Sample 2 contains only madder. Sample 3 reveals the same composition as sample 1 but an additional dyestuff, Brazil-wood, is clearly to be detected. In the Middle Ages dyeing with Brazil-wood was only allowed in shading another stable dye because of its poor fastness to light. Its presence on the yarns proves that the document was not often exposed to the light.

[8] See, for example, L. Masschelein-Kleiner in *Mikrochimica Acta*, VI (1967), pp. 1080–5).

Part Two

9   The Charter of the Clothiers' Guild of Lier, 1275[1]

Herman van der Wee and Erik van Mingroot

The study of medieval guilds and corporations has not always had the attention it deserves. H. Pirenne, in his *Histoire de Belgique*, did not find it necessary to treat the history of the towns of Brabant extensively and contented himself with indicating in a couple of pages the most important points which distinguish the development of the towns in Brabant from those in Flanders.[2]

A whole series of important local studies about the early guilds and trades in Brabant can of course be cited: for example, for Leuven (Louvain) the works of H. Vander Linden, J. Cuvelier, J. Verhavert and R. Van Uytven, for Brussels those of G. Des Marez, P. Bonenfant and F. Favresse, for Antwerp those of Fl. Prims and Fr. Blockmans, for Malines those of J. Laenen and H. Joosen, for 's Hertogenbosch the work of N. H. L. Van den Heuvel, for Diest the publication of J. Vannerus. However, there is no real synthesis for Brabant. The only fortunate exception is the important comparative study by Carlos Wyffels about the origin of the merchant and craft guilds in Flanders and Brabant.[3]

Editions of texts about early craft and merchant guilds in Brabant can be found in the works of H. Joosen, F. Favresse, J. Vannerus and others. Unfortunately there is no general collection, as for Flanders.[4]

---

[1] This essay is the result of a joint research effort. Van der Wee discovered the error of misdating the charter and wrote the first two parts. Van Mingroot is the editor of the charter given in the third part, and is the author of the fourth part.

[2] H. Pirenne, *Histoire de Belgique* (Brussels, 1909), part I, pp. 286–8 (quoted by H. Van Werveke, 'L'oeuvre de Félicien Favresse' in F. Favresse, *Etudes sur les métiers bruxellois au moyen âge* (Brussels, 1961), p. 22).

[3] C. Wyffels, *De oorsprong der ambachten in Vlaanderen en Brabant* (*Verhandelingen van de Koninklijke Vlaamse Academie voor Wetenschappen, Letteren en Schone Kunsten van België. Klasse der Letteren, XIII, 13*) (Brussels, 1951).

[4] G. Espinas and H. Pirenne, *Recueil de documents relatifs à l'histoire drapière en Flandre. Première Partie: des origines à l'époque bourguignonne*, 4 vols. (Brussels, 1906–24); H. E. De Sagher, J. De Sagher, H. Van Werveke and C. Wyffels, *Recueil de documents relatifs à l'histoire drapière en Flandre. Deuxième Partie: le sud-ouest de la Flandre depuis l'époque bourguignonne* (Brussels, 1951–61).

As a result some important documents, treating craft and merchant guilds during the Middle Ages, have remained unknown. A representative example is the 'Ouden Gulden Charter' of the town of Lier, a ducal cloth-guild charter, which has always been considered by the local historians as having been granted in 1475. A correct reading of the text leads to the conclusion that it was in fact granted in 1275 rather than in 1475.[5] The thorough diplomatic analysis, which follows the edition of the text given here, proves the authenticity of the document.

I Historical framework

The correct dating of the charter of Lier as 21 April 1275 has great significance. With the exception of the document from Lier and two texts from Leuven (Louvain) of 1221 and 1271,[6] the oldest known cloth-guild charters of Brabant all concern the socially turbulent period of the early years of the fourteenth century. In Flanders the social agitation connected with the battle of the Golden Spurs in 1302 had given the signal for the breakthrough of the corporative era, while in Brabant the unrest gave the duke the chance to place the local cloth guilds under strict central and municipal control. The cloth guilds of Brabant at that moment were officially integrated in the patrician rule of the towns, so that their loyalty towards the established order was guaranteed. They were also obviously the ideal instrument to regulate the local textile industry and to ensure its control by the patriciate. Such privileges were granted by the dukes in 1302 for Malines,[7] in 1306 for the towns of Leuven, Brussels and Tienen, and in 1308 for Antwerp.[8]

The town of Lier was not granted a guild privilege in this period. There was undoubtedly a special reason for such an omission: on 21 April 1275, Lier had received a cloth-guild privilege which already contained all the basic elements for regulating local economic life included in the other guild charters of the beginning of the fourteenth century.

---

[5] H. Van der Wee, 'Het sociaal-economisch leven te Lier in de Middeleeuwen', *'t Land van Ryen* (1952), II, pp. 51–2.

[6] The duke of Brabant already granted a first charter to the guild in Leuven in 1221 (H. Vander Linden, *Histoire de la constitution de la ville de Louvain* (Ghent, 1892), p. 160ff; it was followed by a new ducal guild privilege in 1271, where the authority of the guild over the cloth industry is explicitly recognised (R. Van Uytven, *Stadsfinanciën en stadsekonomie te Leuven van de XIIde tot het einde der XVIde eeuw* (*Verhandelingen van de Koninklijke Vlaamse Academie voor Wetenschappen, Letteren en Schone Kunsten van België. Klasse der Letteren, XXIII, 44*) (Brussels, 1961), p. 347.

[7] J. Laenen, *Geschiedenis van Mechelen tot op 't einde der middeleeuwen* (Malines, 1926), p. 136, n. 2. In fact this concerns the confirmation of the earlier privilege of 1276.

[8] C. Wyffels, *De oorsprong der ambachten* (see n. 3), pp. 29–31; P. Bonenfant, 'Le premier gouvernement démocratique à Bruxelles (1303–1306)', *Revue de l'Université Libre de Bruxelles* (1920), pp. 578–94.

Why was a basic charter granted to the local cloth guild in Lier more than thirty years before the other textile towns in Brabant? Three circumstances must be mentioned here. In the first place, by the thirteenth century Lier had already developed into an important centre of textile production. This is shown by a number of documents. In 1242 an agreement was reached between Antwerp and Malines whereby both towns and their respective fullers and weavers undertook not to help fullers and weavers from the other town (in time of revolt) nor to employ weavers from the other town or to associate with them (in case of emigration or banishment). A similar arrangement was again made between Antwerp and Malines in 1249, but this time also with the towns of Brussels, Leuven, Tienen, Diest, St Truiden, Maastricht, Zoutleeuw and Hoei.[9] The town of Lier was not mentioned in the two agreements. A quarter of a century later, on the contrary, Ghent took the same initiative and then Lier was included. Indeed, in 1274 urban agreements were made between Ghent, Brussels, Malines, Leuven, Lier, Antwerp, Tienen and Zoutleeuw.[10] The agreement between Ghent and Lier was even explicitly renewed on 12 June 1277.[11] This leads to the conclusion that, during the third quarter of the thirteenth century, Lier had become so important as a textile centre, that it came to figure among the greater cloth towns in Brabant.

As a second important point the guild charters of Leuven of 1271[12] and of Malines of 28 August 1276[13] must be mentioned. In the privilege of Leuven the authority of the guild over the local cloth industry was explicitly recognised. In the privilege of Malines, which was granted by Walter Berthout (lord of Malines), the important wool and cloth merchants, members of the guild, received special privileges with regard to long-distance trade (that is, beyond the Scheldt and the Maas). It was clear that the lord of Malines wished to grant the cloth guild a monopoly of the export trade, that is, he wanted an osmosis between the important merchants and the patricians, to bring the whole cloth industry under better control of town and lord.

A third essential point concerns the social conflict in Brabant between the important cloth merchants, who increasingly assumed the role of merchant-contractors, and the weavers and fullers who were reduced to a subordinate social and economic position. In the guild

[9] H. Joosen, *Recueil de Documents relatifs à l'Histoire de l'Industrie drapière à Malines (des origines à 1384)* (Brussels, 1935), pp. 394–6.
[10] F. Prims, 'De eerste eeuw van de lakennijverheid te Antwerpen (1226–1328)', *Antwerpsch Archievenblad* (1928), 2nd ser., III, p. 131.
[11] E. Mast, *Geschiedkundig Liersch Dagbericht* (Lier, 1888), p. 154.
[12] See n. 5.
[13] H. Joosen, *Recueil de Documents* (see n. 9), pp. 401–4.

charter of Malines of 1276 the weavers and fullers who wanted to participate in long-distance trade directly suffered especially from the obligatory payment of a special tax, which was double that which a merchant who was not a member of the guild had to pay. Moreover, in May 1275, that is, immediately after the 'Ouden Gulden Charter' in Lier was granted by Duke John I, the magistrates of the town of Lier came to an agreement with the corporation of the fullers and with all master fullers of Lier, whereby they agreed, on oath and under threat of banishment and fine, not to create any more revolt in the town, not to enlarge the organisation of the fullers' corporation, not to increase its taxes and dues, and not to imprison or put to work exiles without permission of the elected representatives.[14] Offenders would have to pay the fine to the count and would be at either his mercy or the mercy of his sheriff. The magistrates of Lier were obviously acting in accordance with, or probably on the orders of, the duke.

If the three above-mentioned situations are set side by side, the following hypothesis can be formulated. The social unease which occurred in Brabant about the middle of the thirteenth century, especially in the circles of weavers and fullers, as a reaction against the growing importance of the big merchant-entrepreneurs, had not led to important explosions; probably it had died down partly through the influence of the agreements between the towns of 1242 and 1249. A quarter of a century later a new flood of social malaise developed in the cloth centres of Brabant. In the old textile town of Leuven the cloth guild sought preventive measures and obtained, in 1271, a ducal charter which made it possible to order and control the *wollewerc* (wool trade) in a more thorough and effective way. In most centres, however, only defensive measures were taken. The most important towns in Brabant again tried to solve the unrest by a series of agreements, which came to a final conclusion in 1274 and had in view combined action against rebellious fullers and weavers. In Lier the agreements led to great irregularities. Probably Lier had grown, after the mid-thirteenth-century tribulations which had most affected Antwerp and Malines, into a young dynamic centre halfway between both cities where greater freedom and lower wages still prevailed. During the unrest of 1274–75, exiled fullers who sought shelter in Lier, were imprisoned there and put to work for very low wages. Such action seemed too much; the cloth industry in Brabant needed thorough regulation by the authorities. So the duke took some measures. He used the rebellion of the fullers in Lier as an excuse to issue the 'Ouden

---

[14] The text of this agreement was published in H. Van der Wee, 'Het sociaal-economisch leven te Lier' (see n. 5), p. 166.

Gulden Charter'. On the example of the 1271 guild charter of Leuven the local cloth industry was placed under the authority of the cloth guild of Lier. But the duke clearly went further: he integrated the merchant guild of Lier in the patrician town magistrature, in this way creating a fusion between the local landed gentry and the moneyed aristocracy, and founding the basis for a broader oligarchy which would mean a better guarantee for consolidating ducal control over the towns in Brabant.

The charter of Lier served as a model for the guild charter of the neighbouring big cloth centre Malines, which was granted by Walter Berthout, lord of Malines: a good example of the demonstration effect of the ducal policy on the lord of Malines. The social unrest which disrupted Flanders and Brabant in 1302 and which in several places led to the victory of the corporations, provided the duke of Brabant with the excuse to submit also the other towns in Brabant to the doctrine which he had developed in the guild charters of Leuven and Lier.[15] Even Leuven, where the ducal doctrine had only been introduced as a partial beginning in 1271, received a new guild charter. In Malines, which had now come under Brabant's jurisdiction, confirmation of the charter of 1276 was sufficient.[16] In Lier, where the ducal doctrine had received a more complete form for the first time, a charter seemed superfluous and was not granted. Additions to the 1275 charter were only made on 20 October 1326 in the ducal privilege 'van de Hoge Halle'.[17] The cloth industry in Lier was at that moment at the beginning of a new, impressive flowering, which would continue till the beginning of the fifteenth century.

II Economic analysis of the text

A thorough examination of the contents of the 'Ouden Gulden Charter' of Lier is justified by its importance for the development of guilds and corporations in Brabant, as explained above.

In the *notificatio–narratio* the guild of Lier is officially recognised by the duke as an institution of private law of the town. It is possible that the charter of 1275 was not the first official ducal recognition but an earlier one seems improbable; the town of Lier had originated only relatively recently (it became a town in 1212),[18] and in the 'Oudt Privilegieboeck van de Stad Lier', the charter of 1275 figures as the oldest guild charter.[19] It can furthermore be concluded from the

---

[15] C. Wyffels, *De oorsprong der ambachten* (see n. 3), pp. 29–31.

[16] See n. 6.

[17] H. Van der Wee, 'Het sociaal-economisch leven te Lier' (see n. 5), pp. 53–4.

[18] H. Van der Wee, 'Een stad groeide uit het moeras', *'t Land van Ryen* (1962), XIII, pp. 98–105.

[19] Town archives, Lier: Algemene Bronnen, Oudt Privilegieboeck.

notificatio–narratio that the cloth guild already existed in Lier before 1275 and was already well established. At the moment of official recognition in 1275 it had, moreover, already developed into an organisation which counted mostly merchant-entrepreneurs active in the cloth industry. It probably was ruled by custom, but received at this moment explicit regulations, which, as the text illustrates, were issued with ducal permission, on the advice of the sheriff and under the control of the magistrates. Consequently, the charter was the result of conscious ducal policy, which in exchange for official protection, wanted to bind the cloth guild tightly to the municipal authority of sheriff and magistrates. The first section of the charter provides an interesting insight into the social and institutional structure of Lier. In 1275 already there was an obvious distinction between the merchants and the artisans in Lier, and this social breach was underlined in the charter. A rich textile or other merchant, of the same social level as the merchant-entrepreneurs, then the only group which counted in the guild, could, by paying an entrance fee, become a member. A member of a lower social level, for example, an independent craftsman, such as a leather worker, a shoemaker or a weaver, could also become a member of the cloth guild by paying an entrance fee if he relinquished his old trade: so the craftsman had to become a merchant or be so rich that he could live on his private means.

The mixing of the commercial aristocracy, principally represented by the cloth guilds, and of the landed gentry, represented by the patrician town government, is clearly shown by the rule that a merchant wanting to become a member of the cloth guild and who was the son of an alderman, dean or magistrate, only had to pay 30 per cent of the entrance fee mentioned above, and especially in the rule that magistrates and stewards of the town automatically became members by paying a stoup of wine. However, the cloth guild in Lier was not yet a closed society which, as a public institution, possessed a complete monopoly in trade. It was still a free organisation, open to newcomers, even from lower social groups. The stratification, however, into higher and lower categories was already clearly defined. Moreover, the osmosis in the higher level between the new group of rich merchants and the older group of patricians traditionally mono-polising political power was already well under way. Unfortunately it is not known where the origins of the patrician landed gentry in Lier should be sought. In the fourteenth and fifteenth centuries representatives of certain noble families were still regularly cited as magistrates of Lier.[20]

[20] L. Gijsemans, 'De Lierse plutocratie der 14de en 15de eeuw. Aantekeningen over de sociale positie van de Lierse Schepenen', *'t Land van Ryen* (1968), XIX, pp. 32–7.

Does the mention of these families refer to the long-established political monopoly of the 'family clans' as we find it in Brussels, Leuven, Antwerp and Zoutleeuw?[21] Was their dominating influence connected with the important domain of the chapter of St Gummarus or with the domain Anderstad,[22] as had happened similarly in Leuven, where in the beginning of urban expansion the domain and chapter of St Peter had played a crucial role?[23] We do not know the answer. However, it is beyond question that the political supremacy of the patrician families in Lier had to make way for an alliance with those who, especially in the growing cloth industry and trade, had acquired a fortune quickly, as early as 1275, which means much earlier than in most other towns in Brabant.[24]

In the next sections of the charter the cloth guild is assigned complete control of the town's cloth industry. Thus the transition from a private to a public institution was prepared, a transition achieved in the privilege 'van de Hoge Halle' in 1326. The consolidation of the monopoly of the guild was indicated by the charter of 1275, principally concerning the regulation of the production process. All merchant-entrepreneurs and others who had cloth made for their own account, whether members of the cloth guild or not, were subject to the metrological rules about the use of raw materials and about the production or improvement of the fabrics imposed by the guild. Somebody, who was not a member of the guild and who wanted to start a retail cloth business in Lier, could not obtain a sales counter in the town hall for this purpose, and could not even lay claim to a covered booth near the cloth hall. Although retail business was not forbidden for non-members of the guild, it certainly was made very difficult.

The existence of an organised cloth hall in Lier in 1275 is thus implicit in the text. Moreover, from the remark about the covered booths outside the walls the impression is given that the existing building was at that moment already too small, which clearly indicates the importance of the textile industry in Lier in 1275. On the other hand, from an urban account, which has subsequently been lost, through Van Graesen, lord mayor in the early seventeenth century, it is known that in 1367 a new cloth hall with a belfry was built.[25] If

---

[21] F. Favresse, *L'avènement du régime démocratique à Bruxelles pendant le moyen âge (1306–1423)* (*Académie Royale de Belgique, Classe des Lettres. Mémoires en — 8°, Tome XXX, 1*) (Brussels, 1832), pp. 24–31; idem, *Etudes sur les métiers Bruxellois au moyen âge* (Brussels, 1961), p. 215 n. 1.

[22] H. Van der Wee, 'Een stad groeide uit het moeras' (see n. 18), pp. 1–10.

[23] J. Cuvelier, *La formation de la ville de Louvain des origines à la fin du XIVe siècle* (Brussels, 1935).

[24] F. Favresse, *Etudes* (see n. 21), pp. 213–52.

[25] H. Van der Wee, 'Het sociaal-economisch leven te Lier' (see n. 5), p. 54.

no new cloth hall was built in Lier[26] in the intervening period, the text of 1275 and the evidence of Van Graesen confirm the impression that the cloth industry in Lier was stagnant or even depressed about 1300; the pre-1275 building did not have to be extended and only the revival of the cloth industry in the second quarter of the fourteenth century and especially from the third quarter onwards would demand the new building of 1367.

The inclusion of a series of articles referring to the guild officers' immunity in the exercise of their administrative or juridical powers indicates the gradual transition of the guild towards a public institution. The authority over the guild was in the hands of aldermen and deans and was officially recognised by the duke. This meant that when aldermen and deans consulted together concerning the guild or an individual member, and also when they issued decrees in conjunction with the sheriff or magistrates or when they acted in their legal capacity, they could not be held responsible for possible damage or disadvantage. The deans of the guild were even charged with actively tracing irregularities in the use of raw materials during spinning and weaving, in the first place the mixing of *bureelwol* or *kamwol*;[27] they also had to control the wool qualities prescribed by the guild; the deans had even the power to confiscate and burn the goods if they notified the sheriff and magistrates of the town. If the culprit was a member of the guild, he was expelled and could only be readmitted when the guild gave permission. If he was not a member, he was forbidden by the guild to practise his trade for the period of a year and a day. The guild appealed to the sheriff and magistrates for the execution of these punishments and the payment of the fines, which were partly due to the guild treasury. The cloth guild had consequently acquired quite extensive powers of organisation and jurisdiction in matters concerning the cloth industry. These powers were strengthened by the fact that the cloth guild had its own treasury and that the deans could receive all guarantees in the matter of breach of the rules and usages by the members of the guild.

Although the cloth guild in 1275 was still a free private organisation, the transition towards a public role and towards the corporative era

---

[26] For his 'Kronijk van de stad Lier', Richard Van Graesen, several times magistrate and mayor of Lier in the beginning of the seventeenth century, had the use of a series of documents of the fourteenth century, which since then have been lost. Van Graesen does not note the building of a new cloth hall except for the year 1367 (Town archives, Lier, Algemene Bronnen, Kronijk van de stad Lier, copy from Van Graesen (725–1615).

[27] For *Bureel*, 'tissu de laine grossière, médiocrement estimé, ayant un compte et un mode de tissage particuliers' see G. de Poerck, *La draperie médiévale en Flandre et en Artois. Technique et terminologie. III. Glossaire flamand* (Rijksuniversiteit Gent. Werken uitgegeven door de Fakulteit van de Wijsbegeerte en Letteren, no. 112, Ghent, 1951), p. 27. For *Camwulle* (*camwolle, kemwulle*), 'laine à peigner', see ibid., p. 66.

was already completely prepared by the extensive powers of organisation and jurisdiction concerning the local cloth industry granted by the duke. The duke used and consolidated the same principles in the guild charters granted to most of the towns in Brabant after the social unrest of the early fourteenth century. Thus the guild charter of Lier of 1275, itself inspired by the charter of Leuven of 1271, was the example – the prototype – used for the ducal guild charters of early fourteenth-century Brabant. The importance of the charter of Lier in the development of corporatism in Brabant cannot be over-emphasised.

III Edition of the 'ouden gulden charter' of Lier

The original text is not available. What follows is from an early-fifteenth-century copy in the Lier Town Archives, Algemene Bronnen, *Oudt Privilegieboeck* fols. XXVII^{r-v} (XI^{r-v}), under the title: *Den ouden gulden charter.*

Johannes, Dei gratia dux Lotharingie et Brabancie, universis quibus presens scriptum videre contigerit, salutem. Notum vobis facimus quod burgenses nostri Lyrenses, ad confraternitatem parancium pannos laneos, que vulgariter gulda dicitur, pertinentes, constituciones quasdam adinvenerunt, quibus ipsi guldam suam de assensu nostro et consilio sculteti et scabinorum nostrorum Lyerensium regi decreverunt, quarum tenor talis est. (Quicumque vult fieri frater dicte gulde, si sit impertinens utpote pelliparius, sutor, textor et huiussemodi, solvet decem solidos Lovanienses ad opus gulde predicte, et operam quam exercere consuevit penitus abiurabit. Si vero pertinens fuerit, utpote mercator, dabit decem solidos eiusdem ponderis et monete. Si autem filius alicuius senioris vel decani vel alicuius scabini Lyerensis fuerit, dabit tres solidos eiusdem ponderis et monete. Item quicumque eligitur in scabinum Lyerensem, efficitur confrater dicte gulde cum una gelta vini, et similiter is qui in villicum eligitur Lyerensem, dummodo sit burgensis Lyerensis. Item quicumque vult facere parari pannos, faciet eos parari secundum pondus et mensuram a dicta gulda instituta, sive sit pertinens ad illam sive impertinens. Quicumque contra hoc fecerit, committit viginti et quinque denarios Lovanienses ad opus gulde. Item si aliquis, qui ad illam non pertinet, vult incidere pannos Lyere et incisos per ullas vendere, stabit extra domum absque coopertorio. In favorem igitur utilitatis communis, concessimus dictis confratribus quod quocienscumque seniores dicte gulde cum decanis suis tractatum habent de ipsa gulda vel de pertinentibus ad illam, seu quicquid in eadem gulda cum sculteto et scabinis Lyerensibus duxerint ordinandum, et moniti a decanis suis aliquid per jure dixerint, nullum ipsis inferatur propter hoc dampnum vel gravamen. Item indulsimus ipsis quod illi, quos ipsi sibi preferunt in decanos, res gulde sue contrarias, quas in villa ubicumque cas esse sciant vel presumant, et si alicubi in villa repperenint burinem vel lanam pectinum -que vulgariter camwolle dicitur-, mixtam cum lana, filis vel pannis et hui[us]modi, que ipso facto bona condempnata dicuntur, ipsi hoc sculteǫ et scabinis nostris de Lyera intimabunt et ipsi ea comburi facient. Et ille penes quem illa inventa fuerint, solvet nobis viginti et septem solidos Lovanienses, et dicte gulde tres solidos dicte monete, quos scultetus et scabini nostri de Lyera ipsi gulde solvi facient ab illo. Et nichilominus talis si in dicta gulda fuerit, privandus est ea donec de novo eam meruerit rehabere. Si vero impertinens fuerit, operam quam exercere consuevit, per annum et diem abiurabit. Insuper auctoritatem dedimus ipsis confratribus, quod decani ipsorum accipiant vadimonia ab illis qui jura in quibus tenentur gulde, solvere contradicunt. In cuius rei testimonium et stabilitatem, presenti scripto sigillum nostrum duximus apponendum. Datum anno Domini M°.CC°. septuagesimo quinto, dominica qua cantatur *Quasimodo*.

IV   Diplomatic analysis

It is no easy task to prove the diplomatic authenticity of this – or any other – charter of Duke John I of Brabant (1267–94).[28] On the one hand, we have to take into account that there are no studies on this subject and that the preparation of an edition of the charters of John I has only been started recently by the Royal Historical Commission of Belgium.[29] On the other hand, at the end of the thirteenth century the chancery in Brabant was still organised along rudimentary lines;[30] the proper organisation of the chancery was only carried out[31] in the fourteenth century around 1355,[32] and further improved in the

[28] C. Knetsch, *Das Haus Brabant. Genealogie der Herzöge von Brabant und der Landgrafen von Hessen*, I (Darmstadt, 1917), p. 33, nr XIV–5; 'Johann I der Siegreiche', E. Strubbe and L. Voet, *De chronologie van de Middeleeuwen en de Moderne Tijden in de Nederlanden* (Antwerp–Amsterdam, 1960), p. 358; M. Wilberg, *Regenten-Tabellen* (Graz, 1962²), p. 25, nr 57; A. Stokvis, *Manuel d'histoire, de généalogie et de chronologie*, pt III^B (Amsterdam, 1966²), p. 511; W. K. von Isenburg and F. Freytag von Loringhoven, *Europäische Stammtafeln*, II (Marburg, 1976), table 8.
[29] Cf. *Handelingen van de Koninklijke Commissie voor Geschiedenis. Bulletin de la Commission royale d'histoire*, CXXXIX (1973), p. xxix.
[30] E. Reusens, 'Les chancelleries inférieures en Belgique depuis leur origine jusqu'au commencement du XIIIe siècle' in *Analectes pour servir à l'histoire ecclésiastique de la Belgique*, XXVI (1896, p. 148; also, *Eléments de paléographie* (Leuven, 1899; Brussels, 1963²), p. 271; P. De Ridder, 'Een paleografische en diplomatische studie van de oorkonden verleend door hertog Jan II van Brabant (1294–1312) aan Antwerpen (6 December 1306) en Zoutleeuw (7 Mei 1307)', in *Bijdragen tot de geschiedenis*, LVI, 1973, p. 142.
[31] E. Reusens, 'Les chancelleries inférieures' (see n. 30); P. Bonenfant, *Cours de diplomatique*, II (Liège, 1958³), p. 88.
[32] H. Nelis, 'Y a-t-il eu des chanceliers de Brabant au XIVe siècle?' in *Annales de la Société d'Archéologie de Bruxelles*, XX (1906), pp. 487–8 and 492–4 (in the time of Duchess Johanna of Brabant, 1355–1406).

Burgundian period.[33] The result was certainly a number of charters written by the addressee,that is, charters which were issued and sealed in the name of the duke of Brabant,[34] but which received their final external and textual form in the scriptorium of monks, canons, towns, aldermen or craft guilds. The loss of the original of the Lier charter of 1275 makes it even more difficult to prove its authenticity[35] as no reference can be made to the external characteristics of the document. Finally, as far as the dictamen is concerned, we find few formulae typical for Brabant, and moreover, the literal comparison of the formulae is made more difficult by the increasing number of charters in the vernacular, either Dutch or French.

Nevertheless it is possible to use the formulae to decide whether this charter is authentic or false. One or more *notarii, pronotarii, cancellarii, clerici, scriptores, confectores cartae* functioned at the court in Brabant, already under Duke Henry I (1183/1190–1235) and Duke Henry II (1235–48),[36] and they certainly were responsible for a number of the ducal charters.[37] As an example we can cite Johannes Cappellanus in 1277 at the court of John I.[38] The charters written by the addressee were also submitted to a certain control by the 'chancery', for example, concerning the formula.[39] It is thus possible to rely on a certain stability of form in the formula so as to reach a responsible opinion about the charter which is being studied.

Our yardstick is the following: a falsifier who tries to imitate the formula of a much earlier charter, inevitably betrays himself, for example, by combining the wrong formulae, because his artificial construction leads to anacolutha, because the order of the words gives an odd impression, by the insufficient fluency of the formulae, as the formulae fashionable at the time are not taken into account, while the falsifier confuses archaic and modern tendencies in the same chancery, because he commits historic and semantic anachronisms. All these elements have to be checked, if possible, in this particular case.

[33] P. Renoz, *La chancellerie de Brabant sous Philippe le Bon (1430–67)* (Brussels, 1955), p. 17 (in the time of Duke Antony of Burgundy, 1406–15); H. Loyens, *Tractatus de concilio Brabantiae, ejusque origine, progressu, auctoritate et praerogativa* (Brussels, 1667), pp. 12–13; A. Uyttebrouck, *Le gouvernement du duché de Brabant au bas moyen âge (1355–1430)*, I (Brussels, 1975), pp. 205–20.

[34] E. Reusens, 'Les chancelleries inférieures' (see n. 30), p. 149.

[35] A. Giry, *Manuel de diplomatique* (Paris, 1893; New York, n.d.), p. 867.

[36] E. Reusens, 'Les chancelleries inférieures' (see n. 30); P. Bonenfant, *Cours de diplomatique* (see n. 31); G. Smets, *Henri I, duc de Brabant, 1190–1235* (Brussels, 1908), pp. 260–3; A. Wauters, 'De quelques difficultés que présente la chronologie des diplômes, bulles et chartes au douzième siècle et au commencement du treizième' in *Table chronologique des chartes et diplômes imprimés concernant l'histoire de la Belgique*, III (Brussels, 1871), pp. xxxix–xli.

[37] P. Bonenfant, *Cours de diplomatique* (see n. 31), G. Smets, *Henri I* (see n. 36), p. 264.

[38] E. Reusens, 'Les chancelleries inférieures' (see n. 30), pp. 149 and 159.

[39] G. Smets, *Henri I* (see n. 36), p. 265. The early chancery notes of the end of the thirteenth century are also revealing: M. Martens, *L'administration du domaine ducal en Brabant au Moyen Age (1250–1506)* (Brussels, 1954), p. 17.

A first indication is the language used. A falsifier, for example, of the fourteenth–fifteenth century, working in a period when the vernacular was the normal language for charters,[40] would have had a tendency in this direction, possibly towards French, the more so because it can be noted that the charters of John I, especially after 1280,[41] are drawn up in this language, which was the everyday speech of the nobility,[42] and of the smaller southern part of the duchy,[43] more probably still towards Dutch,[44] as could be expected in the guild of Lier: it is there that we would have to look for the falsifier, on the principle *cui prodest*, or, as the judge would put it, where 'motive, means and opportunity' exist. But none of this is relevant, because the charter was drawn up in Latin, as was still mostly the case in Brabant around 1275.[45]

The influence of the vernacular, specifically in the institutional and metrological terminology (*gulda, scabinus, scultetus, gelta*),[46] the use of words from the vernacular (*camwolle*),[47] a few orthographic peculiarities (*huiussemodi, constituciones, parancium, quocienscumque*; *dampnum, condempnata* with epenthetic *p*; genitive with single *e*),[48] are typical for

---

[40] P. Bonenfant, *Cours de diplomatique* (see n. 31), II, pp. 72, 82, 95; A. Giry, *Manuel de diplomatique* (see n. 35), p. 471; H. Bresslau, *Handbuch der Urkundenlehre für Deutschland und Italien*, II (Berlin, 1968⁴), pp. 383, 388; A. De Boüard, *Manuel de diplomatique française et pontificale*, I (Paris, 1929), p. 251.

[41] Compare the analyses of the charters of Brabant (and the text of the *datatio*) in A. Wauters, *Table chronologique des chartes et diplômes concernant l'histoire de la Belgique*, V (Brussels, 1877), pp. 386–666 and 716–27; VI (1881), pp. 5–441 and 727–39; VII–2 (1889), pp. 991–1147; S. Bormans and J. Halkin, *Table chronologique* ... , XI 2 (Brussels, 1912), pp. 271–445; J. de Sturler, 'Actes des ducs de Brabant conservés à Londres' in *BCRH*, XCVII (1933), pp. 1–38.

[42] H. Pirenne, *Geschiedenis van Belgïe*, I (Brussels, n.d.), pp. 207–8 and 483.

[43] A. Wauters, *Le duc Jean Ier et le Brabant sous le règne de ce prince (1267–94)* (Brussels–Liège, 1862), p. 390.

[44] P. Bonenfant, *Cours de diplomatique* (see n. 31), II, p. 95 (obviously in use under John I of Brabant since 1274); cf. F. Van Mieris, *Groot charterboek der graven van Holland, van Zeeland en heeren van Vriesland*, I (Leiden, 1753), p. 374 (2 July 1274). H. Obreen, 'L'introduction de la langue vulgaire dans les documents diplomatiques en Belgique et au Pays-Bas' in *Revue Belge de Philologie et d'Histoire*, XIV (1935), pp. 95–7 (in Brabant for the first time in 1254; first original in 1280).

[45] H. Pirenne, *Histoire de Belgique* (see n. 2), I, p. 207.

[46] J. F. Niermeyer, *Mediae latinitatis lexicon minus* (Leiden, 1967²), p. 468ᵃ, s.v. *gilda* (*gulda*), p. 941ᵃ, s.v. *scabinus*, p. 949ᵖ, s.v. *sculnetus*; E. Habel, *Mittellateneinisches Glossar* (Paderborn, s.d.²), col. 167, s.v. *gilda*, col. 353, s.v. *scabinus*, col. 357, s.v. *scultetus*; R. Latham, *Revised Medieval Latin Word-List from British and Irish Sources* (London, 1965), p. 211ᵇ, s.v. *gilda* (gelda, guilda, gulda), p. 421ᵃ, s.v. *scabinus* (Flanders), p. 424ᵃ, s.v. *schultetus* (Antwerp); H. Doursther, *Dictionnaire universel des poids et mesures anciens et modernes* (Amsterdam, 1965²), p. 158, s.v. *gelta* (lot); H. Van der Wee, *The Growth of the Antwerp Market and the European Economy*, I (The Hague, 1963), pp. 78–9, Figure 3.

[47] J. Verdam and C. Ebbinge Wubben, *Middelnederlandsch handwoordenboek* (The Hague, 1949), p. 281ᵇ, s.v. *camwolle*.

[48] Compare K. Langosch, *Lateinisches Mittelalter. Einleitung in Sprache und Literatur* (Darmstadt, 1963), pp. 53–4; K. Strecker and R. Palmer, *Introduction to Medieval Latin* (Dublin, 1968), p. 60; G. Cremaschi, *Guida alle studio del latino medievale* (Padua, 1959), pp. 58–9; L. Traube, *Einleitung in die lateinische Philologie des Mittelalters* (Munich, 1962²), pp. 93–4.

Note: This is only valid in so far as the manuscripts faithfully reflect the original; the date of origin of the copy guarantees against possible renewal of the language.

the Middle Latin which is used. This immediately proves that this is certainly not a humanistic falsum.[49] Whether or not there is a semantic evolution of a classically considered lemma as *tractatus*[50] is also significant; it is in the thirteenth century that this word completely took on the meaning of treaty.[51] In the text, however, the word still has its more classical meaning, and this also guarantees the date of origin of the document.

The structure, that is, the outline of the charter, also contains proof of its authenticity. In practically all John I's charters, and also in this charter of 1275, there is a *corroboratio* (with the exception of a few cases conceived as mandate) and a *datatio*. Considering the introductory protocol, there are principally two sorts of charters of John I. A first sort (*en forme de charte*)[52] consists of: *intitulatio–notificatio–inscriptio–(narratio)–dispositio–corroboratio–datatio*. A second, often employed sort (*en forme de lettre*),[53] which uses the traditional form of address of a letter in the introductory protocol, we recognise in our text: *intitulatio–inscriptio–salutatio–notificatio–(narratio)–dispositio–corroboratio–datatio*.[54] The same structure is used in a whole series of charters of John I of Brabant:[55]

A. MIRAEUS, J.-F. FOPPENS, *Opera diplomatica et historica*, pt I, Brussels, 1723, pp. 775–6 (1285); pt II, 1723, p. 864 (1271), p. 871 (1280); pt III, 1734, p. 687 (1276); pt IV, 1748, pp. 259–60 (1292).

C. BUTKENS, *Trophées tant sacrés que profanes du duché de Brabant*, pt I, The Hague, 1724, *Preuves*, p. 104 (1272), p. 120 (1287).

F. VAN MIERIS, *Groot charterboek der graven van Holland, van Zeeland en heeren van Friesland*, pt I, Leiden, 1753, p. 374 (1274).

J.F. WILLEMS, 'Codex diplomaticus' in *Chronique de Jean van Heelu, ou relation de la bataille de Woeringen*, Brussels, 1836, p. 396, nr IV (1270), p. 567, nr CCVII (1293), p. 570, nr CCXI (1272), pp. 571–2, nr CCXIII (1277), pp. 572–3, nr CCXIV (1283).

---

[49] H. Quirin, *Einführung in das Studium der mittelalterlichen Geschichte* (Brunswick, 1964³), pp. 81–2.

[50] A. Forcellini, J. Furlanetto and J. Perin, *Lexicon totius latinitatis*, IV (Bologna–Padua, 1965⁶), p. 759ᶜ, s.v. *tractatus*, nr II.

[51] J. F. Niermeyer, *Mediae latinitatis lexicon minus* (see n. 46), p. 1035, s.v. *tractatus*, nr 9; C. Du Fresne du Cange, *Glossarium mediae et infimae latinitatis*, VIII (Graz, 1954⁶), p. 144ᵃ, s.v. *tractatus*, nr 6.

[52] P. Bonenfant, *Cours de diplomatique* (see n. 31), II, p. 96; A. De Boüard, *Manuel* (see n. 40), I, p. 263.

[53] G. Tessier, *La diplomatique* (Paris, 1966³), p. 43; C. Cheney, *English Bishops Chanceries* (Manchester, 1950), p. 57. A number of texts, which show a variation here or there, must also be taken into account: for example, the addition of a *invocatio*, *arenga*, *petitio*, *sanctio*, *subscriptio*, placing the *inscriptio* in front or leaving out the *notificatio*, so that the character of a letter is underlined.

[54] *Invocatio, arenga, sanctio* and *subscriptio* remain rare (cf. P. Bonenfant, *Cours de diplomatique* (see n. 31), concerning *sanctio* and *subscriptio*).

[55] In view of clarity the charters for comparison were chosen from those editions which contained a number of charters of John I. In the matter of the structure of the charter, charters in other languages can, of course, be taken into account (although there the charter type is more prominent).

J.F. WILLEMS, 'Codex diplomaticus' in *Les gestes des ducs de Brabant, par Jean de Klerk*, Brussels, 1839, pt I, pp. 682–3, nr LXXVII (1292).

PH. DE BRUYNE, *Histoire du règne de Jean Ier, duc de Brabant*, Namur, 1855, pp. 163–4 (1283).

P. DE RAM, *Johannis Molani Historiae Lovaniensium libri XIV*, pt II, Brussels, 1861, p. 1209, nr LIX (1270), pp. 1209–10, nr LX (1270), p. 1210, nr LXI (1270).

L. ENNEN, *Quellen zur Geschichte der Stadt Köln*, pt III, Cologne, 1867, p. 274, nr 298 (1288).

Analectes pour servir à l'histoire ecclésiastique de la Belgique, pt IX, 1872, p. 279, nr XVI (1274).

V. BARBIER, *Histoire de l'abbaye de Floreffe, de l'ordre de Prémontré*, pt II Namur, 1892, pp. 145–6, nr 321 (1276), pp. 157–8, nr 339 (1279).

S. BORMANS E. SCHCOLMEESTERS, *Cartulaire de l'église Saint-Lambert de Liège*, pt II, Brussels, 1895, p. 487, nr DCCCXV (1292), p. 512, nr DCCCXXXIII (1293).

The *intitulatio, inscriptio, salutatio, notificatio, corroboratio* and *the datatio*[56] are, moreover, the formula parts where we can expect fixed phrases.

Intitulatio: Johannes, Dei gratia dux Lotharingie[57] *et Brabancie*
The *intitulatio* of the charters of John I is always conceived as in the charter of 1275 under study here:

– the name of the issuer of the charter is more frequently not accompanied by the pronoun *ego* or *nos* (which moreover often indicates a charter written by the addressee).[58]

– the devotional formula *Dei gratia*,[59] in this order, has become very characteristic in this group, and has passed into the French charters (for example, *'par la grasce Diu'*; *'par le grace de Dieu'*)[60] as well as

---

[56] Cf. E. Strubbe, 'Diplomatiek' in *Historische W.P. Encyclopedie*, I (Antwerp–Brussels, 1957), p. 64 (*salutatio, datatio*).

[57] For the origin and the meaning of the title 'duke of Lorraine' we refer to E. Strubbe and L. Voet, *De chronologie* (see n. 28), pp. 390–1.

[58] For example, in eight charters for the abbey of St Michael in Antwerp, from 1284–93 (J. F. Willems, *Chronique*, p. 573–8).

[59] P. Bonenfant, *Cours de diplomatique* (see n. 31), II, p. 36: taken from the French royal diplomas. Cf. R. Delort, *Introduction aux sciences auxiliaires de l'histoire* (Paris, 1969), p. 91: France; T. Bishop, *Scriptores regis* (Oxford, 1961), p. 19: England.

[60] S. Bormans and E. Schoolmeesters, *Cartulaire de l'église*, pt II, pp. 315–16 nr DCCCXV (1280), pp. 338–9, nr DCCCXXV (1281), p. 362, nr DCCCXLIV (1283), p. 363, nr DCCCXLV (1283), p. 364, nr DCCCXLVI (1283), p. 376, nr DCCLII (1284), etc. S. P. Ernst, *Histoire du Limbourg*, VI (Liège, 1847), p. 316, nr CCLVI (1283), pp. 318–19, nr CCLIX (1284), pp. 341–2, nr CCLXXIX (1288), pp. 343–5, nr CCLXXXI (1288), pp. 399–400, nr CCCX (1289), p. 400, nr CCCXI (1289), p. 416, nr CCCXX (1292), pp. 416–18, nr CCCXXI (1292; 'par le gracie de Dieu'); *Bulletin de l'Académie royale des sciences, des lettres et des beaux-arts de Belgique*, 2nd ser., XL (1875), pp. 389–94, nr VIII (1270; 'par le gratie de Deu'); K.-F. Stallaert, *Geschiedenis van hertog Jan van Brabant en zijn tijdvak* (Brussels–The Hague–Ghent, 1859), pp. 305–6, nr V (1270), pp. 309–10, nr VIII (1283); T. Rymer, *Foedera, conventiones, literae, et cujuscumque generis acta publica*, pt 1–2 (Farnborough, 1967), p. 167 (1278), pp. 167–8 (1278).

into the Middle Dutch charters (for example, '*by der gratien Godts*').[61]
- John's title is always indicated by the word *dux* (only exceptionally *marchio* is added).
- the placing in the framework of the *intitulatio* formula is usually as here (more exceptionally it is placed between the place names, or at the end of the *intitulatio*).
- the indications of territory are themselves stereotype: they also appear in this form in the circumscription of the ducal seal.[62] At the most the order is turned round, and later, only starting in 1287, the addition *Lymburgie* or *Lymburgensis* can be noted.[63]

A few documents with an identical *intitulatio* to the one of the charter of Lier, can be found in:

A. MIRAEUS J.-F. FOPPENS, *Opera*, pt I, p. 209 (1280); pt II, p. 864 (1271), pp. 871–2 (1283), p. 872 (1284), p. 1010 (1280); pt III, p. 130 (1275), p. 605 (1270), p. 687 (1276), p. 688 (1271); pt IV, p. 256 (1273), pp. 722–3 (1284).

C. BUTKENS, *Trophées*, pt I, p. 103 (1269), p. 104 (1272), p. 107 (1275), pp. 112–13 (1280), p. 230 (1270).

J. F. WILLEMS, *Chronique*, p. 570, nr CCXI (1271), pp. 571–2, nr CCXIII (1277) pp. 572–3, nr CCXIV (1283), p. 573, nr CCXV (1283).

P. DE RAM, *Historiae*, pt II, p. 1209, nr LIX (1270), pp. 1209–10, nr LX (1270), p. 1210, nr LXI (1270).

Analectes pour servir à l'histoire ecclésiastique de la Belgique, pt II, 1865, p. 458 (1271); pt V, 1868, p. 365, nr XV (1280); pt IX, 1872, p. 279, nr XVI (1274).

V. BARBIER, *Histoire*, pt II, pp. 145–6, nr 321 (1276), p. 150, nr 330 (1278), pp. 157–8, nr 339 (1279).

Inscriptio : universis quibus presens scriptum videre contigerit
The *inscriptio* of practically all of John I's charters shows the general form of address '*universis*' (not, for example, *omnibus*, *cunctis*).[64] In

---

[61] C. Butkens, *Trophées*, pt I, *Preuves*, pp. 205–6 (1284), pp. 124–30 (1293), pp. 147–8 (1293); F. Van Mieris, *Groot charterboek*, pt I, p. 374 (1274), p. 434 (1283); J.-F. Willems, *Les gestes*, pt I, p. 676 (1291), p. 679 (1292); F. Favresse, 'Actes intéressant la ville de Bruxelles, 1154–1302' in *Handelingen van de Koninklijke Commissie voor Geschiedenis. Bulletin de la Commission royale d'histoire*, CIII (1938), pp. 472–3, nr 39 (1289; specifically meant as translation).

[62] See pp. 000–000.

[63] E. Strubbe and L. Voet, *De chronologie* (see n. 28), p. 375 (county duchy Limburg); P. De Ram, *Notice sur les sceaux des comtes de Louvain et des ducs de Brabant (976–1430)* (Brussels, 1852), p. 34; Ph. De Bruyne, *Histoire*, p. 64; C. Knetsch, *Das Haus Brabant* (see n. 1), p. 33.

[64] An important exception is for example the 'omnibus' in a charter of 1276 (A. Miraeus and J.-F. Foppens, *Opera*, pt III, p. 687).

some documents the *inscriptio* is limited to this *'universis'*:[65] this is consequently the essential element.

Nearly all these inscriptions express the idea of being addressed to everyone who might see the charter:[66] in the Latin and Dutch as well as in the French charters. This is expressed in different ways, but the following formulae, for example, can reconcile us to the expression used here: 1290: *universis quibus praesens scriptum contigerit intueri* (twice),[67] 1291: idem.[68]

The *presens scriptum*[69] is to be noted, and can be associated with analogous expressions in the *corroboratio*. The formalistic facet of this expression in the charters in Brabant is proved by the translation into Dutch in a charter of 1274: *'allen den ghenen, die dese jeghenwoordige scrifte zullen sien (ofte hooren lesen)'*.[70]

Salutatio: salutem

All greeting formulae of the charters of John I contain, in the first place, the element *'salutem'*, which is precisely the expression of the principle aim of the *salutatio*.[71] This expression, in its most simple form, is found in charters of 1270, 1286, 1292 and 1293.[72] This expression is also found in all, absolutely all charters, which contain the *salutatio* formula (the above-mentioned letter type), but usually completed in very different ways: the *'salutem'*, however, remains the essential, the indispensable element.

[65] For example A. Miraeus and J.-F. Foppens, *Opera*, pt III, p. 605 (1269); J. F. Willems, *Chronique*, pp. 572–3, nr CCXIV (1284), p. 575, nr CCXIX (1284), pp. 576–7, nr CCXXII (1292), p. 577, nr CCXXIII (1292), p. 578, nr CCXXV (1293); J. F. Willems, *Les gestes*, pt I, pp. 684–5, nr LXXIX (1293); L. Ennen, *Quellen*, pt III, p. 292, nr 323 (1289); K.-F. Stallaert, *Geschiedenis* (see n. 60), pp. 324–5, nr XVII (1289); A. Wauters, *Le duc Jean Ier* (see n. 43), p. 360 (1290); *BCRH*, 4th ser., VIII (1880), pp. 369–71, nr LXXII (1283); *Messager des sciences historiques de Belgique*, A° (1860), pp. 447–8 (1280); H. Laurent, *Actes et documents anciens intéressant la Belgique conservés aux Archives de l'état à Vienne, 1196–1356* (Brussels, 1933), pp. 35–7, nr 36 (1292) M. Martens, *Actes relatifs à l'administration des revenus domaniaux du duc de Brabant (1271–1408)* (Brussels, (1943), pp. 27–8, nr 4 (1290).

[66] A. Giry, *Manuel de diplomatique* (see n. 35), pp. 535 and 547 ('omnibus ad quos presens scriptum pervenerit'); A. De Boüard, *Manuel* (see n. 40), I, p. 263, n. 3 (idem).

[67] J. F. Willems, *Chronique*, pp. 531–4, nr CLXXIII (1290), pp. 534–6, nr CLXXIV (1290).

[68] J. F. Willems, *Les gestes*, pt I, pp. 677–8, nr LXXIV (1291); R. Van Uytven, 'Standenprivilegies en -beden in Brabant onder Jan I (1290–93)' in *Belgisch tijdschrift voor filologie en geschiedenis. Revue belge de philologie et d'histoire*, XLIV, 1966, p. 436.

[69] Cf. also J. F. Willems, *Chronique*, p. 575, nr CCXVIII (1284); J. F. Willems, *Les gestes*, pt I, pp. 675–6, nr LXXII (1290); P. De Ram, *Historiae*, pt II, p. 1210, nr LXI (1270); F. Favresse, 'Actes intéressantes' (see n. 61), pp. 461–2, nr 34 (1285).

[70] F. Van Mieris, *Groot charterboek*, pt I, p. 374.

[71] A. Giry, *Manuel de diplomatique*, p. 536; R. Delort, *Introduction aux sciences auxiliares de l'histoire* (Paris, 1969), p. 92; J. Mazzoleni, *Paleografia e diplomatica* (Naples, 1971), p. 224. Cf. two letters in French, in the real sense of the word, by duke John I, with the expression 'salus' (J. F. Willems, *Les gestes* pt I, pp. 670–1, nrs LXVII–LXVIII).

[72] A. Miraeus and J.-F. Foppens, *Opera*, pt I, p. 438 (1293); pt IV, pp. 259, 260 (1292); J. F. Willems, *Chronique*, p. 567, nr CCVII (1293), pp. 577–8, nr CCXXIV (1293); J. F. Willems, *Les gestes*, pt I, pp. 682–3, nr LXXVII (1292); *Bulletin de l'Académie royale de Belgique*, 2nd ser., XL (1875), p. 38, no. VII (1270); Th. Rymer, *Foedera*, 1–3 (Farnborough, 1967⁴), p. 14 (1286).

Notificatio : *Notum vobis facimus quod* . . .
About half the documents in this collection of charters contain the
notificatio formula. One of the often used formulae[73] is '*notum facimus*'
in charters of 1269, 1274, 1277, 1280, 1282, 1284, 1286, 1287, 1288,
1289, 1290, 1292 and 1293.[74] The '*scavoir faisons/fesons*' or '*faisons a
savoier*' in Middle French and the '*maken condt*' in Middle Dutch[75]
documents also have to be noted. The identical formula (with the
personal pronoun) can, for example, be found in the *promulgatio* of
charters of 1279 and 1280.[76]

Corroboratio : *In cuius rei testimonium et stabilitatem presenti scripto sigillum
nostrum duximus apponendum*
In the charters of John I of Brabant the *corroboratio* always makes
room for the mention of the *conscriptio* (as '*presens scriptum*', '*presentes
litterae*', referring to the *instrumentum*) and especially for the announce-
ment of the *sigillatio*. The expression of these two composing elements
can turn out differently (for example, sometimes stated separately),
but a number of charters illustrate the fact that this formula was in
use at the time.

1269:   *In cujus rei testimonium sigillum nostrum praesentibus duximus
apponendum.*[77]

1270:   *In cujus rei testimonium nostrum sigillum presentibus litteris
duximus apponendum.*[78]

1271:   *In quorum testimonium et munimen . . . sigillum nostrum praesentibus
duximus apponendum.*[79]

1274:   *In cujus rei testimonium praesenti scripto sigillum nostrum duximus
apponendum.*[80]

---

[73] A. Giry, *Manuel de diplomatique* (see n. 35), p. 547; R. Delort, *op. cit.*, p. 92.
[74] A. Miraeus and J.-F. Foppens, *Opera*, pt III, p. 138 (1282), p. 139 (1282), 605 (1289); pt IV,
pp. 301–2 (1289), p. 610 (1280); J. F. Willems, *Chronique*, pp. 397–8, nr VI (1274), p. 399, nr
VIII (1274), pp. 399–400, nr IX (1274), pp. 401–2, nr XIII (1277), pp. 501–2, nr CXXXIX
(1289), pp. 520–1, nr CLIX (1290), pp. 573–4, nr CCXVI (1284), p. 575, nr CCXVIII, (1284),
p. 575, nr CCXIX (again 1284), pp. 575–6, nr CCXX (1287), p. 576, nr CCXXI (1289),
pp. 576–7, nr CCXXII (1292), p. 577, nr CCXXIII (1292), p. 578, nr CCXXV (1293); J. F.
Willems, *Les gestes*, pt I, pp. 667–8, nr LXV (1286), pp. 675–6, nr LXXII (1290), pp. 684–5,
nr LXXIX (1293); K.-F. Stallaert, *Geschiedenis*, p. 310, nr IX (1282), pp. 321–2, nr XIV (1283),
pp. 324–5, nr XVII (1289).
[75] Cf. principally F. Van Mieris, *Groot charterboek*, I, pp. 433–547, passim.
[76] *Analestes pour servir à l'histoire ecclésiastique de la Belgique*, pt II, 1865, p. 458 (1271); A. Miraeus and
J. F. Foppens, *Opera*, pt II, p. 1010 (1280)
[77] C. Butkens, *Trophées*, pt I, p. 103.
[78] *BARB*, 2nd ser., XL (1875), p. 388, nr VII.
[79] J. F. Willems, *Chronique*, p. 570, nr CCXI.
[80] Ibid., p. 399, nr VIII.

1277:   *In cujus rei testimonium et munimen praesentibus litteris sigillum nostrum duximus apponendum.*[81]

1280:   *In quorum omnium testimonium et munimen et ad perpetuam stabilitatem, sigillum nostrum praesentibus litteris dignum duximus apponendum.*[82]

1283:   *In cujus rei testimonium et munimen sigillum nostrum presentibus duximus apponendum.*[83]

1284:   *In cujus rei testimonium presentibus litteris sigillum nostrum duximus apponendum.*[84]

1284 and 1286:   *In cujus rei testimonium sigillum nostrum praesentibus duximus apponendum.*[85]

1286:   *In cujus rei testimonium et munimentum, sigillum nostrum praesentibus litteris duximus apponendum.*[86]

1287 and 1289:   *In cujus rei testimonium sigillum nostrum praesentibus litteris duximus apponendum.*[87]

Moreover, especially after 1280, a number of other (sometimes similar) formulae appear to express the corroborative idea. It is, however, certain that '*in cujus rei testimonium*'[88] as introductory formula and the construction '*sigillum nostrum . . . duximus apponendum*'[89] (with reference to the personal intervention of the duke), were frequently used during the first half of John's rule.

It is even more important that the formula used here was still in preparation before 1274, and started to evolve again after 1275, while in the above-mentioned charter of 1274 the formula is all but identical. Proof can be found in a Dutch charter of the same year:[90]

[81] Ibid., pp. 401–2, nr XIII; Th. Lacomblet, *Urkundenbuch für die Geschichte des Niederrheins*, II (Aalen, 1960²), p. 409, nr 699.

[82] A. Miraeus and J.-F. Foppens, *Opera*, pt IV, p. 610.

[83] *BCRH*, 4th ser., VIII (1880), pp. 369–71, nr LXXII.

[84] M. Martens, *Actes relatifs à l'administration*, pp. 23–4, nr 2.

[85] J. F. Willems, *Chronique*, p. 575, nrs CCXVIII and CCXIX; J. F. Willems, *Les gestes*, pt I, pp. 667–68, nr LXV.

[86] Th. Rymer, *Foedera*, 1–3, p. 14.

[87] J. F. Willems, *Chronique*, pp. 575–6, nr CCXX, and p. 576, nr CCXXI.

[88] A. Giry, *Manuel de diplomatique* (see n. 35), p. 575; A. De Boüard, *Manuel* (see n. 40), I, p. 292. Remark also the formula in the French charters of the duke: 'en tesmoignage de laquele chose', 'en tesmongnage de la kele choese' (S. P. Ernst, *Histoire de Limbourg*, VI, p. 316, nr CCLVI, a° 1283; *BCRH*, 3rd ser., II (1861), pp. 473–4, nr XXVI, a° 1280; *AHEB*, IX (1872), p. 280, nr XVII, a° 1275; *BARB*, 2nd ser., XL (1875), p. 395, nr IX, a° 1274; S. Bormans and E. Schoolmeesters, *Cartulaire de l'église*, pt II, p. 363, nr DCCCXLV, a° 1283; pp. 398–9, nr DCCLXVII, a° 1286; pp. 406–7, nr DCCLXXIII, a° 1287).

[89] Cf. also *BCRH*, 4th ser., X (1882), p. 73, nr XXVII (1269); *MSHB*, A° (1860), pp. 447–8 (1280) 'Nos itaque in omnium et singularum rerum supra dictarum evidentiam, testimonium et munimen, sigillum nostrum presentibus litteris duximus apponendum.'

[90] F. Van Mieris, *Groot charterboek*, pt I, p. 374.

'*In kennisse der saken ende vestenissen* [stabilitatem], *so hebben wy dese scrifte met onsen seghel doen stercken*'.

The fact that the addressees of the two Latin charters, of 1274 and 1275, and of the Dutch charter of 1274 are totally different (Lier, Dordrecht and Tiel)[91] and that completely different subjects are concerned,[92] is decisive,[93] so that the similarity of the formulae must be traced to the 'chancery' of Brabant. This basically proves the authenticity of the Lier document of Duke John I: it would be impossible for a falsifier to adhere so accurately to the evolution of the formulae in John's charters, and to the fashion of the time in the formulating of the *corroboratio*!

Datatio: Datum anno Domini M°.CC°. septuagesimo quinto, dominica qua cantatur 'Quasimodo'

The dating formula is, as usual,[94] composed of the following parts:

- the introductory formula '*Datum* . . . ', in John I's charters hardly ever completed by *actum*, and only very exceptionally replaced by it;[95]
- the characteristic, and very stereotype, indication of the year by *anno Domini*,[96] which appears in practically all Latin charters of John I. It is undoubtedly sufficient proof to submit a number of date formulae in the original or in a vidimus.

A. VERKOREN, *Inventaire des chartes et cartulaires des duchés de Brabant et de Limbourg et des pays d'Outre-Meuse. Chartes originales et vidimées,*

---

[91] Lier: Belgium; Dordrecht, Tiel: Holland. W. Moore, *The Penguin Encylopedia of Places* (Harmondsworth, 1971), p. 222, 'Dordrecht', p. 428, 'Lierre' (Lier); M. Gysseling, *Toponymisch woordenboek van Belgë, Nederland, Luxemburg, Noord-Frankrijk en West-Duitsland (vóór 1226)*, I (n.p., 1960), p. 280ᵃ, 'Dordrecht', p. 614ᵇ, 'Lier', II (n.p., 1960), p. 965, 'Tiel'; J. Graesse, F. Benedict and H. Plechl, *Orbis latinus* (Brunswick, 1972), I, p. 662ᵇ, 'Dordracum'; II, p. 399ᵃ, 'Lira'; III, p. 491ᵇ, 'Tillum'.

[92] A. Wauters, *Table chronologique*, V (Brussels, 1877), p. 545 (Tiel); C. Hermans, *Analytische opgave der gedrukte charters . . . betrekkelijk de provincie Noord-Brabant, van het jaar 704 tot en met het jaar 1648* (Bois-te-Duc, 1844), p. 42 (Dordrecht).

[93] About this method of comparing the dictamen of independent charters (method Th. von Sickel): E. Boshof, 'Diplomatik' in E. Boshof, H. Kloft and K. Düwell, *Grundlagen des studiums der Geschichte* (Cologne–Vienna, 1973), pp. 145 and 148; G. Tessier, 'Diplomatique' in Ch. Samaran *et alios*, *L'histoire et ses méthodes* (Paris, 1961), p. 659; W. Bauer, *Einführung in das Studium der Geschichte* (Frankfurt/Main, 1961), p. 201.

[94] Beside the series of editions, for the study of the date formula, see A. Wauters, S. Bormans and J. Halkin, *Table chronologique*, V, VI, VII–2, XI–2 (see above), A. Verkooren, *Inventaire des chartes et cartulaires des duchés de Brabant et de Limbourg et des pays d'Outre-Meuse. Chartes originales et vidimées,* vol. I (Brussels, 1910), pp. 68–116; A. Verkooren, *Inventaire . . . Cartulaires,* vol. I (Brussels, 1961), pp. 132–88.

[95] Cf. A. Miraeus and J.-F. Foppens, *Opera*, pt III, p. 688 (1271); A. Verkooren *Inventaire . . . Cartulaires,* (see n. 94), vol. I, p. 134 (1271), p. 176 (1291). Does this not indicate the redaction in a scriptorium?

[96] A. Giry, *Manuel de diplomatique* (see n. 35), p. 90; E. Reusens, *Eléments de paléographie et de diplomatique du moyen âge* (Leuven, 1891), p. 90.

vol. I, Brussels, 1910, p. 70, nr 89 (1269), p. 71, nr 90 (1270, vidimus), p. 75, nr 96 (1274), p. 83, nr 106 (1283, vidimus), p. 86, nr 111 (1283), p. 87, nr 112 (1284), p. 94, nr 125 (1285), p. 95, nr 126 (1287, vidimus), p. 97, nr 131 (1288, vidimus), p. 98, nr 133 (1289, vidimus), p. 108, nr 144 (1289), p. 109, nr 146 (1290), p. 114, nr 150 (1292).

The Dutch version of this formula can also be noted: '*Int jaar ons Heeren*';[97]

– the date is strange in that way that part of it is expressed in Roman figures (decimals and units) and part in letters (thousands and hundreds). In so far as this is not the result of the transmission in writing, a connection can be seen with the ducal charters of Brabant of 1270, 1281, 1283, 1284, 1285, 1287, 1289, 1290, 1291, 1292 and others;[98]

– the date according to the *temporale*, a part of the liturgical calender, as became the habit in the first half of the thirteenth century (habit which already fell into disuse from the beginning of the fourteenth).[99]

The construction with '*dominica qua cantatur*'[100] still appears in charters of John I from 1274, 1277 and 1290.[101] This expression consequently was part of the diplomatic formula, if the situation occurred (Sunday was not the most usual day for the issuing of a charter). A few other cases are known where the liturgical date formula, with reference to the incipit is used, but without the '*qua cantatur*'.[102]

---

[97] A few examples: A. Verkooren, *Inventaire ... Chartes originales*, vol. I, p. 99, nr 134 (1289); *Inventaire ... Cartulaires*, vol. I, p. 177 (1291), p. 179 (1292); F. Favresse, 'Actes intéressant' (see n. 61), pp. 469–71, nr 38 (1289), pp. 474–80, nr 40 (1291); P. De Ram, *Chronique des ducs de Brabant par Edmond de Dynter*, pt II (Brussels, 1854), pp. 454–8 (1291); J. F. Willems, *Les gestes*, pt I, p. 676, nr LXXIII (1291), p. 679, nr LXXV (1292), pp. 684–5, nr LXXIX (1295); F. Van Mieris, *Groot charterboek*, p. 374 (1274), p. 462 (1285), p. 465 (1286), p. 541 (1291), p. 542 (1291), p. 547 (1292).

[98] A. Verkooren, *Inventaire ... Chartes originales*, vol. I, p. 87, nr 112 (1284), p. 90, nr 117 (1285) , p. 94, nr 125 (1285), p. 95, nr 126 (1287), p. 108, nr 144 (1289), p. 109, nr 146 (1290); *BCRH*, 4th ser., III, 1876, p. 191 (1281), pp. 191–2 (1283), p. 194 (1291); P. De Ram, *Historiae*, pt II, p. 1209 (1270); J. F. Willems, *Les gestes*, pt I, pp. 675–6 (1290), p. 679, nr LXXV (1292; Dutch), pp. 682–3, nr LXXVII (1292); F. Van Mieris, *Groot charterboek*, pt I, pp. 433–4 (1283). Other examples are *legio*. A number have only the thousands in numbers, or only the units in letters.

[99] E. Strubbe and L. Voet, *De chronologie* (see n. 28), p. 75; H. Bresslau, *Handbuch* (see n. 40), II, p. 405. Numbers of charters of John I were dated by this heortologic system.

[100] E. Strubbe and L. Voet, *De chronologie* (see n. 28), p. 42.

[101] A. Verkooren, *Inventaire ... Chartes originales*, I, p. 75, nr 96 (1274); *Inventaire ... Cartulaires*, vol. I, p. 137 (1274), p. 143 (1277); J. F. Willems, *Chronique*, pp. 397–8, nr LVI (1274); *Les gestes*, pt I, p. 672, nr LXIX (1290); G. Aders, 'Regesten aus dem Urkundenarchiv der Herzöge von Brabant, c. 1190–1382' in *Düsseldorfer Jahrbuch*, XLIV (1947), p. 35, nr 58 (1274), p. 36, nr 64 (1277). It must be noted that two of these examples date from round 1275.

[102] For example, L. Ennen, *Quellen*, pt III, p. 274, nr 298 (1288). Cf. for the date formula used: F. Ginzel, *Handbuch der mathematischen und technischen Chronologie*, III (Leipzig, 1914), p. 203.

The date formula also makes it possible to complete the dating of the charter. As '*quasimodo geniti*' is the incipit of the introit of the first Sunday after Easter,[103] and as Easter in 1275 (with Sunday letter F) was on 14 April,[104] the precise date of the charter is: 21 April 1275;[105] also after having to take into account the *stilus paschalis* in use in Brabant.[106]

The *validatio* of the charters of Brabant at that time, was principally composed of the seal of the duke, as issuer and sealer of charters, as dignitary who guaranteed the validity of the document issued.[107] The ducal seal is announced everywhere; it also can be found[108] – or there are at least traces of it – on all charters of John I, and for a few of the originals we know about the seal from the vidimus or the transumpt.[109] It is only in exceptional cases that other seals appear, those of nobles or officials and court dignitaries from Brabant, who then added their seal, mainly as witnesses (this is also announced in the *corroboratio*). This is not the case here.

Incidentally, it is possible to visualise the lost seal. John I used three different seal matrices:[110] a hunting seal, a horseman's seal of the military type (from 1277) and an amplified version of the same type (from 1289). During the period from 1267[111] until 1277[112] he consequently used the hunting seal:[113] the duke, bareheaded and dressed in a long tunic, is seated on a horse walking towards the left (diplomatic right), his head is turned towards a falcon on his left hand, and he holds the reins in his right. There is also a sparrow-hawk on the wing (in front of the horse), a walking hound (underneath) and the lion

---

[103] E. Strubbe and L. Voet, *De chronologie* (see n. 28), p. 519.

[104] Ibid., p. 121.

[105] C. Cheney, *Handbook of Dates for Students of English History* (London, 1945), table 24; J. Grotefend, *Taschenbuch der Zeitrechnung des deutschen Mittelalters und der Neuzeit* (Hanover, 1971[11]), p. 190.

[106] E. Strubbe and L. Voet, *De chronologie* (see n. 28), p. 58 (mos Brabantinus); P. Bonenfant, *Cours de diplomatique* (see n. 31), I (Liège, 1958), p. 55; A. Cordoliani, 'Tableau des dates du début de l'année' in *L'histoire et ses méthodes*, p. 1562.

[107] W. Ewald, *Siegelkunde* (Munich, 1914), p. 25; J. Roman, *Manuel de sigillographie française* (Paris, 1912), pp. 3–5.

[108] Cf. the description of the original charters of John I in A. Verkooren, *Inventaire . . . Chartes originales*, vol. I, pp. 75 (1274), 86 (1283), 90 (1285), 114 (1292); J. Schoonbroodt, *Inventaire analytique et chronologique des chartes du chapitre de Saint-Lambert, à Liège* (Liège, 1863), pp. 92–3, nr 353 (1280), pp. 93–4, nr 357 (1281), p. 100, nr 381 (1283), p. 104, nr 394 (1287).

[109] A. Verkooren, ibid., p. 68; K.-F. Stallaert, *Geschiedenis* (see n. 60), pp. 306, 325; J. F. Willems, *Chronique*, p. 396.

[110] P. De Ram, *Notice*, pp. 32–4; A. Wauters, *Le duc Jean Ier*, pp. 245–6.

[111] John I, who became count after the abdication of his brother, Henry IV (1261–67), after 25 May 1267, had not yet got a ducal seal when a charter was issued on 29 June 1267 (J. F. Willems, *Les gestes*, pt I, pp. 664–5, nr LXII).

[112] A. Wauters, 'De quelques difficultés . . . ', p. XLIII. This change in the seal was due to his knighting in 1270 (ibid., bl. XLII XLIII; A. Wauters, 'Jean Ier, dit le Victorieux' in *Biographie nationale de Belgique*, X (Brussels, 1888/89), col. 203).

[113] Cf. the illustration in O. Vredius, *Genealogia comitum Flandriae a Balduino Ferreo usque ad Philippum IV. Hisp. Regem*, I (Brussels, 1642), p. 76; and C. Butkens, *Trophées*, pt I, p. 107 (according to charter of 1275).

rampant of Brabant (behind the horse). The legend is: +*Sigillvm Iohannis Dvcis Lotharingie et Brabancie.*[114] The counter-seal often shows the impression of a seal ring with an antique stone (representing a head) and the inscription *Secretum ducis.*[115]

Although it is often not taken into account, it is essential that the diplomatic study and the comparison with other documents guarantee the usability and the dependability of the charters before the contents can be studied.[116] There are a whole series of charters of John I in the original[117] which can be used as background for the textual characteristics of the Lier document. But there are also about 250 edited charters which can be used to compare the formula.[118] From this material it appears that the stability of the formula and the unity of structure was not very advanced in the first decennium of John's rule, and also that the number of charters increased after 1280. However, all verifiable elements of the formula appear to be acceptable and can be fitted into the diplomatic usages in Brabant around 1275 and into the picture of the Dutch and west European diplomatic of the end of the thirteenth century. In so far as this can be verified, all formalised elements of the text are perfectly in accordance with what one would expect of a charter of Duke John I of Brabant at that time. Consequently, there appear to be enough reasons to give this document a place in the development of the charter formulae, ducal and others, in Brabant. Therefore it is permitted to use the contents – always taking into account a possible positive or negative interpolation[119] – for further study. These contents, which fit into the institutional, social and economic framework of the last quarter of the thirteenth century, can in their turn help prove the authenticity of the document.

[114] O. Vredius, *Genealogia*; C. Butkens, *Trophées*; P. De Ram, *Notice*, p. 32; A. Wauters, *Le duc Jean I*ᵉʳ, p. 245; idem, *De quelques difficultés*, p. xliii; A. Verkooren, *Inventaire . . . Chartes originales*, vol. I, p. 75, nr 96 (according to charter of 1274); G. Demay, *Inventaire des sceaux de la Flandre*, I (Paris, 1873), p. 38, nr 239 (according to letter of 1274).

[115] O. Vredius, *Genealogia* (underneath); P. De Ram, *Notice*; G. Demay, *Inventaire*, I, p. 38, nr 1283 (with picture).

[116] L. Santifaller, *Urkundenforschung. Methoden, Ziele, Ergebnisse* (Cologne–Graz, 1968²), pp. 7 and 42; L. Genicot, 'Les actes publics' in *Typologie des sources du moyen âge occidental*, fasc. 3 (Turnhout, 1972), p. 7.

[117] Compare, for example, a series of charters in Brussels, *Algemeen Rijksarchief, Charters van Brabant* (A. Verkooren, *Inventaire . . . Chartes Originales*, vol. I, pp. 68–116, passim). Cf. also a reproduction in E. Reusens, *Eléments de paléographie*, plate XXXVIII (January 1288).

[118] For comparison: Mr P. De Ridder, at Dilbeek (Belgium), has found the textual tradition of 546 charters of John I (cf. a letter from 14 June 1977).

[119] L. Santifaller, *Urkundenforschung*, p. 42; A. Von Brandt, *Werkzeug des Historikers* (Stuttgart, 1971), p. 122.

10 Cloth in Medieval Literature of Western Europe
Raymond van Uytven

I

For the student of the medieval cloth industry in the Netherlands and on the Continent there is no equivalent to the marvellous series of statistics that Professor Carus-Wilson and Miss Coleman have provided for England.[1] For evaluating the importance of the famous cloth-making towns of Flanders and Brabant during the Middle Ages, quantitative material is either entirely lacking or much less systematic. In an attempt to overcome this shortage of information, scholars have been obliged to look through all sorts of historical sources in search of references to Netherlands cloth in various places.

Their impressive picture of the diffusion of Flemish and Brabant woollens risks overstating the case for the scale of output and of the export trade. Cloth of the Netherlands was in fact an expensive commodity. One single ell (about 0.7 metres) of the cloth Ghent bought in 1362–63 for the town's soldiers cost from 1 shilling to 1s 4 *groot* (1 *groot* = about 1 gram 75 fine silver). For a complete outfit, a surcoat, a coat, a hood and a pair of trousers, some fifteen ells were needed,[2] and at the time a master carpenter earned only 6d *groot* a day. A whole piece (about thirty ells) cost about 30s 4d *groot*, but there were also pieces costing £2 5s 0d, £2 10s 0d, and £4 12s 6d, whereas a scarlet cost as much as £8 1s 6d *groot*. In the hierarchy of values cloth ranked high, as an *ame* of wine (about 135 litres) cost £1 4s 0d and a basket of fresh herrings cost 4s 3d. A mark (about 245 grams) of wrought silver was worth about 11s 6d.[3] A fine Brussels cloth was worth about

---

[1] E. M. Carus-Wilson and O. Coleman, *England's Export Trade, 1275–1547* (Oxford, 1963).
[2] 'Caxton's dialogues', J. Gessler (ed.), *Le Livre des Mestiers de Bruges et ses Dérivés* (Bruges, 1931), p. 19.
[3] A. and H. Van Werveke (eds.), *Gentse Stads- en Baljuwrekeningen (1351–64)* (Brussels, 1970), pp. 561–80.

800 grams of gold, equivalent to one diamond, five rubies and five emeralds or some thirty kilos of pepper, a proverbially high-priced spice.[4]

As a craftsman had to spend between a third and a half of his earnings on food for his family,[5] it is clear that his purchases of clothing would be limited in volume and in value. Only an exclusive upper-class person could afford to wear the quality cloth of the Netherlands and therefore even a modest production of luxury woollens called for distribution over a very extensive area. The bulk of our information, originating from toll lists, market ordinances and other such sources, does not prove the actual presence of a single cloth and it is not unreasonable, in fact, to assume that the passing of a few cloths along the traditional trade routes was considered as a major event at each of the successive commercial centres. On the other hand, the surviving quantitative data concerning actual transactions or cargoes are isolated and accidental, and it would be hazardous to generalise on the basis of these exceptional references.

Such objections may be more or less disregarded when we come to deal with purely literary texts. To captivate an audience a work of fiction must seem real. A writer may idealise persons, things or situations and his imagination can be hyperbolical, but the concrete representation of his images will always reveal features of the real world around him. His casual remarks and comparisons will reflect the common opinion of his public and other generally acknowledged facts of the time.[6] The knights in an epic are doubtless richer and bolder than they usually were, the ladies lovelier and more elegant, but for them to be seen in this way the author has to dress them in the richest clothes he actually knew. The numerous literary allusions containing textiles from the Netherlands sum up, so to speak, the contemporary view of the place these cloths occupied in the economy of the time and the part they played in medieval life. In this sense, literary sources attain a degree of objectivity and a general significance seldom realised by official records. The samples discussed in this essay will show that the information concerning cloth-making centres found

[4] R. H. Bautier, 'La place de la draperie brabançonne et plus particulièrement bruxelloise dans l'industrie textile au Moyen Âge', *Annales Société Royale d'Archéologie de Bruxelles*, LI (1962–66), pp. 45–6.

[5] E. Scholliers, *Loonarbeid en Honger. De Levensstandaard in de XVe en XVIe eeuw te Antwerpen* (Antwerp, 1960), pp. 171–80.

[6] J. C. Payen *et alios*, *Le Roman* (*Typologie des Sources du Moyen Age occidental, 12*) (Turnhout, 1975), pp. 19 and 61–6; O. Jodogne, *Le Fabliau* and J. C. Payen, *Le Lai Narratif* (*Typologie ... 13*) (Turnhout, 1975), pp. 26–8 and 61–3; A. Sempoux, *La Nouvelle* (*Typologie ... 9*) (Turnhout, 1973), pp. 22–30.

in medieval literature is much nearer to reality than F. Michel and K. Zangger, for instance, were willing to admit.[7]

II

A historical survey of cloth-making in western Europe usually opens with an examination of the fascinating 'Frisian' cloths. Professor Doehaerd recently assembled all kinds of literary references to them in sources ranging from biographies to letters.[8] The only real piece of poetry among them may be singled out. The *Carmen in honorem gloriossimi Pippini regis* composed by Ernoldus Nigellus, an exiled courtier, about 826–8 quotes the Rhine speaking to the Vosges:

Utile consilium Frisonibus atque marinis
Vendere vina fuit et meliora vehi . . .
Nam toga vestit eos vario fucata colore,
Quae tibimet nusquam, Wasace, nota foret

(It was a useful decision to sell wine to the Frisians and coastmen, and to import better ware . . . For, a coat dresses our people in a variety of colours, that never was known to you, O Vosges)[9]

A few purely literary references should be added to the dossier concerning 'Frisian' cloths. In *Partonopeu de Blois*, a French romance of the twelfth century, a knight was dressed 'd'un fres palie de Frise' (a bright cloth of Frisia), a present from the emperor.[10] A character in *Li romans de Dolopathos* (about 1222–26) wears a cloak 'd'un drap de Frise (a cloth of Frisia).[11] The actual origin of the 'Frisian' cloths is still a matter of discussion and it is not clear whether they were actually woven in Frisia or whether they were only called 'Frisian' because the merchants of that region were dealing in them. In this debate the following literary texts have been overlooked. *Li romans de Berte aus grans piés* by Adenet le Roi (dating from the second half of the thirteenth century) describes a cloak 'et le drap en fut fait el réaume de Frise', that is to say its cloth is specifically stated 'to be made in the kingdom of Frisia'.[12] The contemporary *Roman d'Auberi* similarly refers to

---

[7] K. Zangger, *Contribution à la Terminologie des Tissus en ancien Français* (Zurich, 1945), p. 1; F. Michel, *Recherches sur le Commerce, la Fabrication et l'Usage des Etoffes de Soie, d'Or et d'Argent et autres Tissus précieux en Occident* (Paris, 1852–54), p. 337.

[8] R. Doehaerd, *Le Haut Moyen Age: Economie et Sociétés* (Nouvelle Clio, 14) (Paris, 1971), pp. 232–4.

[9] E. Faral (ed.), *Ermold le Noir, Poème sur Louis le Pieux et Epitres au Roi Pépin*, (Les Classiques de l'Histoire de France au Moyen Age (Paris, 1932), p. 210; see also p. 88, vv. 1124–5.

[10] J. Gildea (ed.), *Partonopeu de Blois. A French Romance of the Twelfth Century*, I (Villanova, 1967), p. 468, vv. 1700–1.

[11] C. Brunet and A. De Montaiglon (eds.), *Li Romans de Dolopathos* (Paris, 1856), pp. 134–5, especially v. 3880.

[12] P. Paris (ed.), *Li Romans de Berte aus grans Piés* (Paris, 1832), p. 46: XXXI.

'Mantelet cher, que tessurent Frisons' (a costly cloak, the Frisians wove).[13] We would not overestimate the cogency of these texts, but they do nevertheless corroborate other evidence for the production of cloaks (*sagi*) and cloths in Frisia itself. The Latin sources and diplomatic documents concerning Frisian cloth leave little room for doubt that the French poets did indeed mean Frisia and not Phrygia, as A. Schultz supposed.[14] That Frisia was called a kingdom by Adenet le Roi does not contradict this identification because the mythical kings of Frisia are a commonplace in medieval historical literature.[15]

It has been argued that the 'Frisian' cloths were, in fact, Flemish woollens. By the eleventh century Flanders was certainly exporting cloths of various colours. In the words of the poet Winric of Trèves, who wrote his *Conflictus ovis et lini* (Conflict between Sheep and Flax) around 1068–70, Flemish cloth was worthy of a lord to wear:

hunc tamen egregium facit hec provincia pannum
qui viret aut glaucus aut quasi ceruleus.
Has vestes dominis gestandas, Flandria, mittis,
has flocco crispans leniter, has solidans.[16]

(This province makes this excellent cloth in green or blue–green or deep-blue colours. Those clothes, worthy of lords to wear, Flanders, you are exporting, are slightly crisping in the wool; some are more solid.)

In a recent paper, these verses have been quoted by Professor Verlinden to substantiate his theory concerning a technical revolution in cloth-weaving in Flanders during the eleventh century. The word *pannum* instead of *pallia* or *vestes* would mean that a new type of cloth woven in standard-sized pieces was being produced and that consequently a new kind of loom was being used.[17] But this argument is not plausible since a *capitulare* of as early as 805 already used the expression *panni integri* (whole cloths).[18]

Professor Carus-Wilson has herself utilised another literary text, a comment on the Talmut by Rabbi Solomon Izhagi (commonly called

---

[13] Cited by N. W. Posthumus, *De Geschiedenis van de Leidsche Lakenindustrie*, I. *De Middeleeuwen* (The Hague, 1908), p. 2 n. 3.

[14] A. Schultz, *Das höfische Leben zur Zeit der Minnesinger*, I (Leipzig, 1889), p. 337.

[15] A. G. Jongkees, *Het Koninkrijk Friesland in de 15de Eeuw* (Groningen, 1946); idem, 'Gondebald, Koning van Friesland', *Tijdschrift voor Geschiedenis*, LXXIV (1961), pp. 309–29.

[16] A. Van de Vijver and C. Verlinden, 'L'auteur et la portée du Conflictus ovis et lini', *Revue Belge de Philologie et d'Histoire*, XII (1933), pp. 59–81.

[17] C. Verlinden, 'Marchands ou tisserands? A propos des origines urbaines', *Annales ESC*, XXVII (1972), pp. 396–406. His theory has met severe criticism, cf. *Bulletin Critique d'Histoire de Belgique et du Grand-Duché de Luxembourg 1972–73* (Ghent, 1974), pp. 187–8.

[18] A. Boretius (ed.), *Capitularia regum Francorum*, I (Monumenta Germaniae Historica. Leges, Sectio II) (Hanover, 1883), p. 125.

:

Rashi), who lived at Troyes between 1040 and 1105, to argue that the horizontal treadle loom, operated by professional weavers, had been introduced into northern France by the early eleventh century.[19]

The cloths of northern France and nearby Flanders were not only woven professionally, but they were also dyed with great skill. The French poet William Britto (d. *c.*1227) in his epic *De Philipidis* characterised a number of Flemish towns as follows:[20]

Ypra colorandis gens prudentissima lanis (v. 92)

Atrebatum, potens urbs antiquissima, plena
Divitiis, inhians lucris et fenore gaudens . . . (vv. 94–5)

Brugia que caligis obnubit crura potentum
Frugibus et pratis dives portuque propinquo (vv. 103–4)

Insula villa placens, gens callida lucra sequendo
Insula que nitidis se mercatoribus ornans
Regna coloratis illuminat extera pannis. (vv. 110–2)

The ancient and rich city of Arras was naturally described as a centre of usury.[21] Bruges was described as a rich town with its nearby seaport of Damme and its surrounding orchards and meadows. Its manufacture of trousers, which impressed Britto, has received little attention in the historical literature, although it must have been of international importance. The French poet who during the thirteenth century composed *Le Dit d'un mercier* thought it fit among the commodities a Parisian mercer was offering[22] to include trousers of Bruges; and the Vienna citizen, Jansen Enikel, wrote, about 1280, that a proud Hungarian wore such trousers together with scarlet cloth, gold and silk.[23] The 'fabliaux' *Des deux Bordeors ribauth* in the thirteenth century presented two well-dressed characters:

Vois quiex sollers de Cordoan
et com bones chauces de Bruges[24]

(Soft shoes of Cordovan leather and good trousers of Bruges).

---

[19] E. Carus-Wilson, 'Haberget: A medieval textile conundrum', *Medieval Archaeology*, XIII (1969), pp. 165–6.

[20] G. Waitz (ed.), *Willelmus Britto. De Philipidis* (Monumenta Germaniae Historica, Scriptores, XXVI) (Hanover, 1882), pp. 321–2.

[21] G. Bigwood, 'Les financiers d'Arras. Contribution à l'étude du capitalisme moderne', *Revue Belge de Philologie et d'Histoire*, III (1924), pp. 465–508, 969–1000; IV (1925), pp. 110–19, 379–421.

[22] P. Ménard (ed.), *Le Dit d'un Mercier, Mélanges de Langue et de Littérature du Moyen Âge et de la Renaissance J. Frappier*, II (Geneva, 1970), p. 799, v. 67.

[23] P. Strauch (ed.), *Jansen Enikels Werke* (Monumenta Germaniae Historica, Deutsche Chroniken, III) (Hanover, 1900), p. 652, v. 2741.

[24] A. De Montaiglon (ed.), *Recueil général et complet des Fabliaux des XIIIe et XIVe Siècles*, I (Paris, 1872), p. 1.

Eustache le Moine also has an interesting statement: 'De Bruges en Flandre venoie cauches de saie' (From Bruges in Flanders came trousers of serge).[25] The people of Ieper (Ypres) were praised by Britto for their ability to dye wool and the merchants of Lille were praised for their exports of dyed woollens to several foreign countries. Both Winric of Treves and William Britto were impressed by the technical know-how of Flemish cloth-makers and by the variety and splendour of their dyeing. It was probably the deep colours of Flemish woollens that struck the French poet Jean Renart when writing his *L'escouffle*, an adventurous romance, in the early years of the thirteenth century. Its noble hero, when preparing himself for a honeymoon, asks for the best Italian mules and for appropriate travelling coats 'd'un drap de Flandres poleté' (of a dark cloth of Flanders).[26]

In a versified French version of the legend of St Catherine, originating about 1250 in Verona, the noble lady is dressed

d'un ver de Gant
E d'un gris le meilor del mont.[27]

Obviously 'a green cloth of Ghent and the world's best grey cloth' went well together. The lovely lady whom William of Lorris in his famous *Roman de la Rose* (about 1236) planted at the gate of Love's garden, was dressed 'd'un riche vert de Ganz' (a rich green cloth of Ghent).[28] Green cloth of Ghent had its part in *Le tournoiement d'enfer*, a satire of the second half of the thirteenth century, where a cloth merchant is found singing the praises of his green and brown woollens:[29]

Veez comme est doujce et nete

(Look how soft and clean it is)   (vv. 552–6)

But the noble customer objects:

Elle ne fut pas fete a Gant.

(It was not made at Ghent)

[25] Cited by A. Schultz, *Das höfische Leben* (see n. 14), I, p. 293.
[26] F. Sweetser (ed.), *Jean Renart. L'Escouffle, Roman d'Aventure* (Paris, 1974), p. 116, v. 3585.
[27] H. Breuer (ed.), *Eine gereimte Altfranzösisch-Veronische Fassung der Legende der Heiligen Katharina von Alexandrien* (Halle, 1919), p. 254, vv. 2090–1.
[28] E. Langlois (ed.), *Le Roman de la Rose par Guillaume de Lorris et Jean de Meung*, II (Paris, 1920), p. 30, v. 564.
[29] A. Langfors (ed.), 'Le Tournoiement d'Enfer. Poème allégorique et satirique', *Romania*, XLIV (1915–17), p. 532.

So the seller insists:

> Sire, mès car ostez vos guant
> Si la bailliez a la main nue
> Elle n'est pas grosse ne vellue

> (Sir, do take off your gloves
> If you take it in your bare hand
> It is not coarse nor hairy.)

The green cloth of Ghent clearly enjoyed very high esteem during the thirteenth century.[30]

The expensive cloths (*chiers dras*) of Flanders were on sale at all the great fairs. Hervis of Metz, the hero of a thirteenth-century epic, for instance, bought such cloth along with other luxury goods like furs and Paris jewels at Provins, Lagny and Lendit (Compiègne).[31] The merchant in the 'fabliaux', *De pleine bourse de Sense* by John le Galois, travelled to the fair at Troyes, where he only bought:

> escarlate tainte en graine
> de bon pers et de bone laine
> de Bruges et de Saint Omer!

> (scarlets of Bruges and of St Omer, dyed in grain (or kermes), from good colour and good wool)

He did not like even the cloth of Bruges or of St Omer as a personal gift for his wife, and he went to the Ieper (Ypers) hall at Troyes to buy her

> bonne robe de bons pers d'Ypre
> Il n'a meillor de ce en Cypre.[32]

> (a good dress of a good blue cloth of Ypres; there is no better from here to Cyprus.)

In another 'fabliaux', composed by Guillaume le Normand, *Du prestre et d'Alison*, a shrewd woman recruits an accomplice by making her great promises:

---

[30] Cf. E. Faral, *La Vie Quotidienne au Temps de Saint Louis* (Paris, 1938), p. 74, who completely mistook the passage.

[31] E. Stengel (ed.), *Hervis von Metz. Vorgedicht der lothringer Geste* (Dresden, 1903), I, pp. 13–14, vv. 300–8, pp. 16, 25, vv. 590–4 and p. 123, vv. 3030–3.

[32] A De Montaiglon and G. Raynaud (eds.), *Recueil général* (see n. 24), III (Paris, 1878), pp. 91, 94.

Et bone cote à mon savoir
De vert de Doai trainant.[33]

(and a good green train-gown of Douai.)

Gerard of Amiens in his *Escanor* (about 1280) also seems to have held in high esteem the rich cloths of Douai, Ghent, Lille and other Flemish towns:

Riches escarlates vermeilles,
Noires et blanches et sanguines
I troivissiez bien d'aussi fines
Comme en trovast in nule terre
Et qui pers ou vert vausist guerre
De Douai, de Gant ne de Lille . . .

(Rich scarlets vermilion,
Black and white and blood-coloured,
Would you find there, as fine
As one can find in any country
And well worth a blue or green
Cloth of Douai, Ghent or Lille)[34]

In an early-thirteenth-century German epic, *Moriz von Craûn*, Flanders was the manufacturer *par excellence* of red scarlets:

Ze Vlandern er hâte
Nach rôtem scharlate
Ein karich gesant.

(To Flanders he sent for red scarlet.)[35]

Wolfram von Eschenbach, the best of the German courtly poets of the time, dressed his knights and their ladies in *Parzival* and *Willehalm* in:

Brunez Scharlach von Gint
Daz man heizet brûtlachen[36]

(Brown scarlet of Ghent called broadcloth)

[33] A. De Montaiglon and G. Raynaud (eds.), *Recueil général* (see n. 24), II (Paris, 1877), p. 13.
[34] Cited by A. Schultz, *Das höfische Leben* (see n. 14), I, p. 355.
[35] Cited by A. Schultz, ibid., I, p. 354.
[36] W. J. Schröder and G. Hollandt (eds.), *Wolfram von Eschenbach. Willehalm. Titurel* (Darmstadt, 1971), p. 55, LXIII, vv. 15–16.

and in

Ein brûtlachen von Gent
Noch plâwer denne ein lâsûr

(A broadcloth of Ghent, even more blue than a lazuli)[37]

Another contemporary, Heinrich von den Turlin, in *Diu Crône* needed fifty-seven verses to praise a scarlet of Ghent:

Sine varwe als ein viure . . .
Linde was er an dem griffe . . .
Kleine gespunnen, dicke geweben
Und ûf den vadem geschorn . . .
Diu Wolle, lûter uzerkorn.[38]

(Its colour as a fire . . .
Soft was it to touch . . .
Thinly spun, thickly woven
and thoroughly shorn . . .
The wool, the most selected.)

In the second half of the thirteenth century, Konrad von Stoffeln of Swabia wrote an epic about *Gauriel von Muntabel* in which there is a richly dressed knight:

Fritschal von Gent was in den roc
Von Yper blô sin schaperun.[39]

(His coat was of Ghent cloth,
His cap of blue cloth of Ypres.)

About 1280 Jansen Enikel of Vienna thought a garment of Ieper (Ypres) cloth 'daz beste daz ieman dâ weste' (the best, which any knew), but he also cited cloth of Ghent and trousers of Bruges.[40] A few years later another Austrian author, Seifried Helbing, also mentioned cloth of Ghent.[41]

---

[37] G. Weber (ed.), *Wolfram von Eschenbach. Parzival* (Darmstadt, 1967), p. 263.
[38] G. H. F. Scholl (ed.), *Die Crône von Heinrich von dem Türlin* (Bibliothek des litterarischen Vereins in Stuttgart, XXVII) (Stuttgart, 1852), p. 84, vv. 6832–57.
[39] A. Schultz, *Das höfische Leben* (see n. 14), I (Leipzig, 1889²), p. 353.
[40] P. Strauch (ed.), *Jansen Enikel, Werke* (Monumenta Germaniae Historica. Deutsche Chroniken, III) (Hanover, 1900), p. 437, vv. 22472–4 and p. 605, vv. 331–3.
[41] T. G. Von Karajan (ed.), 'Seifried Helbing', *Zeitschrift für deutschen Alterthum*, IV (1844), p. 43: II, v. 77.

The poet of *Von den ledigen wiben* highly esteemed the cloth of Ghent and of Ieper (Ypres) :

> Beidiu, rok und mandel
> In rôter varw der guoten
> Von Iper . . .

(Both coat and cloak in red colour, of good cloth of Ypres)

and

> Rok und mantel dû mir bring
> Von Gent des guoten . . .

(Coat and cloak of good cloth of Ghent you bring me)

The author of *Des Teufels bâbest*, on the other hand, was most impressed by Ieper (Ypres) cloth:

> Do gab man im klaider an
> Fon Yper daz beste . . . [42]

(One gave him then the best clothes of Ypres to dress)

The prevailing impression is that it was Ghent more than Ieper or Douai – and certainly more than Bruges, Lille or St Omer – which had the lead in cloth-making in thirteenth-century Flanders. The level of output of Ghent cloth was considered so high in the twelfth century that the author of the Flemish epic *Vanden Vos Reynaerde* (About Renard the Fox) used the volume of cloth produced at Ghent to express an enormous quantity. 'If all the cloths made at Ghent were parchment, he claimed, they would be insufficient to contain the records of all the rogeries of the Fox' :

> Al ware al tlaken paerkement
> Datmen maket nu te Ghent
> In ne gescreef niet daer an . . . [43]

Until the end of the thirteenth century, Flemish cloths, especially those of Ghent, Ieper and Douai, had practically no competition. It was very rare for literary writers to bother to mention any other clothing towns.

[42] Cited by A. Schultz, *Das höfische Leben* (see n. 14), I, p. 355.
[43] W. G. Hellinga (ed.), *Van den Vos Reynaerde, I. Teksten* (Zwolle, 1952), pp. 8–9.

An exception was Hartman van Aue in his *Erec* (about 1190) who knew of English cloth

> Den besten brûtlach den man vant
> Uber allez Engellant.

(the best scarlet that was found in all England.)[44]

Seifried Helbing, almost a century later, mentions 'einem guoten stampfhair'.[45] However, 'a good Stamford' (possibly derived from *stamen forte*) could merely be a type of cloth, as it probably was in the 'fabliaux', *Du vallet qui d'aise a malaise se met*. The lad in this tale saved all his earnings to have 'une cote en son dos de bleu, de rouge ou d'estainfort' (a coat in its back blue, red or of stamford).[46] Criticising the luxury taste and the easy way of life of the Dominican friars, the troubador Peire Cardenal (*c.* 1190–1271) portrays them as eating the nicest chickens, drinking excellent French wines, and wearing elegant clothes and shoes of fine Marseilles leather. Their soft cassocks were woven of English wool ('tescutz de lan engleza'). Cardenal was perhaps thinking of an English fabric, but he is more probably referring to Flemish cloth made of English wool. It is true when sneering about the subtle speeches of the Dominicans, he alludes to an English textile: 'plans plus c'obra d'englés' (more close than English work).[47] This 'obra d'englés', however, is the equivalent of the Latin *opus anglicanum*, which usually designates English embroidery work. In this field England enjoyed such an esteem that Pope Innocent IV, in 1236, ordered vestments embroidered in England, a command which Mathew Paris in his chronicle said 'did not displease the London merchants who traded in embroideries'.[48] An old French romance, recorded by Jean Renart about 1228, in his *Roman de la Rose*, depicts a lovely maiden at work:

> sor ses genouls une paile d'Engleterre
> et a un fil i fet coustures beles![49]

(on her knees a textile of England . . . and with a thread she is making nice sewings on it)

[44] E. Schwarz (ed.), *Hartmann von Aue. Erec. Iwein* (Darmstadt, 1967), p. 58, vv. 1986–7.
[45] T. G. Von Karajan (ed.), 'Seifried Helbing' (see n. 41), IV (1844), p. 43, v. 73.
[46] A. De Montaiglon and G. Raynard (eds.), *Recueil général* (see n. 24), II, p. 157.
[47] H. Gougaud (ed.), *Poèmes politiques des Trobadours* (Paris, 1969), pp. 60–2.
[48] G. Wingfield Digby, 'Technique and production', *The Bayeux Tapestry. A Comprehensive Survey* (London, 1965), pp. 42–5; M. Fitch, 'The London makers of Opus anglicanum', *Transactions of the London and Middlesex Archaeological Society*, XXVII (1976), pp. 288–96.
[49] F. Lecoy (ed.), *Jean Renart. Le Roman de la Rose ou de Guillaume de Dole* (Paris, 1962), p. 37, vv. 1184–5.

This girl is probably embroidering a piece of textile, but it is not clear whether it is woollen or linen. However, in another passage of this work an allusion is made to 'une escarlate d'Engleterre' (a scarlet of England).[50]

In the thirteenth century, Bertold von Holle in his *Dêmantin* also refers to 'scharlachen von Engelant' and Ulrich von dem Türlin mentions 'Zwelf scharlachen ûz Engelant' (twelve scarlets of England).[51]

A French metrical list of English places, dating from the middle of the thirteenth century, enumerates four cloth-making towns and their fabrics:

> *Escarlate de Nichole* (Lincoln)
> *Haubergé de Estanford* (Stamford)
> *Blaunket de Blye* (Blyth)
> *Russet de Colcester* (Colchester).[52]

In the accounts of Henry III of England, Professor Carus-Wilson found indeed purchases of scarlets of Lincoln, habergets of Stamford and russets of Colchester.[53] The thirteenth-century *Dit de l'apostoile* listed the good white cloth of Lincoln,[54] and Chrétien de Troyes in his *Conte du Graal*, at the end of the preceding century, gave a description of the great city of London with its great variety of merchandise including 'de panes veires et grises' (green and grey cloths).[55] Two French clothing towns also attained some literary notice during the thirteenth century. *Huon de Bordeaux* dating from about 1216–29 mentions 'dras de Biauvesis' (Beauvais)[56] and Ulrich von dem Türlin of Augsburg referred to 'kaemmlin von Pruvis' (camlets of Provins). In the twelfth-century version of the romance of Tristan by Beroul King Arthur is dressed in cloth of Ratisbon.[57]

[50] Ibid., p. 137, v. 4489.

[51] A. Schultz, *Das höfische Leben* (see n. 14), I, p. 354.

[52] Cited by E. Carus-Wilson, 'Haberget: A medieval textile coundrum' (see n. 19), pp. 149–50. Modern edition in D. C. Douglas (ed.), *English Historical Documents*, III (London, 1975), p. 881.

[53] E. Carus-Wilson, 'The English cloth industry in the late twelfth and early thirteenth centuries', *Economic History Review*, XIV (1944), reprinted in her *Medieval Merchant Venturers. Collected Studies* (London, 1954), pp. 211–15.

[54] Crapelet (ed.), *Proverbes et Dictons populaires*, p. 14.

[55] W. Foerster and A. Hilka (eds.), *Chrétien de Troyes. Perceval ou le Conte del Graal* (Halle, 1932), v. 5781.

[56] P. Ruelle (ed.), *Huon de Bordeaux* (Université Libre de Bruxelles, Faculté de Philosophie et Lettres, XX) (Brussels, 1960), p. 118, v. 774.

[57] H. Ammann, 'Deutschland und die Tuchindustrie Nordwesteuropas im Mittelalter', *Hansische Geschichtsblätter*, LXXII (1954), p. 31; A. Ewert (ed.), *The Romance of Tristan by Beroul*, I (Oxford, 1977), p. 111, vv. 3721–2.

III

According to literary sources of the type cited here, competition grew more severe for the Flemish cloth industry during the fourteenth and fifteenth centuries. For instance, the Viennese physician Henry of Neustadt, in the early fourteenth century, mentioned 'stanford' and 'gewant von Schalawn' (cloth of Châlons)[58] and the contemporary story *Lohengrin* alludes to 'scharlach . . . uz Engellant' (scarlet from England).[59] A broad view of the great cloth-making centres of north-west Europe at the beginning of the fourteenth century is provided by the famous *Dit du Lendit*.[60] This versified pamphlet[61] flatters the merchants frequenting the fair of Lendit at Compiègne near Paris, 'la plus roial foire du monde' (the most royal fair in the world) (v. 5). The poet was right in considering this fair as the most important one of the time, because the Champagne fairs were already declining by the end of the thirteenth century. Although 'tiretaine dont simple gent son revestu de pou d'argent' (a light woollen, dressing poor people for little money) was also sold at Lendit, the author was chiefly concerned with the woollen draperies. He enumerates some eighty centres, ranging from Brittany up to the Meuse area, most of them north of the Loire (Figure 10.1). The famous Flemish centres – Ghent, Ieper (Ypres), Douai and St Omer – were represented at the Compiègne market, together with some minor towns like Dendermonde (Termonde), Poperinge, Kortrijk (Courtrai), Aire, Geraardsbergen (Grammont), Lille, Arras and Bailleul. Flanders had to reckon with competition from the other towns of the Netherlands, especially with those of Brabant, Hainaut and Liège and with a host of French centres. Normandy and Ile-de-France, each with some fifteen centres, were quantitatively more strongly represented than Flanders; and as for quality, Brabant did not lag far behind Flanders:

> Gant et Ypre et puis Douay
> et Maaline et Broiselles
> Je les doi bein nommer com celles
> qui plus belles sont a voir (vv. 92–5)

[58] S. Singer (ed.), *Die Werke Heinrichs von Neustadt* (Deutsche Texte des Mittelalters, VII) (Berlin, 1906), p. 12, vv. 604, 607.

[59] Th. Cramer (ed.), *Lohengrin. Edition und Untersuchungen* (Munich, 1971), p. 385, v. 3845; for the date: H. Thomas, 'Der Lohengrin, eine politische Dichtung der Zeit Ludwigs des Bayern', *Rheinische Vierteljahrsblätter*, XXXVII (1973), pp. 152–90 and H. Wenzel, 'Die Datierung des Lohengrin. Beiträge zu einer Forschungskontroverse, *Rheinische Vierteljahrsblätter*, XLI (1977), pp. 138–59.

[60] G. Flagniez (ed.), *Documents relatifs à l'Histoire de l'Industrie et du Commerce en France, II. XIVe et XVe Siècles* (Paris, 1900), LXXIX, pp. 173–9.

[61] For the dating, see R. H. Bautier, 'La place de la draperie brabançonne et plus particulièrement bruxelloise dans l'industrie textile du Moyen Âge', *Annales Société Royale d'Archéologie de Bruxelles*, LI (1962/66), p. 35 n. 6.

(Ghent and Ieper and Douai
And Malines and Brussels
I must name those as those
That are the nicest to see.)

Bruges cloth is missing in this list, probably because in so great an international market, the town's commercial functions had largely superseded cloth-making for export. Nor is there any trace of English cloth at Compiègne. Half a century later it was absent at the Bruges market itself, naturally enough since the import of English cloth in

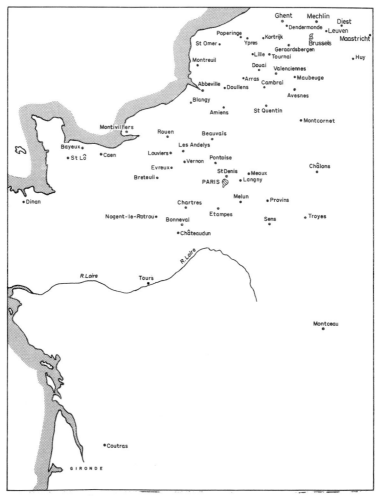

10.1   Cloth-making centres of north-west Europe, early fourteenth century (*from the* Dit du Lendit)

Flanders had been prohibited.[62] A survey of the kinds of cloth for sale in Bruges occurs in a manual for learning French and Flemish composed by a Bruges schoolmaster in about 1369. His *Livre des Mestiers* was a series of sentences translated on daily life including the buying of cloth. For this purpose he listed a lot of cloths available at Bruges (see Table 10.1 and Figure 10.2). A few years later another edition of his book specified that cloth from Ghent, Bruges, Ieper (Ypres) and Kortrijk (Courtrai) was for sale in the cloth hall and that a variety

[62] W. Brulez, 'Engels Laken in Vlaanderen in de 14e Eeuw en 15e Eeuw', *Handelingen Genootschap 'Société d'Emulation' te Brugge*, CVIII (1971), pp. 6–25; J. Munro, 'Industrial protectionism in medieval Flanders' in H. A. Miskimin (ed.), *The Medieval City* (New Haven, 1979), pp. 229–53.

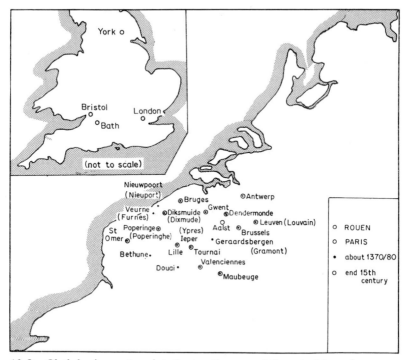

10.2   Cloth-buying centres, late fourteenth century (from the Livre des Mestiers)

Table 10.1   References to cloth towns in various editions of Livre des Mestiers

	Edition of c. 1369	Edition of c. 1380	Edition of c. 1483	Edition of c. 1500
Bruges	*	*	*	*
Ghent	*	*	*	*
Ieper (Ypres)	*	*	*	*
Diksmuide (Dixmude)	*	*	*	*
Lille	*	*	*	*
Tournai	*	*	*	*
Menen (Menin)	*		*	*
Kortrijk (Courtrai)	*	*		*
Wervicq	*			*
Bailleul	*	*	*	*
Poperinge (Poperinghe)	*		*	*
Oudenaarde	*	*		*
St Omer	*	*	*	*
Brussels	*	*	*	*
Leuven (Louvain)	*	*	*	*
Mechlin (Malines)		*	*	*
Antwerp		*	*	*
Dendermonde (Termonde)		*	*	*
Geraardsbergen (Gramont)		*		
Bergues-Saint-Winoc		*		
Veurne (Furnes)		*		
Nieuwpoort (Nieuport)		*		
Bethune		*		
Valenciennes		*	*	*
Maubeuge		*		*
Douai		*		
London			*	
York			*	
Bristol			*	
Bath			*	
Paris			*	
Rouen			*	
Aalst (Alost)			*	
Hondschoote				*
Ronse (Renaix)				*

of other woollens were presented at the market place.[63] William Caxton, once governor of the English merchants at Antwerp and the first printer in England, published a French–English version of this

---

[63] I *Livre des Mestiers*, and II *Gesprächsbuchlein* in J. Gessler (ed.), *Le 'Livre des Mestiers' de Bruges et ses Dérivés* (Bruges, 1931), I, pp. 15–17 and II, p. 13. For a precise dating: R. Van Uytven, 'De Datering van het Brugse *'Livre des Mestiers'*, *Archief- en Bibliotheekwezen in België*, XLVIII (1977), pp. 642–53.

Bruges conversation handbook about 1483. It summed up the cloths that were available at the fairs of Bruges, Antwerp, Bergen op Zoom, Stourbridge, Salisbury, London (on St Bartholomew's Day), Cambridge, Westminster and Châlons.[64] The appearance of Châlons-sur-Saône instead of the fairs of Champagne is not incorrect, since this fair maintained itself well as a cloth market long after the thirteenth century.[65] Around 1500 a further edition of this handbook was printed, giving a list of the woollens sold at the markets of Bruges, Thorout, Menen (Menin), Lille, Ieper (Ypres), Damme, Roeselare (Roulers), Châlons, Montreuil-sur-Mer, Provins and Arras.[66]

At the end of the fourteenth century, Bruges could evidently offer only cloths produced in the southern Netherlands; but a century later the fabrics of England and Normandy were a common merchandise at the fairs of north-west Europe. Among the Flemish textiles, the fabrics from Hondschoote also made their appearance (Figure 10.2).

In the fifteenth century a French paltry rhymer composed *Le Dict des Pays*, a colourful enumeration of the specialities of many towns. It records:

A Londres escarlates fines
Et bons draps vermeilz a Malines
A Nicolle est le bon fil blanc
Et bons drapz royez sont à Gand
Bon vert et bon pers sont en Ypre
Les bonnes sarges sont à Rains
Et à Nevers sont les bons tains
Bons draps gris à Montevillier

(In London fine scarlets
And at Malines vermilion cloths
At Lincoln is the best white yarn
And at Ghent are good striped cloths
At Ieper are fine green and blue
At Reims are the good serges
And at Nevers are the good dyes
Good grey cloths are at Montivilliers)

A variation of this printed in 1597 does not mention Ghent cloth and reads as follows:

[64] III *Ryght good lernyng* in J. Gessler (ed.), *Le 'Livre des Mestiers'* (see n. 63), pp. 21–2.
[65] R. H. Bautier, *The Economic Development of Medieval Europe* (London, 1971), p. 176.
[66] IV *Vocabulaer* in J. Gessler (ed.), *Le 'Livre der Mestiers'* (see n. 63), pp. 25–6.

Les bon camelots sont à Ypres
Anvers est le lieu des bons tains
Les draps blancs à Montevillier

(The good camlets are at Ieper
Antwerp is the town of good dyes
The white cloths at Montivilliers)[67]

Nevertheless during the first half of the fourteenth century the traditional clothing towns of Flanders still dominated the market. The second tale of the eighth day of the *Decameron*, in which Boccaccio (d. 1375) tells of the amorous adventures of the parish priest of Varlungo (near Florence) provides a convincing illustration.

The object of the priest's longings, Belcolore, earned her income from spinning. Each Saturday she brought her yarn to Florence, the centre of a considerable clothing industry. Belcolore was not averse to selling her favours to supplement her earnings. Willing to give her lover some credit, she accepted the priest's cloak as a pledge. This blue cloak, he told her, was of great value being fine cloth of Douai. He had bought it as a second-hand bargain for seven lires, but it was worth at least five shillings more.[68] The priest's speech may sound like the product of Boccaccio's satirical fantasy, but it was true enough that in every medieval town a flourishing trade in old clothes was practised. The famous woollens were so durable that they did not easily wear out, and the rich usually preferred to dispose of their old-fashioned clothes by selling them. An old cloth from Douai thus appears to have been highly valued even in Florence.

In *Le roman du comte d'Anjou*, written by Jehan Maillart in 1316, a duchess of Anjou, wishing to endow a prioress with the richest cloths she had at her disposal, offered her

une brunecte bonne et noire
et un camelin de Douai
molt bon et molt fin.

(A fine black-brown cloth and a camel-coloured one of Douai, very good and very fine.)

She also had coloured cloths and furs, but those were not fitting for a religious woman.[69] In one of his satirical bucolics Jean Froissart

[67] A. De Montaiglon (ed.), *Recueil de Poésies Françaises des XVe et XVIe Siècles*, V (Paris, 1958), pp. 106–16.
[68] V. Branca (ed.), *G. Boccaccio. Decameron*, II (Florence, 1960²), p. 314.
[69] M. Roques (ed.), *Jehan Maillart. Le Roman du Comte d'Anjou* (Paris, 1964), p. 205, vv. 6274–84.

(1333–*c*.1400) introduced a shepherd dreaming of an *houppelande*, the new-fashioned long dress in vogue with courtiers from 1360:[70]

> g'irai à Douai samedi
> s'acheterai une aune entiere
> de drap, se ferai la plus fiere
> qu'on vit ains porter.

(I'll go to Douai next Saturday and buy an entire ell of cloth and have made a long cloak, the most superb one ever saw.)

When he realises that he needs a quarter of a cloth piece and also nine ells 'd'un grant drap d'Irlande' (of a great cloth of Ireland) for the lining, he wisely concludes

> trop me poroit couster
> à vestir une houpelande[71]

(It is too costly for me to wear a long cloak)

The shepherd probably thought of buying Douai cloth in that town, but he could find cheaper fabrics from the newer centres at the Saturday market there. In his chronicle Froissart himself recounts that men of Lille, Douai, Artois and Tournai were large buyers of cloths from Wervicq, Messines, Poperinge and Comines. Ieper (Ypres), the famous old clothing town, was a great centre of this trade. When the French conquered Ieper in 1382, their booty was not Ieper cloths, but mainly woollens from the nearby places on the Leie (Lys) and from Poperinge.[72] Froissart was well aware of the extent to which Flanders was industrialised when he remarked: 'sans la drapperie ne povient-il nullement vivre' (without the woollen industry they could not live).[73] Ottokar von Steiermarken in his *Österreichische Reimchronik*, at the beginning of the fourteenth century, knew of no better way to praise the splendour of a kingly wedding dress than by saying:

> ... sogetanen gewant,
> Des man ze Flandern vindet niht
> In so chostleicher angezicht.

(Such a cloth, that one even in Flanders would not find one which looked so rich.)[74]

---

[70] M. Beaulieu and J. Baylé, *Le Costume en Bourgogne de Philippe le Hardi à Charles le Téméraire* (Paris, 1956), p. 48.

[71] K. Bartsch (ed.), *Romances et Pastourelles françaises des XIIe et XIIIe Siècles* (Leipzig, 1870), p. 322.

[72] J. Kervyn de Lettenhove (ed.), *Oeuvres de Froissart, Chroniques*, X (Brussels, 1870), p. 149.

[73] Ibid., VIII (Brussels, 1869), pp. 77–8.

[74] F. Lichtenstein and J. Seemuller (eds.), *Ottokars Österreichische Reimchronik* (Monumenta Germaniae Historica, Deutsche Chroniken, V, 2) (Hanover, 1890), p. 913, vv. 69051–7.

In Bavaria the famous Lohengrin, composed in the beginning of the fourteenth century, mentions 'vil tuoch von Gente ein teil scharlach geverbet' (much cloth of Ghent, a part dyed in scarlet).[75]

Ieper and Ghent were still outstanding for their technical knowledge of cloth-making in the eyes of that well-informed English customs official – and poet – Geoffrey Chaucer. He knew of no higher praise for that remarkable cloth-making wife of Bath than to compare her favourably with the drapers of those towns:

> Of clooth-making she hadde swiche an haunt
> She passed hem of Ypres and of Gaunt.[76]

Half a century later, about 1436, even the chauvinistic author of *The Libelle of Englyshe Polycye* had to admit that:

> Fyne cloth of Ipre [Ypres] that named is better than ours
> Cloth of Curtrycke [Kortrijk (Courtrai)], fyne cloothe of all colours.[77]

The French poet Eustache Deschamps (d. 1406/07) in *Le Miroir de Mariage* evokes the troubles of a married man who has to go to great expense on account of the fancies of his wife, who asks for golden cloth, silk dresses and 'fin blanc d'Ypres' (fine white cloth of Ypres).[78] That passage inspired the anonymous writer who composed *Les. XV. Joies de Mariage* about 1400. One of the fifteen affections of a husband is the dissipation of his wife, always longing for 'robe d'escarlate ou de Malignes, ou de fin vert, fourrure de bon gris ou de menu ver' (a gown of scarlet or of Malines (Mechlin) cloth or of fine green cloth and linings of good squirrel fur or of ermine). The newly-married man cannot refuse her such a costly dress, since she claims that all her friends have as much. The dress costs him fifty or sixty golden *écus* (1 écus = about 4.5 gram gold), money he really needs to furnish the house, to repair his farm and to buy cattle for his tenants.[79]

It seems that in the fifteenth century Malines (Mechlin) had superseded Ieper (Ypres) as the leading producer of luxury cloth. Even the much earlier *Le dit du Lendit* had suggested that Brussels and

---

[75] Th. Cramer (ed.), *Lohengrin* (see n. 59), p. 309, v. 3083.

[76] F. N. Robinson (ed.), *The Works of Geoffrey Chaucer* (London, 1968), p. 21, vv. 447–8.

[77] G. Warner (ed.), *The Libelle of Englyshe Polycye* (Oxford, 1926), p. 5.

[78] G. Raynaud (ed.), *Oeuvres complètes d'Eustache Deschamps*, IX (Paris, 1894), p. 43, vv. 1221, 1226.

[79] J. Rychner (ed.), *Les XV. Joies de Mariage* (Paris, 1967), pp. 8–11. A woman in an analogous scene in a story of the sixteenth century complained in her turn: 'il n'y avait femme si petite de l'estat dont je suis qui n'eust robbe neuve d'escarlate de Paris ... (E. Mabille (ed.), *Nicolas de Troyes. Le Grand Paragon des Nouvelles* (Paris, 1869), p. 272.)

Malines were rapidly catching up with the Flemish centres. Further-more we have some Spanish evidence to corroborate this from Juan Ruiz (d. 1350) who wrote his *Libro de buen amor* about the middle of the century in the vicinity of Madrid.[80] One of his characters promises his mistress all kinds of gifts amongst which were 'los panos de Melinas' (cloths of Malines).[81] Even more revealing are a few passages in the *Rimado de Palacio*, composed in the last decade of the century by the chancellor of Castile, Pero Lopez de Ayala (d. 1407). He extolled

> escarlates de Brujas e de Melinas
> veynte annos ho que nunca fueron en esta tierra tan finas   (vv. 300–1)
>
> (scarlets of Bruges and Malines, within twenty years there have not been such in this land)

In the meantime he blames the dishonest shopkeepers who show their woollens in a dark corner to their clients:

> Por Brozelas muestran Ypre, por Melinas Rroan   (vv. 310–11)
>
> (Instead of Brussels they show Ieper, for Malines, Rouen)[82]

It is obvious that to him Brussels cloth was superior to Ieper cloth and that Malines woollens are more expensive than those of Rouen. About 1388 the idealistic dreamer and French counsellor Philippe de Mézières condemned the consumption of Brussels and Malines cloths by the royal court as too expensive a luxury in *Le Songe du vieil pélerin*, a plea for reforming the French government.[83]

Before the end of the century, the great Brabantine clothing towns were already on the decline, but secondary centres like Lier (Lierre) maintained themselves better.[84] An anonymous Flemish poem of the early fifteenth century states that all the scholars of Europe would not suffice to describe half the stupidity of the villains:

[80] C. Verlinden, 'Panos belges en fuentes literarias españolas medievales. Poesia e historia economica', *Cuadernos de Historia de España*, XXIX–XXX (1959), pp. 218–30.

[81] H. Gumbrecht (ed.), *Juan Ruiz, Arcipreste de hita. Libro de buen amor* (Munich, 1972), p. 374, v. 1394.

[82] A. F. Kursteiner (ed.), *Poesias del Canciller Pero Lopez de Ayala* (New York, 1920), pp. 51, 53, 80 (v. 468)

[83] G. W. Coopland (ed.), *Philippe de Mézières. Le Songe du vieil Pélerin*, II (Cambridge, 1969), p. 357.

[84] R. Van Uytven, 'La draperie brabançonne et malinoise du XIIe au XVIIe siècle: grandeur éphémère et décadence', *Produzione, Commercio e Consumo dei Panni di Lana nei Secoli XII–XVIII* (Florence, 1976), pp. 85–97.

Ja! Al waert oec altemael papier
Dat laken datmen maect te Lier[85]

(Even if all the cloth made at Lier [Lierre] would be paper)

The two verses echo, as it were, verses of the twelfth century poet of *Vanden Vos Reynaerde* cited earlier. The fifteenth-century author reproduced them, except in substituting paper for parchment and Lier (Lierre) for Ghent.

The emergence of Brabant's woollen industry as against that of Flanders received due notice in England and Germany. To Ranulph Higden (d. 1363) in his description of the world, the *Polychronicon*, Flanders was still the homeland of cloth-making and its fabrics were exported all over Europe: 'Flandra ... gens opere lanifico praeclara quo toti pene Europae submunistrat' (Flemish people famous for its woollens it is supplying to nearly the whole of Europe). Brabant, however, was almost its equal:

Brabantia ad Eurum Flandriae situata, terra mercibus copiosa, potissime lanis ordiendis instar Flandriae indulget quo fit ut lanas quas de Anglia recepit in pannos multicolores convertit multisque provinciis refundit.[86]

(Brabant, situated at the eastern border of Flanders, is a country filled with merchandise. It strongly indulges in working wool in the same way as Flanders. From the wools it received from England, it produces multi-coloured cloths and re-exports them to many countries.)

In the first quarters of the fourteenth century, Henry of Neustadt describes in his Apollonius van Tyrland a vessel loaded with all kinds of treasures and among them:

Scharlach und gar vil gutt gewantt
Von Flander and von Prabantt

(Scarlet and plenty of good cloth of Flanders and of Brabant)[87]

From the fourteenth century on, a third competitor made a remarkable appearance in the international market. Before the middle of the fourteenth century, Normandy was represented at the Compiègne

---

[85] E. Verwys (ed.), 'Van Vrouwen ende van Minne', *Middelnederlandsche Gedichten uit de XIVe en XVe Eeuw* (Groningen, 1871), p. 76, vv. 197–8.
[86] C. Babington (ed.), *Polychronicon Ranulphi Higden*, I (London, 1865), p. 288 and II (London, 1868), pp. 16–17.
[87] S. Singer (ed.), *Die Werke Heinrichs von Neustadt*, p. 15, vv. 779–80.

fair, as described in *Le Dit du Lendit*. The language manual of Caxton, at the end of the fifteenth century, also took notice of it. In Spain, Chancellor Ayala criticised – at the end of the fourteenth century – the tricky shopkeepers who sold Rouen cloth pretending it was from Malines. These dishonest practices were greatly facilitated by the Norman practice of imitating Brabantine cloths. The town of Brussels, for example, formally lodged complaints about this.[88] One of the best-known medieval farces, *La Farce de Maistre Pierre Pathlin* alludes to these facts. The play may be dated about 1464, and Normandy as well as Paris had been suggested as the place of origin. The market scene it presents seems to fit Paris better. In the market place, a lawyer meets a draper, perhaps from Normandy. The latter, selling his cloth there, states that he is also growing sheep and even buying wool at great expense. When the lawyer asks for a fine cloth dyed in the wool, he is offered 'ung tres bon drap de Roen' (a very good cloth of Rouen). To the question 'Quel lé a il?' (what width is it?) the draper answers 'De Brucelle' (Of Brussels).[89] At the Paris market the Norman cloth-makers in fact offered woollens with the specific dimensions of Brussels cloth! Rouen was not the only clothing town of Normandy making a name for itself. As already mentioned *Le Dit des Pays* knew of Montivilliers cloth at the end of the century. In his *Jehan de Saintré* (about 1455), A. de la Sale refers to cloth of Saint-Lô and of Montivilliers. A noble lady provided the equipment for her serving knight with great liberality. He gets a suit 'de fine brunecte de Saint Lo, qui sera fourru de martres' (of a fine brown cloth of Saint-Lô, with a lining of marten) and another 'd'un fin gris de Monstierviller qui sera doublé d'un fin blanchet' (of a fine grey cloth of Montivilliers, lined with a fine white cloth). His trousers are made of a 'fine brunecte de Saint Lo' (a fine brown cloth of Saint-Lô).[90]

In the same period as this knightly novel, a French writer tried to demonstrate the superiority of his country to England in a dialogue between a French and an English herald. The Englishman boasts about the excellence of English wool, while the Frenchman points to the high quality of the fine dyed cloth of Rouen, Montivilliers, Paris, Bourges and other clothing towns in France. He states that French cloth is always sold one or two *éscus* per ell more than that of England. 'Si, fault dire que nous avons meilleures laines ou que vous estez si peu savans que ne savez faire vos draps' (Thus one might say: either we

[88] M. Mollat, 'La draperie normande', *Produzione, Commercio e Consumo* (see n. 84), pp. 403–21 and R. H. Bautier, 'La place de la draperie' (see n. 4), pp. 58–63.

[89] B. C. Bowen (ed.), *Four Farces* (Oxford, 1967), pp. 63–6, vv. 190–3, 259.

[90] J. Misrahi and C. A. Knudson (eds.), *A. de la Sale. Jehan de Saintré*, (Geneva, 1967), pp. 50, 57–8 and 63.

have better wools or you are so ignorant that you cannot make cloth).[91] Later, about 1549, a merchant adventurers' clerk named John Coke did not question the inferiority of English cloth-making when he wrote a retort to this French pamphlet. Coke took a pride in the large volumes of English trade and especially of its two great companies, 'the ryght worshypful company of marchaunts adventurers and the famous felyshyp of the Estaple of Calais, by whom not only the martes of Barowe [Bergen op Zoom] and Antwerpe be mayntened, but also in effect al the townes of Brabant, Holland, Zealand and Flaunders.' Coke's English herald further stresses the huge production of all kinds of textiles in England – 'fyne scarletts, clothes, corseis, stock bredes, fryses, cottons, worsteds, sayes and coverlettes' – and their export to France itself, to all Christian nations and even to the Islamic countries. When his French spokesman pointed out that nevertheless English woollens lack the refinement and the careful finishing of those of France, Flanders, Brabant and Holland, Coke prefers to ignore this remark.[92] His silence amounts to a confession, but such a confession did not shock English ears. As noted earlier, the author of *The Libelle of Englyshe Polycye* had admitted (*c.* 1436) that Ieper cloth was considered better than English fabrics. Even though Chaucer claimed that the wife of Bath surpassed the people of Ghent and Ieper in cloth-making, English merchants were realistic enough to know that even their best cloths had to be dyed and finished in the Netherlands. The sixteenth-century edition of *Le Dit des Pays* recognised that Antwerp was unequalled for the dyeing of cloth.

Refined and dyed in the Netherlands, English woollens could be exported throughout Europe, competing effectively with the most luxurious cloths. Thanks to their relatively low price, they succeeded in displacing most cloths of the Netherlands from the international market during the sixteenth century. Erasmus, in one of his *Colloquia* (1518), introduces two good wives discussing a new dress. Impressed by the elegance of her companion's outfit, the first woman assumes that it is English cloth: 'Nihil jam diu vidi elegantius. Suspicor pannum esse Britannicum.' (I have not seen anything more elegant for a long time. I suppose it is English cloth.) Her friend replies: 'Lana Britannica est, tinctura Veneta' (the wool is English, the dyestuff Venetian).[93] It did not even occur to Erasmus that such a nice cloth could be a

[91] L. Pannier and P. Meyer (eds.), *Le Débat des Hérauts d'Armes de France et d'Angleterre, suiri de The Debate between the Heralds of England and France by John Coke* (Société des anciens textes français) (Paris, 1877), pp. 35–6 and 45.
[92] Ibid., pp. 105, 114–17.
[93] W. Welzig (ed.), *Erasmus von Rotterdam. Ausgewahlte Schriften. VI. Colloquia Familiaria; Vertraute Gespräche* (Darmstadt, 1967), p. 145.

product of his homeland, the Netherlands. Patriotism, to be sure, never did rule the heart of the great humanist; but he might have at least added that the English cloth was dyed at Antwerp.

More revealing still is a passage by Johan Butzbach (d. 1526) censuring the wealth and the worldly pride of the German high clergy. He portrays those bold prelates in their rich outfits made of the finest English cloth, riding on horse-back, their hands loaded with costly rings.[94] A century earlier, the luxury shown here by the wearing of English cloth would have been associated with cloth from either Flanders or Brabant. This is the more striking as Butzbach, who had served as an apprentice tailor about 1495, remembered having worked with 'the costliest textiles, especially scarlets, English woollens, cloth of Liège, Rouen, Grenoble, Bruges, Ghent and Aix'.[95]

IV

From certain medieval tracts we can also learn much about the manner and techniques of manufacturing quality woollens. The extensive division of labour is well illustrated by that Bruges language manual from the end of the fourteenth century. Among the eighty professions discussed, nine concerned the making of cloth. Three of them were typically female occupations: combing, spinning and knotting. The absence of carding is undoubtedly no mere oversight, for the use of carded wool was treated with suspicion or actually prohibited in the great clothing towns of the Netherlands until the late fourteenth century. The Bruges schoolmaster even knew of the prevailing bias against the spinning wheel; the yarn produced by the wheel, he said, had too many knots. His spinster preferred working with the distaff to produce yarn for warp, rather than spinning at the wheel for weft, because working with the distaff paid better. The different manner of spinning for warp and for weft was a common practice during the later Middle Ages in the Netherlands.[96] The Bruges manual listed, as male occupations, the wool beater, the weaver, the fuller, the shearer and the dyer. Those people worked the wool for 'the rich draper' and he paid them piece-work. The Bruges schoolmaster knew several different types of woollens, and so did his imitators – see Table 10.2.[97]

---

[94] J. R. Hale, *Renaissance Europe 1480–1520* (Fontana History of Europe) (London, 1971), p. 224.

[95] D. J. Becker (ed.), *Chronicon eines fahrenden Schülers oder Wunderbüchlein des Johannes Butzbach* (Ratisbon, 1869), p. 122.

[96] For the prevailing technical procedures of the Flemish drapery see G. De Poerck, *La Draperie Médiévale en Flandre et en Artois. I. La Technique* (Bruges, 1951).

[97] J. Gessler (ed.), *Le 'Livre des Mestiers'* (see n. 63), I, p. 15; II, pp. 13–14; III, p. 18; IV, pp. 21–2.

Table 10.2 Kinds of cloths in the various editions of the Livre des Mestiers

A Edition of c. 1369		B Edition of c. 1380		C Edition of c. 1483		D Edition of c. 1500	
a	b	a	b	a	b	a	b
gheminghede	melleis	mellees	ghemenghede	meslés	medleyed		
rode	vermaus	vermelles	root	rouge	red	rouge	root
				vermeil	reed	vermeil	root
groene	werds	verds	grüene	vert	grene	vert	groene
swerte	noirs						
witte	blancs						
sciere	camelins	camelins	sciere				
graeuwe	gris						
blaeuwe	bleus	bleus	blauwe	bleu	blyew	blau	blau
strypte	royés	royets	strijpte	royet	raye	royet	ghestrypt
tierteine	tierteine					tiertaine	tretaine
		gaunes	gheluwe	gaune	yelow	giaune	ghelu
		pers	brune				
		asurés	azúre	assuret	y-asured	asuret	gheazuert
		vergaudes	licht grüene				
		entre pers	zad blaeuwe	entre pers	sad blew	entre pers	satblau
		eskeleis	ghescakelde	esquickeliet	chekeryd	esquicqueleit	ghescakiert
				morret	morrey	moret	moreyt
				saye blanche	saye white	saye blanche	sarck wit
				saye bleu	saye blew	saye bleue	sarck blau
				escarlate en grain	scarlet in grayne	escharlate	schaerlaken

It is worth quoting that the fourteenth-century language manuals (Table 10.2, *A* and *B*) considered 'camelin' to be some colour probably a shade between white and grey, as did the Englishman John of Garlande (1180–*c*.1252) in his *Dictionarius*[98] and that *eskeleis* has been translated by *chekeryd* (Table 10.2 *C*) and *ghescakelde* (Table 10.2, *D*) thus recalling the pattern of a chess-board. The usual interpretation – a kind of blue – such as that of the columbine (in French *ancolie*, in Flemish *akelei*)[99] could thus be wrong.

The fourteenth-century language manuals also deal with kinds of wool. The Bruges schoolmaster ranges them according to their quality – English, Scottish and Flemish. He explicitly states that 'the Scots bring wools from Scotland that are not so good as the English are'. His silence about Spanish and Irish wool cannot be overlooked. Spain became important as a source of wool for the Netherlands only during the fifteenth century, and the place of Irish wool in cloth-making in the Netherlands has been largely overstated due to a misinterpretation of the medieval Flemish word *hierlandsch* (home grown) in many of the records.[100]

The superiority of English wool was a commonplace in medieval literature. Certainly Englishmen could grow lyrical about their country's wool. John Gower (d. 1408), in his *Mirour de l'Omme* (before 1381), called the wool 'that noble lady, goddess of the merchants', 'so nice, so white, so soft',[101] John Lydgate (d. *c*.1450) in his *Horse, Goose and Sheep* (about 1436–40) celebrated:

Of Brutus Albion his wulle is chief richesse
In prise surmounting eny othir thyng
Sauff grayne and corne; marchauntes all expresse
Wulle is chief tresour in this land growing

All natiouns afferme op to the fulle
In all the worlde ther is no bettir wulle   (vv. 351–7)

Lydgate was well aware of the international importance and the political influence of the English wool trade:

---

[98] Edited by G. De Poerck, *La Draperie Médiévale* (see n. 96), I, pp. 317–18, who nevertheless denies the well-foundedness of this interpretation (p. 211, n. 4).

[99] G. De Poerck, ibid., I, p. 167 and III, p. 1,

[100] A. Verhulst, 'La laine indigène dans les anciens Pays-Bas entre le XIIe et le XVIIe siècle', *Revue historique*, XCVI (1972), pp. 281–322; R. van Uytven, '"Hierlandsche" Wol en Lakens in Brabantse Documenten (XIIIe–XVIe Eeuw)', *Bijdragen tot de Geschiedenis*, LIII (1970), pp. 5–16.

[101] G. C. Macaulay (ed.), *Complete Works of J. Gower*, I (Oxford, 1899), pp. 280–1.

> The sheepe is cause and hath be ful long
> Of newe stryf and of mortal werre.
> The wulle was cause and grete occasioun
> Why that the prowde forsworn duke of Borgon
> Cam before Caleys, with Flemynges not a fewe
> Which gave the sakkis and sarpleres of that towne
> To Gaunt and Bruges, his freedom for to shewe
> And of thy wolle hiht hem possessioun   (vv. 409–17)[102]

Of course the nationalistic court official who wrote *The Libelle* of *Englyshe Polycye* stressed the superiority of English wool and the Low Countries' dependence on it:

> By draperinge of oure wolle in substaunce
> Lyvene here commons: this is here governaunce
> Wythoughten whyche they may not leve at ease
> Thus moste hem sterve or wyth us most have peasse.

or:

> The grete substaunce of youre cloothe at the fulle
> Ye wot ye make hit of oure Englissh wolle.

and:

> They may not liven to maintein her degrees
> Withoughten oure Englyshe commodytees
> Wolle and tynne, for the wolle of Englande
> Susteyneth the comons Flemmynges . . .

Not even the growing import of Spanish wool in to Flanders can smother his high spirits:

> Hit is of lytell valeue, trust unto me
> Wyth Englisshe wolle, but if it menged be.[103]

More than a century earlier, Ranulph Higden (d. 1363) had recognised the economic dependence of Flanders and Brabant on English wool because 'Anglia lanas optimas producat' (England produces the best

---

[102] M. Degenhart (ed.), *J. Lydgate, Horse, Goose and Sheep* (Münchener Beiträge zur romanischen und englischen Philologie, XIX) (Leipzig, 1900), p. 65, vv. 351–7; also pp. 68–9, vv. 409–23.
[103] G. Warner (ed.), *The Libelle of Englyshe Polycye* (see n. 77), pp. 5ff.

wools) and therefore 'lanam ejus zelat Flandria' (Flanders envies its wool).[104] More striking still are the circuitous arguments of the French author of *Le débat des hérauts d'armes*, who resorted to great subtlety to contradict the undeniable statement of his English herald:

> Angleterre est fort garnie de bestail . . . et par especial de bestes à laine comme de brebis qui portent la plus fine et la plus singuliere layne que on puisse savoir nulle part . . . Et les marchans dudit royaume les portent vendre en divers royaumes et pays et si y en croit si largement qu'ils en tiennent les taples communes à Calays.

> (England is well supplied with cattle . . . and especially with wool-wearing beasts like sheep that wear the most fine and most particular wool one might find anywhere . . . And the merchants of the realm export it to different realms and countries and there grows so much of it that they keep a common staple at Calais.)[105]

Although the nearly contemporary *Libelle of Englyshe Polycye* deplored the 'racket' of the Italians and other foreigners who bought English wool under the natives' noses, and dominated the market at Bruges,[106] it is clear that in the fifteenth century the bulk of the English wool trade was in the hands of English merchants. Their staple at Calais was the major international wool market both for the French author of *Le débat des hérauts* and for his English opponent John Coke, about 1549.

In previous centuries, however, the export of wool from England had been a foreigner's business. In the thirteenth century *Dit des marcheans* by Philippot, it was clearly stated that merchants from the Continent 'vont en Engleterre, laines et cuirs et bacons querre' (go to England and fetch wool, leather and bacon).[107] Northern France, including Flanders and Artois, had taken the lead in this search for English wool. An Arras poet from about 1270 used the expression 'En Engleterre envoia laine' (he sent wool to England) as one would say now taking coals to Newcastle.[108]

About the middle of the century an Arras *jongleur*, in a satire against a group of well-known citizens, refers to an Englishman who had to collect on behalf of his aunt the debts for fourteen sacks of wool sold three years before to men of Arras. Among the wools there was also

---

[104] C. Babington (ed.), *Polychronicon Ranulphi Higden*, I, p. 288 and II, pp. 16–17.
[105] L. Pannier and P. Meyer (eds.), *Le Débat des Hérauts d'Armes* (see n. 91), pp. 35–6.
[106] G. Warner (ed.), *The Libelle of Englyshe Polyche* (see n. 77), pp. 23–4.
[107] A. De Montaiglon and G. Raynaud (eds.), *Recueil général* (see n. 24), II, p. 125.
[108] A. Jeanroy and H. Guy (eds.), *Chanson et Dits Artésiens du XIIIe Siècle* (Bibliothèque des Universités du Midi, II) (Bordeaux, 1898), p. 100, v. 102.

'laine d'Escoce et de celi de Wales' (wool of Scotland and that of Wales), but Irish wool once again is not mentioned.[109]

The very first recorded import of English wool in Flanders (about 1113) is found once again in a literary text. The *Miracula S. Mariae Laudunensis,* written by the monk Herman (about 1145–50), recounts the misfortune that overtook a number of Flemish merchants when sailing from Wissant to England to buy wool with some 300 marks of silver. Threatened by pirates, the merchants vowed to donate all their money to Our Lady of Laon; but once out of danger, they soon forgot their promises. They travelled almost throughout England and spent their money on large quantities of wool and stored them in a big house at Dover. The night before their departure for Flanders Our Lady punished the merchants, for the building in which the wool was kept burned to the ground.[110]

The story demonstrates that buying wool in England was already a common practice for the Flemish and their neighbours about 1100. In the previous century, however, Flanders relied primarily on home-grown wool. Even around 1070 Winric of Treves considered Flanders as the homeland of sheep: 'Nostra Flandria' (Our Flanders) it was affectionately called by the sheep.[111] A version of the life of St Macharius confirms that during the eleventh century the landholders of the Tournai region sold their wool at Ghent. The *Vita prima S. Macharii* (about 1013–14) cites the fame of the annual fair of St Bavo (1 October) at Ghent, which attracted a host of strangers. One of them, a certain Otherland, took a ship loaded with wool from the harbour of Tournai to Ghent.[112]

The reactions of medieval literary writers suggest that neither the initial great availability of Flemish wool nor even the later access to excellent English wool, gave Flanders and the Netherlands the lead in cloth-making. What impressed them and probably all their con-temporaries most were the superior finishing and especially dyeing techniques of the Netherlands cloth industry. From Winric of Treves and William Britto onwards, they all were obviously fascinated by the rich variety of brilliant colours of Netherlands cloths. The Englishman Ranulph Higden not only marvels about the 'pannos multicolores' (multi-coloured cloths) of Brabant and Flanders, but he explicitly evokes the superiority of the dyeing techniques in Flanders and

---

[109] Ibid., pp. 79–81. For the date see also A. Guesnon, *La Satire à Arras au XIIIe Siècle* (Paris, 1900), pp. 65–6.

[110] J. P. Migne (ed.), *Patrologia Latina,* CLVI (Paris, 1853), p. 975; cf. J. S. Ptatlock, 'The English journey of the Laon canons', *Speculum,* VIII (1933), pp. 454–64.

[111] See n. 16.

[112] *Monumenta Germaniae Historica. Scriptores,* XV, 2 (Hanover, 1888), p. 616; see also F. Vercauteren, *Etude sur les Civitates de la Belgique Seconde* (Brussels, 1934), p. 252.

Brabant to explain the fact that England, in spite of its excellent wool, could not compete with them:

> aquas tamen tinctura tam accomodas sicut Flandria vel Brabantia non habet. Est tamen apud Londonium fons quidam et apud Lincolniam determinatus locus in rivulo per transversum urbis decurrente quorum ope optimum scarletum efficitur.

> (England, however, has no waters that are so suited for dyeing as those of Flanders or Brabant. Although there is a source in London and a certain spot in the little river crossing Lincoln by which the best scarlet is achieved.[113]

It may be tempting to disregard Higden's explanation in terms of the different qualities of the water as too superficial and commonplace, but the fact of the Netherlands' superiority in the field of dyeing cannot be questioned. In the sixteenth-century version of *Le Dict des Pays*, Antwerp was the town *par excellence* for dyeing[114] and this opinion was commonly shared by the English merchants, who had their cloths dyed and finished there.[115] By allowing them to do so, the Netherlands fatally undermined its surviving cloth industry, which had really been doomed from the very moment that England had begun to work the bulk of its wool at home.[116]

V

It will be obvious to the scholar of medieval cloth-making how fairly medieval literature reflected the fortunes of the woollen industry in the Netherlands and of its competitors in Normandy and England. However, one might wonder about the reliability of our literary samples about cloth-making at Leiden and in other towns in Holland, although their break-through in international trade has been well-documented otherwise.[117] The bulk of the growing exports were directed to eastern Europe, and it is natural it did not receive full attention in the literature of western Europe. However, Holland's cloth-makers were not overlooked completely. The author of the *Libelle of Englyshe Polycye* knew of them:

---

[113] C. Babington (ed.), *Polychronicon* (see n. 104), I, p. 288.

[114] A. de Montaiglon (ed.), *Recueil de Poésies Françaises* (see n. 67), V, p. 113.

[115] O. De Smedt, *De Engelse Natie te Antwerpen in de 16e Eeuw*, II (Antwerp, 1954), pp. 353–68.

[116] J. Munro, *Wool, Cloth and Gold. The Struggle for Bullion in Anglo-Burgundian Trade* (Brussels and Toronto, 1973), pp. 180–9, and 'Industrial protectionism in medieval Flanders' (see n. 62), pp. 229–67.

[117] See for instance: H. Ammann, 'Deutschland und die Tuchindustrie Nordwesteuropas im Mittelalter', *Hansische Geschitsblätter*, LXXII (1954), pp. 19–57; N. W. Posthumus, *De Geschiedenis van de Leidsche Lakenindustrie. I De Middeleeuwen* (The Hague, 1908), pp. 238–51.

But thy of Holonde at Caleyse byene oure felles
and oure wolles that Englysshe men hem selles.[118]

He duly stressed the great importance of their purchases of wool-fells at Calais, which differentiated them from other wool buyers there.[119]

In his dialogue of about 1540 John Coke also expressively mentioned cloth-making in Holland as well as in Flanders and Brabant. He showed himself to be a keen observer of the Continental woollen industry. He knew that English wool was worked in France, as well as in the German empire, into says, tapestry, worsteds, cloths and carpets. The growth of tapestry weaving and the emergence of a 'new' lighter drapery of says and worsteds are well-known features of the fifteenth and sixteenth centuries, particularly in the Netherlands. Coke explicitly mentioned the worsteds of Lille.[120] He perhaps overstated the contrast between England and the Continent concerning cloth-making, but nevertheless a contrast there was. Cloth-making in England was a natural complement of wool growing as 'we have shepe berying woll of the worlde, whose valure in the olde tyme was estemed to the weyght of golde'. It went along with farming and husbandry in the countryside. English clothiers were usually farmers. In France and in the Netherlands, on the contrary, the woollen industry was legally concentrated in the towns, and industrial regulations and official inspections resulted in the production of well-finished quality fabrics. Whereas the English cloth-making farmers only employed the labour available on the spot, on the Continent a host of different specialised artisans for spinning, carding, weaving, fulling, shearing and dyeing were employed. Cloth-making also attracted tailors and hosiers to the Continental towns and of course such people in their turn attracted supporting trades and retail traders such as barbers, brewers, bakers and the like.[121]

The examples used in this essay are but the fruit of occasional reading; more systematic gathering would easily amplify them. As they are, they will suffice to demonstrate that medieval literature has a lot to say to the student of social and economic history. Literary quotations have often been used to illustrate the results of research based upon specific and often quantitative records, but their validity

[118] G. Warner (ed.), *The Libelle of Englysshe Polycye* (see n. 77), p. 28, vv. 545–6.
[119] N. W. Posthumus, *De Geschiedenis* (see n. 117), pp. 184–204; E. Power, 'The wool trade in the fifteenth century', *Studies in English Trade in the Fifteenth Century*, E. Power and M. M. Postan (eds.) (London, 1933), pp. 60–2.
[120] For the textile industry at Lille see for instance: P. Deyon and A. Lottin, 'Evolution de la production textile à Lille aux XVIe et XVIIe siècles', *Revue du Nord*, XLIX (1967), pp. 23–33.
[121] L. Pannier and P. Meyer (eds.), *Le Débat des Hérauts d'Armes* (see n. 91), pp. 104–5 and 114–18.

goes beyond mere illustration. A close analysis of medieval literature may throw light upon patterns of demand and consumer behaviour that would otherwise be hard to uncover, and in some way the objectivity of its incidental information is such that it is often more reliable than most quantitative sources.

11 The Rise of the Florentine Woollen Industry in the Fourteenth Century
Hidetoshi Hoshino

I

Judging from the surviving documents, the beginnings of the export trade in Florentine woollen cloth dates from the early decades of the thirteenth century. We have evidence of Florentine cloth being exported to Venice in 1225[1] and Palermo in 1237[2] followed by Macerata in 1245[3] and Lucca in 1246,[4] while documents from 1252 reveal the presence of Florentine products at Genoa and Ragusa (Dubrovnik).[5] These represent the earliest documented examples of the Florentine woollen cloth trade, yet the price level of these products was very low when compared with prices charged for cloth which was imported from the northern countries during the same period. This phenomenon is historically conceivable when one considers the great commercial expansion of northern woollen cloth throughout the whole of Europe.[6]

Responding to the demand of the Italian textile market, the highly industrialised area of Flanders invaded the Italian peninsula with

---

[1] R. Cessi (ed.), *Deliberazioni del Maggior Consiglio di Venezia*, I (Bologna, 1950), p. 80.

[2] U. Monneret de Villard, 'La tessitura palermitana sotto i Normanni e i suoi rapporti con l'arte bizantina', *Miscellanea Giovanni Mercati*, III (Città del Vaticano, 1946), p. 484.

[3] R. Davidsohn, *Forschungen zur Geschichte von Florenz*, III (Berlin, 1901), reg. 29; L. Pratesi, 'I Paganelli delle Marche e lo statuto più antico del Comune di Macerata (1245)', *Atti e memorie della R. Deputazione di storia patria per le Marche*, new ser., X (1915), pp. 341–2.

[4] R. Davidsohn, *Storia di Firenze*, IV, 2 (Florence, 1973), pp. 138 and 835.

[5] R. Lopez, 'L'attività economica di Genova nel marzo 1253 secondo gli atti notarili del tempo', *Atti della Società ligure di storia patria*, LXIV (1935), p. 226; C. Jireček, 'Die Bedeutung von Ragusa in der Handelsgeschichte des Mittelalters', *Almanach der kaiserlichen Akademie der Wissenschaften* XLIX (Wien, 1899), p. 420 n.42.

[6] Compare H. Laurent, *Un grand commerce d'exportation au Moyen Age. La draperie des Pays-Bas en France et dans les pays méditerranéenne (XII–XV siècles)* (Paris, 1935); H. Ammann, 'Deutschland und die Tuchindustrie Nordwesteuropas im Mittelalter', *Hansische Geschichtsblätter*, LXXII (1954); Ch. Verlinden, 'Contribution à l'étude de l'expansion commerciale de la draperie flamande dans la péninsule ibérique au XIIIᵉ siècle', *Revue du Nord*, XXII (1936); idem, 'Draps des Pays-Bas et du Nord de la France en Espagne au XIVᵉ siècle', *Le Moyen Age*, XLVII (1937).

woollen materials of various types and places of origin. They included not only luxury items from Ghent, Ieper (Ypres), Douai and Châlons, but also those of inferior quality produced in many different Flemish cities. However, since transportation costs had, of course, to be included in the price for the Italian market, the Florentine products which were of a lesser quality maintained a competitively lower price throughout the thirteenth century.[7] In fact, there is no documentary evidence in existence to suggest that Florence produced cloth of a quality comparable with that imported from the northern countries – cloth which we shall label, in accordance with established terminology, *panni franceschi.*

If we accept the fact that Florence in this period had not yet begun to specialise in high-quality manufacture, but instead produced material qualitatively similar to the common, cheap cloths, then the market demand for Florentine woollen material must have been very limited, since many other Italian cities probably produced similar fabrics. Because of the demand for common cloth, many cities competed for the same market with materials which were qualitatively identical. Yet it is necessary to point out that, with regard to luxury material, Flemish cloth had acquired a true monopoly over the Italian market. We should ask ourselves, therefore, how and when this monopolistic hold over the Italian market weakened to such an extent that several openings were made for Italian, and especially for Florentine, woollen products.

Considering the data regarding the sale of Florentine cloth which we have collected, the inferior quality of the Florentine product remained, to a large extent, until the end of the 1320s, as a comparison of the prices of Florentine and *franceschi* cloth demonstrates. This same phenomenon is noticeable in another documentary form: the extensive custom and duty taxes which survive for the thirteenth and fourteenth centuries for many Italian cities. An analysis of these documents reveals that *panni franceschi* were subjected to a duty which was higher than that levied against Italian cloth and that, among the Italian products themselves, the cloth produced in Florence, Como, Milan and Verona were distinguished by their frequent appearance in these records as well as by the large total sums of duty which they were charged. In effect, these four cities represent the top level of Italian industrialisation, in so far as they were in a position to produce several types of cloth for a market which obtained for a long time. We can state, therefore, that the level of production in Florence was nearly

---

[7] For the following description, we cannot present here documentary proof. The arguments will be discussed in detail in our forthcoming book: *L'arte della lana in Firenze nel basso Medioevo. Il commercio della lana e il mercato dei panni fiorentini dei secoli XIII–XV.*

equal to that of several of the more industrially advanced cities of Lombardy. In fact, Lombard woollen cloth was imported into Florence, where it was copied or dyed by the manufacturers of that city.[8] In addition, we are aware that in Florence, cloth manufactured at Como and Milan was sold at a price which was competitive with that of the Florentine products themselves.[9] Lombard cloth was diffused, together with Florentine products, all over the Italian market, and particularly in the south where the production of higher-quality textiles was non-existent. The industrial importance of Milan during this period should not be underestimated simply because of the nearly complete absence of documentation. According to the duty estimate compiled at Milan, most probably around 1320, Milanese cloth, together with that produced at Como, was valued at £28 per piece followed by Florentine and Veronese at £24.[10]

Except for a certain amount destined for the Levant, Italian woollen cloth, Florentine included, was consumed within the ambit of the Italian peninsula and never crossed the Alpine frontiers to be marketed in the countries of north-west Europe. It was not even distributed in Germany where the development of the woollen industry was immature, because of the commercial expansion of *panni franceschi*. To this can be added the fact that the papal court at Avignon always purchased *panni franceschi* and never showed the slightest interest in Italian products. Moreover, Italian cloth within the Italian market itself always remained a product of secondary importance with regard to the general scale of prices at this time. Not even the Florentine products were an exception, and as we have already mentioned, until about 1320 one cannot speak of Florentine cloth which was competitive with the *panni franceschi*.

Only after 1320 did Florentine products begin to improve in quality. As has occurred in all phases of the history of industrialisation, Florence, which was initially backward, began this process of qualitative improvement by imitating the products of the more advanced countries. We are able to document, in a rather concrete manner, this process of imitation. The expression *panni alla francesca* appeared for the first time in the statutes of the Wool Guild (*Arte della Lana*) in 1331.[11] However, although the date of approval for these statutes is listed as 1331, we are certain that the major part of the rubric was compiled

---

[8] A. M. E. Agnoletti (ed.), *Statuto dell'Arte della Lana di Firenze (1317–19)* (Florence, 1940), pp. 119–20 and 125–6; *Archivio di Stato di Firenze*, (abbreviated *ASF*), *Arte della Lana*, n. 2, II, 32; n. 6, III, 2.

[9] Compare U. Dorini (ed.), *Statuti dell'Arte di Por Santa Maria del tempo della Repubblica*, p. 99; *Biblioteca Riccardiana, Codice*, n. 2526, c. 3; *ASF, Tribunale di Mercanzia*, n. 4120, c. 88ᵗ.

[10] A. Noto (ed.), *Liber datii mercantie Communis Mediolani. Registro del secolo XV* (Milan, 1950), pp. 16–17.

[11] *ASF, Arte della Lana*, n. 2, II, 49 and 52.

during the years 1326–27.[12] Therefore, the first mention of this
terminology should be placed within these dates, while in the preceding
statutes of 1317 this expression is not to be found.[13] In order to confirm
our dating, we can cite another document: the commercial accounts
of the Rinucci company of the Wool Guild for the years 1322–25,
where the dates for the sale or acquisition of Florentine cloth are
recorded. According to these commercial records, the Rinucci company began selling cloth *alla francesca* in May 1323, while previously
they had always sold cloth of inferior quality such as *saia* or *tritana*.
But the cloth sold by the company after this date was composed for
the most part of products labelled *mescolati* or *mischiati a la francescha*.[14]
It seems, therefore, that this type of woollen cloth was one of the
superior northern cloths which had been imitated for the first time by
the Florentine manufacturers. We shall postpone until later a discussion
of the marketing techniques of this imitation cloth in order to keep to
the logic of our argument.

II

There are several reliable documents which serve to clarify the development of the production of woollen fabrics in Florence during the first
half of the fourteenth century.

A Two notebooks kept by an official of the *Mercanzia* for the years
1321–22, where the movement of goods between Florence and Pisa
is recorded.[15] From these we can extract the value of a bale or a piece
of Florentine cloth sent to Pisa based on the duty estimates for exportation. These two notebooks are especially interesting for the information
which they contain regarding the various qualitative types of cloth
which were produced during this period, but since the registers
served only as a record of the trade between the two cities, neither the
name of the destination nor that of the sender is recorded. It is important to point out that during this period goods which were sent to
Pisa from Florence were completely free from taxes.[16] We believe,
therefore, that in the present case the duty estimates are reliable and
precise, even though, as economic historians have often noted, such
documents do not necessarily reflect the true market price of the listed
items. However, one major defect does exist in the use of these documents, in so far as the amount of cloth contained in a bale is not always

[12] *ASF, Arte della Lana*, n. 2, IV, 28: in the statute is inserted a rubric written in December 1327.
[13] *Statuto dell'Arte della Lana* (see n. 8).
[14] *ASF, Carte Del Bene*, n. 63, cc. 110–41, passim.
[15] *ASF, Tribunale di Mercanzia*, nn. 14141, 14142.
[16] Compare P. Silva, 'Intorno all'industria e al commercio della lana in Pisa' in C. M. Cipolla (ed.),
Storia dell'economia italiana. Saggi di storia economica, I (Turin, 1959), pp. 129–47.

listed. We have assumed that a bale contains four pieces of cloth; this seems to represent the *minimum* number contained in a bale, and therefore the price of a piece of cloth obtained by dividing the value registered for a bale by four represents the *maximum* level theoretically possible. This fact has been taken into account in the compilation of Table 11.1.

B   The second set of documents derive from the commercial book of the Rinucci company, which was mentioned above, and from which we have extracted sales information for cloth *alla francesca* which had been definitely produced in Florence.[17] From this data we can obtain price levels for higher-quality material which the city was itself producing during this period.

C   Thirdly, we have the commercial book of the Covoni company[18] which, in the years 1336–39, sent various types of Florentine cloth to a Paduan agency which was connected with the central Covoni company. Custom duties charged at the city gates was always included in the prices listed for this cloth. However, since this expense represented approximately 1.1 per cent of the total value during this period (a fact which is ascertainable from the other documentary sources),[19] this defect can be easily overcome.

D   Finally, we have another commercial register from the same period, and this time originating from the Bencivenni company which was located in Venice and which provides a description of the prices of cloth sent from Florence to Venice.[20] All of this information is summarised in Table 11.1.

During the years 1321–22, Florence produced a great quantity of cheap fabric, as indicated by column *A*, the qualitative level of which did not differ from that of the provincial products; in 1324 and 1332, cloth from Casentino was valued at s. 22 and s. 19 respectively per canna.[21] Based on the fact that in 1324 a certain cloth of an unknown origin was valued at s. 27 per canna and was described as *panno grosso*,[22] we can include in the category *grosso* all cloth the value of which was below s. 30 per canna. As one can see from column *D*, the production of common cloth was continued by the Florentine manufacturers throughout the 1330s and the 1340s.

On the other hand, if we compare the data from columns *B* and *C* with that of column *A*, several interesting points can be observed which

[17] *ASF, Carte Del Bene*, n. 63.
[18] A. Sapori (ed.), *Libro giallo della compagnia dei Covoni* (Milan, 1970).
[19] *ASF, Carte Del Bene*, n. 64, c. 153.
[20] *ASF, Carte Del Bene*, n. 64.
[21] *ASF, Tribunale di Mercanzia*, n. 1041, c. 8ᵗ; n. 4134, c. 109.
[22] *ASF, Tribunale di Mercanzia*, n. 1041, c. 9ᵗ.

Table 11.1   *Prices of Florentine cloth, 1321–40* (soldi a fiorini per canna)

	A 1321–22		B 1323–25		C 1336–39		D 1337–40	
	Cloth	Percent-age	Cloth	Percent-age	Cloth	Percent-age	Cloth	Percent-age
over s. 5–10	3	1						
10–15	15	3						
15–20	79	14			16	1	9	5
20–25	168	30					52	31
25–30	86	16			6	0	35	21
30–35	120	22	11	4	20	2	23	14
35–40	52	9	12	5	52	4	23	14
40–45	13	2	13	5	81	7	7	4
45–50	16	3	34	13	625	52		
50–55			128	49	279	23	10	6
55–60			28	11	117	10		
60–65			37	14				
65–70					8	1	5	3
70–75							3	2
75–80								
80–85					1	0		
Total	552		263		1205		167	

have significance with regard to our present arguments. In the years 1321–22, a great part of the cloth (68 per cent) was concentrated within the categories which range from s. 20 to s. 35 per canna, as opposed to the cloth of a much higher value of s. 45 to s. 55 per canna, which represents the major part (75 per cent) of cloth for the years 1336–39. This rise in the value of Florentine cloth during the 1320s and 1330s – nearly a doubling in value – confirms our view that the process of qualitative improvement began in the 1320s. It is necessary to remember that the value of cloth for the 1320s is probably overrated, due to those documentary difficulties which have already been mentioned. On the other hand, the documentation used for compiling column *C* is exceptionally rich with respect to the prices of Florentine cloth and merchandise sent to Padua, and it is important that these products were acquired by the Covoni company from various merchants and manufacturers. The price information which it contains is not, therefore, simply representative of a single producer but is a cross sample of several manufacturers.

Column *B* represents valuable evidence of the beginning of the improvement of Florentine cloth. If one only takes into consideration the cloth which is valued at s. 50 to s. 55, it will be seen that this alone represents nearly one-half (49 per cent) of the total, and is on a corresponding level with the cloth which constitutes the majority of column *C*. One can conclude that Florentine standard cloth, which was of an improving quality in the first half of the fourteenth century, was manufactured from products whose value per canna oscillated, generally speaking, from s. 45 to s. 55, or at the most to s. 60.

How did the price level of the standard Florentine cloth compare with the various *panni franceschi* which were sold on the same Florentine market? An answer to this question is possible, based on documents which have survived from the Del Bene commercial company – an enterprise which specialised in the sale of *panni franceschi* in Florence.[23] Although these documents refer to the years 1318–23, an examination of later sources reveals the stability of prices for *panni franceschi* after 1320, and therefore we can use this documentary source with confidence for cloth prices throughout the first half of the fourteenth century.[24]

Table 11.2   Prices for panni franceschi *sold in Florence by the Del Bene company, 1318–23* (soldi a fiorini per canna)

Origin	Price (maximum and minimum)	Origin	Price (maximum and minimum)
Douai	162–92	Caen	76–39
Malines	152–58	Orchies	68–53
Brussels	!23–85	Hondschoote	63–41
Châlons	123–63	Arras	50–49
Ghent	107–55	Paris	50–45
Ieper (Ypres)	106–43	Poperinghe	47–38
Lille	89–59	Saint-Denis	29
Alost	87–69	Ghistelles	24–21

A comparison of Tables 11.1 and 11.2 reveals that Florentine cloth in the first half of the fourteenth century never reached the high qualitative level of the textiles produced in several of the great industrial cities of Flanders and Brabant, such as Brussels, Châlons, Douai, Ghent, Malines and Ieper (Ypres). In addition, the price level of the standard Florentine cloth, that is, the improved type of

[23] A. Sapori, *Una compagnia di Calimala ai primi del Trecento* (Florence, 1932), pp. 282–303. Unfortunately, the price per canna is not available from the commercial book of the Del Bene company (cf. *Carte Del Bene*, n. 2), while the length of a piece of *panni franceschi* varies according to the types and the origins. We have utilised the average among the maximum and minimum length found in the description of the famous Pegolottian manual. F. B. Pegolotti, *La pratica della mercatura*, edited by A. Evans (Cambridge, Mass., 1936).

[24] Cf. the prices of cloth acquired by the Peruzzi for domestic use, such as the products of Brussels, Douai, Alost, Provins and Châlons. A. Sapori (ed.), *I libri di commercio dei Peruzzi* (Milan, 1934), pp. 25, 65–7, 92, 95–6, 99, 114, 146, 149, 181, 199 and 256.

this period, is in fact comparable with that from Hondschoote and Poperinghe or from Arras and Paris – the first two cities having had a secondary importance during this period, and the last two, formerly great centres of production, had already declined economically. The price of the Florentine standard cloth was nearly equal to certain kinds of cloth of secondary quality produced in the great Flemish–Brabant cities such as the *couverture* of Ieper.[25]

On this subject, we should recall the economic activity of the great Italian merchant-entrepreneurs who operated in England until the 1340s. These Italian merchants, in addition to being financiers, dealt above all in English wool. But when the Tuscan merchants such as the Riccardi, the Frescobaldi, the Bardi, the Peruzzi, and many others exported English wool to their own native city, was it not English wool of the highest quality? Given that the quality of the primary material was decisive for the production of expensive cloth, why then did there exist this great difference between the price of Florentine cloth and *panni franceschi*?

III

The importation of English wool was an early enterprise and already by 1317 there is evidence of a vast Genoese organisation established in Florence for the sale of English wool.[26] In succeeding years, there is ample documentation available, including that from the Bardi company, confirming the continuation of this commerce in English wool in Florence. However, the information which is available does not have much importance for our argument because, given its sporadic nature, it is not possible to extract any reliable statistical measurements.[27] Therefore, we have analysed this phenomenon from the qualitative point of view, which is the basis of the present study.

Of all the wool produced in the late Middle Ages, that produced in England was amongst the finest. This fact is incontestable, but it is true only in a general sense. According to Pegolotti, a Florentine merchant and author of the famous manual for merchants, English wool was classified into three categories according to its quality: *buona*, *moiana* and *locchi*.[28] In other words, English wool included several types of inferior quality which were not suited to the production

---

[25] For the price of *couverture* of Ieper (Ypres), see the same sources cited in note 23. However, we should mention that the length of this type of cloth was the half of a normal Flemish piece.

[26] R. Davidsohn, *Forschungen* (see n. 3), reg. 691.

[27] For the business of the Bardi company regarding the English wool in Italy, only two small notions for the years 1330–33 are available. A. Sapori, *La crisi delle compagnie mercantili dei Bardi e dei Peruzzi* (Florence, 1926), p. 218; G. Bigwood, 'La politique de la laine en France sous les règnes de Philippe le Bel et de ses fils', *Revue Belge de Philologie et d'Histoire*, XV (1936), p. 444, n. 2.

[28] F. B. Pegolotti, *La pratica della mercatura* (see n. 23), p. 258.

of highly valued items. In Florentine commercial documents, however, this Pegolottian classification was almost never used, but rather the terms *lana lunga*, *lana gentile*, *lana agnellina* and *boldrone* were preferred. According to the Florentine documents, it appears that the first two categories of wool (*lunga* and *gentile*) corresponded to the Pegolottian category *buona* and *agnellina* to *moiana*, while the term *boldrone* appears only in official documents as, for example, in the custom tax lists of Florence for 1326[29] or in the documents of the Wool Guild and never in ordinary commercial documents.

Although information relative to the sale of English wool is very scarce, we do know that in Florence during the first half of the fourteenth century, the importation of *agnellina* wool from England was rather common. This type of wool is frequently mentioned in the various commercial and official documents of the period. In 1316, the Albizzi company, which had extremely close ties with the Wool Guild throughout the fourteenth century, acquired 82 bales of English *agnellina* wool through a Genoese commercial firm.[30] During the years 1322–25 several Florentine merchants, including the Bardi and Peruzzi, sent to Lombardy by way of France a large amount of *agnellina* wool.[31] This type of wool is also mentioned in the brokerage taxes levied on the sale of this wool to members of the Wool Guild which are listed in the statutes of 1317, 1333 and 1338,[32] in addition to also appearing in the custom tax records of 1326.

It is also possible to document in certain cases the marketing of long wool of high quality. We know, that in addition to the Alberti company, several powerful commercial firms during the years 1323–25 had sold English long wool to the manufacturer Rinuccio di Nello Rinucci. These prices are summarised in Table 11.3 which, because of the scarcity of this kind of documentation, represents an extremely valuable source.[33]

Unfortunately, these documents do not state the place of production and we are not able to compare the prices for this type of wool with those for *agnellina* wool due to the lack of documentary information for this latter category. But calculation based on sales information for *agnellina* at Venice confirms that the price oscillated between £16 and £21 (Florentine value) during the years 1336–38.[34] From this we

[29] L. Cantini (ed.), *Legislazione toscana*, (Florence, 1800), pp. 302–3.
[30] *ASF, Notarile antecosimiano*, R 348, cc. 16–16ᵗ.
[31] G. Bigwood, 'La politique de la laine' (see n. 27).
[32] *Statuto dell'Arte della Lana* (see n. 8), pp. 86–7; *ASF, Arte della Lana*, n. 3, I, 48; n. 5, I, 50; *Legislazione toscana* (see n. 29), pp. 302–3.
[33] *ASF, Carte Del Bene*, n. 63, cc. 8ᵗ–9, 10ᵗ, 11ᵗ, 14–14ᵗ, 15ᵗ, 16ᵗ–17.
[34] *ASF, Carte Del Bene*, n. 64, cc. 162 and 175ᵗ.

Table 11.3   Prices for English long wool in Florence, 1323–25

Date	Quantity (bale)	Price (£ for 100 lb)	Importer
9 September 1323	4	25	Matteo Biliotti
11 September 1323	8	25	Rinuccio di Cocco
20 October 1323	6	28	Gualterotto de' Bardi
9 November 1323	2	24	Niccolò di Nello Rinucci
8 February 1324	6	$25\frac{3}{4}$	Gualterotto e Doffo de' Bardi
5 April 1324	5	26	Luzio Guidalotti
7 April 1324	6	33	Bernardino da Massa
14 June 1324	3 (great bales)	$27\frac{1}{2}$	Tommaso Peruzzi
21 August 1324	10	$25\frac{1}{2}$	Dino Rinieri da Massa
17 February 1325	10	25	Gualterotto e Doffo de' Bardi
? March 1325	2	$24\frac{1}{2}$	Nello Rinucci
5 March 1325	2	28	Gualterotto e Doffo de' Bardi
5 March 1325	2	24	Gualterotto e Doffo de' Bardi
11 April 1325	9	$26\frac{1}{2}$	Gualterotto e Doffo de' Bardi
8 May 1325	7	$27\frac{1}{2}$	Gualterotto e Doffo de' Bardi
23 May 1325	8	27	Gualterotto e Doffo de' Bardi
11 July 1325	6 ⎱ 2 ⎰ (great bales)	$25\frac{1}{4}$	Francesco Buonfigliuoli

are able to confirm the qualitative superiority of long wool over *agnellina* wool. However, the documents used to compile Table 11.3 included an entry for the sale of a large quantity of *agnellina* from Burgundy, which was transacted by the Peruzzi company in 1322 at £28, a price which is not far from those listed in this table.[35] The *agnellina* of Burgundy was a rather important product in both Lombardy and Tuscany at this time.[36] It also appears that one could find English long wool of mediocre quality. According to a document dated 1 November 1329 from the Alberti company, eight bales of this type of wool which were stored in a warehouse were estimated at about £13 per 100 lb, while the English black wool was valued at approximately £18.[37]

The better English wools are identified in the early-fourteenth-century documents by their place of origin. Among the few examples

[35] *ASF, Carte Del Bene*, n. 63, c. 6.
[36] G. Bigwood, 'La politique de la laine' (see n. 27), passim.
[37] A. Sapori (ed.), *I libri degli Alberti del Giudice* (Milan, 1952), p. 101.

available we find several places connected with wool production: *Bincestro* (Winchester, Hampshire), *Contisgualdo* (the Cotswolds, Gloucestershire), *Elmetta* (Elmet, Yorkshire), *Linsea* or *Lindisea* (Lindsey, Lincolnshire), *Marcia* (the Marches, Shropshire) and *Sant'Albano* (St Albans, Hertfortshire).[38] For wool from *Contisgualdo*, *Lindisea* and *Marcia* it is possible to ascertain their prices in Florence in 1334: £35 for the first and £37 for the last two at 100 lb.[39] A comparison between these prices and those listed in Table 11.3 clearly reveals the distinct quality of these famous English wools. It seems that the products of *Marcia* were even more expensive than those of *Contisgualdo*. Toward the middle of the fourteenth century, in the market of Bruges, these two types of wool cost respectively 24–24½ marks for the *Marcia* and 18 marks for the *Contisgualdo*.[40]

Various qualities of English wool were imported to Florence even after the collapse of the Bardi and Peruzzi companies in England. In addition to the purchase of the higher-quality wool already mentioned in 1344 by a group of Florentine merchants consisting of Giovanni, his son Tommaso and Francesco Dardi, Dino Burci and Piero di Bertolo Bertaletti from the Genoese commercial firm of Sismondo Grillo (31 bales of *Lindisea* and *Marcia* and 22 bales of *Contisgualdo*), we also know of a large quantity of English wool of secondary quality acquired in 1345. Jacopo di Gherardo Gentili, a Florentine merchant and formerly a member of the Peruzzi company in London, together with a certain Johannes de Bosulim, a London merchant, with whom he divided half of the profits, had arranged with a Spanish ship for transportation to Biscaia of 320 sacks of English wool (*grossa* and *agnellina*) destined for Florence.[41]

In addition to England, there was another major European centre for wool production during the Middle Ages – the western Mediterranean, from the western coast of Africa across the Iberian peninsula to southern France.[42] The wool produced in this area, as we can infer from the documents, was qualitatively inferior and commanded a

---

[38] *ASF, Carte Del Bene*, n. 64, cc. 161 and 175. The *Marcia* is not mentioned in the Pegolotti's manual. But we are sure that it regards Shropshire borderlands (the *Marches*) if we consider the highest price of the wool. Cf. E. Power, *The Wool Trade in English Medieval History* (Oxford, 1941), p. 23; T. H. Lloyd, *The Movement of Wool Prices in Medieval England*; *Economic History Review Supplement*, 6 (Cambridge, 1973), p. 71.

[39] *ASF, Tribunale di Mercanzia*, n. 1100, cc. 172–6ᵗ.

[40] *ASF, Tribunale di Mercanzia*, n. 1111, s.n. (28 June 1351).

[41] *ASF, Tribunale di Mercanzia*, n. 1105, s.n. (19 April 1348).

[42] R. Lopez, *Studi sull'economia genovese nel Medio Evo* (Turin, 1936), pp. 33–4; A. Schulte, 'Garbo und Florenz. Zur Geschichte der Wollproduktion im Mittelalter', *Zeitschrift für die gesamte Staatswissenschaft*, LVIII (1902), pp. 39–47.

much lower price. Florence often used this wool in the production of cloth throughout the thirteenth century as well as during the early decades of the fourteenth century, during the period when the importation of the higher-quality English wool was still minimal. But following this period, are we actually speaking of a total conversion of the Florentines to English wool?

The truth is that the intense activity of the Florentines in England, where the high-quality wools were selected for exportation, has given rise to this legend, which is supported by the data offered by the chronicler Giovanni Villani regarding Florentine cloth production in 1338. According to our information, there does not exist the slightest documentary evidence, even of an indirect nature, to support the theory of a quantitative superiority of English wool within the Florentine market in the first half of the fourteenth century. This is not to say, however, that we are utilising here an *argumentum ex silentio*; both in the commercial documents as well as in the statutes of the Wool Guild for the years 1317, 1331 (compiled in 1326–27), 1333 and 1338, we find mention of wool originating from the Mediterranean area,[43] and, in fact, the places of origin of the wool used in Florence during the first half of the fourteenth century were more varied than they were during the later period, including the fifteenth century.

We have compiled the following two tables to illustrate the Florentine situation with regard to the acquisition of its raw materials. Table 11.4 is based on the brokerage tax which the manufacturers had to pay to the Wool Guild for wool acquired through middlemen. Unfortunately the year 1331 is missing from the statutes because the part which contained the relative rubric has been lost.[44] Table 11.5 is compiled on the basis of the Florentine *libro di gabelle*.[45] It is not possible to date with any great precision this well-known source, but it is certain that it pertains to the first half of the fourteenth century or, at least, reflects the situation of that period, given the fact that it employs the archaic means of the English wool classification such as *agnellina* and *boldrone* and lacks any qualitative denomination which is higher than these two categories.[46]

[43] *ASF, Arte della Lana*, n. 2, II, 38 and IV, 29; n. 3, II, 37; n. 5, II, 37; A. Doren, *Die Florentiner Wollentuchindustrie vom 14. bis zum 16. Jahrhundert* (Stuttgart, 1901), pp. 507 and 509.
[44] *ASF, Arte della Lana*, n. 2.
[45] *Biblioteca Riccardiana, Codice*, n. 2526; A. Doren, *Die Florentiner Wollentuchindustrie* (see n. 43), pp. 494–6.
[46] *Ponzo* in Table 11.4 is most probably Saint-Pons de Tomière in southern France, an important commercial centre. See R. Davidsohn, *Storia di Firenze* (see n. 4), IV, 2, p. 117.

Table 11.4 Brokerage tax on the acquisition of wool, 1317–38 (soldi per 100 lb)

	Lana lunga Washed	Lana Not washed	Lana Washed	Lana agnellina Not washed	Lana agnellina Not washed	Lana agnellina Washed	Lana agnellina Washed	Boldrone Not washed
	1333, 1338	1317	1333, 1338	1317	1333, 1338	1317	1333, 1338	1317
Crete					1		$1\frac{1}{2}$	
Cyprus		1			1		$1\frac{1}{2}$	
Garbo	1		3					
Majorca					2		3	
Minorca					2		3	
Narbonne				2	2	3	3	$\frac{4}{5}$
Perpignan				2	2	3	3	
Ponzo					2		3	
Provence				1	1	2	$1\frac{1}{2}$	
Puglia				1	1	2	$1\frac{1}{2}$	
San Matteo					2		3	
Sardinia				1	1	2	$1\frac{1}{2}$	

	Washed fioretto	Lana lunga	Lana lunga	Lana agnellina	Lana agnellina
	1333, 1338	1317	1333, 1338	1317	1333, 1338
Burgundy	5	3	3	3	3
Flanders		3	3	3	3
France		3	3	3	3
Germany	5	3	3	3	3
England	5	3	3	3	3

Table 11.5   Custom tax for wool, first half of the fourteenth century (£ per 450 lb)

	Lana		Lana agnellina		Boldrone	
	Not washed	Washed	Not washed	Washed	Not washed	Washed
Cyprus	3	4½	3	4½		
Garbo	2 7/10				3	4½
Languedoc	6	6				
Majorca	6	6				
Narbonne	6	6				
Perpignan	6	6				
Provence	3	4½	3	4½		
San Matteo	6	6				
Verona	6	6				
Burgundy			9	9		
Germany	6	6				
England			9	9	6	7½

It is obviously impossible to extract from the data presented in these two tables any indication of the quantity of high-quality wool imported into Florence. However, it would be reasonable to state, given the extreme range of prices for Florentine products, that Florence during this period imported all types of wool from every wool-producing area. Mediterranean wool did not necessarily play a minor role in the manufacturing of cloth, especially if one takes into consideration the importance of cloth of the lighter type produced using local wool and destined for the various Mediterranean markets, such as the Aragonese, Barcelonean and Perpignan cloths. It was, in fact, the great variety of the origins of the raw material which was one of the major reasons why Florentine merchants were referred to during the golden age as the 'fifth element of the world'.

IV

The major Florentine products of the fourteenth century were always identified by the names of various types, such as *tintillano*, *mescolato*, *saia*, *stametto*, *tritana*, *mezzalana* and *grosso*.[47] The last three products were clearly of common quality, as is reflected in the terminology itself. The *saia* and *stametto*, on the other hand, belonged to the light

---

[47] For the definition of these various types of cloth, cf. F. Edler, *Glossary of Mediaeval terms of business, Italian series 1200–1600* (Cambridge, Mass., 1934); F. B. Pegolotti, *La pratica della mercatura* (see n. 23), (*Glossary* by A. Evans); A. Castellani (ed.), *Nuovi testi fiorentini del Dugento*, 2 vols. (Florence, 1952), (Glossario); A. Zonghi (ed.), *Statuta artis lanae terrae Fabriani (1369–1674)* (Rome, 1880), (Glossarium).

fabrics created exclusively with combed wool used as either weft or warp. It is important to note that these Florentine fabrics were for the most part diffused throughout the Italian and Levant markets during the first half of the fourteenth century,[48] and that in addition, they were not always fabrics of a modest price.

The *tintillano* and *mescolato* did not originally represent the valuable luxury fabrics *sui generis*: the first was a woollen cloth which had been dyed before being spun, while the second was a type of cloth obtained by utilising various threads which had each been dyed a separate colour, with the result that a single colour was obtained in the mixing of the different individually coloured threads.

However, in the commercial documents of the fourteenth century, the term *tintillano* is never used in reference to *panni franceschi*, even though such a form of cloth undoubtably existed in the market place of the city, but we often find the term *mescolato* (or *mischiato*) used to refer to northern products. Therefore, *tintillano* must not have been a technical term as much as a commercial or marketing expression, and was applied to a type of Florentine cloth which included *mescolato*, given that the two types of cloth share many technological elements in common, especially the dyeing of the wool before it is woven.

In the statutes of the Wool Guild for 1317, the manufacturers were already forbidden to use *loto*, a dyeing substance of inferior quality, in the preparation of *tintillano* cloth.[49] This prohibition was applied to the imitation cloth *alla francesca* only in the later statutes of 1331: *panno tintillano fiendum a la francescha*.[50] In the same statutes appears a phrase which is significant for the clarification of the characteristics of this kind of cloth: *panni qui fieret a la francescha sive cum scardassis*.[51] One can deduce from the use of the phrase *cum scardassis* that in the *tintillano* or *mescolato* cloth, the primary material was operated *cum scardassis*, that is, it was wool which had been carded for use as weft, as opposed to the types labelled *saia* and *stametto* which were always made with combed wool. That the improvement of Florentine woollen products began with the imitation of northern cloths can be reconfirmed by a rubric of the communal statutes of 1415: cloth *qui fierent more gallico, videlicet tintillanis, mescolatis, seu saggis lingias*, etc.[52]

It was always forbidden to use *agnellina* wool in the manufacturing

---

[48] Cf. the list of the Florentine cloths registered in the custom tariff of Ferrara (1326). *Statuta provisiones et decreta gabellarum civitatis Ferrariae* (Ferrara, 1624), p. 46.

[49] *Statuto dell'Arte della Lana* (see n. 8), pp. 26–7.

[50] *ASF, Arte della Lana*, n. 2, II, 52.

[51] *ASF, Arte della Lana*, n. 2, II, 49.

[52] *Statuta Populi et Communis Florentiae*, II (Fribourg, 1778), p. 198.

of the types of cloth mentioned above[53] and this indicates that *agnellina* was not adapted to the production of cloth *alla francesca* for technological reasons – that is, the difficulty of dyeing *agnellina* wool, or at least the impossibility of obtaining a profound dye deep within the fibre, as well as the difficulties connected with the process of fulling due to the extreme softness of the fibres which did not offer any resistance to this treatment.[54] *Agnellina* was the primary material used for the production of light cloths, such as *saia* and *stametto*. Therefore, the new product being produced by the Florentines in the 1320s required an adequate supply of high-quality wool which was elastic and resistant, and only England, given the geographical pattern of production, was in a position to offer this type of merchandise.

As we have already mentioned, there are no direct statistics regarding the importation of English wool into Florence. However, we can assume that from a qualitative point of view, the Florentines began importing high-quality English wool in the 1320s in connection with their imitation of the expensive northern cloths, *panni alla francesca*.

On the other hand, we cannot assume that the importation of English wool occurred either in a regular or constantly increasing pattern until the formation of the vast Flemish–Brabant industrial complex which was a major consumer of English wool. During the entire fourteenth century, Florence continued to produce various types of cloth which did not require the use of *Marcia* or *Contisgualdo* wool, and for which *agnellina* from England, Burgundy or any Mediterranean wool supplier was sufficient.

To conclude this section, we have compiled Table 11.6, which lists the various prices for Florentine cloth according to their different categories. Column *A* is based on data from the commercial book of the Bencivenni company which has already been cited,[55] while column *B* lists the cloth stored in the shop of a bankrupt merchant of Por Santa Maria, and which was estimated by a committee of merchants appointed by the *Tribunale di Mercanzia*.[56] The document does not specifically mention that these were Florentine products, but it is certain that they were made in Florence given the descriptive categories used, as well as the fact that Por Santa Maria Guild, particularly in the first half of the fourteenth century, frequently dealt in cloth manufactured in Florence.

[53] *ASF, Arte della Lana*, n. 2, 11, 52; n. 3, 11, 51; n. 5, II, 51; n. 6, II, 36.

[54] Duhamel du Monceau, *Il lanaiuolo ovvero l'arte di fabbricare i panni di lana, principalmente intorno a ciò che appartiene a' panni fini* (Florence, 1776), pp. 2 and 7.

[55] *ASF, Carte Del Bene*, n. 64, cc. 141–1ᵗ, 143, 144, 145–7ᵗ, 149ᵗ, 150ᵗ–4ᵗ.

[56] *ASF, Tribunale di Mercanzia*, n. 1070, cc. 315–18.

Table 11.6   Prices for Florentine cloth according to type-names, 1337–40 (soldi a fiorini per canna)

Cloth	A 1337–40	B 1340
tintillano	72–66	64–44
mescolato	55–53	64–46
stametto	52–40	16–14
saia cotonata	44–37	
saia lingia	37½	42
saia piana	33–22	
stametto altopascino	24½–20	
trafilato		19–17
tritana		11
taccolino		5

V

The great Flemish industrial crisis began around 1320. Ieper (Ypres), one of the most important cities within the production complex of Flanders, reached its peak in 1318. The decline itself was a gradual one, with high levels of production being maintained throughout the second half of the fourteenth century. Due to the lack of information with regard to other Flemish cities, this pattern of a gradual decline has come to be generally accepted by most historians. It is worth noting, however, that the Flemish decline was in part accentuated by the industrial activity of several cities of Brabant, such as Brussels, Malines, Leuven and perhaps Alost also. The products of Brussels and Malines were already on the point of surpassing, in terms of quality, those from the older cities of Flanders such as Douai, Ghent and Ieper.[57]

This commercial activity in Brabant was short lived, and endured only until about 1340. It is interesting to note that at this same moment, England was establishing the foundation for her long history of industrial development. Because of the reorientation of commercial activity towards her internal market, the traditional Flemish products

[57] H. van Werveke, 'De omvang van de Ieperse lakenproductie in de veertiende eeuw', *Mededeelingen van de koninklijke Vlaamsche Academie voor Wetenschappen, Klasse der letteren*, IX, 2 (Antwerp, 1946); R.-H. Bautier, 'La place de la draperie brabançonne et plus particulièrement bruxelloise dans l'industrie textile du Moyen Age', *Annales de la Société Royale d'Archéologie de Bruxelles*, LI (1962–66); R. van Uytven, *Stadsfinanciën en stadsekonomie te Leuven van de XIIᵉ tot het einde der XVIᵉ eeuw* (Brussels, 1961), pp. 353–7; idem, 'La draperie brabançonne et malinoise du XIIᵉ au XVIIᵉ siècle: grandeur éphémère et décadence', *Produzione, commercio e consumo dei panni di lana (nei secoli XII–XVIII)*, edited by M. Spallanzani (Florence, 1976).

disappeared from England around 1340.[58] More than the Flemish crisis during the last years of the thirteenth century, the period 1320–40 was a true turning point in the history of the medieval European woollen industry and was much more than simply a second industrial crisis.

Curiously, the beginning of the production of cloth *alla francesca* by Florence corresponded chronologically with the initial stages of the decline of the Flemish industry, and it is impossible not to draw the conclusion that the importation of high-quality English wool into Florence, necessary for the production of the cloth *alla francesca*, must have had some connection with the industrial situation in Flanders where the Italian merchants, and particularly the Florentines, were the major suppliers of the raw wool. In other words, the Flemish crisis had two major economic results which were directly tied to the interests of the Florentine merchants operating in Flanders and England: first, there was the loss of the Flemish market for English wool, and secondly there was the simultaneous decline in Flemish high-quality products as exported by the Italian merchants, that is, in the decline of *panni franceschi*. These economic effects would have been even more profound if the same crisis had affected the Brabant industry. Most probably the Florentine merchants were forced by these circumstances to export to their native city the only merchandise which they had in England, even though the voyage was much longer and more dangerous. English woollen cloth of this period was not yet an important export. Although the quality was rather good, it was not equal to that of the Flemish or Brabant centres, and in any case the volume was insufficient to support such a trade.

The growing scarcity of *panni franceschi*, and in particular the higher-quality varieties, within the Italian market and consequently in the Levant, was a factor of major concern not only for the Italian merchants living in northern Europe, but also for those who resided in the turbulent Calimala Street of Florence, because the city itself was a great redistribution centre of *panni franceschi* for the entire peninsula.[59] These were the circumstances which brought the Florentine economy to the edge of 'industrialisation', that is to say, to the specialised production of highly valued cloth.

It is possible to document clearly the fact that Florentine cloth, produced as an imitation of the Flemish–Brabant products, followed several specific models. For the highly valued cloth, it seems that the

---

[58] E. M. Carus-Wilson, 'Trends in the export of English woollens in the fourteenth century', *Medieval Merchant Venturers. Collected Studies*, 2nd edn (London, 1967), pp. 241–3.
[59] Cf. A. Sapori, *Una compagnia di Calimala* (see n. 23), ch. III.

products of Douai, Brussels and Malines were the examples which those Florentine specialists in the production of luxury cloth sought to imitate. A company of the Wool Guild, directed by Cione and Neri de' Pitti, an old mercantile family from the Oltrarno, sold its own products to a southern merchant in Naples in 1341. The list of these products included, in part, cloth which was identified *a modo di Borsella*, *a modo di Mellino*, and *a modo di Doagio*. These were the original names, registered in a commercial book of this company kept at Naples.[60] We can add that the cloth labelled a *modo di Doagio* of the Pitti company was the most expensive fabric produced in Florence, as many commercial documents from the early fourteenth century clearly reveal. The Florentine woollen industry, therefore, was substituting imitated products for the traditional *panni franceschi* both in the Italian market as well as that of the Levant. This gradual process of substitution also continued during the second half of the century; the documents sometimes mention Florentine cloth *a Borsella*.

In fact, with regard to the second half of the century, we have available several documents of primary importance with which to demonstrate the continuous acquisition on the part of the Florentines of the higher-quality English wools. One example is provided by the Del Bene company, which specialised in the high-quality *tintillano* cloth. The agency acquired between 28 April 1355 and 7 July 1368 a total of 147944 lb of wool, and produced 2023 pieces of cloth. Except for a small proportion which was Burgundian wool (1959 lb), the rest was English wool of the highest quality, such as *Marcia* or *Contisgualdo*.[61] Another example comes from the Lucchese company of Guinigi which sold in Florence a large quantity of the same kind of wool to various manufactures in 1369–70;[62] the fine wool was imported continuously in the city even after the Ciompi's revolt of 1378.[63]

It seems, therefore, that the prices for English wool imported in Florence throughout the period remained high. The reason for this can certainly be traced, in part, to the famous customs policy passed by England shortly after the beginning of the Hundred Years War.[64] On the basis of the Florentine documents, however, it does not appear that this policy vitally affected its woollen industry; generally speaking,

[60] *ASF, Tribunale di Mercanzia*, n. 1076, cc. 10–10ᵗ; n. 1090, cc. 13–13ᵗ, 39ᵗ–41ᵗ; n. 4165, cc. 54–5; n. 4166, s.n. (29 October 1342).

[61] *ASF, Carte Del Bene*, n. 5, passim; n. 12, cc. 1–4ᵗ.

[62] *ASF, Tribunale di Mercanzia*, n. 1157, cc. 107ᵗ–112, 132–7ᵗ.

[63] *Archivio di Stato di Prato, Datini*, n. 1186, cc. 59, 66, 79; n. 1187, cc. 187, 194ᵗ, 234ᵗ, 255–5ᵗ, 260ᵗ, 264ᵗ, 271.

[64] E. M. Carus-Wilson and O. Coleman, *England's Export Trade 1275–1547* (Oxford, 1963), pp. 194 and 196.

it was in the second half of the century that many manufacturers specialised in the luxury cloth utilising the English wool of fine type.

Without a doubt, these new taxes certainly affected prices for wool of an inferior quality, because in the customs assessment the quality of the wool was not considered. Therefore, it might also have been that the diminished volume of business in England forced the Florentine merchants to concentrate their economic interests in high-quality wool for exportation – a situation completely the opposite of that which occurred in the first half of the century when they were involved in the exportation of every kind of English wool.

But was it only for these purely 'economic' motives that the Florentine merchants of the second half of the century continued to export to their country the best English wool? We ask ourselves how the workshop could have operated without anticipating, to some degree, the market within which its products would realise their economic potential. We believe that there was a continuation of this activity for a very precise reason, which was determined by the structure of the cloth market during this period: the acquisition of high-quality primary material was the *conditio sine qua non* of the woollen industry of Florence, finding itself, as it did, faced with a market both in Italy and the Levant wherein highly valued cloth was in short supply. Although several examples of the presence of Brabant cloth, such as that produced at Alost, Brussels and Malines, are documented as existing in the Florentine market at rather high prices when compared to the preceding epoch,[65] the process of imitation has greatly advanced in Florence with the passage of time. By 1388–90 several examples of Florentine cloth *a Borsella* can be found in the inventories of the workshops of a few manufacturers, along with quality cloth dyed in grain.[66]

Therefore, the collapse of the so-called *grande draperie* of northern Europe at the end of the fourteenth century was certainly fortunate for the Florentine woollen industry and from this moment onwards, the Arno city achieved an almost total monopoly over the Mediterranean world, or more exactly in the Italian and Levant markets, in terms of luxury cloth, and in the commercial documents of the period there begin to appear references to the famous *panno di San Martino*, that is, cloth manufactured, by definition, with the fine-quality English wool and deriving its name from the neighbourhood of medieval Florence which specialised in the production of this quality fabric. It seems that only the cloth manufactured at Milan and Venice can be

---

[65] *ASF, Carte Del Bene*, n. 6, cc. 53ᵗ, 79Gᵗ, 79Rᵗ and 79Tᵗ.
[66] *ASF, Pupilli avanti il Principato*, n. 1, cc. 135ᵗ, 282ᵗ–3, 425ᵗ–6.

considered at all equal to the quality products which the Florentines placed on the Italian market during the second half of the century.[67]

We should add, in closing, that the manufacturing of products which employed Mediterranean wool continued in Florence, and simultaneously with the creation of the *San Martino* cloth category, the Mediterranean products acquired the name of *Panno di Garbo*. Such standardisation of products – *San Martino* and *Garbo* – was the result of a long and gradual evolution of the Florentine woollen industry in the fourteenth century.

[67] Cf. T. Bini, *I lucchesi a Venezia. Alcuni studi sopra i secoli XIIIe–XIV, parte seconda* (Lucca, 1856), pp. 398–9 (doc. XI, 8) and 404–5 (doc. XI, 10).

12 The Woollen Industry in Catalonia in the Later Middle Ages
Manuel Riu[*]

The study of the woollen textile industry in medieval Catalonia has not undergone any significant new developments in the years that have passed since Miguel Gual Camarena, the author of other important works on the subject, presented his detailed paper in Prato in April 1970 on the available source materials and bibliography.[1] In this paper, published six years later together with those of Claude Carrère,[2] Francisco Sevillano,[3] and Valentín Vázquez de Prada and Pedro Molas Ribalta[4] (all of which examine different aspects of the Catalan, Aragonese and Majorcan woollen industries), can be seen the progress that has been made towards a better understanding of the origins and growth of woollen textile manufacture in the area and the period that concern us. These studies also make it unnecessary for me to include here the earlier bibliography relevant to many aspects of the subject.

[*] *Translator's note*: This article has been translated from Castilian, but the numerous Catalan terms and expressions in the original have been retained for obvious reasons; an English translation of these has been provided in parentheses.

I have been very greatly assisted in my work by my father, Jack Walker, who put a lifetime's experience of the woollen industry at my disposal and spent much time patiently explaining to me the different processes involved in cloth-manufacture. I am also deeply indebted to Margaret Johnson of the British Library's Department of Printed Books, who not only helped me with bibliographical problems, but also read the whole typescript and made several valuable suggestions for its improvement. Neither of these persons, of course, is responsible for any inaccuracies and infelicities that may remain. (*Roger M. Walker*)

[1] M. Gual, 'Orígenes y expansión de la industria textil lanera catalana en la Edad Media' in Marco Spallanzani (ed.), *Produzione, commercio e consumo dei panni di lana (nei secoli XII–XVIII)*. Atti della Seconda Settimana di Studio, 1–16 aprile 1970, Istituto di Storia Economica F. Dantini, Prato, Pubblicazioni, II (Florence, 1976), (hereafter *Produzione*), pp. 511–23. Other papers in the collection, by R. Carande and J.-P. Le Flem, deal with the Castilian woollen industry.

[2] 'La draperie en Catalogne et en Aragon au XVe siècle', ibid., pp. 475–509. This author also includes a detailed study of the textile industry in Barcelona between 1380 and 1462 in her book *Barcélone, centre économique à l'époque des difficultés, 2 vols.* (Paris, 1967), esp. pp. 421–528.

[3] 'Artesanía textil de la lana mallorquina (siglos XIV–XV)' in *Produzione*, pp. 537–52.

[4] 'La industria lanera en Barcelona (siglos XVI–XVIII)', ibid., pp. 553–65.

It cannot be said, however, that research into the origins and development of the woollen textile industry in Catalonia and into various related topics is – except in certain specific cases – in any sense complete, in view of the mass of unedited documentation preserved in the archives both of Catalonia and of other countries which, like the Archivo Dantini in Prato, could much improve our overall knowledge of the subject.

Origins of the woollen industry in Catalonia: the domestic phase

In the medieval period it is possible to discern in the Catalan woollen industry two distinct phases, which are clearly delimited by the reorganisation which began in the fourteenth century. The first phase, the domestic or family phase, can be traced back to the eleventh century through indirect evidence such as toponomy, which has preserved for us the place-name *Vila-mantells* (town of blankets), founded or at least supported by a monastery of Mozarabic origin, Sant Llorenç de Morunys, which existed in the eleventh century and which was also to establish a *Villa-de-olleriis*, specialising, as the name implies, in the manufacture of stoneware. This case of a monastery in the high Middle Ages supporting two manufacturing centres specialising in the production of woollen cloth and of pottery, which arose close to the monastery but which were clearly separate from it, is not, in our view, unique. At all events, it leads us to seek the possible origins of the Catalan textile industry in the busier rural centres of the Pyrénées or Pre-Pyrénées, where the sheep which provided the essential raw material were plentiful, and especially in the monasteries, which certainly figured among such centres.[5]

The present state of our research does not allow us to trace the development of these local manufacturing centres step by step. We do, however, have scattered pieces of evidence which, for example, confirm the presence in El Vallès of a dyer called Ennecò in the year 1052, of a weaver named Llop Sanç in 1057, and of a draper or clothier called Pere in 1164.[6] These facts alone testify to the existence of a woollen industry as early as the middle of the eleventh century in the upper Cardenar and lower Llobregat valleys, two Catalan regions closely connected with one another. Moreover, in Vic the existence of woollen cloth production can be traced back to 1060.[7] In Llagostera

[5] See M. Riu, 'La villa franca de Sant Llorenç dels Piteus y su antigua industria lanera', *Pirineos* (Zaragoza), VI, nos. 17–18 (1950), pp. 535–47.
[6] See Mn. J. Mas, *Libri Antiquitatum* (Barcelona, 1909–14), rubrics 643, 717 and 1875 respectively.
[7] Biblioteca de Catalunya (Barcelona) (hereafter BC), MS 729, vol. I, 85.

and Caldes de Malavella also, in the first half of the twelfth century, there were many young weavers,[8] even though the local industry there was going through a difficult period owing to the depredations of a nobleman, who took advantage of the Count's absence to harass his subjects. It seems, then, that working in the textile trade offered certain economic attractions to the young people in the countryside, and if this was the case, the manufacture of cloth had probably already gone beyond the purely domestic circle.

There is evidence for the existence of fairs and markets in different towns in Catalonia, from Seu d'Urgell down to Barcelona, from the eleventh century onwards, and for the possible use of the system of compound interest in Barcelona from the beginning of the eleventh century.[9] Fairs and markets, as they developed during the twelfth and thirteenth centuries, must have encouraged the national cloth trade as well as stimulating local production. For information on the commercial practices of twelfth-century Catalonia, especially with regard to maritime trade, mercantile societies and some features of an incipient capitalism, one should consult the works of Dom Agustín Altisent,[10] especially the thought-provoking study which postulates the existence at the end of the twelfth century of a workshop in Lérida belonging to Nicolau de Sarlat, which was engaged in the production of cloth, probably made of a mixture of hemp and wool, as was to become normal practice in other places in the interior of Catalonia.[11] The blending of hemp and wool for the manufacture of cloths intended for the markets in the mountains could well be an innovation brought from Sarlat, in Périgord, where the production of such cloths was already known at this period.

There is one exceptional piece of needlework from this period, the famous 'Tapestry of the Creation', recently restored and preserved in the Cathedral Museum of Gerona. This tapestry, which was executed at the beginning of the twelfth century, probably in the Gerona area, is carefully embroidered with strands of different-coloured wools,

[8] Archivo de la Corona de Aragón (Barcelona) (hereafter ACA), document of Ramón Berenguer IV, quoted by E. de Hinojosa, *La cuestión agraria* . . . (Barcelona, 1905), p. 271 n. 1.

[9] See G. Feliu, 'Interès compost en un document barceloní de l'any 1011?', *Estudios Históricos y Documentos de los Archivos de Protocolos* (Barcelona, 1978), VI, pp. 75–83. C. Batlle, 'Sobre la fira de Barcelona (segle XIII)', *Cuadernos de Arqueología e Historia de la Ciudad* (Barcelona, 1977), XVII, pp. 129–39, collects bibiographical and documentary references to markets and fairs in Catalonia. See also P. Bertrán Roige, 'Concessió de mercat i fira a Vilanova de Corbins per Pere el Catòlic (1213)', *Cuadernos de Historia Económica de Cataluña* (Barcelona, 1977), XVI, pp. 7–10.

[10] Especially 'Comerç marítim i capitalisme incipient. Episodis de la vida econòmica d'un matrimoni tarragoní (1191–1203)' in R. Saladrigues (ed.), *Miscel.lània Històrica Catalana* (Abadía de Poblet, 1970), pp. 161–80.

[11] 'Una societat mercantil a Catalunya a les darreries del segle XII', *Boletín de la Real Academia de Buenas Letras de Barcelona*, XXXII (1967–68), pp. 45–65.

which is evidence of excellent wool-dyeing techniques. It is clear that it was the existence of such techniques which later permitted the importation of undyed cloths to be dyed and finished in Catalonia. Fulling mills along the rivers Ter and Segre, near to Gerona and Lérida, are known to have existed in the twelfth century; Lérida was celebrated for the excellence of its dyeing in the early thirteenth century and Barcelona in the mid-thirteenth century. From the beginning of the thirteenth century there are more frequent references to woollen centres, apprenticeship indentures, weavers, dyers and fullers, as well as to the construction of new fulling mills and to different quality cloths. Nevertheless, it is surprising that there is a dearth of definite references to the woollen industry in Barcelona before 1253.[12]

The 1258 *lleuda* (a form of purchase tax) accounts for Cambrils, in the Camp de Tarragona, studied by Gual, record the dyestuffs arriving in the area, and these point to a not inconsiderable activity in textile production and dyeing: kermes, indigo, lake, vermilion, quicksilver, orpiment, gall, orcil, alum, woad from Languedoc, antimony, verditer, etc., as well as fuller's earth, and raw materials for textile manufacture.[13] In the Barcelona exchange-brokers' tariff, drawn up in 1271, it was laid down that on every *quintal* (46 kgs) of wool the buyer and the vendor would pay 1 *diner* tax, and there would be a further charge of 1 *diner de reva* (a tax paid by the buyer to the owner of the premises where the transaction took place); a similar amount would be levied on a *quintal* of hemp yarn.[14] We know that cloths arrived in Barcelona from Flanders, Arras, Paris, England, Bruges, Valenciennes, Béziers, Narbonne, Châlons, Provins, St Omer, Montelieu (in the district of Carcassonne), from various places in Catalonia, such as Lérida, Sant Daniel and Valls, and also from Valencia, all with a minimum piece-length of ten *canes* (16 metres). In the *lleuda* accounts for Valencia during the thirteenth, fourteenth and fifteenth centuries, there are listed imports of wool and cloth from Avignon, Arras (a Flemish town from which a fine-quality woollen cloth called *staminis fortis* was imported), Narbonne, Genoa and other places, among them once again Lérida, which shows the wide market already reached by Lérida cloth, stretching at least from Barcelona

[12] See A. D[urán] S[anpere], 'Historia industrial de Barcelona. Fabricación de paños en los siglos XIII, XIV y XV' in A. Durán Sanpere (ed.), *Divulgación histórica de Barcelona* (Barcelona, 1946), II, pp. 123–7.

[13] M. Gual, 'La lezda de Cambrils (1258)', *Boletín Arqueológico* (Tarragona, 1966), LXVI, pp. 113–28.

[14] See J. Corominas, 'Tarifa dels corredors de Barcelona l'any 1271' in F. Pierce (ed.), *Hispanic Studies in Honour of I. González Llubera* (Oxford, 1959), pp. 119–27.

to Valencia.[15] However, the cash-flow could not have been very great, since in Barcelona from the middle of the thirteenth century cloth was sold on credit, payable in monthly instalments. This credit-buying suggests that cloth sales had reached a consumer market which had only limited resources, but which was reacting to social pressure.

The tariffs of the Montblanc fair of 1281 and the *lleuda* accounts of Cotlliure for 1317 (the latter published by Jaume Sobrequés), besides mentioning specifically the importation of cloth from Avignon, Genoa, France and Arras, on which was paid a tax of 4 *diners* per piece, whatever its provenance, also mention Lérida cloth, on which 2 *diners* was paid, and other local cloths, fustians and serges, which realised 1 *diner* per piece. The duty on a bale of wool weighing 3 *quintals* was 1 *sou* and 6 *diners*.[16]

In all these tax accounts and tariffs, as well as in the records of foreign cloths – principally French and Flemish, but also English and Italian – one finds evidence of a home market for local cloths and of dealings in raw materials, particularly wool, scouring agents and dyestuffs (principally for blue, red, green and black dyes), and also implements for spinning, carding and combing wool, all of which testifies to a steady growth in the manufacture of woollen textiles. Examples of this growth could be multiplied simply by referring to published work on the subject, but we do not feel this to be necessary.

The increasing importance of dealings in locally manufactured woollen cloths at Catalan fairs in the fourteenth and fifteenth centuries is clearly shown in the concessions and privileges granted at the fairs of Cervera and Cardona.[17] These are but one example of the demarcations drawn up in order to prevent a clash of interests.

Origins of the woollen industry in Catalonia: the industrial phase

Until the early part of the fourteenth century, the Catalonian consumer market was dominated by foreign textiles. Its own products were destined only for the rural markets, with rare exceptions, such as Lérida cloths. In the urban markets and fairs one tended to find foreign products, mainly Flemish, French and Brabantine, which were

[15] See M. Gual, 'Arancel de lezdas y peajes del reino de Valencia (siglo XV)', *Anuario de Historia Económica y Social* (Madrid, 1968), I, p. 685; ibid. (1969), II, pp. 32 and 34.

[16] For the fair of Montblanc, see ACA Cancillería, Reg. 44, fol. 200ᵛ; and *Memorias de la Real Academia de Buenas Letras* (1901), VI, p. 553. For Cotlliure, see J. Sobrequés, 'La lleuda de Cotlliure de 1317' in *Cuadernos de Historia Económica de Cataluña: Primer trimestre del curso 1969–70* (Barcelona, 1970), pp. 65–84.

[17] See M. Gual, 'La feria de Cervera y sus privilegios (siglo XIV)' in F. Udina (ed.), *Homenaje a Martínez Ferrando, Archivero* (Madrid, 1968), pp. 181–196.

more sought after by the town-dwellers because of their superior quality. The ships which transported these cloths, whether Catalan or foreign, were usually of medium size: their average tonnage, until the early part of the fourteenth century, was only some 150 tons.[18] Even at the end of the fourteenth century, despite all the advances made in commercial navigation, one finds references to ships of 600 *botti* (about 450 present-day tons), although there existed ships of twice that tonnage.

The origin of the woollen mills in Catalonia in the early part of the fourteenth century was largely brought about, as Juan Reglá has pointed out, by the harassment which the Catalan merchants who bought cloth in France suffered at the hands of French royal officials between 1283 and 1313.[19] This harassment was due to the political tensions which existed at the time between the Crown of Aragon and France. The Catalan merchants used to take to France horses, silver plate, and ready cash, in order to buy good-quality cloths, mainly woollens, both dyed and undyed. This thirty-year period of disruption to the normal supply of textiles culminated in the French being forbidden to accept Catalan currency, to advise Catalan merchants in their purchase of cloth,[20] to form business associations with Catalans, and to sell them undyed cloth, so as to prevent them from dyeing it red in Catalonia. All this was more than enough to encourage the manufacture in Catalonia of products that could only with great difficulty and at considerable expense (tolls, taxes, entry and exit dues, stamp duties, etc.) be obtained in Marseilles or in Montpellier (since the journey through Aigues Mortes was unavoidable), especially since Catalan and Valencian buyers still sought them.

These difficulties caused an immediate drop in imports, and as cloth became scarcer and as there was no fall in demand, prices rose in the Catalan urban markets. The value of a ship's cargo varied between 400 and 600 *lliures* (pounds), and the losses alleged by the merchants in one of their complaints to the king amounted to over

---

[18] Licences granted to Spaniards in England to export wool were still rare in 1273, at which date one has the names of only seven Spaniards, and these seven were exporting wool from England to Flanders, not to Spain, because they could make bigger profits that way. The profit could be as high as twenty times the original cost. See T. Lloyd, *The English Wool Trade in the Middle Ages* (Cambridge, 1977), pp. 50 and 58. Touchard has observed that Spanish merchants who went to Britain used to go principally to Wales in the early days, although never in great numbers; on the other hand, in Bristol they outnumbered the Bretons from the end of the fourteenth century and throughout the fifteenth; see H. Touchard, 'Marins bretons et marins espagnols dans les ports anglais à la fin du Moyen Age', *Cuadernos de Historia* (Madrid, 1968), II, pp. 81–91.

[19] 'El comercio entre Francia y la Corona de Aragón en los siglos XIII y XIV y sus relaciones con el desenvolvimiento de la industria textil catalana' in Instituto de Estudios Pirenaicos, *Actas del Primer Congreso Internacional de Pireneistas* (Zaragoza, 1950), pp. 1–22.

[20] See H. Finke, *Acta Aragonensia* (Berlin–Leipzig, 1923), III, doc. 70, pp. 155–62.

5600 *lliures*. The local textile industry, which at first was ill-equipped to supply the markets with products of equivalent quality, was forced to make a great effort to modernise itself very rapidly and change the domestic structure, a change that was difficult and never totally achieved.

In this connection there is a very significant letter written by the bailiff of Barcelona, Romeu de Marimón, on 13 April 1304, to King James II of Aragón, in which he informs the king that in various parts of the city of Barcelona there had been set up in recent years *grans companyîes* (large concerns) for the manufacture of *draps de lana* (woollen cloths), that weavers of both sexes had arrived from other countries, that the buildings required for the development of the industry had been constructed, that the quality of their products was approaching that of the French ones, and that their prices were cheaper; all of which should enable them to win markets in the kingdom of Castile. [21] The reference to the construction of new buildings may imply large factories with several weaving-sheds, warehouses, dye-houses, etc., but the texts do not provide further details.

Although the treaties signed by Philip IV and James II in April and May 1313 put an end to the dispute between France and the Crown of Aragon, and although the harassment of Catalan merchants stopped, in the intervening years the expansion achieved by the Catalan woollen industry had become irreversible. It seems, therefore, misguided to attribute, as Wolff has done, an alleged decline in the Catalan cloth trade to the French prohibition of 1318 (withdrawn in 1333), although it may temporarily have adversely affected Perpignan, where 40 000 pieces a year from various sources were finished. [22]

Alongside the consideration of this expansion of the woollen textile industry in Catalonia, one should also take into account the imposition of the *bolla* which, from the end of the thirteenth century (from 1289?) until its abolition in 1770, placed a duty on both foreign and home-produced cloths as they entered or left the country. This was payable at the time of inspection and a lead or wax seal was affixed at one of the various *taulas* or tax-offices situated in twenty-seven Catalan towns, some on the frontiers, some in the interior: Barcelona, Lérida, Gerona, Perpignan, Sant Joan de les Abadesses, Olot, Empúries, Camprodón, Figueres, Vic, Manresa, Berga, Tàrrega, Ripoll, Tarragona, Mont-blanc, Cervera, Vilafranca del Penedès, Pallars, Tortosa, Puigcerdà, Cardona, Seu d'Urgell, Prades, Bagà, Castellbó and Santa Coloma

[21] See J. E. Martínez Ferrando, *Jaime II de Aragón, sus hijos y su vida familiar* (Barcelona, 1948), II, p. 463.

[22] See P. Wolff, 'Esquisse d'une histoire de la draperie en Languedoc du XIIe au XVIIIe siècle' in *Produzione*, pp. 435–65.

de Queralt. From 1363, or perhaps earlier, these were the most important centres of woollen manufacture in Catalonia. The Catalan government received the duty, which was set at 4 *sous* for a piece of cloth up to 12 *canes* (about 20 metres) in length, plus 4 *diners* for every *palmo* (about 8 inches) by which it exceeded this length.[23] It has been estimated that this duty brought in an annual revenue of some 40 000 *lliures* in the first third of the fifteenth century, which would presuppose a production or sale of at least 200 000 pieces of cloth a year.[24]

With regard to the collection of other taxes by the different municipalities, particularly from the fourteenth century onwards, one should consult the work of José María Font y Rius on the economic administration of the Catalan towns, with special reference to Barcelona, Manresa and Vic.[25]

The Church was also, to a certain extent, able to benefit from this expansion of the woollen industry, since the demand for wool inevitably led to an increase in the size of flocks and in the need for summer and winter pasturage, with a consequent increase in the returns on grazing land.[26] In this respect, it is worth noting the judgement given in April 1307 by Ramón Embestat, the Judge of Cerdaña, in favour of Bernat Ferrer, the priest of the church of Santa María del Castell in Bagà, by which the heirs of Pere de Prat were ordered to make over to the priest half the wool from 1000 sheep which for five years (that is, from 1302) had been grazing in the Serra del Cadí.[27] The fact that the Bagà area supplied wool to the new Catalan drapers is attested by a contract of 30 November 1322, by which Jaume Ralter, a cloth-manufacturer from Manresa, acquired in that town in upper Llobregat 90 pounds of pure wool to be shorn from the rams and ewes of a flock that was still at pasture.[28]

From the first decades of the fourteenth century industrial development advanced rapidly, not only in Catalonia, but also in Majorca and Aragon, both great centres of wool production and of exporting of wool to Catalonia. Between 1302 and 1319 weavers and dyers from

[23] See F. Torrella Niubó, 'El impuesto textil de la bolla en la Cataluña medieval', *Hispania* (Madrid, 1954), LVI, pp. 339–64.

[24] This figure is not as exorbitant as it seems if we remember that in the three mountain woollen-manufacturing centres alone (Bagà, Pobla de Lillet and Ripoll) in the mid-fifteenth century there were about two hundred heads of families engaged in the textile industry, representing 46 per cent, 39 per cent and 53 per cent respectively of the total population of those places (see Carrère, 'La draperie en Catalogne' – see n. 2 above).

[25] 'Órganos y funcionarios de la administración económica en las principales localidades de Cataluña' in *Finances et comptabilité urbaines du XIIIe au XVIe siècle. Historische Uitgaven*, VII (1964), pp. 257–78.

[26] See M. Riu, 'Transhumància de la Vall de Lord a les comarques centrals de Catalunya', in C[entre] E[studis] C[omarcals] d'I[gualada], *Actas y Comunicaciones de la I Asamblea Intercomarcal de Investigadores del Penedès y Conca d'Odena* (Martorell, 1950), pp. 150–60.

[27] ACA, Consejo de Ciento, Beneficios eclesiásticos, doc. 10.

[28] See J. M. de Mas y Casas, *Ensayos históricos sobre Manresa* (Manresa, 1882), p. 157.

Puigcerdà and Perpignan came to Manresa, at the confluence of the rivers Llobregat and Cardener, and proceeded to ply their trade there. In Barcelona at the same period English wool was already being used, and figures relating to production costs, employment of manpower, and profits were being worked out. It was calculated at that time that twenty workshops could make enough money to support five hundred people, and that the profit was in the region of 60 per cent, after the costs of buying raw materials and dyestuffs and labour costs had been deducted. This estimated profit margin seems rather optimistic if we remember that commercial profits in these same two decades did not usually exceed a maximum of 20 per cent, and not infrequently only reached 10 or 12 per cent. This was because, despite the fact that a *quintal* (46 kgs) of wool cost no more than 32 *sous*, and that half a *quintal* would be sufficient to weave a piece 15 *canes* (about 25 metres) in length, the 12 pounds of kermes necessary to dye such a piece could cost up to 36 *lliures*.

Nevertheless, it is clear that in 1334 six textile centres in the interior (Bagà, Berga, Sant Daniel, Valls, Pobla de Lillet and Sant Llorenç de Morunys) were exporting their products not only to the other territories of the Crown of Aragon, particularly to the Aragonese north-east, but also to Castile. And ten other more important centres (Banyoles, Barcelona, Bellpuig, Lérida, Manresa, Perpignan, Puigcerdà, Ripoll, Sant Joan de les Abadesses, and Vilafranca de Conflent) were sending theirs to the ports and great markets of the western Mediterranean (Almería, Genoa, Pisa, Naples, Palermo), the eastern Mediterranean (Rhodes, Beirut, Damascus, Famagusta, Alexandria), and particularly north Africa (Tunis), with a piece of cloth fetching on average between 10 and 15 gold florins, from the mid-fourteenth to the mid-fifteenth century.

The municipal by-laws usually lay down the conditions under which cloth-dealings are to be transacted. Those of the town of Falset in 1348, for example, after specifying how much could be charged, according to the quality of the cloth, by the merchants or brokers (*corredors de drap*) 'who pass through the town carrying cloth on their backs' (*que porten roba a coll per vila a vendrer*), state explicitly that no one may deal in his own cloth or in any cloth in which he may have a share.[29] After the disruption caused by the Black Death in 1348, monarchs were obliged to rule on the competence of those who practised as drapers. Peter III did so in 1349 in an attempt to prevent the damage being done by incompetent drapers in Barcelona.[30]

[29] BC, MS 729, vol. IV, pp. 560ff.
[30] ACA, Cancillería, Reg. 961, of Peter the Ceremonious, fol. 129ᵛ.

However, although the public weighers and town councillors laid down standards and prohibitions to guarantee the quality of Catalan products and prevent frauds,[31] Court officials continued to wear cloth from Saint Denis or Narbonne, as the Treasury accounts show. Fine cloths were now being manufactured in Catalonia, but the Royal Household still preferred foreign goods.

In fact, the export of Catalan cloths abroad did nothing to stop the continued importation into Catalonia of high-quality foreign cloths. Consequently, with a view to protecting local products, the Cortes (parliament) which met in Barcelona in 1365 levied duties, which varied between 40 and 60 *sous* a piece, on all cloths coming into Catalonia from Malines, Florence, Brussels, Leuven, Ieper (Ypres), Bruges, Kortrijk (Courtrai), and other places in Flanders and France. Cloths made from English wool were charged a duty of only 20 *sous* and those from Languedoc a mere ten.[32] All cloths had to bear the wax seal of the customs-office where payment of the duty had been made.

As the exports and imports of woollen cloths continued to increase, a development took place in Spain which, as Roberto S. López pointed out, once its effect was felt on the peninsular raw materials, was to produce great changes in the woollen industry and the wool trade, since it both increased the exports of wool to other countries and also enabled the quality of home-produced cloths to be improved at less cost. This development was the cross-breeding of coarse-woolled ewes with north-African fine-woolled rams, which produced in the mid-fourteenth century, a new strain of sheep, the merino, whose wool was of a sufficiently fine quality to compete in international markets. Soon Italy began to import significant quantities of Spanish wool. The Medicis, through their agent Andrea dei Pazzi, the Manellis, the Alessandris, the da Uzzanos, and the Datinis, among others, set up agencies in Barcelona.[33] The role of Barcelona, however, in this traffic was a minor one, because the wool which was particularly sought after in Italy, and especially in Florence, came from Minorca, Majorca and the Maestrazgo (the northern area of the province of Valencia). In the markets of northern Europe Spanish wools, mainly from Castile,

[31] Archivo Histórico de la Ciudad de Barcelona (hereafter AHCB), Ordinacions especials, Llibre del Mostaçaf de Barcelona, vol. I, fol. 24ᵛ (1352), fol. 51ᵛ (1353), fol. 72ʳ (1354). These concern the prohibition of wool-spinning in the Pescatería area, near to the basilica of Santa María del Mar, which was under construction.

[32] See *Cortes de Cataluña*, Academia de la Historia edn (Madrid, 1899), II, 390.

[33] See F. Melis, 'La lana della Spagna mediterranea e della Barberia occidentale nei secoli XIV–XV' in Marco Spallanzani (ed.), *La lana come materia prima: Atti della Prima Settimana di Studio*, Istituto di Storia Economica F. Dantini, Prato, Pubblicazioni I (Florence, 1974), pp. 241–51, esp. p. 242.

did not begin to compete favourably with English wools until later. In Bruges, at the beginning of the fifteenth century, Spanish wools were still regarded as being of only average quality, and they were used, like Scottish wools, to make serges or lower-quality textiles, whilst some Spanish merchants, who exported English wools to the Mediterranean countries, obtained immunity from customs duty in England, as the records from the third decade of the fifteenth century clearly show. On the other hand, with the decline of Ieper (Ypres) at the end of the fifteenth century, the purchase of Spanish wool increased in Bruges (1494), and the new Flemish drapers expanded their exports to the Mediterranean area. Spanish wool was adopted for use in Ghent, Brussels and Malines, and eventually replaced English wool in Bruges in 1544.[34]

These changes in the international wool trade should not make us forget the efforts that were being made at the same time to encourage and control the textile industries at home, in particular the Catalan woollen industry, to which we now turn our attention. Although throughout the fourteenth century there was no shortage of measures designed to regulate the practice of the different textile crafts – measures drawn up by the craftsmen themselves – as we shall see, from the end of the fourteenth century the intervention of the municipal authorities in the different manufacturing centres was becoming more and more obtrusive and oppressive. The Consell de Cent (Council of One Hundred) in Barcelona, for example, on 17 November 1416 fixed cloth measurements at '12 *ramos*, each of which must measure exactly 13 *palms*, so that the piece would measure 19 and a half *canes* in the warp'. This apparently innocuous decree, aimed at standardising the length of pieces, basically profited the drapers and finishers at the expense of the weavers, since the latter, who received a fixed price per piece, were obliged to make the pieces longer, which benefited those who supplied the raw materials and those who took the pieces for finishing. How had this come about? Simply because those who made the municipal decisions, through being members of the Council, were the drapers, not the weavers. Local politics influenced economic decisions and affected industrial production, benefiting one social group at the expense of another which was dependent on it. Political considerations and economic interests led to the resolutions of the Cortes of 1422 and to the general decrees of 1424, which were the key measures taken to reorganise the cloth

---

[34] See J. H. Munro, *Wool, Cloth and Gold: The Struggle for Bullion in Anglo-Burgundian Trade 1340–1478* (Brussels, 1972), pp. 4–5, 86, 183. In 1776 Adam Smith would write that all fine cloths are woven from Spanish wool and that English wool could not be mixed with it without a loss of quality.

industry in Barcelona with a view to putting an end to a protracted crisis.

The divergence of interests which had arisen in the meantime, since the second half of the fourteenth century, between the different sectors of the textile industry, and even within the woollen sector itself because of the increasingly greater specialisation within the trade, brings us now to a consideration of a still largely unexplored aspect of the question, namely the effect of the *confrarias* (charitable brother-hoods) on industrial problems. *Confrarias* and guilds are constantly spoken of and written about as if they were parallel institutions, without any recognition of the fact that, even if their evolution was parallel, their interests were often opposed. The growth of the *confrarias* of artisans in the last decades of the fourteenth century and the first decades of the fifteenth, under the protection of the Crown and with the support of the more restless elements in the Church (particularly the Franciscan and Dominican communities), was due to the control that the municipal authorities had succeeded in gaining over the guilds. Consequently, the new *confrarias*, which brought artisans together for religious or social purposes, did not neglect the opportunity to unite their members also for industrial purposes so that they could, when the need arose, defend their own interests. As we have already noted, the interests of the weavers now tended to be very different from those of the drapers, although neither group could do without the other.

Although the manufacture of low- and medium-quality cloths amply met the demands of the home market and even allowed for some profitable exports, the importation of fine woollens into Catalonia continued during the late fourteenth and early fifteenth centuries, to such an extent that in the years 1436–38 the Consellers (Councillors) of Barcelona consulted experienced drapers and merchants as to whether it would be advisable to increase local production and begin the manufacture of finer cloths.[35] Inevitably the response was affirma-tive, and so the Council set up a large-scale operation to acquire fine wools in Flanders and England, with the object of reselling them to the weavers of Barcelona, either on credit or to be paid for in instalments.[36] On 21 November 1438 the Consellers of Barcelona themselves produced a detailed decree concerning the methods and practices to be observed in the working of English wool: this wool would be worked on its own (that is, unmixed with any others) and the cloths produced would be marked with an escutcheon with a cross in the middle and the letter B (for Barcelona) at the side. The finest cloths would have 32 picks and

[35] See C. Batlle, *La crisis social y económica de Barcelona a mediados del siglo XV* (Barcelona, 1973), I, pp. 186–8.
[36] See A.-E. Sayous, *Els mètodes comercials a la Barcelona medieval* (Barcelona, 1975), p. 136.

the medium-quality ones at least 28. The manufacture must be absolutely perfect. To strengthen the cloths only lard (obtained from pig fat) would be used, and it was forbidden, on pain of a fine of 300 *sous*, to dye them with 'gall or vinegar, or vitriol, or batches of ground pigment, or *excoxa de vern* [alder bark]', which were cheaper dyestuffs and dyeing techniques, but of inferior quality.[37]

Although some technical improvements were introduced (such as combs 14 *palms* long), and although attempts were made to produce other materials such as satin and silk,[38] this endeavour to revitalise the Barcelona woollen textile industry was on the whole a failure, on account of the greed of some speculators. In order to understand the question fully, one would have to find out which textile craftsmen held decisive power on the Council during the period, and also ascertain their financial resources, since one gets the impression that it was someone with more speculative ability than ready cash who tried to set up the operation with public funds (the money deposited in the *Taula de Canvi*, the municipal bank, which I have written about elsewhere) at least as much for his own profit as for the benefit of the community. In the Barcelona of 1440 there were more than a hundred heads of families involved in the woollen industry: sixty-four drapers, forty-five weavers and ten dyers. The majority of woollen cloths being produced were of mediocre quality and their value varied between 60 and 100 florins a *bala*, a unit of packaging in which between eight and eleven pieces could be transported, depending on their thickness. The price of these cloths varied, then, between eight and nine florins per piece.

Municipal intervention was to continue in the following years. New by-laws in 1448 and 1457 show how rigorously the Council of Barcelona carried out this intervention: the payment of a duty of six *diners* on every piece taken to the communal *Tirador* (tenter), the obligation to state the weight on every piece, etc.[39] Thus, within this second, industrial phase in the development of woollen textile manufacture in Catalonia, one must recognise a long period of municipal intervention, during which the Crown seems to have lost control of the guilds. Further research needs to be done on this topic.

For the mid-fifteenth century Claude Carrère has provided us with a well-documented study of the different aspects of the Catalan woollen industry, in which she stresses both the relative and absolute im-

---

[37] See A. de Capmany, *Memorias históricas sobre la marina, comercio y artes de la antigua ciudad de Barcelona* 4 vols. (Madrid, 1779), II, pp. 427–32, doc. 287.

[38] See Batlle, *La crisis social* (see n. 35), I, p. 192.

[39] See de Capmany, *Memorias históricas* (see n. 37), II, pp. 439–47, doc. 292, and II, pp. 360–1, doc. 242.

portance of the industry to the economy of the principality, where between 40 and 60 per cent of the population in manufacturing centres were engaged in the woollen industry and were largely supported by it.[40] But the second half of the fifteenth century, the period when, as Federigo Melis points out, the great Catalan industrial centres grew up alongside those of Genoa and other Italian states, is still largely unstudied.[41] Moreover, the so-called 'great triangle' of Barcelona, Valencia and Majorca still offers numerous opportunities for research, not only to determine the part played by the industrialisation of textiles in the economic awakening or *redreç* (raising up) of the last third of the century, but also to estimate the contributions made by the 'wool region' (the Maestrazgo, San Mateo, the Balearics) and the 'dyes region' (Alicante and Murcia) to the industrialisation of Catalonia, where basic raw materials for the manufacture and dyeing of cloth were in short supply. Furthermore, on Melis's excellent map of the centres of wool production and woollen manufacture Catalonia is left blank, except for the region around Tortosa, which borders on the Levantine zone of Castellón de la Plana.[42]

Pierre Bonnassie has studied the organisation of the Barcelona woollen industry at the end of the fifteenth century, with special reference to the decree of 1499 and other legal documents.[43] I know of no overall study devoted to the fortunes of the Catalan woollen industry in the sixteenth century. There are, however, some important partial studies, among which one should single out for mention that of Valentín Vázquez de Prada and Pedro Molas on the industry in Barcelona in the sixteenth and seventeenth centuries, in which they examine the long period of decline which followed the *redreç*, the successive ordinances and the efforts of the drapers to maintain control of production through the City Council and the guilds, thus putting pressure on the weavers and other cloth-workers who depended on them.[44] The new concepts of political economy, which we have seen developing throughout the fifteenth century, had little effect in this area. The threefold social function of the Catalan textile guilds in the sixteenth century – mutual aid, education, town government – has been noted by F. Torrella.[45] Nevertheless, the point needs stressing.

---

[40] See Carrère, 'La draperie en Catalogue' (see n. 2).

[41] 'I rapporti economici fra la Spagna e l'Italia nei secoli XIV–XVI' in F. Ruiz Martín (ed.), *Mercaderes italianos en España, siglos XIV–XVI* (Seville, 1976), pp. 179–99.

[42] The map is reproduced in *Mercaderes italianos* (n. 41), between pp. 156 and 157.

[43] *La organización del trabajo en Barcelona a fines del siglo XV*, Anejos del *Anuario de Estudios Medievales*, 8 (Barcelona, 1975), pp. 147–59.

[44] *Produzione*, pp. 553ff.

[45] 'Aspectos sociales de los antiguos gremios textiles catalanes', *Hispania* (Madrid, 1958), LXXII, pp. 1–18.

It seems that in an attempt to save the Catalan textile industry from the decline which was threatening it, in 1511 Ferdinand the Catholic, after confirming the privileges granted by his predecessors,[46] as was normal, authorised the immigration of workers from Flanders and northern Italy who could instruct the Catalan craftsmen in new techniques. These measures were to prove insufficient, and Charles V had to allow the importation of foreign cloths once more,[47] although certain duties were levied on them in 1519,[48] as had been the case centuries before. His son, Philip II, was to follow the same policy, imposing a duty of 20 per cent on French cloths in 1547.[49] This protectionist policy of taxing imports was accompanied by an expansion of the guilds and by new decrees. But new guilds and new decrees did not mean that the crisis, which was largely one of production, had been resolved.

Let us take one example. After a succession of individual regulations,[50] the guild ordinances of the Barcelona drapers were drawn up in final form in 1599. The drapers once more reorganised their guild to give it greater pre-eminence over the weavers' guilds, taking advantage, as they had done before, of their active participation in the government of the city. The privileges accorded to the sons of master-craftsmen in the examinations and the exclusion of new masters from the prime wardenship of the guild, together with other restrictive practices, show that the expansionist phase of this traditional industry had come to an end.[51] Naturally enough, the weavers reacted against the drapers, who went on treating them as a simple labour force to serve their interests; and it seems symptomatic that the weavers should act not through their enfeebled guilds, but through the *confrarias* of which they were members. They sought a solution to a problem which, as we have seen, was not a new one, but at least two centuries old. So we find the weavers of wool, hemp and flax, belonging to the *confraria* of Saints Iu and Sever in Seu d'Urgell, drawing up new *Ordinacions* (ordinances) for themselves on 20 April 1613;[52] the wool and flax weavers of Balaguer doing the same thing on 15 July 1618;[53]

[46] ACA, Cancillería, Reg. 3558, of Ferdinand II, fol. 146ᵛ.

[47] See F. Torrella, 'Le règne des corporations', *Cahiers Ciba*, III (Barcelona, 1963), p. 14.

[48] ACA, Consejo de Ciento, doc. 111, 7 December 1519.

[49] ACA, Consejo de Ciento, doc. 60, 6 December 1547.

[50] For example, BC MSS 1028 and 1036, which concern the varying fortunes of the drapers and weavers of Vic during the sixteenth century and contain a register of their respective trade marks from 1548.

[51] The text of the *Ordinacions* of the drapers, weavers and dyers of Barcelona between 1474 and 1669 can be seen in BC MS 1991.

[52] Archivo de la Catedral de Urgell, *Llibre de les Ordinacions*, 20 April 1613. The text is approved and confirmed by the bishop, Friar Bernat de Salba.

[53] ACA, *Co. Do. In*, vol. VIII, p. 531.

and the weavers of the *confraria* of Santa María in Vilafranca del Penedès drawing up theirs on 6 December 1618.[54]

Organisation of the guilds

In view of the importance of the guilds in the evolution of the textile industry, we shall explore the subject a little further. Almost from the very beginning of the industrial phase in textile manufacture one comes across weavers, dyers, fullers, drapers and clothiers forming themselves into guilds or *confrarias*. The crafts within the industry become more diverse: there appear *verberatores* (beaters) of wool; carders and card-makers; combers and *fullones* (fullers); male and female spinners; winders who prepare the bobbins of yarn; weavers of wool, flax and cotton; drapers, or *paratores pannorum lanae* as the industrial cloth-makers are usually called (although a distinction is sometimes made between the two in documents, since the drapers did not always merely finish their own cloths but also acquired and dressed wool which they handed over to the weavers, by which they became the real textile industrialists and the others their subordinates). Scourers, dyers, fullers, warpers, grinders of cropping shears (*smolatores de tesores de baxar*), cloth-shearers or croppers (*abaixadors*), merchants, tailors, etc. followed other trades closely connected with the textile industry. When their interests coincided, they did not hesitate to join together in the same guilds. But as their interests diverged more and more, new guilds and *confrarias* were formed. The creation of a guild has been often identified with the appearance of industrial activity in a particular place, but this may not always be the case. *Confrarias* and guilds, as has already been pointed out, arise in very different circumstances in response to very varied needs. One gets, then, a rather false picture if one studies the guilds without taking these circumstances and needs into account.

The first known guild ordinances seem to be those of the blanket-weavers of Valencia and of the wool-dealers of Perpignan, dating from 1283 and 1298 respectively, followed by those of the Barcelona woollen-weavers in 1308,[55] and those of the Valencian drapers and dyers in 1311. On the one hand, these ordinances, which first make their appearance in the big cities, are intended to ensure the quality of the products, prevent unfair competition, punish dishonest practices, etc. On the other hand, they lay down the requisites for the products: the

---

[54] Archivo de Protocolos de Vilafranca del Penedès (Museum of Vilafranca), Confrares de la Confraria de Santa María, 1618.

[55] These have been transcribed and studied by us elsewhere: see 'Aportación a la organización gremial de la industria textil catalana en el siglo XIV', in *VII° Congreso de Historia de la Corona de Aragón* (Barcelona, 1962), II, pp. 547–59.

types of raw material, blends, weight and length of pieces, number of threads, types of cloths, trade-marks, etc. The ordinances regulate the combing, carding, spinning, weaving and dyeing processes, and become loaded with more and more technical details as we move into the fourteenth and fifteenth centuries. These detailed requirements may certainly have put constraints on expansion, which was sacrificed for the security of guaranteed profits.

The ordinances of the guilds and *confrarias*, on the one hand, and the decrees of the Cortes and the municipalities, on the other, delimit more and more clearly the respective functions and rights of the different crafts. If one makes a comparative study of the privileges and successive ordinances of the drapers of Cervera (1343) and Perpignan (1380), of the weavers of Vilafranca del Penedès (1374), Berga (1374) and Gerona (1377), of the dyers of Perpignan (1378), of the weavers, drapers and dyers of Barcelona (1380, 1383 and 1386), of the drapers of Gerona (1387) and Puigcerdà (1396), of the woollen-weavers of Barcelona (1387 and again in 1402), and of the many others that exist, one is provided with ample information about the legal position of the Catalan textile manufacturers and operatives in the closing centuries of the Middle Ages and the first centuries of the modern era.[56]

The following are a few points relevant to this topic; they make no claim whatsoever to be exhaustive. When King Peter III, on 4 April 1343, granted his permission for the drapers of Cervera to form a guild, he authorised them to adopt the statutes which the drapers of Camprodón had drawn up for themselves, empowering them to meet two or three times a year in a convenient place, to collect dues and to elect two masters of their craft, or more if they wished, to administer their wealth.[57] The textile industry was, then, by now sufficiently well established in Cervera and Camprodón for the drapers to need administrators of their communal wealth, which derived from the dues paid by the members of the guild.

Other guild statutes, such as those of the weavers of Vilafranca del Penedès, which were presented for approval in 1374, claim to have been drawn up to prevent dishonest practices and stipulate that for *el bon regiment de la art de draperia* (the proper running of the cloth-trade) the *jurats* (elected leading citizens) should each year choose one draper and the weavers should choose one draper and two weavers, who would be familiar with the ordinances and would swear on oath to ensure that these ordinances were carried out. These four *sobreposats* (supervisors)

[56] See E. Asensio, 'El gremio de tejedores de Barcelona a finales del siglo XIV', ibid., II, pp. 407–16.
[57] See R. Freitag, 'Die katalanischen Handwerkorganisationen unter Königsschutz im Mittelalter', *Gesammelte Aufsätze zur Kulturgeschichte Spaniens* (Munster, 1968), XXIV, pp. 41–226, esp. 183–6.

or *veedors* (overseers), as they were called, would be empowered to inspect *les peses et los pesals et les canes* (the weights, the scales, and the measuring rods) of drapers and weavers, to destroy defective weights and scales, and impose a fine of 2 *sous* for the offence; they could also appropriate and destroy any rods for measuring cloth which turned out to be inaccurate, and impose in this case a fine of 5 *sous*. They would also be authorised to inspect linen, hemp and woollen cloths, and the combs (*pintas*) and other implements in the workshops. Anyone who refused them entry to their premises would be liable to a fine of 50 *sous*. The statutes specifically refer both to master- and mistress-weavers (*maestre* and *mestressa*) and to apprentices of both sexes (*fadrins* and *fadrines*). No one should be allowed to take over a weaving-shop (*obrador de la art de texidoria*) unless he had practised the trade for four years, on pain of a fine of 20 *sous* and confiscation of all his implements. No female weaver would be permitted to buy a workshop if she had not been in the trade for two years, on pain of a fine of 10 *sous* and the loss of all her implements (*tots los arreus*). Apprentices must not do work on their own account until they had completed three years of their apprenticeship. Those craftsmen who worked for a master must not work for another without their own master's knowledge. Finally, weavers were forbidden to weave secretly, and it was stipulated that all workshops should open on to the street and should remain open from sunrise to sunset.

The relations between drapers and weavers were not always cordial, as we have noted. The disputes between the weavers and drapers of Berga, for example, brought about the intervention of Peter III in 1374.[58] On 3 April 1373 the king had granted the drapers of Berga permission to meet, elect *sobreposats* or *majorals*, and draw up ordinances. The weavers rejected these ordinances because they felt that they were harmful to their interests, and the king resolved the problem by decreeing that the weavers should draw up their own ordinances. Drapers and weavers nominated their respective representatives, two from each guild, and between them they decided that each year the drapers should elect one trusted member from their guild and the weavers one from theirs, and that these two should be empowered to measure and weigh the woollen cloths woven in the town as well as the unfinished cloths that came into it. The official weighers would affix a lead seal (with the Berga mark) to the cloths which they found

---

[58] A somewhat later document, dated 28 April 1391, gives us the information that in Berga there were fifty-five weavers, fifty drapers, fourteen dyers and thirty-seven merchants, who were all heads of families; the woollen textile industry was thus by far the majority occupation in the town. See Archivo de la Cofradía dels Colls (Museo del Patronato Vall de Lord, Sant Llorenç de Morunys), doc. 79.

to be of the correct weight. Since it was possible for a piece to have left the workshop in perfect condition and then to have been badly finished by the draper and badly dyed by the dyer, the drapers and weavers agreed that the finishing operations should be supervised by the *sobreposats*, who would be empowered to impose fines of up to 60 *sous* on anyone who breached the regulations.

Equally interesting, as far as one can see, are the ordinances of the *confrarias* approved by John I before his accession to the throne.[59] Let us take just one example. Prince John, on 21 February 1376, recognising that the ordinances agreed by the drapers of the city of Gerona would help to increase religious observance, at their request authorised them to establish a *confrarias* in honour of St Francis, in the Franciscan house in Gerona. In the statutes or ordinances of this *confrarias* it was stipulated that members would not work on the saint's feast-day, 'and that no dyer would put cloth into his vat during that week, nor would any fuller use the day to repair his mill, nor any draper spread cloth on his tenter'. All those members who happened to be in the city on that day must attend Mass, unless they were ill. They would be organised into groups of ten, headed by a *deener* (leader of a group of ten). They would have a chest in which would be kept the funds of the *confraria* into which they would each pay 1 *diner* every Saturday; and none of these funds could be spent without the knowledge of the 'four worshipful councillors of the craft' elected by the members of the *confraria*. When a member died, he had to bequeath 5 *sous* to the *confraria* and pay off any arrears of dues. The bell of the *confraria* would not be tolled in mourning until these dues had been paid.

More or less all the statutes of the *confraria* contain regulations of this kind. But alongside these rules there are others, such as the following: 'Item: all those who belong to a *decena* [group of ten] shall attend a meeting whenever and wherever summoned by their *decenero* [leader] for whatever purpose, whether in connection with the affairs of the *confraria* or those of the craft, and anyone who fails to attend shall pay 12 *diners* into the chest of the *confraria*.' Another regulation informs us that money may be paid out of the chest 'for the defence of the *confraria*'. The *confrarias*, then, do not ignore matters concerned with their craft, matters which would seem to be more the province of the guilds in normal circumstances, nor do they ignore the fact that the defence of their members' interests may involve them in expense.

Regulations of this kind, slipped in amongst others designed to protect the moral and social welfare of the members, may pass unnoticed. But alongside the injunctions to all master-craftsmen and

---

[59] See Freitag, 'Die Katalanischen Handwerkorganisationen' (see n. 57), pp. 189–92.

apprentices (*macips*) to give alms to fellow-members who are poor or sick, to attend members' funerals and to recite 25 paternosters and 25 Ave Marias for the repose of their souls, and to attend the brotherhood feast on St Francis's Day in the convent of the Minors, one should also remember the oath which was sworn upon admission to the *confraria* not to act against the king, his heir or the 'commonweal'.

On 30 October 1377 Prince John, Duke of Gerona, granted the weavers of Gerona the right to assemble, 'as they had done of old', in order to elect representatives (*suprapositos*) to govern their trade, to draw up ordinances, to safeguard the interests of their craft, and impose penalties, as they used to do. In the little under two years which had elapsed between the approval of the ordinances of the drapers' *confraria* and the granting of these protective measures to the weavers, the conflict between the two crafts had become intensified on account of the divergence of their interests.

The drapers were more powerful and so could pay for royal protection. It is not surprising, then, that on 9 May 1386 Peter III received 1000 gold florins from the drapers of Perpignan in return for granting them the right to reorganise themselves after they had lost all their documents 'as the result of something which happened in the building where they were kept'. They were thus empowered to meet, to draw up new statutes, to elect three *rectors* for their guild and fifteen assistant *rectors*, to charge for the use of the *Tiradors* (tenters), and 'to summon together the members of the guild on matters affecting their craft'.[60]

Despite the regulations, there were many breaches of them. In 1396 John I, now king, had to summon the drapers of Puigcerdà, on pain of a fine of 500 florins, to meet in the Dominican house there in order to annul the appointments of those they had chosen to manage their affairs and to elect new ones, since the earlier appointments had been made contrary to the rules.[61] The weavers of Perpignan also seem to have ignored their rules, to judge by what Martin I tells us when he approved their new statutes on 25 October 1400.[62] Perhaps because of the pressures put on them by the drapers of the town, several weavers, finding themselves unable to earn a living, had become bandits, footpads, pimps, swindlers, etc. in their search for new means of subsistence. However, sometimes they returned to weaving 'to the discredit of the craft', and the guild of weavers succeeded in banning them from practising their trade, on pain of a fine of 100 Barcelona *sous*. And the case of the Perpignan weavers is far from being unique. The disputes between the different craftsmen

[60] Ibid., pp. 200–1.
[61] Ibid., p. 207.
[62] Ibid., pp. 214–19.

within the textile trade increased as time went on. Their interests not only diverged; they often proved directly opposed to one another. In the records of the Cortes of 1481, *drapers* (drapers), *perayres* (clothiers), *botiguers* (merchants) and *sastres* (tailors), because of the opportunities they had to buy and sell cloth by the length (*drap a tall*) rather than by the piece, were expressly forbidden to hold the offices of tax-collector (*cullidor*) or keeper of the lead seals or seal-casts, or be in possession of the pincers used to affix the wax duty-paid seals of the *bolla*, since they might seal lengths of cloth that did not meet the required conditions for sale.

Centres of woollen cloth production

Miguel Gual, after collecting a great deal of information, drew up a map of the centres of textile production in Spain.[63] Amongst the 140 towns identified and recorded on this map, thirty are to be found within the old boundaries of Catalonia (which includes those areas which in modern times passed to France). Six of them can be documented in the twelfth century: Prats de Molló (now French), Gerona, Salt, Caldes de Malavella, Llagostera and Lérida. A further thirteen are referred to in thirteenth-century texts: Perpignan and Pont d'Armentera (1229), Vic (1238), Ripoll (1238), Barcelona (1253), Berga and Bagà (1255), Banyoles, Sant Daniel and Valls (1271), Igualada (1283), Gósol (1291) and Puigcerdà (1293). Another six places are added for the fourteenth century: Sant Llorenç de Morunys and Manresa (1302), Pobla de Lillet (1321), Bellpuig (1334), Camprodón (1350) and Torroella de Montgrí (1392). Five more are recorded in the fifteenth century: Castelló d'Empúries (1405), Ceret (1426), Almenar (1444), Tortosa (1457) and Sant Joan de les Abadesses (1461). Gual added to these a further nine places which were difficult to locate precisely: for example, la Vall d'Aràn, Rósellon, Llobregat, Ter, etc. refer either to quite extensive areas or to water courses where the fulling mills, which were generally close to the textile centres, were probably situated. Later, in 1970, Gual designated a further eighteen places as textile centres; among them were Balaguer, Besalú, Capellades, Cardona, Cervera, Martorell, Molins de Rey, Montcada, Ripollet, Sabadell, Sant Celoni, Sant Feliu de Torelló and Solsona. The total number of documented centres of textile manufacture thus rose to fifty-five and the list cannot be considered complete. One ought at least to add Peralada (from 1261), Sallent (already very active in 1449), Ribas de Fresser and Queralps. As well as taking into account

---

[63]'Para un mapa de la industria textil hispana en la Edad Media', *Anuario de Estudios Medievales* (Barcelona, 1967), IV, pp. 109–68. There is a folding map between pp. 128 and 129.

the Catalan centres in the south of France, such as Montpellier, Prats de Molló, Vilafranca de Conflent, etc., it should also be pointed out that several monastic centres gave rise to a flourishing textile industry: into this category come Sant Martí de Canigó, Santa María de Ripoll, Sant Joan de les Abadesses, Sant Pere de Camprodón and Sant Llorenç de Morunys, to cite only some of the best-known cases.

Catalan textiles

Not all the centres of production were engaged in manufacturing the same textiles or products of identical quality. This resulted in some highly esteemed products being copied in other places: Gósol blankets, for instance, were sometimes made in Bagà, and Banyoles textiles were copied in Barcelona. Sometimes merchants, clothiers or drapers from a place with a high reputation for cloth bought products from other centres in order to resell them with the mark of their own town, thus meeting a demand which local production could not cope with alone. In other cases, weavers moved to another town where there were better opportunities, taking with them their local skills.

It is mainly through the tax records and the ordinances of the guilds that we can find out about the great variety of woollen cloths manufactured in Catalonia, about the blending of wool with flax, hemp, camel-hair or goat-hair, as well as about the blending of different-quality wools. We have already mentioned the possible Gallic origin (from Sarlat) of the cloths that were manufactured in Lérida in the twelfth century. The cloths of Sant Llorenç de Morunys, in the upper valley of the Cardener, may have originated in Poitou, since they were popularly known as *draps piteus* (Poitevin cloths) until their production ceased in the nineteenth century. *Burells*, *sargil* or *sarzil* (serge), *estamenya* or *stam* (worsted) figure amongst the most common types of Catalan cloths in the thirteenth and fourteenth centuries, alongside the *draps anglesos* (English cloths), so called because they were made from English wool, the *pentinats* (combed cloths) which were woven from combed wool, and the *vervins*, copied from the cloths of the Flemish town of Wervicq. Amongst the most sought-after cloths in the local markets were those from Lérida, to which we have referred on several occasions, the black and white cloths from Ripoll, and the serges from Banyoles, which were copied in Barcelona, as we have said.

When the cloth left the workshop it could vary in length between 12 and 20 *cans* of eight *palms* (1 *palm* = 8 inches), a maximum of some 30 metres; but it would shrink to 27 or 23 metres, or even less, during the finishing. We have seen how the drapers took good care to keep increasing the length of the pieces during the period under consideration. The length, the width or number of threads, and the weight of cloths were the subject of numerous decrees throughout the period which concerns us.

In Catalonia cloths were called after their place of manufacture (*banyolencs*: from Banyoles; *cadins*: from Cadí) or place of origin (*eixelons*: from Aix; *piteus*: from Poitou; *vervins*: from Wervicq), after their colour (*blanquets*: white; *negres*: black; *vermells*: red), after their raw material (*canamillana*: hemp; *mesclats*: mixtures; *de mija lana*: half wool), after the number of threads in the weft (*devuytens*: eighteens; *vintens*: twenties), after their length (*migans*: halves) or their width (*strets*: narrows), after the dyeing process used (*de molada*: with batches of ground pigment), after their pattern (*listat*: striped) or lack of it (*pla*: plain), according to whether or not various coloured wools had been used in weaving the piece. There is, then, no uniformity in the industrial and commercial terminology of the period.

The problem of the cost of textiles is still unresolved; but it is worth recording here the findings of Melis, which refer principally to the end of the fourteenth century and the beginning of the fifteenth. The price paid for wool in Majorca or Minorca (which was between 60 and 70 per cent of the price of English wool, to which it was inferior in quality) had multiplied sevenfold by the time the cloth was made, and the cost of transportation was equivalent to 21 per cent of the initial price of the wool, that is, only some 3 per cent of the final cost of the cloth.[64] To fix the sale price one would have to add the profit margin, which would be between 10 and 12 per cent, to the total.

Techniques and implements

The appearance in the tax records of the thirteenth century of *pintes de fust de pentinar draps* (wooden combs for combing cloth) and *torns de filar llana* (spinning-wheels) is significant as an indication of the increasing industrialisation of textiles. The technical aspects of cloth manufacture, however, have been the least studied of all. Wooden cards greased with lard and combs for combing long wools were improving. From the end of the thirteenth century there is no lack of evidence concerning technical advances made in Catalonia, such as the spinning-wheel, invented in Tortosa by Roiç Ximeneç from La Cenia in 1457 and awarded a prize of ten florins by the town council of Tortosa because 'it did the work of three women'. Nevertheless, the wheel did not succeed in replacing the spindle totally even as late as the nineteenth century.

It seems that the narrow loom with *dues calques* (two treadles), for a single weaver, male or female, was predominant in Catalonia until

---

[64] 'I rapporti' (see n. 41), p. 194.

the sixteenth century. There was still a large proportion of narrow looms in the countryside in the eighteenth and nineteenth centuries. The looms that are preserved in the museums of Sabadell, Tarrassa, Berga, Ripoll and the Ethnographic Museum of the Spanish People of Monjuic (Barcelona) are all narrow looms, although most of them are not earlier than the eighteenth century and none dates from the medieval period. Some of them have a rather archaic appearance, despite the fact that they were built in the eighteenth or nineteenth centuries, like the one in Berga. On the other hand, the one in the Museum of the City and Region of Igualada is a broad loom, with four treadles, for a pair of weavers. A comparative study of the different mechanisms and fittings of the looms that have been preserved could well prove very fruitful.

The fulling mills, powered by water and located on the rivers Ter, Segre, Cardener, Llobregat, Besós, Francolí, etc., documented from the twelfth century onwards, were constantly improving; but the noise produced by the blocks made it necessary to build them some distance from the towns.[65] In the early fifteenth century (1417) some more detailed inventories describe them as already having water channels; a wheel which drives the mill-shaft, reinforced with copper hoops, which in its turn moves the milling machine (*noc* or *nyoc*) with its heavy double wooden blocks which beat the cloth to scour and strengthen it; *sotsbarber* (graters), *taleres* (shafts), *claviots* (pegs), *llevadors* (carriers), *tayes* (pulleys), etc., and auxiliary fitments of iron and copper, such as troughs for washing the cloth. The whole framework is still wooden, but iron and copper are used to reinforce the key points of the mechanism so as to prevent its wearing and deteriorating. The proprietors of these mills are the local counts or the king or bodies (such as the canons of Gerona or the hospitals of Barcelona) to whom they granted permission to construct and work them, on payment of an annual rent.

The organisation of the tenter-grounds (*estricadors*), with their wooden frames called *tiradors* or *estiradors* (tenters) for drying and stretching the cloth, often figures in guild and municipal ordinances. Situated on the outskirts of the towns, these grounds were at first privately owned, but the guilds and town councils soon assumed responsibility for their installation and maintenance, as is made clear, for example, by the ordinances of the Mostaçaferia (Mustard Fair) of Barcelona.[66] In the ordinances of the Igualada public weighing-

---

[65] Thus the bailiff of Barcelona in 1255 laid down the limits within which the fullers of fustian could carry out their trade; cf. S. Sanpere y Miquel, *La Rodalía de Corbera* (Barcelona, 1890), doc. 60, fol. 203.
[66] AHCB, Vegueria, Crides, vol. II, fols. 66ff. and fol. 70 (1373).

office[67] it was forbidden to tenter cloth on the city walls, because the clothiers' guild owned its own tentering grounds.[68]

The cards for raising cloth, used by the clothiers for finishing, and the shears used by the croppers (*abaixadors*) to reduce the nap, complete this list of implements. Finally, to measure the cloth when it was sold not in pieces but in lengths (*a tall*), that is to say, cut up, the merchants carried with them a half-*cana* (1 ell) and a half-ell, made of iron, hinged and engraved with the mark or seal of their place of origin. In the Museum of the Patronat Vall de Lord in Sant Llorenç de Morunys (Lérida) several examples have been preserved, together with loom-weights, boxwood truckles and several fragments of cloth.

[67] See Gabriel Castellà (ed.), *Llibre la Mostaçaferia* (Igualada, 1954), p. 69, rubric 150.
[68] J. Riba i Ortínez, *La industria tèxtil igualadina: Història d'un gremi* (Igualada, 1958), pp. 33–9.

13 Cloth Merchants' Inventories in Dijon in the Fourteenth and Fifteenth Centuries
Françoise Piponnier

I

Among the rich collection of probate inventories dating from the late fourteenth century surviving in the town hall at Dijon, there are eight dealing with cloth merchants.[1] They date from the period 1389 to 1438, and provide long lists of cloths, giving their places of origin, their prices and their various colours. These inventories reveal the composition and extent of the fortunes of the deceased persons; they also provide an insight into a commercial network which extended far beyond the capital of Burgundy. This study deals only with the way in which the cloth merchants were supplied with their materials. When further statistical analysis of the data provides a stronger basis, a study will be undertaken of other social and economic aspects such as the extent of their fortunes, their way of life and their place in the life of the city.

An obvious objection can be made that eight inventories of cloth merchants do not constitute a sufficient statistical series, even if one

---

[1] The documents used here all come from the series of probate inventories in the municipal archives of Dijon (Departmental Archives of the Cote d'Or, Series B II 356). Throughout this essay they are designated by the following letters:

A Probate inventory of Philippot Geliot, son of Philippe Geliot, citizen of Dijon (1392)
B Probate inventory of Belot, wife of Jean de Beaufort (1404)
D Probate inventory of Jeannote, wife of Perrenot Jaqueron (1411)
E Probate inventory of Guillote, wife of Simonot Vaichet (1419)
F Probate inventory of Guillote, wife of Jacquot Lerousselet called Laborde, cloth merchant (1427)
G Probate inventory of Jean Petit, d'Aiserey (1427)
H Probate inventory of Etienne Lachèvre, merchant (1427)
J Inventory of goods left on deposit at Monin de Bretennières by François and Jacques Serras, brothers, merchants (1433)
K Probate inventory of Henry Maistre, merchant (1438)
L Inventory of a bale of cloth (1389)
M Probate inventory of Jean de Somme, Hosier (1400)

adds the two lists of cloths left on deposit in Dijon by foreigners, and the recorded stock of a hosier. But for this period one cannot overlook the slightest bit of information, however fragmentary. The stocks listed in these inventories are considerable and examination of their places of origin reveals a remarkable pattern of variety.

Over the fifty years from 1389 to 1438, the procedure for drawing up the inventories varied. Each time, the contents of the store were carefully laid out. In the majority of cases, every piece of cloth was separately specified. The experts dictated the places of origin, the length and the value of each cloth to the clerk who drew up the text of the inventory. Unfortunately, in the case of the extensive stocks of Henry Maistre, they were content merely to indicate the number of pieces of each colour and their total value, pile by pile, often omitting to state the place of origin.

The period under consideration was characterised by a succession of crises and considerable monetary instability, so it would be difficult to attempt to calculate and compare the value of goods from the different cloth-manufacturing centres. It is not yet possible to calculate these prices in constant terms, since the relationship between prices and monetary fluctuations are too poorly understood in this period. The quantitative study of the goods also runs into other obstacles – particularly the diversity of units of measurement on the one hand, and the variations in the cloth widths on the other. The latter difficulty raises insoluble problems in the present state of knowledge. It has not been ignored here, but left on one side. As for the units of measure, only once was the ell which the experts used to measure the stock defined; in this case, it was the ell of Paris. It is specified in the inventory of the cloth left on deposit in the city by the two foreign merchants (stock J) and since they felt it necessary to specify this unit, it was probably not the normal standard of measure at Dijon. Lacking other indications, it has had to be assumed that all the stocks were evaluated using the same unit of measure.

These inventories – despite their insufficiencies, despite a certain lack of homogeneity and despite their low number – are of exceptional interest because they offer some perspectives on the production and distribution of cloth at the end of the Middle Ages which go far beyond the limits of Dijon.

II

In order to present the data retrievable from these documents with the maximum clarity, a series of maps have been produced. Figure 13.1 shows the location of all the cloth-manufacturing centres specifically mentioned.[2] The identification of the place-names, sometimes encountered with whimsical spellings (Cintron for Saint-Trond, for example) was not easy. A number of them did not correspond to any known centre of cloth manufacture. In two cases, attempts at identification had to be abandoned: Disquine and Durlan. These might refer to Dixmude (Flanders) and Durban (Aude), but they are too uncertain to be retained. Other identifications remain doubtful: Dreston in England and Laborde. The only French community presently bearing the name of Laborde is situated in the Hautes Pyrénées, a good way from all the Dijon supply centres.

Looking at the map of the cloth-manufacture centres supplying Dijon, it is clear that there was a heavy preponderance of the regions to the north and north-west of Dijon. The almost complete absence of southern cloths, in particular those from Languedoc, is undoubtedly due only to the distance. The same reason also accounts for the small number of Norman and Breton centres represented. Within the supply region, the number of centres called on by the merchants of Dijon is impressive. This was a period in which cloth entered extensively into commerce, and the inventories used here supply information concerning products destined for the average customer, rather than the sort of material referred to in the accounts of the aristrocracy.

Figures 13.2 and 13.3 attempt to shed light on the relative importance of the different centres supplying Dijon. Figure 13.2 shows the amount of cloth from each source measured in terms of length, and Figure 13.3 shows the total value of the cloth from each centre of supply. A comparison between these two figures brings out the discrepancy between the quantities and the prices; this can be readily explained by the extremely variable values of textile products. A region like Lorraine, which is represented by considerable quantities, loses a great deal of its importance when the value of its cloth is taken into account. On the other hand, Flanders, Brabant and Normandy which produce highly priced cloth take the lead in terms of value. Figure 13.3 places the regions which produce high-quality cloth in the limelight, while the preceding figure shows up the supply centres for products of volume distribution.

After taking an overview of the stocks of cloth found in this collection of documents, it seems desirable to analyse the composition of each stock as a function of its origin. Figure 13.5 synthesises the data and underlines the contrast between the first two stocks and all the other

---

[2] To give an idea of the precision of the inventories used, the percentages of the total value of the stock whose origin could be identified were as follows: A 86 (per cent); B 97; D 85; E 84; F 63; G 99; H 94; J 99; K 97.

13.1–13.6   Origin of cloths found in the stocks of nine drapers, Dijon, 1392–1437

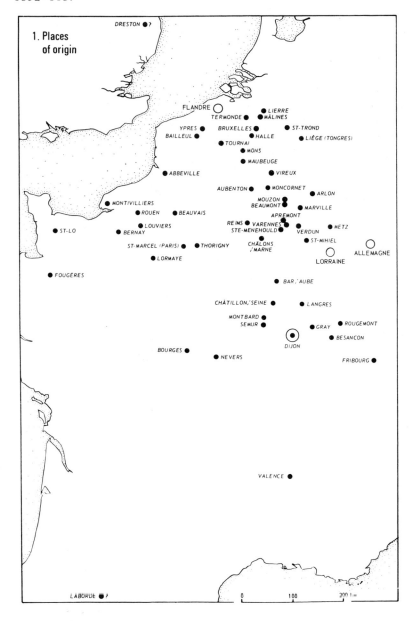

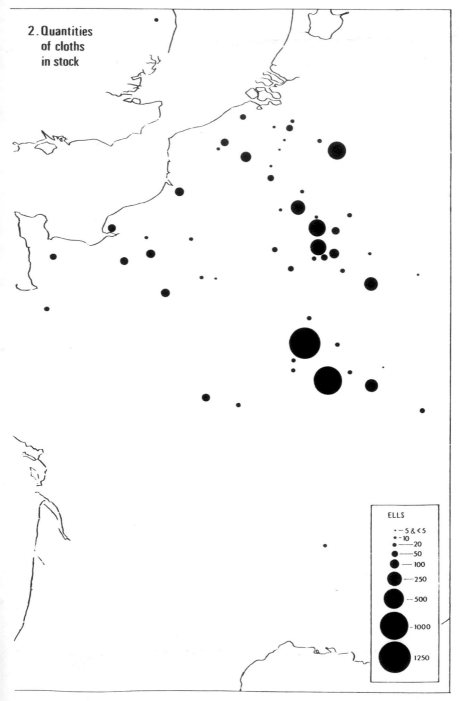

2. Quantities
of cloths
in stock

ELLS

· — 5 & < 5
• — 10
● — 20
● — 50
⬤ — 100
⬤ — 250
⬤ — 500
⬤ — 1000
⬤ — 1250

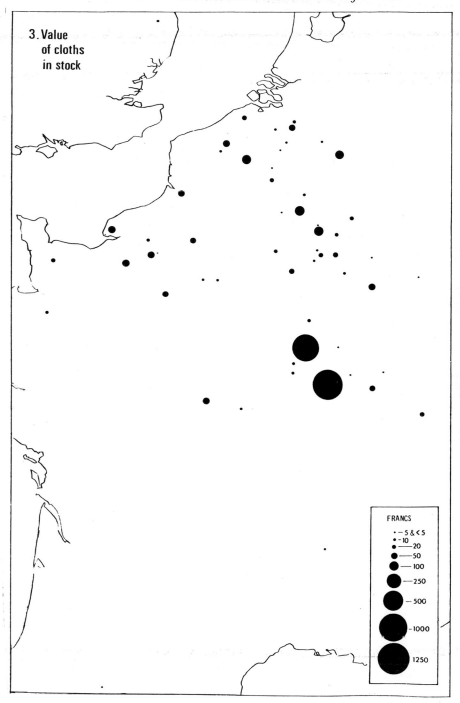

3. Value
of cloths
in stock

FRANCS

• – 5 & < 5
• – 10
— 20
— 50
— 100
— 250
— 500
– 1000
1250

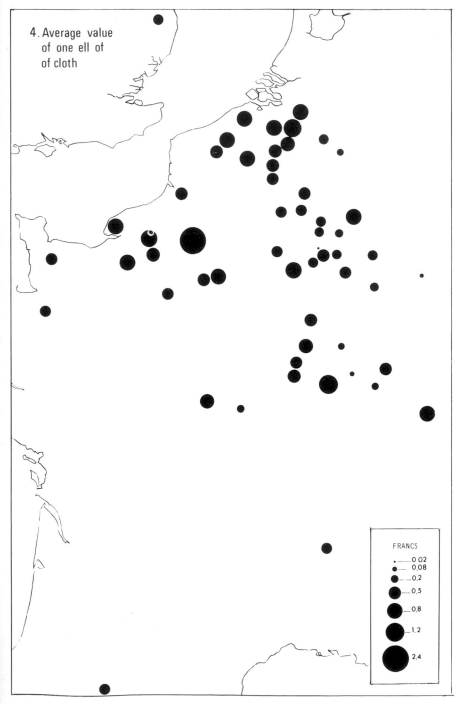

4. Average value
of one ell of
of cloth

FRANCS

· ———— 0 02
· — 0,08
● —0,2
● —0,5
● —0,8
● —1,2
● 2,4

stocks. Stocks A and B were very diversified and offered cloth from twenty-eight and twenty-three sources respectively. Leaving aside stocks L and M, which are not representative of the Dijon cloth merchants, the remaining seven stocks were made up of cloth from between four and thirteen sources only.

Among these, the goods of three tradesmen whose inventories reveal that they were not only cloth retailers must be put aside. When their inventories were drawn up, Jacquot Lerousselet (F), Jean Petit (G) and Henry Maistre (K) were in possession of large quantities of raw materials and machinery, showing that they belonged to the world of production and not only to the world of commerce. The house of Lerousselet possessed a large quantity of weaving equipment, since the minor heirs saw themselves being awarded as their part some 'looms, cards, some mounted and . . . all tools used by the said weaver of cloth'. At Henry Maistre's, the presence of a 'dyeing boiler' and 'shearing scissors' at his domicile suggests the finishing of cloth woven elsewhere. Vegetable dyestuffs, galls and woad of Picardy, as well as a reference to cloth belonging to him still 'on the weaver's loom' confirm the range of his activities. Moreover, the considerable quantities of wool which these merchants kept in their houses set them apart from the others. Sometimes it is raw wool whose origin is occasionally indicated – Berri in F and G, Provence in K – and sometimes it is wool that has undergone one or more stages of treatment – carded wool, carding 'to make cameline' (G), even wool dyed before having been spun or woven (F and G). Among the yarns, a careful distinction is made for those which have been done 'à la cologne', that is, 'à la quenouille' (K) and even the unbleached cloth woven with this yarn (G). The experts made distinctions between the yarn intended for the warp of the cloth, the selvages, and for the weaving of certain types of cloth, like that of 'sargi warp' (G).

It is not surprising to find that products 'Dijon style' constituted a substantial proportion of the stocks of these three cloth merchants. Such products constituted 47 per cent and 78 per cent respectively of the total value of the stocks of (F) and (G). In the case of the third (K), cloth from Dijon and Châtillon is counted together making a separate evaluation impossible for 98.5 per cent of the stock. Taking into account the quantity of the products from Besançon held by Lerousselet (F), 23 per cent of the total, the amount of cloth imported into Burgundy is limited to 30 per cent (F), 21 per cent (G) and 1.5 per cent (K) of the total value of all the stock. It might be added that the number of cloth-manufacturing centres outside the region covered by these small percentages is quite limited: in the case of (F), five for (G) and two for (K).

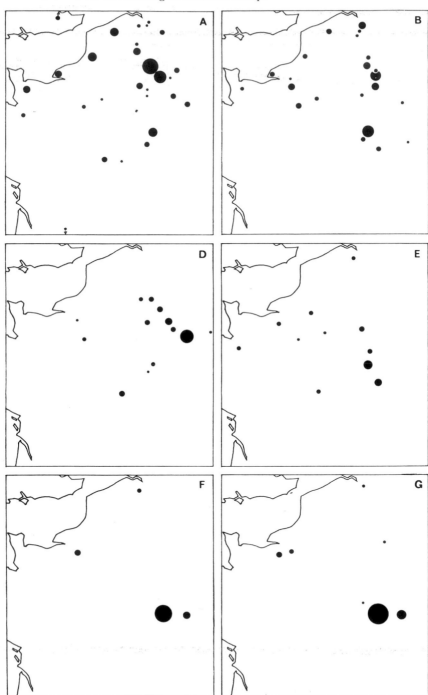

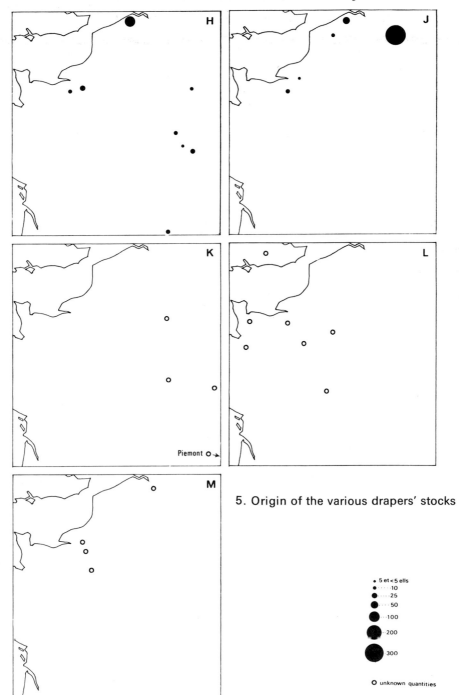

5. Origin of the various drapers' stocks

Even among the merchants whose role was solely concerned with the retailing of cloth, the considerable differences in the variety of cloth from different places offered to their customers is noticeable. The breakdown is as follows:

Date	1392	1404	1419	1419	1427	1433
Stock	A	B	D	E	H	J
Number of centres cited	28	23	13	10	8	7

From the dates, one might think of a secular shrinking of the supply market in a troubled period during which the circulation of goods might be difficult beyond the boundaries of Burgundy. This does not seem to be the case. In fact, the percentage of the value of cloth from Burgundy fluctuated widely throughout the period:

Stock	A	B	D	E	H	J
Percentage	9	32	7	42	6	0

Many factors other than the political situation must have intervened – the economic situation, the relative dynamism of the cloth-producing regions, the evolution of their production and the facility to adapt to the fashions of the day. The disappearance of the cities of Champagne and especially of Lorraine is evident, as is the falling-off of the northern provinces of Burgundy in relation to Normandy, which firmly maintained its position, and the appearance of centres such as Langres and Fribourg. Of course, in these comparisons between stocks, account ought to be taken of other factors, such as the social background of the customers, or the level of stock turnover. Unfortunately there are no data at our disposal on these matters.

III

Comparison of Figures 13.2 and 13.3 brings out the disparity between the quantity and the value of the products of the different cloth-manufacturing centres, and consequently between the prices of the cloth offered to the clientele of Dijon as shown on Figure 13.4. Although one of the fundamental variables, the width of the cloth, is missing, it still seems that the unit price of the cloths constitutes a sufficiently reliable basis for forming a classification. Insufficient data exist for stocks F, K, L and M; all the cloth figuring in the other seven inventories has been classified in terms of its price per ell. Figure 13.6 shows the relationship between the quantities and the value of the cloth making up each stock.

The majority of the fabric offered by the Dijon retailers had a price between 0.2 and 0.6 francs per ell. All of them carried a relatively large quantity of low-priced fabrics, less than 0.2 francs per ell, and with the exception of Perrenot Jaqueron (D), they also offered a choice of expensive cloth, priced between 0.8 and 1.2 francs per ell. The stock of G differs primarily from that of the other retailers by its small proportion of low-priced cloth. The quantity of the stock does not seem to have an effect on its composition. The most limited one (H) has the highest proportion of stock among the higher price levels, but as with the others, low-priced and expensive fabrics with a very wide range of prices are all offered. It might be added that the stock with the highest-priced fabrics is the one with the largest inventory.

While most of the retailers provide a large range of higher-priced goods to satisfy the requirements of their demanding clients, some of them, on the other hand, offer no expensive cloth (D) or a reduced selection (B). A smaller range of prices may be an indication of a business oriented toward a more modest clientele. This seems evident in the case of Perrenot Jaqueron: the majority of his goods were priced between 0.2 and 0.3 francs per ell, and fabrics valued at more than 0.5 francs per ell make up less than 10 per cent of his stock. In spite of the abundance of very low-priced fabrics at Jean de Beaufort's (B), there are a good many middle-priced goods, while his choice of expensive fabrics is considerably more limited than at Simonot Vaichot (E), Philippot Geliot (A) and even Etienne Lachèvre (H).

The information revealed by the inventories is not limited to the price and the quantity of the fabric; a study of their terminology allows us to go a little further in analysing the stocks. It is only at the bottom of the hierarchy of the fabrics, as defined by their unit prices, that one finds a certain diversity in the designations. The summit is occupied by fabrics designated for the most part by their colour. An exception is '*la brunette*', the high price of which classes it among the luxury fabrics. *Beige* and *tiretaine* are found at the lowest price level. The standard technical works on medieval fabrics overlook *beige*, and the descriptions in the inventories do not allow us to come any closer to the reality. The only two centres of production are cited as Gray and Langres. The inventory of de Beaufort (B) contains two statements about *beige* with which this merchant was well-supplied. *Boige de villaige* seems to indicate a source or a type of rustic cloth; *boige de pelongey* suggests the raw material, the *pelon* or *pelisse*, removed from the skin of the sheep,

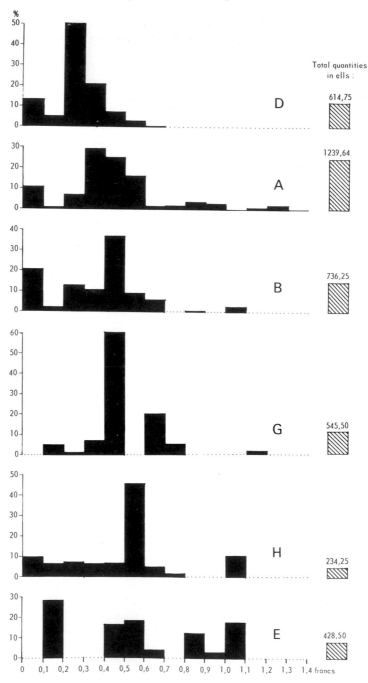

6. Distribution of cloths according to their value, in the various stocks (percentages)

that is, a wool of mediocre quality.[3] In this inventory *burel* is crossed out and replaced with *boige de villaige*; this correction could suggest that the two fabrics known as *beige* and *burel* resembled each other. As for the colour, the standard texts sometimes qualify *beige* as white; it is known that this adjective is a synonym for light. The fact that *beige* may be striped (K) does not prevent the cloth from being recorded as undyed.

By contrast, *tiretaine* is well-known to the specialists in medieval fabrics. It was a fabric made of mediocre wool with a linen or cotton warp. Furthermore, they were characterised by their narrowness, and they could be striped.[4] This information relates to the *tiretaines* of Douai, while those encountered in Dijon were from 'Germany', that is, from Lorraine (D) and Châtillon (B). Nevertheless, we find striped *tiretaines* mentioned in (H).

In the next higher price categories '*bureau*' (H), '*brifaudeure*' or '*brifaudine*' (A and B), '*laveure*' (D) and *cameline* (A, B, D and E) are characterised by the use of raw materials of second quality, which does not stop some of them from being dyed like that 'gros bureaul noir' of Etienne Lachèvre (H).[5] The only colours ascribed to *cameline* are '*white*' and '*brun*', synonyms for light and dark, which could refer to natural-coloured fabrics. Besides Dijon and Bar-sur-Aube, all the *cameline* manufacturing centres cited are in Lorraine – Beaumont-en-Argonne, Marville and Verdun.

Velu and *frise* are clearly distinguished from the other fabrics, although their technical characteristics are unknown to us. Of three mentions of *velu*, two refer to a fabric dyed black. Although measurements are lacking in the inventories, making it impossible to calculate unit prices, the *serpillères* and fustians of Piémont belonging to the Serras brothers (J) must also be classed at the lower end of the scale of fabrics in current use. The fustians of Piémont were cotton fabrics; the characteristics of the *serpillères* of Fribourg remain unknown except that they were used to wrap the other fabrics.

The serges were identified by the thread from which they are woven as well as by their weave.[6] Sometimes they were of fabric composed of wool and another fibre, like the 'serge demi-fil' of Jean Petit (G) which originated in Besançon. Other pieces were made in Apremont (K), and some were of local production (B). The *sargerie* was actually very active in Dijon during this epoch. Like *tiretaines*, serges could also be striped.

[3] G. de Poerck, *La draperie médiévale en Flandre et en Artois: Technique et terminologie* (Bruges, 1951), I, pp. 31–2.
[4] Ibid., pp. 231–2.
[5] Ibid., II, *s.v. burel*, p. 30; *s.v. briffaudure*, p. 26; *s.v. laveton*, p. 113; *cameline*: I, pp. 210–11.
[6] Ibid., II, *s.v. sarge*, and I, pp. 216–31.

When it comes to the *brunettes* and the *yrenes* which now and then reached the prices of the highest-quality fabrics, it seems that we are dealing with fabrics which are characterised mainly by their dyeing. If one can believe de Poerck, *brunette* would be a quality fabric most often of a very dark blue bordering on black and the *yrene* or *araigne* an orange-coloured cloth.

Table 13.1 lays out the hierarchy of the fabrics and the cloth-making cities using a classification by unit price and centre of production. At the top one notes the pre-eminence of the northern provinces of Burgundy as well as Normandy, with a slight advantage in favour of the latter. Only Champagne, with Châlons, and Burgundy with Châtillon are able to rival them at the highest level. At the lower end of the scale, one notes the centres in Lorraine and Burgundy. However, it must be recalled that the large quantity of undyed cloth – much cheaper than after it had been dyed – in the inventories leads to a certain downgrading in these statistics of the products of Dijon itself. The same is probably true for certain centres of great renown such as Halle and Termonde, which are represented in the shops of Dijon only by white cloth. Finally, we note that the cloth from Brussels that is found here is narrow, '*à la petite moison*'; so that a fabric which we know occupied a place at the summit of medieval cloth manufacturing occupies only a lowly place in our table.[7]

IV

Looking merely at the geographical aspects of these inventories, we can observe that the goods stocked by Dijon cloth merchants reveal a mass of information concerning the commerce and the production of textiles during the Middle Ages. The system of trade in textiles, with its hub in the capital of Burgundy, stretched out especially towards the west and north-west. A comparison with the provisioning of the court of Anjou shows some important differences, due in part to the social level of the consumers.[8] The Anjou princes used large quantities of valuable Norman fabrics. The situation of the court in Anjou and in Provence explains the reliance for moderately priced fabrics on the cloth manufacturers of Bourges and of the Languedoc region. The use of cloth from Barbary and Turkey is without doubt an expression of the exotic taste of King René, the fantasies of a prince which find no echo in the shops of Dijon. Other interesting comparisons could be

[7] R. H. Bautier, 'La place de l'industrie brabançonne et plus particulièrement bruxelloise dans l'industrie textile au Moyen Age', *Annales de la Société Royale d'Archéologie de Bruxelles*, LI (1966).
[8] F. Piponnier, *Costume et vie sociale* (Paris, 1970), p. 331.

Table 13.1   Classification of cloths according to their price per ell

Price per ell	Cloth place of origin	designation	Other materials place of origin
0–0.19 F	Lorraine	beige bureau cameline tiretaine velu	Gray, Langres, village Beaumont, Marville Châtillon
0.20–0.39 F	Beaumont Dijon Fougères Laborde Langres Lormaye Lorraine Marville Metz Montcornet Mouzon Reims Saint-Lô Saint-Trond Sainte-Menehould Semur Verdun	brifaudeure cameline frise laveure serge velu	Nevers Beaumont Dijon, Lorraine, Marville, Verdun Dijon
0.40–0.59 F	Abbeville Bailleul Beaumont Beauvais Bourges Brussels Châtillon Dijon Dreston Durlan Fougères Fribourg Halle Liège Lierre Lormaye Lorraine Louviers Maubeuge Montcornet Mons Montbard	brunette cameline	Bourges, Virieux Beaumont

continued overleaf

Table 13.1 continued

Price per ell	Cloth place of origin	designation	Other materials place of origin
	Reims		
	Saint-Lô		
	Saint-Marcel		
	Saint-Mihiel		
	Sainte-Menehould		
	Tournai		
	Valence		
0.60–0.79 F	Abbeville	brunette	Rougemont
	Bernay		
	Bourges		
	Brussels		
	Châlons		
	Dijon		
	Disquine		
	Lormaye		
	Louviers		
	Montbard		
	Rouen		
	Saint-Lô		
	Termonde		
	Ieper (Ypres)		
0.80–0.99 F	Arlon		
	Châlons		
	Châtillon		
	Flandre		
	Louviers		
	Malines		
	Montivilliers		
	Thorigny		
	Tournai		
	Ieper (Ypres)		
1.00–1.19 F	Arlon		
	Bailleul		
	Bernay		
	Châlons		
	Châtillon		
	Lierre		
	Lormaye		
	Montivilliers		
	Rouen		
1.20–1.39 F	Arlon		
	Montivilliers		
	Rouen		

drawn with the provisioning of the papal court at Avignon; and with the transactions concerning cloth at the fairs of Châlon.[9]

As for cloth production, the Dijon documents offer a mass of information, very fragmentary it is true, on the fabrics manufactured in the centres supplying the city, their names, colours and prices. They have brought to light some little-known centres because their products were to satisfy a level of popular consumption, difficult to grasp in the usual medieval documents. For the city of Dijon itself, the inventories reveal even better than the rules of the trade the concrete reality of production conditions, raw materials, workshop equipment, and the exact composition and amount of the merchant's capital investment. It is unfortunate that the examples are so few.

[9]R. Delort, 'Note sur les achats de draps et d'étoffes effectués par la Chambre apostolique des papes d'Avignon (1316–1417)', *Mélanges d'Archéologie et d'Histoire publiés par l'Ecole française de Rome* (1962), p. 215–88; H. Dubois, *Les Foires de Chalon et le commerce dans la vallée de la Saône à la fin du Moyen Âge* (Paris, 1976), p. 159–71.

14 The Textile Trade of Poland in the Middle Ages
Jerzy Wyrozumski

The formation of nation states in central and east Europe during the tenth century was bound to influence the economic development of the countries of western Europe. The courts of the new sovereigns and the social élite developing at their side exhibited a growing demand for non-agricultural products. This acted as a stimulus to the growth of a number of branches of industry and trade, and to increasing specialisation. While the demands of military garrisons and of lower- and middle-rank officials were comparatively easy to meet, the situation was quite different in the case of the high dignitaries and courtiers who were much more exacting and difficult to please. This was especially true for textiles. In the highest social class, clothes were not only designed to protect the human body against cold and damp, but also to distinguish the wearer from the rest of the community. In the new social system that was emerging, elaborate and rich ways of dressing became a token of high office and dignity.

From time immemorial, the production of textiles was among the principal skills in the Slavonic countries. Woven cloth was used as a fairly frequent means of payment, the verb *płacić*, to pay, in all Slav languages being derived from *płat*, a piece of cloth.[1] Textile crafts had been, however, originally mainly a female occupation and for a long time – up to the thirteenth century – remained a domestic concern.[2] The archaeological findings show that Slavonic skill in textile production was relatively high;[3] but it did not rise above the level of folk culture, which soon ceased to be adequate for the requirements of

[1] S. S. Ciszewski, *Placidla pierwotne, Prace etnologiczne* (Warsaw, 1929), II, pp. 1–75.
[2] K. Tymieniecki, *Organizacja rzemiosla wczesnosredniowiecznego a geneza miast polskich*, Studia Wczesnosredniowieczne, III (Wroclaw, 1955), pp. 9–86; J. Wyrozumski, 'Tkactwo w Polsce w X–XIII wieku', *Kwartalnik Historii Kultury Materialnej*, XIII, 3 (1965), pp. 499–519.
[3] G. Sage, 'Die Gewebe aus dem alten Oppeln', *Altschlesien*, VI (1936), pp. 322–32; W. Holubowicz, *Opole w wiekach X–XII* (Katowice, 1956); J. Kaminska and A. Nahlik, *Wlokiennictwo gdanskie X–XIII wieku* (Łódź, 1958); A. Nahlik, 'Tkaniny z XIII–XIV-wiecznego cmentarzyska w miejscowosci Rownina Dolna, pow. Ketrzyn', *Rocznik Olsztynski*, I (1958), pp. 171–91; J. Kaminska and A. Nahlik, 'Etudes sur l'industrie textile du haut moyen âge en Pologne', *Archeologia Polona*, III (1960), pp. 89–119; A. Nahlik, *Tkaniny wsi wschodnioeuropejskiej X–XIII w.* (Łódź, 1965).

the royal court and the élite. Describing the visit paid by Emperor Otto III to Poland in the year 1000, a contemporary observer of the event, Thietmar Bishop of Merseburg, stressed the great splendour and munificence with which King Boleslaus the Brave had received his imperial guest.[4] A century later, the anonymous chronicler known as Gall, founding himself upon an early-eleventh-century source (no longer extant), also emphasised the great wealth and variety of dress among the Polish king's retinue at the same event, referring to the variety of fabrics used for the ceremony.[5] It is beyond doubt that most of them must have been imported, although some might have constituted war booty and some were possibly local products.

[4] M. Z. Jedlicki (ed.), *Kronika Thietmara* (Poznań, 1953), pp. 203–4: 'Qualiter autem cesar ab eodem tunc susciperetur et per sua usque ad Gnesin deduceretur, dictu incredibile ac ineffabile est'.

[5] *Monumenta Poloniae Historica*, 2nd ser., II (Kraków, 1952), p. 21: 'A camerariis vero palia extensa et cortinas, tapetia, strata, mantilia, manuteria, et quecumque servicio presentata fuerunt, iussit similiter congregare et in cameram imperatoris comportare'.

14.1   Poland, showing its mid-thirteenth century frontiers

Between the eighth and eleventh centuries, central Europe could be reached from the West along the following trade routes: the Baltic route, which in the period under discussion went mostly to the Prussian harbour of Truzo near the present-day Elblag;[6] an inland route going from Bavaria into the Danubian lands, reflected in the Raffelstetten tariff, revised in the years 903–5;[7] another inland way, which evolved from this as early as the tenth century, if not before, went to Prague and thence via Kraków to the Kiev region, a route described by the Arabic traveller Ibrahim ibn Jacob in 965–6.[8] In the ninth and tenth centuries the role of textile products in the commerce between East and West remained quite insignificant, as there is no special reference to it in the Raffelstetten tariff. There, the main stress was laid on two articles of exchange – slaves and salt. The situation changed with the gradual growth in importance of the early feudal central European states. Certainly, by the beginning of the thirteenth century there was a custom-house in Gdańsk where customs duty was paid mostly on woollen cloth. It was brought there, along with salt, by Lübeck merchants, to whom the Duke of Pomerania granted *libertatem inauditam* in 1224–26. In all probability this importation had been carried on for some time, as there was mention even of the different sorts of cloth which used to be transported, viz., *burnit* and *frizal*.[9] The tariff issued in the second half of the twelfth century for Masovia in central Poland mentions cloth among the principal goods transported there by both land and water.[10] There are records from the first half of the thirteenth century to show that in this way cloth used to be supplied to the Court of Masovian Princes.[11] It is difficult to establish when the inland routes from Germany to Poland began to be used, but it is clear that after the Teutonic Order had founded its state in Prussia (after 1226) the route from Frankfurt-an-der-Oder to Prussia became much more active. The customs treaties of 1238 and 1243 connected with this route mention textile articles brought from the West, among them woollen cloth, *brunetum, viride et scarletum*, and linen cloth called *pannus lineus*.[12]

Only some of the textiles imported into Poland from western Europe were consumed in the country at the royal, ducal and other noble courts, while some passed through the country east and southwards.

[6] The Anglo-Saxon version of Orosius – G. Labuda (ed.), *Zrodla skandynawskie i anglosaskie do dziejow Slowianszczyzny* (Warsaw, 1961), p. 69.

[7] G. Friedrich (ed.), *Codex diplomaticus et epistolaris Regni Bohemiae* (Prague, 1904–07), I, no. 31.

[8] *Monumenta Poloniae Historica*, 2nd ser., I (Kraków, 1946), p. 146.

[9] M. Perlbach (ed.), *Pommerellisches Urkundenbuch* (Gdańsk, 1882), no. 33.

[10] J. K. Kochanowski (ed.), *Codex diplomaticus et commemorationum Masoviae generalis* (Warsaw, 1919), nos. 88, 464.

[11] Ibid., no. 362.

[12] *Codex diplomaticus Maioris Poloniae* (Poznań, 1877), I, nos. 207–37.

Gall, the chronicler already cited, recorded in the early years of the twelfth century that 'regio Polonorum ab itineribus peregrinorum est remota et nisi transeuntibus in Russiam pro mercimonio paucis nota'.[13] The source is a highly trustworthy one and there is good reason to suppose that, since during the following century Russia was importing textile fabrics, in particular woollen cloth, then in the twelfth century too foreign merchants must have brought such goods to that country. Again, if we can trust the information contained in a source no longer extant and untraceable that after 1214, the merchants of Wroclaw had been granted the right to store their goods at Novogrod Vyelikij,[14] and in this trade woollen cloth must also have played a very important part.

Textiles began to be transported through Poland to Hungary probably at a later date than they were to Russia. Hungary lay in the sphere of Danubian trade and that was the first route by which it received textile products from western Europe.[15] With the growing importance of the textile trade in the Baltic, central Europe received more and more of the products of the expanding cloth-weaving centres of Flanders and northern France via Poland, especially since there was also trade in the opposite direction when Hungarian copper was transported to the Baltic coast and on westwards to Bugia. The first mention of woollen cloth in this trade was in 1265, in the tariff of Twardoszyn, near the Hungarian–Polish border.[16] Woollen cloth was referred to along with salt and lead imported into Hungary from Poland, but it was certainly merely a transit merchandise. This transit trade grew considerably in importance in the following years, and competition developed between Kraków and Sacz for participation in it.[17] In Hungary, the town of Koshice endeavoured to control the trade, or to have the greatest share in it.[18]

Towards the middle of the thirteenth century, Poland started on a period of economic development which manifested itself in the improvement of agricultural techniques, in the gradual spread of rent payments, in the advancement of the mining industry, of various arts and crafts, the use of money, and in the establishment of a number of urban communities. This sort of change at approximately the same time also affected the other countries of central Europe, first in the

---

[13] *Monumenta Poloniae Historica*, 2nd ser., II, p. 6.
[14] M. Scholz-Babisch and H. Wendt (eds.), *Quellen zur schlesischen Handelsgeschichte* (Breslau, 1940), no. 57.
[15] F. Bastian, 'Die Legende von Donauhandel im Frühmittelalter', *Vierteljahresschrift für Sozial- und Wirtschaftsgeschichte*, XXII (1929), pp. 289–330.
[16] G. Wenzel (ed.), *Codex diplomaticus Arpadianus* (Budapest, 1872), no. 499.
[17] F. Piekosinski (ed.), *Codex diplomaticus civitatis Cracoviensis* (Kraków, 1879), I, nos. 7, 13, 16.
[18] O. R. Halaga, *Kosice – Balt. Vyroba a obchod v styku vychodoslovenskych miest s Pruskom (1275–1526)* (Koshice, 1972).

west and then in the east. The further eastwards, the later these changes came. In Poland (if we exclude Silesia which held the leading position in this respect), the culmination of these changes came in the fourteenth century. As regards the trade we are here concerned with, these developments were visible in the development of professional textile production in towns, first of woollen cloth, and somewhat later of linen. Technical progress was much easier to achieve in towns, while in former times most of the fabrics had been woven at home.[19] Many foreign weavers, chiefly Germans, but others as well, began to flock into Polish towns. Thus in Wrocław, for example, there was a whole colony of Walloon weavers whose origins can be traced back possibly to the twelfth century.[20] The big landowners began to take greater care of their sheep and to introduce better breeds. The records of the time contain mentions of *oves selectae* and *oves Gallicae*.[21] The growing supply of wool to the market was coupled with an improvement in its quality.

Besides these tendencies towards a more advanced textile production evident in some towns such as Wrocław, Świdnica, Kraków, Biecz and Krosno upon the Wisłok, there were a number of other towns where the traditional craft was carried on with the aid of weavers from the neighbouring villages, where woollen cloth and linen of poor quality was produced, usually undyed, but accessible at a price the poorer classes could afford. A number of production centres of this type evolved, at such small towns in southern Poland, for example, as Lelów, Chęciny, Szydłowiec, Strzyżów and others. Many villagers, too, continued to weave cloth, linen more than woollen. For several centuries to come weaving was to remain one of the most active folk industries, supplying goods to town markets as well as purely local ones. In the seventeenth and eighteenth centuries, Polish village linen became an article of exportation. In the course of the fourteenth century village woollen cloth was well-known in Kraków and the adjoining town of Kazimierz (now incorporated into Kraków). The cloth was known as *pannus terrester* or *pannus terrenus albus vel griseus* and was brought to the town markets both by the peasants and by the landed gentry.[22] That this was a fairly common custom can be seen

[19] J. Wyrozumski, 'Tkactwo w Polsce' (see n. 2).
[20] T. Goerlitz, 'Das Breslauer Wallonenviertel', *Beiträge zur Geschichte der Stadt Braslau*, III (1937), pp. 77–106.
[21] R. Grodecki (ed.), *Księga henrykowska* (Poznań–Wrocław, 1949), p. 319; G. A. Tzschoppe and G. A. Stenzel (eds.), *Urkundensammlung zur Geschichte des Ursprings der Städt* (Hamburg, 1832), p. 153 n. 3.
[22] S. Krzyzanowski (ed.), *Acta scabinalia Cracoviensia 1365–76 et 1390–97* (Kraków, 1904), no. 1081; A. Chmiel (ed.), *Acta consultaria Casimiriensia 1369–81 et 1385–1402* (Kraków, 1932), p. 152.

from an Act passed in 1423, where woollen cloth is mentioned among the *res terrestres* supplied to the town by the peasants.[23]

In the development of the textile trade in fourteenth- and fifteenth-century Poland, two provinces were particularly active and prominent – Silesia, which from the 1330s was largely a fief of the kingdom of Bohemia,[24] and Little Poland.[25] But the trade played an important part also in other provinces, especially in central Poland (the provinces of Łęczyca and Sieradz), and in the north-east, in Masovia, where many small production centres were scattered about.[26] In the north-west of Poland, that is in Little Poland, the textile trade was later to play an important part in the economy after the sixteenth century.[27]

Polish textile products soon came to be exported. There was great demand for them, especially in western Russia, and their popularity was soon extended to Moldavia and Hungary. These were the main destinations of the export trade. In a charter granted in 1264 to Połaniec, a small town in Little Poland, the inhabitants were authorised to go 'versus Russiam cum pannis vel quibuscumque talibus aliis mercibus'.[28] This cannot have referred to the transit of woollen cloth of foreign make, since this was carried on almost exclusively by the major towns, but to the exportation of cloth of local production in the region. This trade began developing quickly from the middle of the fourteenth century when the Ruthenian provinces of Halicz and Vladimir were incorporated into the Polish kingdom. It was probably then that Polish woollen cloth first crossed the borders of Russia, paving the way to Moldavia, and then further on to the south.[29] The rise of this export trade was of great significance for the Polish economy, as it stimulated the economic activities of a great many small towns, scattered throughout almost the whole of the country, while the transit trade contributed towards the enrichment of a few major towns only.

The way towards the export of Polish cloth to Hungary had been paved by the transit trade referred to above. But it was only in the fourteenth century that this export trade was really consolidated. Woollen cloth is mentioned in the tariff of the road from Buda to

[23] J. V. Bandtkie (ed.), *Ius Polonicum* (Warsaw, 1831), p. 220.

[24] A. Schodrok, *Die schlesische Tuchweberei und Tuch Handlung von den Anfängen bis 1526* (Freiburg im Breisgau, 1948).

[25] J. Wyrozumski, *Tkactwo malopolskie w poznym sredniowieczu* (Kraków, 1972).

[26] J. Kaminska and I. Turnau (eds.), *Zarys historii wlokiennictwa na ziemiach polskich do konca XVIII wieku* (Wrocław, Warsaw and Krakow, 1966), p. 134.

[27] A. Maczak, *Sukiennictwo wielkopolskie XIV–XVII wieku* (Warsaw, 1955).

[28] F. Piekosinski (ed.), *Codex diplomaticus Poloniae Minoris* (Kraków, 1886), II, no. 473.

[29] L. Charewiczowa, *Handel sredniowiecznego Lwowa* (Lwów, 1925), pp. 67, 80, 93, 106; J. Wyrozumski, *Tkactwo malopolskie* (see n. 25), pp. 129–30.

Vienna issued in 1352 and 1394, as well as in that for the road from Poland to Hungary issued in 1434 (at Czchów).[30] Another tariff, issued in 1393 at Nowy Sącz, mentions fustian among the articles exported from Poland.[31] Apart from Kraków and Nowy Sącz, referred to on another occasion, some minor towns such as Biecz, Krosno, Żmigród and others also took part in the exportation of Polish textiles to Hungary. On the Hungarian side, the town which was most involved in the textile trade with Poland was Koshice in Slovakia.[32]

From time to time in the fourteenth and fifteenth centuries Polish woollen cloth, most of it probably from Silesia, also reached more distant lands, though evidently without playing any important part in trading relationships. There are references to such woollen cloth in Styria, Carinthia, Venice and Saxony, and it must have also been known in Switzerland, where it was recorded in the Zurich tariffs of 1379 and 1400.[33]

Side by side with the development of textile production in Poland, the importation of foreign fabrics, especially woollen cloth, continued. Imports and the transit trade did not diminish; on the contrary, imports grew markedly in the course of the fourteenth and fifteenth centuries. It is not difficult to explain why: cloth of Polish make was destined for a different market, for mass demand, whereas imported cloth was sought by the élite, by the upper classes. The drawback to an import trade of this kind was that it did not stimulate a tendency to improve the quality of either the domestic products or the techniques of production. Rather it worked to neutralise any such tendency. On the other hand, the import trade provided profits which helped considerably to enrich the more important towns, especially Gdańsk, Toruń and Kraków. It was through Gdańsk that the main traffic in foreign cloth was conducted, while Toruń tried to monopolise the trade to the south and east. Here, however, it had to face serious limitations with respect to entering into direct trading relations with Russia and Hungary. Kraków was very active as an intermediary in this field, especially as regards woollen cloth being transported from the north to Hungary as well as that transported by land from Germany via Nürnberg (Nuremberg).[34] Another town which profited from

[30] H. Ammann, 'Wirtschaftsbeziehungen zwischen Oberdeutschland und Polen im Mittelalter, l'artisanat et la vie urbaine en Pologne médiévale', *Ergon*, III (Warsaw, 1962), p. 342; F. Piekosinski (ed.), *Codex diplomaticus civitatis Cracoviensis* (Kraków, 1882), II, no. 310.

[31] F. Piekosinski and J. Szujski (eds.), *Libri antiquissimi civitatis Cracoviae saeculi decimi quarti* (Kraków, 1877), II, p. 85.

[32] O. R. Halaga, *Kosice – Balt* (see n. 18), pp. 248–50.

[33] H. Ammann, 'Wirtschaftsbeziehungen' (see n. 30), p. 344.

[34] S. Kutrzeba, *Handel Krakowa w wiekach srednich na tle stosunkow handlowych Polski* (Kraków, 1902), pp. 26–7, 63–4, 84–5, 139–42.

this trade was Łwów, the most important trading emporium in Ruthenia, incorporated in the kingdom of Poland. Towards the end of the Middle Ages two other towns began benefiting by this trade when Poznań and Lublin began to act as intermediaries in the exchange of commodities with the Grand Duchy of Lithuania. It was in this branch of trade, with woollen cloth imported from abroad, that the class of professional clothier-merchants (*pannicidae*) evolved in Poland, while home-produced cloth was frequently sold by the producers themselves; sometimes they even carried it with them to the foreign countries.[35]

The importation of woollen cloth and the transit trade produced other benefits besides the commercial profits. The high-quality foreign woollen cloth used sometimes to be submitted to certain special methods of dressing, particularly to re-shearing and pressing. This was also done at Koshice in Hungary. This type of dressing enhanced the quality of the cloth and enabled the price to be raised, offsetting the costs of reloading and of transport. The tariff for woollen-cloth shearing at the Kraków shearing-house, for example, took into account the following kinds: *brwkesch, florenczesch, eyprisch, mechlesch, herntalesch, balbarth, gemeyn eyprisch, englesch* and, as the last item on the list, *landtuch*.[36]

We will now proceed to review the various textile goods to be found in the Polish markets in the fourteenth and fifteenth centuries, particularly in Kraków which was the central emporium of the Polish textile trade. This will help us to establish the countries and towns from which the different fabrics were brought to Poland,[37] as well as to determine the relation between the respective prices of imported and domestic cloth. The main sources making such a review possible are the tariff of payment for cloth-shearing in Kraków (1364) and the Kraków maximum-prices tariff (1396),[38] as well as a number of bills and accounts dating from the late fourteenth century to the last quarter of the fifteenth.[39] It should be stressed that throughout this period the

---

[35] J. Wyrozumski, *Tkactwo maloplskie* (see n. 25), pp. 122–5.

[36] *Codex diplomaticus civitatis Cracoviensis*, II, no. 262.

[37] C. Verlinden, 'Brabantsch en Vlaamsch laken te Krakau op het einde der XIV-e eeuw', *Mededeelingen van de Koninklijke Vlaamsche Academie voor Wetenschappen, Lettern en Schoone Kunsten, van Belgïe*, V, 2 (1943); idem, 'Dwa bieguny ekspansji sukiennictwa flamandzkiego i brabanckiego w XIV w.: Polska i Polwysep Iberyjski', *Sprawozdania z posiedzen Komisji Naukowych Oddzialu PAN w Krakowie* (January–June 1967), pp. 119–22.

[38] *Codex diplomaticus civitatis Cracoviensis*, II, no. 286.

[39] F. Piekosinski (ed.), *Rachunki dworu krola Wladyslawa Jagielly i krolowej Jadwigi z lat 1388 1420* (Kraków, 1896); *Libri antiquissimi civitatis Cracoviae* (see n. 31), II; J. Karwasinska (ed.), 'Rachunki zupne bochenskie z lat 1394–1421', *Archiwum Komisji Historycznej* (Kraków, 1939), XV, pp. 123–232; S. Gaweda, Z. Perzanowski and A. Strzelecka (eds.), *Rachunki krolewskie z lat 1471–72 i 1476–78* (Wroclaw and Kraków, 1960).

prices for the different sorts of woollen cloth were fairly stable in Poland.[40]

The most popular Italian textile in Poland was Florentine woollen cloth (*pannus Florentinus, florenczesch*). It was one of the oldest imported products on the Polish market. Three colours are mentioned, brown, red and yellow. It was lavishly bought at the royal court; the king used to make gifts of it, for instance, to foreign envoys. The price of this cloth at that time was approximately 20–2 groszes per ell. There was also a semi-Florentine variety, no doubt derived from the Florentine cloth proper.

A very important position in the import trade was held by English woollen cloth (*pannus de Anglia, Angliciensis, preciosus Angliensis, englesch gewant*). It was fairly differentiated as to quality; in a short interval of time its price in Kraków varied from 14 to 24 groszes per ell. Two colours are mentioned, brown and red. At the royal court it was offered as a gift to envoys of foreign states, officials and the clergy. The cloth that came from Lund (*pannus Lundensis, lunsky, lundysz*), which first reached Poland towards the end of the fourteenth century, was also considered to be an English product. Perhaps originally this name had designated fabrics exported from London; in the course of time it came to be used as the name of a particular sort of expensive cloth, which may explain why a variety of *lundysz*, known as *falendysz*, was considered to be an Italian cloth. The price of this sort of cloth in Kraków in the years 1395–1431 was 12, 14, 16, 18 and 24 groszes per ell.

The woollen cloth of Flanders was represented on the Polish market by several sorts and varieties. It came mainly from Bruges (*brukesch, bruczskie pannus*). During the second half of the fifteenth century its price in Kraków amounted to 30 groszes per ell, the highest price for any woollen cloth in that part of Poland. We should also mention woollen cloth from Lier (*pannus de Lira*). Late in the fourteenth century an ell of this fabric (black in colour) cost 24 groszes, but at approximately the same time it could also be bought for 18 groszes. The Dendermonde cloth (*dillirmundisch, von Derelmunde*) was cheaper and cost 15 groszes per ell. Cloth which came from Kortrijk (Courtrai), commonly known as *koltrysz* (*pannus de Coltres, de Cortir, coltrisch, colcistiense, culcistri, criczsky alias gulcistri, flaveus pannus vulgariter coltrysz*) had been noted to occur for nearly a century at the price of almost 12 groszes per ell. The name designated both the place of origin and a particular sort of cloth. Cloth coming from Ieper (Ypres) (*eypresch, eyprisch*), though known in Kraków from 1364, is not listed in the maximum-prices tariff issued in 1396. It probably did not play a

[40] J. Wyrozumski, *Tkactwo małopolskie* (see n. 25), pp. 133–41.

prominent part, perhaps just being transported through Poland to Hungary. At least two sorts were known: *eyprisch* and *gemeyn eyprisch*. Mention should also be made of woollen cloth from Geeraardsbergen (*de Gersperg, Girinsberg*), which in the late fourteenth century was priced in Kraków at about 12 groszes per ell.

Among the Brabant woollen cloth pride of place belonged to that of Brussels (*pannus de Bressela, Brusliensis, Broslensis, Bruseliensis, brusselskie*). It was known in Poland in several colours – white, yellow, grey, red, green and black. It was differentiated as to quality and towards the end of the fourteenth century its price ranged from 20 to 32 groszes per ell. It was often bought by the royal court. An important part was played by the cloth made at Malines (Mechlin) known as *mechelskie* (*machelsky, pannus Mechliensis, Mechilensis, Machaliensis, de Mechil, von Mechlesch*). In the late fourteenth century it was priced at 17 groszes per ell, and nearly a hundred years later at 15 groszes. There was also woollen cloth made at Leuven (Louvain) (*pannus Levinensis, de Lovana*), which appeared on the Kraków market at the end of the fourteenth century at 16 groszes an ell, but this probably did not play any important part. This was also probably the case with Thynian cloth which was apparently produced at Tirlemont or Thienen (*pannus Thinensis, de Tyn*). It came in two sorts, long cloth priced at the end of the fourteenth century at 14 groszes an ell, and short cloth at 9 groszes. Less frequently the Kraków market got a supply of Herenthals cloth (*herentalesch, pannus Harntaliensis, Aruntaliensis*); in its black variety it cost 18 groszes an ell. Finally, from time to time there was a supply of *ballarth*, formerly identified with English woollen cloth, but now considered to be Brussels cloth, green in colour, that is, *bellaerts*.

Among the French fabrics, we come across woollen cloth made at Enghien in Artois (*pannus Edingensis, Edingi*). It seems to have been of mediocre quality, as its price at the end of the fourteenth century was only 8 groszes an ell. A frequent supply to Poland was the *arras* (*harras, arrasch*), which had derived its name from the town of Arras, but which was soon extended also to designate common cloth of various colours. It occurred in Pomerania, in Poland proper, in Lithuania, Russia and Hungary. In 1396, 1417 and after 1470 its cost was barely 3 groszes an ell. It was very cheap indeed and presented serious competition to the cloth of local make.

The Dutch textiles included *pannus Ostrodomensis* or *Ostrodamiensis*, priced during the fifteenth century at 15 groszes an ell. Usually from the Netherlands also came the *karazje* (*kersey, kirsey, kirsing*), a common cloth priced the same as *arras*, 3 groszes an ell. It was known in Poland during the fourteenth and fifteenth century and was transported through the country to Hungary, and in all probability to Russia and Lithuania as well. Its importation, however, did not develop on a major scale until the sixteenth century.

There is no doubt that in the Polish textile trade in the Middle Ages German cloth played a prominent part. However, it is much more difficult to trace it down in Polish sources since the different sorts were only rarely designated by the name of the town from which they came. Nevertheless, from the late fourteenth century we know woollen cloth from Aachen (*pannus de Aquis*) priced at 8 groszes an ell, and cloth from Zwickau in Saxony (*Czekelische tuch*). Various cloths with German names, such as *Kreptuch*, *Schleftuch* and *Stubreyt*, designate merely the kind of the fabric, leaving the town of origin unnamed.

Comparatively numerous were the cloths coming to Poland from the lands of the kingdom of Bohemia. They were called either *panni Bohemicales*, or, in Lusatian towns, *panni Settavienses* and *Zitavienses*, *panni Gorlicenses*, etc. In the fourteenth century Silesia was also incorporated with the kingdom of Bohemia, and hence we might include into the same group *panni Vratislavienses*, *panni Swidnicenses* and *stamina de Cruczborg*. The price of this cloth ranged between 4 and 5.5 groszes an ell.

Now we can draw a comparison between cloth imported to Poland and cloth of home make as regards their respective prices. The comparison seems instructive, reflecting both the standard of Polish textile production and the structure of the whole textile trade. It is to be regretted that we have no adequate quantitative indicators regarding the share of the different sorts of cloth in the trade. The cost of transport of foreign cloth must, of course, have affected their price, in many cases quite substantially. Italian cloth was priced in the fourteenth and fifteenth centuries at 20–2 groszes an ell, English at 12–24 groszes, Flanders cloth at 12–30 groszes, Brabant cloth at 9–30 groszes (and, in exceptional cases, at 32 groszes), French cloth (from Enghien) at 8, German cloth (from Aachen) at 8, Bohemian cloth at 4–5.5, and only *arras* and *karazja* at 3 groszes an ell, while cloth of domestic Kraków make was sold at a price ranging from 2 to 3 groszes an ell. The cheapest of all was *loden Cracoviensis* at 2 groszes per ell. Cloth of village make, which the town of Kazimierz provided for its shepherds, was priced at 2 groszes an ell. In other Polish towns at that time, where woollen cloth was also produced, it was sold at a price from 2 to 4 groszes. It was in most cases undyed and only semi-finished in an unskilled way. The two markets in Poland were clearly quite distinct.

15 The Fustian Industry of the Ulm Region in the Fifteenth and Early Sixteenth Centuries
Hermann Kellenbenz

I

In southern Germany the weaving of fustian (*Barchent*), a textile made from a mixture of flax and cotton, began in the fourteenth century. The stimulus came from northern Italy where fustian weaving had already developed, especially in the area around Milan. The flax was to be found in abundance in the extensive area between Lake Constance and the Danube and beyond, and from the Swabian Alps to the river Lech. The cotton came from Venice or from Genoa. The ships of these two republics brought it from the Levant, and the southern German merchants, who had good trading relations with both towns, bought it or exchanged it for their goods. The German towns which had the best trade relations with northern Italy were Augsburg, Ulm and Nürnberg (Nuremberg) which at that time was beginning to push Regensburg from its dominant commercial position.

Fustian weaving in Ulm arose out of the earlier traditions of woollen and linen weaving. Woollen weaving was at its height before the end of the thirteenth century, after which linen and then fustian weaving began their expansion. Within the Swabian linen-weaving area as a whole, the Ulm region stretched from the Jura across the Danube valley and the valley of the Iller.[1] Linen weaving in this region was an old tradition, but it came to be of importance for the export trade from the twelfth century. In the course of the fourteenth century woollen and linen weaving was partially replaced by fustian weaving in the whole north-east of the Swabian linen area, especially in Augsburg, Ulm, Memmingen, Biberach and Kaufbeuren and in the north as far as Nördlingen. The reason why fustian weaving gained

---

[1] Hektor Ammann, 'Die Anfänge der Leinenindustrie des Bodenseegebiets', *Alemannisches Jahrbuch* (1953), pp. 251–313.

at the expense of linen must be seen in the growing relations with Italy and the influence coming from there in matters of fashion. Fustians were finer and softer than the coarser linen. Moreover, it must have impressed Ulm and Augsburg merchants who came to Italy how fustian weaving expanded in the course of the fourteenth century in Lombardy. Merchants of Ulm visited Como and Milan as well as Venice.

It is not known exactly when it was that fustian weaving began in Ulm. But we do know that Johannes Vol of Ulm bought cotton in Milan in 1375, that the Nürnberg merchant Claus Rummel sold '*Ulmer Barchent*' with the trade mark of the 'grape' at Cologne in 1389, and that another Ulm merchant, Ulrich Strölin, sold fustians with the quality mark of the 'ox' at the Frankfurt fair in 1398. Between 1406 and 1413, 'Zan' Vol was the most important buyer of Syrian cotton from the Venice merchants Donado Soranzo and Fratelli. From as early as 1389, the yearly revenue from the so-called fustian *Schau* is known; it rose from 1257 guilders in that year to 3555 guilders by

15.1   The Ulm fustian region

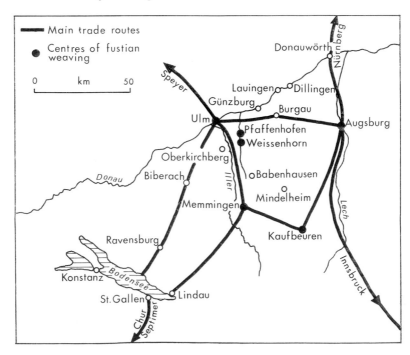

1413. During the fifteenth century, fustian from Ulm was sold as far as Spain, England and the Hanse towns.[2]

In the first woollen weavers' ordinance of February 1403 the Mayor and the Great and Small Councils of Ulm declared that there had been much recent quarrelling because a number of grey cloth-weavers (*Grautucher*) attempted to enter the guild of weavers in order to obtain the right to weave fustians. Previously the Council had not allowed this because of the fear that members of other guilds would do the same. It was decided in 1403 that in future no citizen who was an artisan should be allowed to enter the weavers' guild. The children of citizens could only enter the guild after having served their apprenticeship in weaving; people from the country or from other towns who were weavers (but not those belonging to any other craft) could enter after becoming citizens and staying for five years, as could weavers' journeymen and employees living in the town. Outside the town, that is beyond half a mile from the town, weavers could weave fustians and bring their products to the *Schau* (show), but only if they used cotton which had been inspected in Ulm.[3] Another ordinance in March 1403 forbade moving from one guild to another without the permission of the Council. Ulm merchants had control over the cotton used in Ulm as well as in the surrounding countryside. The country weavers (*Gäuweber*) mostly lived in the region east of Ulm, in the margraviate of Burgau, and particularly in the lordships of Kirchberg, Weissenhorn and Pfaffenhofen. In the same way the towns of Biberach, Memmingen and Augsburg had their country weavers too. In about 1500 the number of country weavers in the Ulm region was between 330 and 600. A document dating from 1513 reveals that every weaver having

---

[2] H. Sieveking, 'Aus venetianischen Handelsbüchern', *Schmollers Jahrbuch für Gesetzgebung, Verwaltung und Volkswirtschaft*, XXVI (1902), pp. 221–3; Aloys Schulte, *Geschichte des mittelalterlichen Handels und Verkehrs zwischen Westdeutschland und Italien*, 2 vols. (Leipzig, 1900–02), II, p. 136; Franz Bastian, 'Regensburger Textilindustrie im späten Mittelalter' in Hermann Heimpel (ed.), *Das Gewerbe der Stadt Regensburg* (Stuttgart, 1926), pp. 184, 187ff, 189, 202, 210–19; idem, *Das Runtingerbuch 1383–1407 und verwandtes Material zum Regensburger und süddeutschen Handel*, 3 vols. (Regensburg, 1944, 1935 and 1943), I, pp. 550–4, 627; II, pp. 68–76, 84, 123, 140–51, 262, 274; III, p. 227; Bruno Kuske, *Quellen zur Geschichte des Kölner Handels und Verkehrs*, 4 vols. (Bonn, 1918–34), I, p. 413; Hektor Ammann, 'Vom geographischen Wissen einer deutschen Handelsstadt des Spätmittelalters', *Ulm und Oberschwaben*, 34 (1955), pp. 39–65; Werner Schnyder, *Handel und Verkehr über die Bündner Pässe im Mittelalter zwischen Deutschland, der Schweiz und Oberitalien*, I (Zürich, 1973), p. 157, nr 128c; Wolfgang von Stromer, *Die Gründung der Baumwollindustrie in Mitteleuropa; Wirtschaftspolitik im Spätmittelalter* (Stuttgart, 1978), pp. 37–8.

Concerning the trade see also H. Wescher, 'Baumwollhandel und Baumwollgewerbe im Mittelalter' in *Ciba-Rundschau*, 45 (Basle, 1940), pp. 1632ff; Wilhelm Stieda and Hildebrand Veckinchusen, *Briefwechsel eines deutschen Kaufmanns im 15. Jahrhundert* (Leipzig, 1921); Aloys Schulte, *Geschichte der Ravensburger Handelsgesellschaft 1380 1530, 3 vols* (Stuttgart/Berlin, 1923), II, p. 97 n. 5; Franz Irsigler, 'Leben und Werk eines spätmittelalterlichen Kaufmanns am Beispiel von Johann von Nuyss' in *Jahrbuch des Kölnischen Geschichtsvereins*, 42 (1968), pp. 117f; von Stromer, *Die Gründung der Baumwollindustrie*, pp. 85ff.

[3] Eugen Nübling, *Ulms Kaufhaus im Mittelalter* (Ulm, 1902), p. 156ff.

one loom kept about seven persons occupied in spinning, and that if he owned three looms he might need twenty-seven or thirty persons for the spinning.

The weavers generally worked for wages, receiving the raw cotton from merchants known as *Wollherren*. Only some of them became independent entrepreneurs, buying the cotton from the *Wollherren*, having it spun by members of their household, then weaving it and selling the unbleached fustian to the fustian merchants. Before the fustian could be sold on the markets it had to be approved by the *Schau* which was a body of about eight or ten persons under the control of the town. The product was destined for sale in the markets of Switzerland, Italy, France, the Netherlands and England, and later in Spain and Portugal too.

The first ordinance of the Ulm *Schau* that has been preserved dates from the year 1419 which was a time of depression and thus the Council of Ulm found it necessary to give stricter orders for maintaining its standards. It laid down rules of procedure for the carders, the wool-beaters and the weavers. A further ordinance in 1424 laid down rules for bleaching.[4] Throughout the fifteenth century, the matter of the country weavers also remained a problem. In 1457 the town weavers obtained a law that no country weaver was allowed to have more than two looms. Moreover at the *Schau* the country weavers had to pay one shilling more than the town weavers for each of the three qualities of cloth (marked with the signs of ox, lion or grape). The weavers of Weissenhorn and of Burgau protested against this measure and the Weissenhorn weavers instigated their Council to ask the Ulm Council to abolish the new ordinance, but the Ulm Council maintained its position. In 1467 there was further trouble. The weavers of Memmingen and of Biberach obtained from their Council a ruling that the country weavers of their region were to be excluded from their *Schau*. These weavers then asked the Ulm Council for permission to have access to the Ulm *Schau*, and the Ulm Council acceded to this request against the wishes of the town weavers. In Ulm itself there was also trouble between the *Wollherren*, who dominated the trade with the cotton markets in Italy, and the retailers and other small traders. The *Wollherren* were eager to maintain their monopoly of cotton and they did not want to allow others to enter the trade in fustians; they endeavoured to see that the weavers were not permitted to buy cotton from retailers and other small traders in exchange for fustians.[5] This

---

[4] Karl Schmid, *Die Entwiklung der Hofer Baumwoll-Industrie 1432–1913* (Leipzig–Erlangen, 1923); von Stromer, *Die Gründung* (see n. 2), p. 37 n. 45.

[5] For instance, in 1460 and 1465; Eugen Nübling, *Ulms Baumwollweberei im Mittelalter* (Leipzig, 1890), pp. 150ff. The following account draws on this source.

was intended to enable them to set the price of raw cotton in their own way. However, the Council compromised with the town weavers in that it lowered the customs duty on cotton, and weavers as well as shopkeepers were allowed to buy the cotton from foreign merchants and not only from the Ulm merchants travelling to Italy. In order to prevent the raising of prices of yarn and weft by any middlemen, an ordinance of 1489 laid it down that only members of the guild of weavers should be allowed to buy yarn or weft (*Wepfen*). Towards the end of the century the Ulm fustian met some competition from the type of linen known as *Golschen* which was woven at Memmingen, Biberach, Weissenhorn, Günzburg, Mindelheim and other places where it was under the control of special ordinances including a *Schau*. There must have been more flax growing than in other periods and certainly more yarn was produced. Generally the good yarn which was used for fustian weaving was separated from the worse qualities and sold for a higher price.

There was a short crisis in 1512 when the war between the Emperor, the Pope, France and the Republic of Venice made the price of cotton rise. At that time the town weavers seem to have felt the competition of the country weavers more strongly than before, and they asked the town Council not to permit the country weavers to make *Golschen* and to forbid them access to the *Schau*, and not to allow any new fustian weavers in the country to attend the *Schau*. The Council decided to continue to allow the *Golschen* weavers who had their own workshops, but that they should be restricted to only one loom, and that no newcomers would be permitted into the trade. This ordinance also applied to the weavers of Söflingen, a village just outside the walls of Ulm. The town weavers were further permitted to obtain yarn in exchange for *Golschen*, while this was forbidden for the country weavers. Thus, the Council made a concession concerning *Golschen* but it did not give way in the question of fustian weaving by country weavers. When in 1513 the town weavers addressed their grievances to the Emperor, he commissioned Adam von Fruntsberg at Mindelheim and Wilhelm Gussen von Gussenberg at Glött to mediate between them and the Council, which they tried to do with negotiations at Dillingen on the Danube. Here the representatives of Ulm stressed that the fustian production was a matter wholly dependent on the Ulm Council and that the town weavers 'being linen weavers' had nothing to do with fustian. They pointed to an interesting fact and foresaw a danger for the Ulm fustian trade: if the Ulm town weavers insisted in their monopolistic policy, there might be more than one organised fustian *Schau* in the surroundings of Ulm such as already existed for *Golschen*. The representatives of Ulm proposed to limit the number of country weavers to 420 and that each one should have no more than two looms.

The weavers replied that during the past year only 330 weavers had 'an die Schau gewirkt'. But the year was, according to the argument of the representatives of Ulm, an exceptional one because of the war; after peace was restored, they claimed, the number would rise to 500 or 600. The Dillingen negotiations ended in August 1513 without a solution having been obtained. In September the Emperor decided that things should remain in the state they had been in hitherto.

II

After 1513 the situation was to change considerably. In competition with Ulm, the Augsburg merchant and banker Jakob Fugger began to develop fustian weaving at Weissenhorn, a small town only a few miles to the south-east. Originally in the hands of Wittelsbach-Landshut, Weissenhorn and the surrounding county of Marstetten became the property of the Emperor Maximilian in 1505. Two years later Maximilian mortgaged it together with the lordships of Ober-kirchberg, Oberpfaffenhofen and Wullenstetten to Jakob Fugger in return for loans which Fugger made to him. Weissenhorn had a tradition of weaving, especially of *Golschen*; from 1480 it had a *Golschen–Schau* which included regulations concerning red and white fustians and the bleaching of fustian. In 1517 the *Bürgermeister* of Weissenhorn decided to establish a *Barchent-Schau*, a development which received support from Fugger who provided the weavers with cotton.[6]

Little can be discovered of how weaving developed in the Weissenhorn region under him. Nikolaus Thoman, the author of *Weissenhornische Chronik*, states that in 1521 only four or five weavers produced their fustians at the *Schau*, but during the following years the situation seems to have improved. Jakob Fugger died at the end of 1525, but under his nephew Anton Fugger, his heir, the fustian trade became a more important factor in the whole Fugger enterprise. As a consequence of religious difficulties at Augsburg, Anton Fugger retired in late 1533 and early 1534 to Weissenhorn, and during the last months of 1535 he was to be found again at Weissenhorn.[7] We may assume

[6] Norbert Lieb, *Die Fugger und die Kunst im Zeitalter der Spätgotik und frühen Renaissance* (Munich, 1952), p. 123ff. Eduard Wylicil, 'Die Weissenhorner Barchentschau', *Zeitschrift des Historischen Vereins für Schwaben*, 60 (1954), gives according to Thoman, 1516 as the year when the *Barchent-Schau* was established; Götz Freiherr von Pölnitz, 'Die Anfänge der Weissenhorner Barchent-weberei unter Jakob Fugger dem Reichen' in *Festschrift für Hans Liermann* (Erlangen, 1964), pp. 196–220, dates the origins of fustian weaving in Weissenhorn back to the 1470s; idem, *Anton Fugger* (Tübingen, 1958), II, p. 303 n. 27; von Stromer, *Die Gründung* (see n. 2), p. 61 n. 63, supposes that fustian weaving began already before 1403.

[7] See Norbert Lieb, *Die Fugger und die Kunst im Zeitalter der hohen Renaissance* (Munich, 1958); Götz Freiherr von Pölnitz, *Anton Fugger*, 3 vols. (Tübingen, 1958–71), esp. I, pp. 277, 290, 295/6, 298, 336, 346, 689 n. 161.

that he used this opportunity to take care of the organisation of fustian weaving there. However, there is little or no clear information about this. The Augsburg inventory of 1533 mentions that the Nürnberg factor Gastel Fugger sent '5 geschnittene Hölzer, damit man die Barchat wird bezeichen zu Weissenhorn'.[8] The Weissenhorn chronicler Thoman records that in May 1534 the Fuggers began to erect a building where the fustians and the cotton had to be weighed, called the *Gret* or *Wag*. During the summer of the next year the plans were modified and a *Schau* for fustian and cotton was established there.[9] The Weissenhorn weavers were ordered not to buy their cotton at Ulm any more, but to obtain it from the Fuggers and not to go to the Ulm *Schau* with their products.

Ulm tried to get Augsburg to intervene with Fugger in its favour. Augsburg in turn was afraid of Fugger's rivalry since its weavers bought their yarn from as far as six miles outside the town and had suppliers of yarn in Burgau and indeed in Weissenhorn itself. Moreover Augsburg was anxious in case other neighbouring areas might imitate Fugger's example and organise their own fustian trade. Fugger's categorical reply was that Augsburg should keep out of everything concerned with his *Barchenthandel*.[10] At the same time he used his relations with the Emperor as well as with Ferdinand and the Upper Austrian government at Innsbruck to assist him against Ulm.[11] On the other side, Ulm tried to influence the members of the Schmalkalden Federation to tell the English representatives that the fustian trade of the Fuggers in England be prohibited. It was claimed that the Fuggers had got a privilege which was directed against the Ulm trade in England.[12] The Emperor was appealed to by Ulm as well as by Augsburg, but both towns were regarded as untrustworthy centres of Protestantism, and neither could get help from the Emperor. In 1538

---

[8] Lieb, *Die Fugger und die Kunst im Zeitalter der hohen Renaissance* (see n. 7), p. 317; von Pölnitz, *Anton Fugger* (see n. 7), I, p. 685 n. 147; Fürstlich und Gräflich Fuggersches Familien- und ·Stiftungs-Archiv Dillingen/Donau (FA) 2.1.22b/42–5, 62f, 88.

[9] Nübling, *Ulms Baumwollweberei* (see n. 5), p. 159 n. 2.

[10] FA 27.4.22/24; von Pölnitz, *Anton Fugger* (see n. 7), I, p. 669 n. 48.

[11] In August 1535 representatives of Augsburg negotiated with Anton Fugger at Weissenhorn and in September with Raymund Fugger at Mickhausen. At the end of November 1535 Ulm representatives came to Weissenhorn in order to speak with Anton Fugger. In January 1536 the Ulm Bürgermeister Jörg Besserer visited Anton Fugger at Augsburg in order to move him to give way. People who intervened for Fugger were the vice-chancellor Dr Held, the councillor Ferenberger, the Freiherr von Völs and the bishop of Vienna: FA 27.4.22; von Pölnitz, *Anton Fugger* (see n. 7), II, p. 303 n. 27. On 20 November 1535, Fugger concluded a contract with the Bürgermeister and Council of Weissenhorn; ibid., p. 305 n. 28.

[12] Nübling, *Ulms Baumwollweberei* (see n. 5), p. 159ff, gives the year 1532, but this seems to refer to 1536; cf. von Pölnitz, *Anton Fugger* (see n. 7), II, p. 305 n. 28. In April 1536 Ulm asked Landgraf Philipp of Hessen if it would be useful to send representatives to Henry VIII concerning the fustian trade or to be content with letters to him; von Pölnitz, ibid., II, p. 307 n. 42.

King Ferdinand received 20000 guilders from Ulm as a loan and in return promised to leave castle and county of Kirchberg, the castle of Illerzell and the lordships of Wullenstetten, Pfaffenhofen, Weissenhorn, Marstetten and Buch to Ulm after the mortgage to Fugger expired in 1568. Nevertheless, in November of the same year he renewed the privilege for the Weissenhorn fustian *Schau*.[13] At precisely the same time, the records of Fugger's relations in Venice show that considerable quantities of cotton were bought there. The accounts for November 1535 reveal orders for 91 sacks of about 760 centners and 23 sacks of 176 centners for the price of 10877 guilders.[14]

A consequence of this new activity in the Weissenhorn region was a shortage of yarn at Ulm and the Ulm Council found it impossible to permit the town weavers a second loom for fustians. After 1543 the yarn boilers were no longer allowed to boil yarn for weavers who worked for the Fugger *Schau* at Weissenhorn.[15] By 1544 the dispute between Ulm and Fugger was clearly growing more fierce. Fugger forbade his weavers to visit the Ulm *Schau* any more. Once again Ulm addressed itself to Augsburg and to King Ferdinand.[16] Ferdinand's vice-chancellor Gienger came from Ulm and he promised to help his native town. Ferdinand's reply was favourable to Ulm, but at the same time Anton Fugger managed to obtain a response from Charles V at Cambrai in September 1544 favourable to himself.

In 1545 there were further complications. Ulm sued Fugger because his *Kastner* forbade the weavers of certain villages to buy cotton from the merchants at Ulm.[17] Ferdinand now again took Fugger's side. He withdrew his support because of Ulm's participation in the Schmalkalden league, and Ulm had to recognise this in 1547 when Fugger's mortgage was extended until 1598.[18] After the revolt of the princes the situation changed fundamentally. From the autumn of 1552 Ulm received increasing support from Ferdinand and the Upper Austrian government at Innsbruck.[19] The good diplomatic relations of Ulm

---

[13] Ibid., II, p. 421 n. 170.

[14] Ibid., I, p. 687 n. 152.

[15] Nübling, *Ulms Baumwollweberei* (see n. 5), p. 161.

[16] Ibid., p. 161; von Pölnitz, *Anton Fugger* (see n. 7), II:2, p. 62 n. 7.

[17] According to von Pölnitz, the villages were Erlishofen, Diepoldshofen, Walkertshofen, Pfaffenhofen, Rothberg and Kadolzhofen. Fugger replied that his *Kastner* only had given a hint; von Pölnitz, *Anton Fugger* (see n. 7), II:2, p. 71 nn. 74 and 76. The document in FA 27.4.22 calls these places 'Flecken' (large villages with markets) and has the names 'Erbishofen, Diepolzhofen, Molckerzhofen, Pfaffenhofen, Weg-, Berg- und Kadolzhofen'. The *Kastner* reported that in the five villages of the Iller valley which were interested in the Weissenhorn *Schau* not more than two or three weavers really went to Weissenhorn; in the Roth valley and in the lordship of Pfaffenhofen there were forty weavers who were ordered by the *Kastner* to bring their products to the Weissenhorn *Schau*.

[18] Von Pölnitz, *Anton Fugger* (see n. 7), II:2, pp. 542, 756 n. 184; FA 212.2 and 213.2.

[19] Von Pölnitz, *Anton Fugger* (see n. 7), II:1, pp. 359ff and 678 n. 215.

with the court of Ferdinand and the Innsbruck government helped to promote the Ulm standpoint. Negotiations at Günzburg in October 1553 between the parties under the mediation of Habsburg commissioners failed.[20] Though the town of Weissenhorn wanted Fugger to continue the production of fustians and the *Schau*, Fugger himself became tired with the matter. He planned to reduce his activities and was finally inclined to give way, or at least to leave things as they had been in 1534.[21] In August 1555 he concluded an agreement with Ulm permitting all fustian produced in and around Weissenhorn to be sold to the Ulm merchants, and even let Ulm buy his supply of cotton stapled at Weissenhorn for 11 000 guilders.[22] Subsequently. the Weissenhorn weavers again brought their products to the Ulm *Schau*.

III

The Weissenhorn enterprise was under the direction of a factor by the name of Valentin Mair, who, when Anton Fugger was not at Weissenhorn, received his orders from the central administration of the Fugger enterprise at Augsburg. The books were kept by a book-keeper called Christoph Müller. The whole business was organised on the basis of the putting-out system. Like the Ulm *Wollherren*, Fugger supplied the weavers with cotton while they provided themselves with yarn spun in the surroundings of Weissenhorn. The yarn was boiled at Weissenhorn by special yarn boilers. There were dyers and cloth-shearers. Ground for two bleacheries was bought by the town of Weissenhorn, where the costs of construction were financed by the town.[23] Orders were made through the Augsburg administration for the purchase of cotton in Venice. The cotton crossed over the Alps and went through Kempten and Memmingen. The Fuggers themselves sold the fustians, and their trading organisation ensured that there was no problem in selling them. Most of the fustians were sold outside Germany, throughout western Europe.[24] In Italy, Venice was the most important distribution centre. The French market, especially Paris, was provided through connections in Strasbourg. A smaller quantity went to Vienna via the Danube.[25] Most of the fustians were sent to Antwerp where they were sold to England, Spain and Portugal.[26]

---

[20] Ibid., p. 420.
[21] Ibid., p. 459.
[22] The centner for 20 guilders; Nübling, *Ulms Baumwollweberei* (see n. 5), p. 162.
[23] FA 37.4.22 and FA 221, 3 nr 21.
[24] In 1536 Cardinal Bernhard of Trient received, through the agency of Hall, cloth from London, Ulm, Augsburg and Öttingen as well as fustian, von Pölnitz, *Anton Fugger* (see n. 7), II, p. 326 n. 155.
[25] Ibid., II, p. 455 n. 291; FA 2.1.22c.
[26] Von Pölnitz, *Die Fugger* (Frankfurt/Main, 1960), pp. 173ff; idem, *Antom Fugger* (see n. 7), II, p. 409 n. 134.

Fugger also bought fustians at Augsburg, besides those made in Weissenhorn.[27]

From the records of the dispute with Ulm and Augsburg, it can be seen that around 1535 Fugger's investment amounted to about 30 000 guilders and that he expected a yearly profit of 2000 guilders. The fustian trade represented only a relatively modest part of his whole enterprise. However, the Ulm and Augsburg fustian traders were afraid that Fugger might raise his production to sixty, seventy or even a hundred thousand pieces of fustian, quite apart from *Golschen*. Fugger denied that this was his intention; some figures show that during the following years production at Weissenhorn increased substantially, but that it never reached the level mentioned by his adversaries.[28]

Transport was undertaken by carters from southern Germany; among others, Fugger used the famous Frammersbacher from the Spessart forest. On the way to the Netherlands, many of the goods passed through Nürnberg, where Gastel Fugger, a relative, directed the agency for some time. After relations with places to the east diminished, he had much to do with arranging transport and settling payments.[29]

For 1539 there exist some figures which give an idea of the actual size of the fustian business, for which a special account was kept in Fugger's books. An entry in that year shows that 17 688 pieces remaining in stock were valued at 32 045 guilders.[30] Between 8 January and 20 May 1539, the administration at Augsburg noted expenses of 44 456 guilders for the Weissenhorn fustians, of which 43 315 guilders were provided in cash. Further cash was provided by the Weissenhorn *Kastner*, Philipp Gugel. At the same time 227 sacks of cotton to the value of 1114 guilders came from Venice where the factor Chrisoph Muelich had to follow the course of the market and send samples of the best qualities.[31] Some of the cotton was sold to weavers at Kaufbeuren. In January 1539 the Antwerp agency recorded 2433 pieces of fustian for 6963 guilders.[32] Between 27 May and 14 August in that year the Augsburg administration spent about 7300 guilders on the Weissenhorn fustian business.[33] Some 102 sacks of cotton came from

---

[27] The Augsburg merchants who sold fustians to Fugger were Jakob Herbrot and Marx Schaller; von Pölnitz, *Anton Fugger* (see n. 7), II, p. 407 n. 134.

[28] FA 27.4.22.

[29] FA 2.1.22c; von Pölnitz, *Anton Fugger* (see n. 7), II, p. 430 n. 22.

[30] In 1536, 18 000 guilders came from Nürnberg to Augsburg, probably mostly for fustians, and 7000 guilders came to Weissenhorn; von Pölnitz, *Anton Fugger* (see n. 7), II, p. 323 n. 147.

[31] Ibid., II, p. 554 n. 67.

[32] Ibid., II, p. 430 n. 22; FA 2.1.22c.

[33] Ibid., p. 445 n. 140; von Pölnitz mentions transports in cash by Swabian, Franconian and Hessian carters, payments by Carl Schiller, Dr Roth, both from Ulm, the Abbot Heinrich of Wiblingen and the Weissenhorn Kastner Gugel who sent money to factor Valentin Mair.

Venice via Kempten and Memmingen and between August and the end of December another 1250 centners were supplied.[34] Between 20 September and 31 December 1539 Mair received about 11 000 guilders from Augsburg, Ulm and Frankfurt. Between 28 November 1538 and 31 December 1539 the expenses of the Augsburg administration for the Weissenhorn business amounted to 63 741 guilders.[35] The Antwerp account of 31 August 1540 mentions 225 bales of fustian for the years 1539 and 1540.[36] Generally a bale contained a *Fardel* which consisted of 45 pieces.[37]

There are other figures for the years after 1544. In the summer of 1544 Hieronymus Reihing at Augsburg had to buy cotton in large quantities.[38] In the autumn Hans Mair, who represented the Fuggers at Kempten,[39] provided transport for 84 sacks of cotton from the agency at Venice which was still under the direction of Muelich. Payment followed from Weissenhorn which, as has been noted, received the money from Augsburg where Reihing was in charge of the fustian business.[40] He organised the transport for which Frammersbach carters were then used.[41] In the spring of 1545 the provision of cotton from Venice seems to have stopped for some time, and Mair at Weissenhorn had to buy cotton from other places to prevent the weavers from having a shortage of the raw material.[42] At that time the fustians were sold at the Frankfurt fairs or were taken by the Ulm merchants.[43] Some of the fustians which went to the Netherlands passed through Erfurt and Hamburg where Fugger was represented by a merchant called Greiner who had business connections in London.[44]

At the beginning of September 1545, Veit Hörl, the then factor at Antwerp, received an order to send fustians from stock to Spain and Portugal by the next fleet in order to avoid losses by price falls in Antwerp. At the same time Hörl had the intention of selling fustians on the English market through Christoph Haintzel, a German

---

[34] For the 102 sacks Hans Rentz at Memmingen put on his account 344 guilders on 12 July and for the 1250 centners 998 guilders; 700 guilders had already been paid at Venice, von Pölnitz, *Anton Fugger* (see n. 7), II, p. 445, n. 140.

[35] FA 2.1.22c; von Pölnitz, *Anton Fugger* II, pp. 445 n. 140 and 455 n. 141.

[36] Von Pölnitz, *Anton Fugger*, II, p. 488 n. 191.

[37] Nübling, *Ulms Baumwollweberei* (see n. 5), p. 128.

[38] FA 2.1.27a/4; 2.1.27b/37, 40.

[39] At Kempten the mintmasters assisted Mair in questions of payments: FA 2.1.27b/63, 71f, 75; von Pölnitz, *Anton Fugger* (see n. 7), II:2, p. 71 n. 74.

[40] Von Pölnitz, *Anton Fugger*, II: 2, p. 629 n. 31; FA 2.1.27b/58f.

[41] Von Pölnitz, *Anton Fugger*, II: 2, p. 141; FA 2.1.27b/141–3.

[42] FA 2.1.27b/88–91, 93.

[43] Hans Philipp Schad bought through the mediation of Bartlme Kobolt; FA 1.2.1a/126f, 132.

[44] Von Pölnitz, *Anton Fugger* (see n. 7), II:2, pp. 640 n. 122 and 631 n. 47. Staatsarchiv Gotha, Geleitsakten Weimar, Cc 764, II, 1544/45: 293, 306, 320, 341, 363, 385, 402, 418, 439, 467.

merchant at London. Christoph Raiser was the representative at Seville, while Jobst Veit worked at Lisbon.[45] At the fairs of Castile, the main agency at the Spanish court sold the fustians.[46]

The English market took a growing interest in Fugger's plans. In October 1545 Christoph Haintzel received some fustians from Antwerp. He was advised to meet Fugger's correspondents in order to raise sales in England, and rooms were hired in London to serve as an agency.[47] At the beginning of 1546, Gaspar Ducci offered the King of England a loan of 40 000 Flemish pounds, given by Fugger, a quarter of which was to be taken in fustians.[48] This seems to have been a project of the Antwerp agency, because Fugger himself feared that Henry VIII might merely use the Weissenhorn fustians for sale below the market price. He was inclined to agree that if the fustians were not sold at the Antwerp market by English merchants, they could be used for English soldiers' and mariners' wear. Moreover, Fugger wanted to combine the transaction with a sale of copper and jewels. Negotiations went on and a contract was concluded according to which the Court of Westminster got a loan of £40 000, a quarter in fustians.[49] A considerable quantity of them were drawn from the stock of Christoph Haintzel,[50] the remainder to be sent from Antwerp and Hamburg.

For some time the market possibilities at Paris were thought to be of interest. The Paris correspondent Roberto de Rossi had to get information concerning whether the French preferred white or coloured fustian. Fustians to be sold at Paris were to be sent via Strasbourg. However, by May 1546 the situation at Paris was so bad that losses of 50 per cent were thought probable.[51] During the summer of 1546, there were changes in personnel which brought difficulties. At Kempten Hans Renz was followed by Hans Mair. At Hamburg Jobst Michel died. Fugger thought of taking his brother Christoph Michel as an agent, because he was the agent of the Schetz. At Antwerp the active Veit Hörl also died. Fugger's nephew Raymund Fugger and Christoph Wolf were charged with responsibility for the agency.[52]

[45] Von Pölnitz, *Anton Fugger* (see n. 7), 11: 2, pp. 621 n. 290 and 626 n. 7; FA 2.1.27b, 41f, 51f, 54.
[46] Cf. Hermann Kellenbenz. 'Fustanes de Weissenhorn en las ferias de Castilla', *Cuadernos de Investigación Histórica*, 2 (Madrid, 1978), pp. 317–34.
[47] Von Pölnitz, *Anton Fugger* (see n. 7), II:2, p. 632 n. 53; FA 2.1.27b/57, 63, 67.
[48] Von Pölnitz, *Anton Fugger*, II:2, p. 141; *Letters and Papers Foreign and Domestic, Henry VIII*, XXI, p. 184.
[49] Von Pölnitz, *Anton Fugger*, II:2, p. 149; FA 2.1.27b/138, 141; *Letters and Papers, Foreign and Domestic, Henry VIII*, XXI, 1, nr 142, 263, 264, 291, 296, 301, 435, 460. There are two dates for the contract: 21 February 1546 and 16 March 1546.
[50] Haintzel had 168 bales in his stock.
[51] FA 2.1.27b/154f.
[52] Von Pölnitz, *Anton Fugger* (see n. 7), II:2, pp. 671 n. 238a and 695f n. 157; FA 2.1.27b/145f, 150, 158f.

Later on Mathias Örtel became the main person at Antwerp. Meanwhile the Schmalkalden war caused great difficulties for the fustian business. Soldiers of the Schmalkalden League occupied Weissenhorn. Ulm and Augsburg were both Protestant towns, on the side of the Schmalkalden League. Anton Fugger himself left Augsburg and transferred his residence to Schwaz in Tyrol. The Augsburg administration of the enterprise remained under the direction of Jakob Sauerzapf. The supply of cotton ceased.

Venice closed the passes, but Fugger managed to get cotton from Antwerp and from Hamburg until the supplies from there ceased too and weeks came when the weavers at Weissenhorn were without any raw materials. Representatives of the weavers went to Augsburg to seek help from Sauerzapf, who proposed to help them to the extent of 4000 or 5000 guilders. Every weaver who was not in arrears with his deliveries was to receive half a centner of cotton for every loom. There were weavers with one loom and others with two. Providing corn was not the solution, Sauerzapf found, because about seventy of the weavers' families had their own farms which could provide them sufficiently with food. But all of them needed money in cash in order to buy linen yarn. If help was not granted weavers might emigrate. However, the situation in the Ulm territory and at Augsburg was not very different. Augsburg weavers were used for building fortification works or served as soldiers.[53] Anyway, the year 1546 concluded with a favourable balance for the Weissenhorn business: 49 939 guilders on the credit side and zero on the debit side.[54] Under commodities, 12 500 guilders for fustians were to be found, but this figure was little in comparison with the stock of copper which amounted to 1.25 million guilders. The Nürnberg agency was now the centre for distribution.[55]

In the early months of 1546 things improved. Through Ulm correspondents, money was transported to Weissenhorn to provide for the weavers. Fugger himself doubted that the markets would improve very rapidly and therefore ordered the production to be dropped. Prechter at Strasbourg hoped to reactivate relations with Paris to get a better sale for the Weissenhorn fustians in France. From May to July goods were supplied through Speyer, Mainz and Cologne to the Netherlands, through Strasbourg and Luxemburg and through

---

[53] Von Pölnitz, *Anton Fugger*, II:2, pp. 205, 213, 219, 246f, 276f, 330f, 658 n. 89, 659 n. 103, 667 n. 181; FA 2.1.27b/113, 122f, 139, 141, 147, 148, 149, 154f. At that time 6000 pieces were at Weissenhorn on stock.

[54] Von Pölnitz, *Anton Fugger* (see n. 7), II:2, p. 330f.

[55] The 49 949 guilders of the activa came from Nürnberg.

Nürnberg, while from the Netherlands came *Lösch*, that is, material for packing the fustians.[56] At this time, white bleached fustians and coloured ones were produced; two-thirds of the latter were black and one-third was grey, the same as earlier.[57] When the fustians arrived in the Netherlands they were calendered. Documentation prior to 1549 is scarce, coinciding with a new slackening of the business at Weissenhorn, but we get some insight into the fustian trade in Spain through the account which was delivered by Justus Walther, the agent at the court, in September 1548.[58] In Spain, Seville and the fairs of Castile were good markets for Weissenhorn fustians. From Seville much of the Weissenhorn products went to America.[59] The Castile fairs were centres for distribution all over Spain. From the end of 1547 until 19 September 1548, when Walther concluded his account, the agency had sold 4062 pieces in white, 1264 in grey, and 1059 in black. Also, 158 chests, 10 small bales and 146 pieces of tablecloth were sold. Additionally, the factory had received another quantity of fustians, 3218 pieces in white, 1076 in grey, and 1076 in black, as well as 179 chests and 179 small bales of tablecloth. Part of these goods had probably already been sent to the fairs, while in the storehouse remained 1770 pieces in white, 470 in grey, and 370 in black, and 76 chests and 89 small bales of tablecloth. The market for them was good. However, too many of the customers bought on credit and this brought losses because several buyers went bankrupt during the 1540s.[60]

The Augsburg records give some details for summer 1549. The war difficulties by then had passed. With new energy the sale of fustians especially through Nürnberg to the Netherlands was organised. From there money was sent to Weissenhorn for the weavers.[61] Dietrich Heufler sent 105 sacks of cotton from Venice with the assistance of Christoph Muelich. It seems that this was the first consignment which crossed the Alps after the Schmalkalden war. New difficulties soon arose with the revolt of the German princes against Charles V, and the war between Charles and Henry II of France. The Weissenhorn

[56] Jörg Thoma was the Fugger agent at Speyer, Jan Pastor at Cologne; in 1543 Hans von Opung was a representative of the Fuggers at Mainz, but it is unknown if he was still alive in 1547; FA 2.1.27b, 193f, 199f, 205, 215f, 227f, 230f; von Pölnitz, *Anton Fugger*, II:2, pp. 360, 438, 479, 512, 762 n. 35, 763 n. 41.

[57] FA 2.1.27b, 215, 218f.

[58] FA 43.2.

[59] Hermann Kellenbenz, 'Die fuggersche Faktorei in Sevilla', *Revue Internationale d'Histoire de la Banque*, 8 (1974), pp. 200–15.

[60] Cf. Kellenbenz, 'Fustanes de Weissenhorn en las ferias de Castilla' (see n. 46), p. 322.

[61] In June 1549, Jörg Stegmann at Speyer sent about 200 taler to Weissenhorn: von Pölnitz, *Anton Fugger* (see n. 7), III:1, p. 83f.

region was occupied by the Elector of Saxony's troops, though the neutrality of Thuringia made it possible to continue the trade in fustians and flax to some degree. Nevertheless, on the route to Portugal there was a heavy loss. Textiles to the value of 10 000 Escudos were taken by the ships of the King of France.[62] After the restoration of peace, Anton Fugger had increasing difficulties with his fustian business owing to the tenacious efforts of Ulm to recover the Weissenhorn output for its *Schau* and to force Fugger to abandon the trade. While negotiations were taking place at Gunzburg in 1553, Mathias Örtel, the factor at Antwerp, was ordered to intensify the fustian trade.[63] A further 2000 pieces of coloured fustians were sent to the Netherlands, and white-bleached fustians were to be dyed and sent on. Francisco de Erasso, the secretary of Charles V, urgently needed money. Fugger was willing to add, beyond the 200 000 guilders on which negotiations took place, 100 000 more guilders when Erasso agreed to get the fustians sold to the soldiers instead of leaving them to merchants.[64] Moreover fustians went to Spain.[65] The Bishop of Bamberg, Weigand von Redwitz, ordered different sorts of fustians for 1000 guilders, probably in connection with a loan. He did it at the Nürnberg agency.[66] In 1552, 295 weavers from Weissenhorn and surrounding villages owed Fugger 675 pieces of the first quality (ox), 782 pieces of the second quality (lion) and 128.51.3 guilders.[67] In the general account of 31 December 1553, the *Barchenthandel* section reveals the following figures for the years 1546–53: *Ausgeben* (debit), 552 guilders; *Einnehmen* (credit), 63 443 guilders. The total credit of the whole enterprise at that time was 4 456 637 guilders; thus the Weissenhorn business remained only a small part of the Fugger enterprise.[68]

---

[62] Ibid., pp. 279, 283, 287.
[63] Ibid., p. 427.
[64] The fardel should be at 27 vl. pounds: ibid., III:1, p. 438f.
[65] Ibid., p. 476.
[66] Ibid., pp. 455, 483; the sum of 1000 is given in ducats.
[67] The document shows the following distribution: Hernach die Weber so gen Weissenhorn wurckhen:

39 Weissenhorner	ox 90	leo 101	fl —.26.—
44 Grauerzhoffer	ox 172	leo 120	fl 12.28.—
43 Auttenhoffer	ox 90	leo 121	fl 5.43. 4
60 Pfaffenhoffer	ox 95	leo 172	fl
26 Bobenhauser	ox 53	leo 50	fl 11.57. 2
26 Hegelhoffer	ox 60	leo 95	fl 69. 7. 1
31 Gannertzhoffer	ox 66	leo 84	fl 29, 9, 2
20 Yberberger	ox 37	leo 28	fl
6 Reichenbacher	ox 12	leo 11	fl
Summa 295 Weber sein schuldig	ox 615	leo 782	fl 128.51. 3 p(er) 1552ᵗ. Jar. FA 27.4.22.

[68] Von Pölnitz, *Anton Fugger* (see n. 7), III:1, p. 481f.

IV

Towards the middle of the sixteenth century, the successful time for fustians seems to have come to an end. Anton Fugger gave way in the dispute with Ulm. He did it probably under the influence of diminishing opportunities on the Antwerp market and elsewhere. He tried to establish the production of fustians at Schwaz, but it proved unsuccessful.[69]

Changes in fashion also took place. Instead of the white fustians which were the speciality of Ulm, the cheaper coloured fustians came on the market. Originally at Ulm only *Brief*, that is the fourth quality, was used for dyeing. From the end of the fifteenth century the neighbouring town of Biberach had begun to specialise in coloured fustians which found a good market in Württemberg.[70] Ulm, too, began to develop coloured fustians, but used only silk dyes whereas the Biberach people dyed with wood chippings. Fustians intended to be dyed black were sent to Augsburg which was known for its black dyeing works. Many Biberach people sent their fustians to Ulm to get them dyed there and sold them as Ulm fustians. In the course of the sixteenth century, the competition from Biberach developed to such an extent that in 1555 the Ulm Council ordered the *Verordneten zum Gewirk* to give advice on how far the Biberach trade was damaging that of Ulm.[71]

Furthermore, bombazine became fashionable. In Italy, where it originated in the region of Milan and Como, it was first a silk textile and later on, silk mixed with wool or cotton. In 1574 a special *Schau* for bombazine was established at Ulm,[72] though at first the Ulm weavers had difficulties in producing good bombazines which could compete in foreign markets. While the fustian trade went into decline more and more, a new time began for linen which was increasingly exported for tropical markets overseas.

V

The Fugger experience in the fustian trade is interesting from several points of view. It is a case of a major merchant house, specialising in banking and the trade in metals, moving for a period into the textile business as a producer. Knowledge of favourable market conditions in distant places, such as Antwerp, London, the Castile fairs and Seville, provided a reason for Anton Fugger from the 1530s to extend the fustian production in which his uncle, Jakob Fugger, had already

---

[69] Von Pölnitz, *Die Fugger* (see n. 26), p. 257.
[70] Dieter Funk, *Biberacher Barchent, Herstellung und Vertrieb im Spätmittelalter und zur beginnenden Neuzeit* (Basle, 1965), pp. 24ff.
[71] Nübling, *Ulms Baumwollweberei* (see n. 5), p. 162f.
[72] Ibid., p. 164.

been interested. The business flourished because of the combination of a good supply of raw material – cotton from Venice and flax produced in the Weissenhorn area – with good market relations for the sale of the finished product. Fugger, however, underestimated the tough rivalry from the important fustian centre of Ulm whose territorial boundaries lay just beyond the lordship of the Fugger family. Augsburg, the other centre of fustian production, produced difficulties too. Augsburg weavers used linen yarn spun over a wide area, including Weissenhorn, and Augsburg feared that the Fugger example might be followed elsewhere. Personal and political reasons caused Fugger to give way and leave the fustian trade to the town of Ulm.

The Fugger case is interesting too from a more general point of view. As von Stromer has shown, the introduction of the fustian trade in East Swabia and the middle Danube region was undertaken by merchants with experience in long-distance trade. They met with success owing to their collaboration with the government of the towns, especially the imperial towns, the imperial prelates and the houses of Wittelsbach and Habsburg.[73] The Fugger enterprise at Weissenhorn was that of a merchant house which had itself become the owner of a territorial lordship and which tried to follow an economic policy of its own. In 1534 the Fugger family obtained from Charles V the right to establish mints in their lordships.[74] Anton Fugger aspired to create a territorial entity in the Danubian area similar to that of the Medici in Tuscany.[75] His ambitions met with no success. The political and economic forces of the large imperial towns were still great enough to enable them to maintain their position against smaller units such as the lordship of Weissenhorn, certainly as far as the fustian trade was concerned. Later, Duke Friederich of Württemberg, neighbour of the Ulm territory on the western side, was strong enough in the early seventeenth century to promote the linen trade of his own of Urach against that of Ulm. His policy was an early example of mercantilism

[73] Von Stromer, *Die Gründung der Baumwollindustrie* (see n. 2), pp. 11ff, 29ff, 134ff. Concerning the economic policy of territorial princes cf., too: Ulf Dirlmeier, *Mittelalterliche Hoheitsträger in wirtschaftlichem Wettbewerb* (Wiesbaden, 1966); Herbert Hassinger, 'Politische Kräfte und Wirtschaft 1350–1800' in H. Aubin and W. Zorn (eds.), *Handbuch der Deutschen Wirtschafts- und Sozialgeschichte*, I (Stuttgart, 1971), pp. 608ff; Hermann Kellenbenz, *Deutsche Wirtschaftsgeschichte*, I (Munich, 1977), pp. 152ff.

[74] Von Pölnitz, *Anton Fugger* (see n. 7), I, p. 304; Robert Mandrou, *Les Fugger, propriétaires fonciers en Souabe 1560–1618, Etude de comportements socio-économiques à la fin du XVIe siècle* (Paris, 1969), pp. 40ff.

[75] Von Pölnitz, 'Fugger und Medici' in *Historische Zeitschrift*, 166 (1942); idem, 'Cosimo I. Medici und die europäische Anleihepolitik der Fugger' in *Quellen und Forschungen aus italienischen Archiven und Bibliotheken*, 31 (1941); idem, *Anton Fugger*, vols. I–III, index Medici.

in the territories of the German princes, a policy which came to be dominant after the Thirty Years War.[76]

Anton Fugger had to give up his Weissenhorn fustian business, but fustian production continued there under the control of the town council and the Bürgermeisters, who generally were merchants involved in the trade. The Weissenhorn fustian was surely not as good in quality as that of Ulm. When, from 1574, Weissenhorn attempted to extend its privileges, it did not succeed owing to the strong opposition from Ulm. The fustian production of Weissenhorn rose to 16 732 pieces in 1618, but declined to an average of about 5000 pieces during the Thirty Years War and fell to 182 pieces by 1642.[77] At Augsburg, by contrast, some 410 000 pieces passed through the *Schau* in 1595 and some 430 000 in 1612. At Ulm at the end of the sixteenth century production was at the level of 100 000 pieces per annum.[78] Compared with the output of Augsburg and Ulm, fustian production at Weissenhorn was a modest affair.

[76] G. Karr, *Die Uracher Leinenweberei und die Leinwandhandlungskompagnie* (1930); Hermann Kellenbenz, 'Unternehmertum in Südwestdeutschland' in *Tradition*, X (1965), pp. 163ff.

[77] Wylicil, *Die Weissenhorner Barchentschau*, pp. 1 and 5ff.

[78] Eckart Schremmer, 'Die oberschwäbische Textillandschaft bis zum Beginn des Merkantilismus' in Max Spindler (ed.), *Handbuch der Bayerischen Geschichte*, III, 2 (Munich, 1972), p. 1083f.

Part Three

16 Medieval Garments in the Mediterranean World
Veronika Gervers

In late antiquity and the early Middle Ages, the major centres of Europe, the Near East and north Africa were all situated on the Mediterranean. It was in such large cities as Rome, Constantinople, Alexandria and Antioch that medieval society and culture evolved from a common Graeco-Roman background and from new influences emanating from 'non-classical' civilisations on the outskirts of the Empire. In turn, this large but closely linked world subsequently formed the basis for three distinct and diverse cultures: Byzantium, western Europe and the Caliphate. Until about the time of Justinian (AD 527–65), there was, as Peter Brown has convincingly argued, a strong horizontal unity in the Mediterranean.[1] Its division into east, west and south was a secondary and chronologically later development, one in which the unifying traditions of the past were retained even when the divisions became clear and unmistakable.

Owing to both its uniformity and its diversity, this pan-Mediterranean culture provides fertile ground not only for historical and artistic research, but for textile studies and especially for the study of costume. The large quantity of textile remains, together with the richness and variety of artistic depictions of contemporary costume as well as the wealth of written references to trade, textile production and actual garments, all provide excellent sources for an examination of Mediterranean textile and costume history.

Despite the abundance of available evidence, no serious attempt has yet been made to consider the problems and evolution of early garments from these lands. The textile historian has hitherto concentrated on the technical and/or stylistic analysis of surviving fabrics,

[1] Peter Brown, 'Eastern and western Christendom in late antiquity: A parting of the ways', *Studies in Christian Thought*, XIII (1976), pp. 1–24.

and not on the garments to which the fragments originally belonged. Similarly the art historian has emphasised the iconographic significance of the pictorial sources, but neglected the realism which is to be found in such individual details as costume. Parallel with these studies, the historian's work has centred on trade relations, the organisation of the textile industry, and on textual examination of the sources, but not on the textiles themselves.

I should like to discuss here, through an interdisciplinary approach, some general problems relating to medieval Mediterranean dress, giving special attention to the construction of garments. I shall emphasise the value of the material remains, most of which have been preserved in the desiccated soil of Egypt. Furthermore, textile finds from Egypt, although usually of local manufacture, reflect an international style that was common throughout the Mediterranean. This is true for clothes produced either in late antiquity, or the early Christian and Islamic periods. I hope to avoid the unsubstantiated discrepancies that arise from the study of pictorial materials or of written sources alone.

Significance of the textile finds from Egypt

Large numbers of textile remains, often complete garments, have come to light at numerous Egyptian sites. The post-Pharaonic material becomes especially interesting and rich from the beginning of the Christian era. The custom of mummification ended with the acceptance of Christianity, and the dead were thereafter buried fully clothed. From the third century AD, therefore, the finds become more complete and the situation remained the same throughout Islamic times.

Egypt was a major cultural centre throughout the period of the late Empire, the early centuries of the Byzantine period, and under the Arabs, who conquered the territory in AD 640. Thus all the finds have considerable historical and social significance. Egypt, moreover, had been famous for its textiles, especially for its linens, since Pharaonic times. From the late Roman period, its woollen fabrics also attained a high reputation and were sought after in many lands.[2] Consequently

---

[2] For Egyptian flax production in the Roman period, see Pliny, *Natural History*, XIX. Linen remained important throughout the medieval Islamic period: Gladys Frantz, 'Textiles in the medieval Egyptian economy (868–1021)', paper read at the Colloquium on Medieval Textiles in the Mediterranean World in 1977; R. B. Serjeant, *Islamic Textiles: Material for a History up to the Mongol Conquest* (Beirut, 1972). Though imported, Egyptian wool was not of first quality in Roman times, see Ewa Wipszycka, *L'industrie textile dans l'Egypte romaine* (Wrocław, Warsaw and Kraków, 1965), p. 27. In the Islamic period, however, Egyptian woollen fabrics and garments gained a high reputation. Djahiz (d. AD 869) noted that 'the best robes are of Egyptian wool, then the Fars–Khuzistan kind, and the fine goat-hair in Fars, the fine Shiraz goat-hair ... ' (Serjeant, *Islamic Textiles*, pp. 49, 75, 136). Miskawaihi also spoke of the 'djubba of Egyptian wool' (AD 929), and said that in AD 995 'a cadi of Baghdad had 1000 garments of Egyptian wool' (Serjeant, *op. cit.*, pp. 136, 138).

the textile finds might be expected to reflect the traditions and achievements resulting from the constant changes of civilisations.

In the first place, the material provides a broad perspective for the existence and survival of classical traditions. The finest late antique examples retain the tendencies of Hellenistic illusionism and are replete with elements of pagan mythology, while the later pieces demonstrate the misunderstood disintegration of this international style and lead eventually to the creation of a folk art, the real 'Coptic' art. Beside the elements stemming from a classical inheritance, costume and textile decoration incorporated expressions of Christianity such as crosses and Biblical scenes from at least the fourth century. Subsequently the arrival of the Arabs introduced new attitudes towards almost all levels of life and art.

The Arabs brought with them a different, more oriental garment tradition that in turn could have influenced the entire textile production of the country. The workmen in the textile industry, however, were largely Copts who, we may assume, continued to use the long-established weaving traditions inherited from their forefathers.[3] The Egyptian material from the early Islamic period provides sufficient grounds for us to conclude that many types of antique and early Christian garments and decorative ideas survived at the same time as new styles were being integrated.[4] The appearance of new weaving techniques together with new loom types or adaptations made to the old looms may be postulated with some certainty. They would lead,

[3] Serjeant, *Islamic Textiles* (see n. 2), pp. 136 (Baladhuri, see n. 4), 138 (Patriarch Dionysos, AD 815), 142 (al-Makdisi, AD 985). Two tapestry-woven *clavus* bands from late Fatimid or Ayyubid Egypt might have belonged to tunics similar to those from late antiquity and the early Middle Ages. They appear to indicate that this classical garment-type survived well into the Islamic period. See A. F. Kendrick, *Catalogue of Muhammadan Textiles of the Medieval Period* (Victoria and Albert Museum, London, 1924), p. 28, pl. 7, nos. 921, 922.

[4] Baladhuri mentions that the inhabitants of Misr (Cairo) in Egypt were required to supply the Arabs with what appears to be a characteristically Muslim woollen outfit, consisting of an upper gown called *djubba suf*, an upper cloak called *burnus*, a turban, trousers and shoes. Instead of the djubba, however, a Coptic garment called *kibti* could be provided (Serjeant, *Islamic Textiles* (see n. 2), p. 136). According to Yedida K. Stillman, the costume of Arab, Jewish and Coptic women did not differ greatly in Fatimid and Ayyubid Egypt ('The wardrobe of a Jewish bride in medieval Egypt', *Studies of Marriage Customs*, Folklore Research Centre Studies, Hebrew University of Jerusalem, IV (1974), pp. 297–303; idem, 'The importance of the Cairo Geniza manuscripts for the history of medieval female attire', *International Journal of Middle East Studies*, VII (1976), pp. 579–89). For the survival and revival of 'Coptic' artistic traditions, see Lisa Golombek and Veronika Gervers, 'Tiraz fabrics in the Royal Ontario Museum' in V. Gervers (ed.), *Studies in Textile History in Memory of Harold B. Burnham* (Toronto, 1977), pp. 82–125; Ernst Kühnel, 'La tradition copte dans les tissus musulmans', *Bulletin de la Société d'Archéologie Copte*, IV (1938), pp. 78–89; Dorothy G. Shepherd, 'An early Tiraz from Egypt', *Bulletin of the Cleveland Museum of Art*, XLVII (1960), pp. 7–14; Deborah Thompson, 'A Fatimid textile of Coptic tradition with Arabic inscription', *Journal of the American Research Center in Egypt*, IV (1965), pp. 145–50, pls. 34–40; and papers presented by Lisa Golombek ('ROM tiraz; problems of patronage'), Louise W. Mackie ('Tulunid textiles'), and Sheila Canby ('A Fayyum textile in the Museum of Fine Arts, Boston') at the Colloquium on Medieval Textiles from the Mediterranean World. See also Ernest J. Grube, 'Studies in the survival and continuity of pre-Muslim traditions in Egyptian Islamic art', *Journal of the American Research Center in Egypt*, I (1962), pp. 76–87.

in turn, to changes in the type of dress. The introduction of cotton cultivation was also to bring about major changes in the textile industry. Andrew Watson's research, however, has shown that cotton became a major crop in Egypt only from the thirteenth century.[5]

Between Roman times and the medieval Islamic period, Egypt maintained important economic ties with the various parts of the Empire, and subsequently of the Caliphate. Textiles played a major role in the export and import trades.[6] Grave goods provide us with both local and foreign products of the textile industry. As only a very limited number of fabrics have survived elsewhere, the international scope of the Egyptian finds is particularly significant.[7] Without them,

---

[5] Andrew M. Watson, 'The rise and spread of old world cotton', in Gervers (ed.), *Studies in Textile History* (see n. 4), pp. 355–68.

[6] Pliny states that Egypt imported the wares of Arabia and India in exchange for linen (*Natural History*, XIX.ii.7). For linens produced outside Egypt in the late Empire, see the references in the Edict of Diocletian on Maximum Prices, with an English translation in Tenney Frank (ed.), *An Economic Survey of Ancient Rome* (Baltimore, 1940), V, pp. 305–421. (See Tables 16.1–16.4) It is clear from other sources that in Roman Egypt, weavers frequently worked exclusively for the eastern trade. Linen goods were in great demand. Garments made of papyrus were exported to Rome (Frank (ed.), *An Economic Survey of Ancient Rome* (1936), II, pp. 335ff). For the trade, see also M. P. Charlesworth, *Trade-routes and Commerce of the Roman Empire*, rev. edn (New York, 1970); Allan Chester Johnson and Louis C. West, *Byzantine Egypt: Economic Studies* (Princeton, 1949), pp. 137–51; E. H. Warmington, *The Commerce between the Roman Empire and India* (London, 1928). For the Islamic period, see Serjeant, *Islamic Textiles* (see n. 2), and S. D. Goitein, *Letters of Medieval Jewish Traders* (Princeton, 1973).

[7] For survivals at Dura-Europos, see R. Pfister and Louisa Bellinger in M. I. Rostovtzeff *et al.*, *The Excavations at Dura-Europos* (New Haven, 1945), IV, pt. II. For those at Halabiyeh see R. Pfister, 'Textiles de Halabiyeh (Zenobia), découverts par le Service des Antiquités de la Syrie dans la nécropole de Halabiyeh sur l'Euphrate', *Institut Français d'Archéologie de Beyrouth, Bibliothèque Archéologique et Historique*, XLVIII (Paris, 1951). For Nubia see William Y. Adams, 'Post-Pharaonic Nubia in the light of archaeology, 1–3', *Journal of Egyptian Archaeology*, L (1964), pp. 102–20; LI (1965), pp. 160–8; LII (1966), pp. 147–62; Elizabeth Crowfoot, 'The clothing of a fourteenth-century Nubian bishop' in *Studies in Textile History* (see n. 4), pp. 43–51; Leonard C. Woolley and D. Randall MacIver, 'Karanog: The Roman-Nubian cemetery' in B. Cox Eckley, Jr, *Expedition to Nubia*, III–IV (Philadelphia, 1910). For Palmyra see R. Pfister, *Textiles de Palmyre, découverts par le Service des Antiquités du Haut-Commissariat de la République Française dans le nécropole de Palmyre*, I–III (Paris, 1934–40). For Persian silks see Pope (ed.), *A Survey of Persian Art from Prehistoric Times to the Present, V: The Art of the Book and Textiles*, pp. 2029–42, and *XIV: New Studies, 1938–60* (London 1964–68), papers by P. Ackerman, E. Kühnel and D. G. Shepherd; Gaston Wiet, 'Soieries persanes', *Mémoires presentées à l'Institut d'Egypte*, LII (Cairo, 1947). See also the recent controversy over the Buyid silks with further bibliography in the *Bulletin de liaison du Centre International d'Etude des Textiles Anciens* (CIETA), XXXVII (1973), studies by M. Lemberg, G. Vial and J. H. Hofenk-De Graaff on the silks of the Abegg Foundation, Riggisberg, Bern; and Dorothy G. Shepherd 'Medieval Persian silks in fact and fancy: a refutation of the Riggisberg report', in ibid., XXXIX–XL (1974). For textiles and garments from European church and royal treasuries, see X. Delaporte, *Le voile de Notre Dame* (Chartres, 1927); H. A. Elsberg and R. Guest, 'The veil of Saint Anne', *Burlington Magazine*, LXVIII (1936), pp. 140–5; Otto von Falke, *Kunstgeschichte der Seidenweberei*, 2 vols. (Berlin, 1913); A. F. Kendrick, *Catalogue of Textiles from Burying-Grounds in Egypt*, I, *Graeco-Roman period* (Victoria and Albert Museum, London, 1920); A. F. Kendrick, *Catalogue of Early Medieval Woven Fabrics* (Victoria and Albert Museum, London, 1925); G. Marçais and G. Wiet, 'Le voile de Sainte Anne d'Apt', *Monuments et Mémoires*, XXXIV (1934), pp. 177–94; Sigrid Müller-Christensen, 'Textiles in Schwaben', in *Suevia Sacra: Frühe Kunst in Schwaben, 7–13. Jahrhundert* (Augsburg, 1973), pp. 51–2, 192–216, Figures 188–214; Paul Perdizet, 'La tunique liturgique historiée de Saqqara', *Monuments et Mémoires*, XXXIV (1934), pp. 97–128 (with reference to the tunic of Moyenmoutier, found in the coffin of Saint Hydulphe, archbishop of Trèves, d. AD 707); W. F. Volbach, *I tessuti del Museu Sacro Vaticano, Catalogo del Museo Sacro*, III (Vatican, 1942).

16.1　Tunic of bleached linen tabby with tapestry-woven decoration in purple wool and linen. Egypt: Byzantine period, fifth–sixth century AD

16.2　Tunic of bleached linen tabby with tapestry-woven decoration in purple wool and linen. Egypt: Byzantine period, fifth–sixth century AD

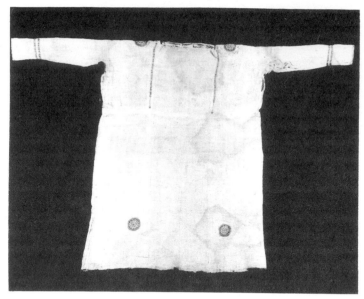

16.3   *Tunic of bleached linen tabby with tapestry-woven decoration in pale purple wool and linen, applied roundels. Egypt: Byzantine period, fifth–sixth century* AD

16.4   *Tunic fragment of weft-faced cream woollen tabby with tapestry-woven decoration in coloured wool, details in linen. Egypt: Islamic period, seventh– ninth century* AD

we would be able to ascertain next to nothing about early silk production in the Near East, about the embroidered or printed and painted
cottons of Persia, Mesopotamia, or even of India, about the art of
the so-called Sassanian compound weaves and the Asiatic tapestries,
or about the *ikat*-dyed and striped fabrics of the Yemen.[8] They provide
an extremely important complement to the testimony of the written
sources. It is only with the aid of the surviving material that we are able
to comprehend the terminology of the documents. We have, on the
one hand, written references and, on the other, archaeological remains;
each needs to be interpreted in light of the other. The written sources
say little about technology, for example, and the textiles themselves
are silent about the social and economic conditions in which they were
produced.

Since textiles of foreign production are relatively rare among the
Egyptian material, we are unable to interpret them as satisfactorily
as the Egyptian work. They naturally reflect the types which Egyptian
taste demanded, rather than necessarily the textiles produced by the
countries in which they originated. Before such distinctions can be
made, we must first learn to separate local and foreign products.
Linen, invariably S-spun, has traditionally been associated with Egypt;
but we know from Diocletian's Edict on Maximum Prices that the
best linens were made elsewhere. These have yet to be identified
among the fragments known to us. Everything found in Egypt may
thus not be Egyptian, although it is likely that all but a small percentage
of the finest pieces are of local manufacture. When working with
specific types of woollen tapestry, or woollen and silk compound
weaves, the question of origin becomes even more complicated, and we
can base our conclusions only on certain assumptions.

Further questions arise concerning the significance of what is known
with some certainty to be Egyptian. Do the surviving fragments
reflect the total output of the country's textile industry and the variety
of its costume? Are they indicative of the whole quality range of
Egyptian textiles? We do not believe so, and consequently the remains
must be viewed with some reservations when general conclusions are
formulated. Some of the difficulties and discrepancies inherent in the
existing material need to be discussed.

[8] See N. P. Britton, *A Study of Some Early Islamic Textiles in the Museum of Fine Arts, Boston* (Boston,
Mass., 1938); Kendrick, *Catalogue of Muhammadan Textiles*; Ernst Kühnel and Louisa Bellinger,
Catalogue of Dated Tiraz Fabrics: Umayyad, Abbasid, Fatimid (The Textile Museum, Washington,
DC, 1952); C. J. Lamm, *Cotton in Medieval Textiles in the Near East* (Paris, 1937). For Indian printed
fabrics, see R. Pfister, *Les toiles imprimées de Fostat et l'Hindoustan* (Paris, 1938); John Irwin and
Margaret Hall, *Indian Painted and Printed Fabrics, Historic Textiles of India at the Calico Museum*, I
(Ahmedabad, 1971), pp. 1–13.

Table 16.1   Prices of linen garments, according to the edict of Diocletian, AD 301

	Shirts (unmarked)	Dalmatics (unmarked) women's	men's	Wraps	Face cloths (unmarked)	Hoods or cloaks	Loin cloths or girdles	Handkerchiefs	Headbands for women
First quality:									
Scythopolis	den. 7 000	11 000	10 000	7 500	3 250	3 500		1 300	
Tarsus	den. 6 000	10 000	9 000	7 000	3 000	3 000		1 000	
Byblus	den. 5 000	9 000	8 000	6 000	2 500	2 500		800	1 500
Laodiceia	den. 4 500	8 000	7 500	5 500	2 250	2 250		600	
Tarsus and Alexandria	den. 4 000	7 000	6 500	4 500	1 750	1 750		500	
Second quality:									
Scythopolis	den. 6 000	9 000	7 500	6 500	2 500	3 000			
Tarsus	den. 5 000	8 000	6 500	5 500	2 250	2 500		700	
Byblus	den. 4 000	7 000	6 000	5 000	2 250	2 250		600	1 200
Laodiceia	den. 3 500	6 000	5 000	4 000	2 000	2 000		500	
Tarsus and Alexandria	den. 3 000	4 500	4 500	3 000	1 500	1 500		400	
Third quality:									
Scythopolis	den. 5 000	7 000	6 000	5 000	2 250	2 500		700	
Tarsus	den. 3 500	6 000	5 000	4 000	2 000	2 250		600	
Byblus	den. 3 000	5 000	4 000	3 500	1 750	2 000		500	800
Laodiceia	den. 2 500	4 000	3 000	3 000	1 500	1 750		400	
Tarsus and Alexandria	den. 2 000	3 000	2 000	2 500	1 250	1 250		300	

Table 16.1 Continued

| | Shirts (unmarked) | Dalmatics (unmarked) | | Wraps | Face cloths (unmarked) | Hoods or cloaks | Loin cloths or girdles | Handkerchiefs | Headbands for women |
		women's	men's						
Made at various places									
First quality	den. 1 500	2 500	2 250	2 250	1 000	1 000	1 000	250	400 plus
Second quality	den. 1 250	2 250	2 000	1 750	750	750	800	200	400
Third quality	den. 1 000	1 750	1 500	1 250	500	600	600	150	300
Coarser linen, used by common people and slaves:									
First quality	den.	1 000	800	800	350		400	120	250
Second quality	den.	800	600	600	225		300	100	200
Third quality	den. 500	600	500	500	200		200	80	150

288 Cloth and Clothing in Medieval Europe

In the first place, the dead were seldom buried in their best garments. Such grave goods as tunics, shrouds and curtains frequently show signs of wear and of ancient repairs. Applied tapestry-woven ornaments sometimes appear to have belonged to older clothes. A papyrus from the second or third century reports that an 'old cloak' was acquired 'for burial' for as little as 24 *obuli*, an extremely low price when we consider that new linen tunics usually fetched from 8 to 32 *drachmae*, and special cloaks cost from 140 to 400 *drachmae*.[9] The custom of burying the dead in valuable dress was criticised by such early Church fathers as St Jerome (*c.* 348–420), St Ambrose (340–97), and St Basil (*c.* 330–79).[10] In view of the prices paid for garments, such an attitude may be quite understandable.

While prices for different articles can be well-documented over several centuries through the evidence of papyri, an excellent source of comparison lies in Diocletian's Edict on Maximum Prices.[11] This edict, dating from AD 301, provides us with a unique schedule of prices determined for that single year (Tables 16.1–16.5), although not all of these prices can be authenticated. The schedule dates from a period of considerable inflation, and its prices are considerably higher than those of the first and second centuries AD, so that comparisons are difficult to make. The edict attempts to lower the high prices then current, and totally disregards regional variations. The figures can probably be considered realistic only in the place where the edict originated, possibly Nicomedia. Despite these considerations, the edict's standards are probably an accurate reflection of the various price levels in the eastern Mediterranean. This enables us to formulate valuable comparisons within the large price-range based on quality and the type of garments. It also provides us with a structure into which the actual textile finds may be placed.

Some of the prices for the different linen garments stipulated by the edict are given in Table 16.1. The horizontal top register indicates the types of garments made of linen. The varying qualities of the different items are shown in the left-hand column. The first three divisions give the cost of the first, second and third qualities of named products from the most highly renowned centres: that is, from Scythopolis, Tarsus, Byblus, Laodiceia and Alexandria. These obviously constituted the

[9] Frank (ed.), *An Economic Survey of Ancient Rome* (see n. 6), II, pp. 318–20.
[10] Kendrick, *Catalogue of Textiles from Egypt* (see n. 7), I (1920), p. 20.
[11] Frank (ed.), *An Economic Survey of Ancient Rome* (see n. 6), V, pp. 305–421; S. Lauffer, *Diocletians Preisedikt* (Berlin, 1971) gives the fullest text (fragments have been found in over thirty cities) with a bibliography and brief commentary. See also Richard Duncan-Jones, *The Economy of the Roman Empire: Quantitative Studies* (Cambridge, 1974), Appendix 17, pp. 366ff; A. H. M. Jones, 'The cloth industry under the Roman Empire', *Economic History Review*, 2nd ser., XIII (1960), pp. 183–92.

luxury items, exported throughout the provinces and worn only by the privileged classes. Then there are another three qualities of garments, which are clearly inferior to the first. These garments, made in many places, formed the bulk of standard, good-quality stuffs, frequently used for clothing the army. In the last category, the coarser linen garments used by common people and slaves are similarly divided into three qualities.

Within this highly elaborate set of categories, we can see, for example, that shirts, presumably under-tunics, were available for prices ranging from as high as 7000 to as low as 500 *denarii*. In other words, the most expensive garment cost some fifteen times more than its coarsest counterpart. The same is true for all the other items shown in Table 16.1. It should be noted that all the prices referred to simple, plain linen garments. Those which were decorated cost considerably more, and ornaments executed in purple wool were especially costly (Table 16.2). While the plain examples of women's dalmatics or over-tunics cost from 600 to 11 000 *denarii*, those with purple stripes, differing in the quality and quantity of the dyed wool used, went for prices ranging from 3500 to 32 000 *denarii*. Silk tunics cost even more, but the edict does not give the exact figures.

For a better understanding of the relative value of these prices, we may note that a linen weaver earned from 20 to 40 *denarii* per day with maintenance (Table 16.3).[12] Thus he would have had to work from 12 to 24 days to earn enough to buy the simplest of the plain tunics which served as the standard costume of the time. Needless to say, no weaver, common labourer, or farm worker could ever have afforded any of the name-brand garments (see Table 16.5).

Since so many degrees of quality can be established for this single year, the Egyptian textile finds might be expected to exhibit a similar range of variation proportionate to cost. In actuality, however, they do not. Very few fragments are of the finest quality, and even the lesser degrees cannot be clearly distinguished. It would seem, therefore, that the finest and most valued garments were not in fact put into the graves at all, but were passed on and worn from generation to generation. Costume formed part of the estate left in prominent families not only in late antiquity and the early Middle Ages, but also into modern times. It has been regarded as a traditional gift, a custom which has continued at least in the Near East to the present day. To underline the importance attached to garments during the Islamic period, we may cite Ibn Khaldun (AD 1332–1406), who noted that al-Mahdi, father of Harun al-Rashid (AD 786–809), used to consult 'his tailors about the mending of the torn garments of his household, for he used

---

[12] Frank (ed.), *An Economic Survey of Ancient Rome* (see n. 6), V, p. 379.

to avoid providing his family with new clothes at the expense of the treasury'.[13]

[13] Serjeant, *Islamic Textiles* (see n. 2), p. 16.

Table 16.2   Cost of textile raw materials according to the edict of Diocletian, AD *301*

Material	Use		Price		
Linen	Not used for clothing, called *tow*:				
		First quality	1 pound	denarii	24
		Second quality	1 pound	denarii	20
		Third quality	1 pound	denarii	16
	Used for garments:				
	A	First quality	1 pound	denarii	1 200
		Second quality	1 pound	denarii	960
		Third quality	1 pound	denarii	840
	B	First quality	1 pound	denarii	720
		Second quality	1 pound	denarii	600
		Third quality	1 pound	denarii	450
	C	Coarse yarn for the use of common people and slaves:			
		First quality	1 pound	denarii	250
		Second quality	1 pound	denarii	125
		Third quality	1 pound	denarii	72
Wool	Natural:				
	from Tarentum, washed		1 pound	denarii	175
	from Laodiceia, washed		1 pound	denarii	150
	from Asturia, washed		1 pound	denarii	100
	washed, of the best middle quality		1 pound	denarii	50
	all other wool, washed		1 pound	denarii	25
	Dyed purple:				
	dyed purple		1 pound	denarii	50 000
	dyed lighter purple		1 pound	denarii	32 000
	dyed bright in Tyrian purple		1 pound	denarii	16 000
	dyed once (in Tyrian purple?)		1 pound	denarii	12 000
	dyed twice in the best genuine Milesian purple		1 pound	denarii	12 000
	dyed twice in the second-quality Milesian purple		1 pound	denarii	10 000
	dyed scarlet with Nicene kermes		1 pound	denarii	1 500
	dyed in best archil purple		1 pound	denarii	600
	dyed in second-quality archil purple		1 pound	denarii	500
	dyed in third-quality archil purple		1 pound	denarii	400
	dyed in fourth-quality archil purple		1 pound	denarii	300
Silk	white		1 pound	denarii	12 000
	raw silk, dyed purple		1 pound	denarii	150 000

Table 16.3 Wages of spinners and weavers, according to the edict of Diocletian, AD 301

Craftsmen	Work involved	Rate	Wage	
Spinners	purple silk for all silk cloth	1 oz	denarii	116
	purple silk for part silk cloth	1 oz	denarii	60
	purple wool of the finest quality, for soft-finished cloth	1 oz	denarii	24
	gold spinner	1 lb	denarii	2500
Those who unravel silk	with maintenance	1 oz	denarii	64
Linen weavers	first-quality work, with maintenance	daily	denarii	40
	second-quality work, with maintenance	daily	denarii	20
Wool weavers	wool from Mutina, with maintenance	1 lb	denarii	40
	wool from Tarentum and Laldiceia	1 lb	denarii	30
	wool for warm clothing	1 lb	denarii	30
	wool of second quality	1 lb	denarii	20
	wool of third quality	1 lb	denarii	15
	Tapestry-woven decoration or 'embroidery' in wool: for mantle of wool of Mutina, cr of Laodiceia, resembling that of Mutina	1 oz	denarii	25
Silk weavers	Plain fabrics: part silk, with maintenance	daily	denarii	25
	unpatterned silk, with maintenance	daily	denarii	25

Continued overleaf

Table 16.3   continued

Craftsmen	Work involved	Rate	Wage	
Silk weavers	Patterned fabrics:			
	silk in diamond weave, with maintenance	daily	denarii	40–60
	'brocade'-maker working in gold, for first quality work	1 oz	denarii	1000
	for second quality work	1 oz	denarii	750
	Tapestry-woven decoration or 'embroidery':			
	in gold filé for all silk fabrics, first quality work	1 oz	denarii	500
	second quality work	1 oz	denarii	400
	shirt ornaments, part silk	1 oz	denarii	200
	all silk	1 oz	denarii	300

Table 16.4   Wages of tailors and fullers, according to the edict of Diocletian, AD 301

Type of garment	Tailors	Fullers	
Shirts			
		made of wool, new	den. 25–20
		made of coarser wool	den. 20
		made of part silk, new	den. 175
		made of all silk, new	den. 250
		made of all silk, unmarked, new	den. 200

Item		den.
Dalmatics without hood, for women	for an ordinary tunic, new	den. 16
	used	den. 10
	attaching a silk neck-band	den. 50
	attaching a part-silk neck-band	den. 30
	made of part silk, unmarked, new	den. 125
Dalmatics with hood	of coarser wool, new	den. 50
	of pure, soft-finished wool, new	den. 100
	of part silk, new	den. 300
	of all silk, new	den. 600
Men's dalmatics or *colobia*	folding and sewing a garment, for a finer piece	den. 6
	for a coarser piece	den. 4
	of part silk, new	den. 200
	of all silk, new	den. 400
Hoods or cloaks, called *caracallae*	for a larger piece	den. 25
	for a smaller piece	den. 20
Mantles or cloaks, called *chlamys*	light, doubled, of wool from Mutina, new	den. 500
	light, single, of wool from Mutina, new	den. 250
	light, of wool from Laodiceia	den. 200
Fibulatoria	of wool of Mutina or Laodiceia, new	den. 200
Hooded cloaks, called *birrus*	for cutting and finishing a *birrus* of first quality	den. 60
	of second quality	den. 40
	of wool from Nervii	den. 600
	of wool from Laodiceia	den. 175
	Dacian	den. 300
	Noric	den. 200
	other	den. 100
	African	den. 50

Table 16.5 List of comparative wages and prices, according to the edict of Diocletian, AD 301

Wages		Prices
Farm labourer, with maintenance	daily	den. 25
Stone mason, with maintenance	daily	den. 50
Worker in marble pavements and walls	daily	den. 60
Worker in wall-mosaics, with maintenance	daily	den. 60
Wall painter, with maintenance	daily	den. 75
Figure painter, with maintenance	daily	den. 150
Shepherd, with maintenance	daily	den. 20
Elementary teacher	monthly per pupil	den. 50
Teacher of Greek or Latin literature, and of geometry	monthly per pupil	den. 200
Barber	per man	den. 2
Shearer, with maintenance	per animal	den. 2
Water carrier, working a full day, with maintenance	daily	den. 25
Maker of models, with maintenance	daily	den. 75
Other workers in plaster, with maintenance	daily	den. 50

Food	Quantity	Prices
Wine	1 Italian pint	den. 30–38
Beer	1 Italian pint	den. 4–2
Oil	1 Italian pint	den. 40–48
Vinegar	1 Italian pint	den. 8
Lamb	1 Italian pound	den. 12
Pork	1 Italian pound	den. 12
Beef	1 Italian pound	den. 8
Ham	1 Italian pound	den. 20
Chickens	1 pair	den. 60
Hare		den. 150
Rabbit		den. 40
Fish	1 Italian pound	den. 24–26
Butter	1 Italian pound	den. 16
Lettuce and cabbage, best quality	5	den. 4
second quality	10	den. 4
Leeks, largest	10	den. 4

Table 16.5 continued

Wages			Food	Quantity	Prices
Polisher, for a sword, used		den. 25	Green onions	25–50	den. 4
Polisher, for a helmet, used		den. 25	Watercress	bunch of 20	den. 10
Polisher, for an ax		den. 6	Melons	2–4	den. 4
Polisher, for a sword scabbard		den. 100	Eggs	4	den. 4
Copper smith, on copper	per pound	den. 6	Chestnuts	100	den. 4
Copper smith, on small vessles	per pound	den. 6	Walnuts	50–100	den. 4
Copper smith, on figurines or statues	per pound	den. 6	Apples	10–40	den. 4
Scribe, for the best handwriting	100 lines	den. 25	Pomegranates	10–20	den. 8
Scribe, for second-quality handwriting	100 lines	den. 20	Figs	25–40	den. 4
Notary, for writing a petition or legal documents	100 lines	den. 10	Olives, ripe	1 Italian pint	den. 4

It is significant that silk, an expensive luxury fabric, is almost non-existent among the grave goods of the late antique and early Christian/Byzantine periods. At the same time, documentary evidence shows that silk was not only widely known in the Roman world, but that silk textiles were actually woven in several cities of the Empire (Tables 16.2–16.4).[14] Tapestry-woven ornaments executed in silk, or in silk and gold filé, were produced together with half-silk and all-silk fabrics. The value of these special textiles is well-documented in Diocletian's edict. Weavers received from 400 to 500 *denarii* for weaving one ounce of tapestry decoration in gold filé, while only 25 *denarii* were paid for an ounce of tapestry-woven ornaments when made with the finest wool (Table 16.3).[15] Under such circumstances, it is hardly surprising that woollen tapestries form the majority of the archaeological finds, and many silk patterns can be reconstructed only through woollen imitations or from artistic representations. Something in the order of 100 000 fragments of so-called Coptic textiles are housed in public and private collections throughout the world today; and while a large proportion of them bear tapestry-woven decoration worked in coloured wool and linen, less than a dozen examples are known to exhibit tapestry-woven ornaments worked entirely in silk, or in a mixture of silk or purple wool and gold filé.[16]

---

[14] For silk and silk weaving in the Roman and early medieval periods of the Mediterranean world, see Pliny, *Natural History* vi.54; Edict of Diocletian, XX (Frank (ed.), *An Economic Survey of Ancient Rome* (see n. 6), V, pp. 377–8); (Tables 16.2–16.4); L. Duchesne (ed.), *Le Liber Pontificalis* (Paris, 1886); W. F. Volbach, *Early Decorative Textiles* (London, 1969), pp. 16–17, 22–4, 30–2; L. M. Wilson, *The Clothing of the Ancient Romans* (Baltimore, 1938), pp. 4–5, 37. For the industry and silk textiles themselves, see Falke, *Kunstgeschichte der Seidenweberei* (see n. 7); R. J. Forbes, *Studies in ancient technology, IV, The Fibres and Fabrics of Antiquity* (Leiden, 1956), pp. 53ff; R. Forrer, *Die römischen und byzantinischen Seiden-Textilien aus dem Gräberfelde von Achmim-Panopolis* (Strasbourg, 1891); Kendrick, *Catalogue of Textiles from Egypt* (see n. 7), I, pp. 22–3, 29, and III, *Coptic Period*, pp. 69–75; M. Khvostov, *Ocherki organizatii promyshlennosty i torgovli v greko-rimskom Egipte, I, Tekstilnaya promishlennost v greko-rimskom Egipte* [Studies of the organisation of industry and commerce in Graeco-Roman Egypt, I, The textile industry] (Kazan, 1914); A. Lucas, *Ancient Egyptian Materials and Industries*, 3rd edn (London, 1948), pp. 170ff; Wipszycka, *L'Industrie textile dans l'Egypte romaine* (see n. 2), pp. 37–9.

[15] Frank (ed.), *An Economic Survey of Ancient Rome* (see n. 6), V, pp. 377–8.

[16] For examples in the Victoria and Albert Museum, London, see Kendrick, *Catalogue of Textiles from Egypt* (see n. 7), I, pp. 22, 29 no. 62 (tapestry-woven decoration in silk, part of a linen tunic; p. 66, pl. 14), no. 113 (tapestry-woven decoration in silk, applied to a linen tunic; p. 79), no. 162 (tapestry-woven decoration in purple wool, and gold filé wound round a silk core, part of a linen cloth; p. 94, pl. 25). For a fragment worked in silk and gold filé in Vienna, see *Kunst und Handwerk*, XIV (1911), p. 253 and Kendrick, *op. cit.*, p. 29. For the golden bands in the Salonika Museum, see Volbach, *Early Decorative Textiles* (see n. 14), p. 22. For a fragment from Kostolats (Colonia Viminacium), decorated with a Victory figure in gold filé (purple silk core, warp of purple silk), dating from the first third of the third century AD, possibly manufactured in Syria, see Agnes Geijer, 'A gold tapestry from the third century AD', *Bulletin de Liaison du Centre International d'Etude des Textiles Anciens*, XXIII (1966), pp. 15–16; Edith B. Thomas and Agnes Geijer in *Meddelande från Lunds Historiska Museum, 1964–65* (Lund, 1965), pp. 223–36. Two fine tunic ornaments are in the collection of the Museum of Fine Arts, Boston.

In Islamic times, according to both the finds and the documents, the use of silk became more widespread, but ornaments woven in gold filé remain rare. Such fabrics, identified by Lisa Golombek as ḳaṣab,[17] appear to have been produced in considerable quantities at both Tinnīs and Damietta, in the Nile delta. Yacḳūbī (AD 891) wrote:

> Tinnīs is an ancient city in which valuable garments of Dabīḳī and ḳaṣab are made, of close texture and fine ... Then comes the town of Damietta in which garments and sharb-linen and ḳaṣab cloths are made.[18]

Nāṣir-i-Khusraw (AD 1047) gave even more detailed information about the centres where ḳaṣab was produced:

> Tinnīs makes coloured ḳaṣab used for turbans, head-dresses, and women's clothing ... White ḳaṣab is made at Damietta ... I have heard that the ruler of Fars had sent 20 000 dinars to Tinnīs to buy a complete set of royal robes ... There are famous weavers there who weave the royal robes.[19]

As was the case with many sought-after fabrics, ḳaṣab was imitated outside Egypt in Iran, Iraq, and the Yemen.[20] Al-Makdisī (AD 985) referring to Kazerun in Fars, noted that:

> It is the Damietta of the Persians, and that is because the linen garments which are of the same make as ḳaṣab resembling the shatawī [from Shata, Tinnīs–Damietta group], even if they are of cotton, are made and sold there.

He went on to say that from Sīnīz, another city of Fars, 'come garments resembling ḳaṣab; sometimes the flax is brought to them from Egypt, but what is made nowadays is grown there'.[21]

Although the tradition of tapestry-woven ornaments in silk and gold filé may well go back to the Egypt of late antiquity, ḳaṣab as a special

---

[17] Golombek and Gervers, 'Tiraz fabrics in the Royal Ontario Museum' (see n. 4); Serjeant, *Islamic Textiles* (see n. 2); and Goitein, *Letters of Medieval Jewish Traders* (see n. 6). Ṭardwaḥsh, manufactured in the tiraz factories of Alexandria, Miṣr (Cairo), and Damascus, may refer to a similar kind of fine, tapestry-woven fabric, using filé of precious metals for the ornaments (al-Makrizi's (d. AD 1442) description of the robe of honour received by important emirs, *c.* AD 1280, quoted by Serjeant, *op. cit.*, p. 150). In the *Arabian Nights*, it is described in the following manner: 'He then unfolded the piece of linen and lo, in it was the figure of a gazelle worked with silk and embroidered with red gold, and facing it was the figure of another gazelle worked with silver, and having upon its neck a ring of red gold, and three beads of silver' (Serjeant, loc. cit.).

[18] Serjeant, *Islamic Textiles* (see n. 2), p. 140.

[19] Ibid., p. 142.

[20] Ibid., pp. 39, 49, 57, 76, 78, 127.

[21] Ibid., pp. 51, 54.

fabric was first recorded in the ninth century. Prior to the eleventh century, however, it is almost non-existent among the archaeological finds. Even in the late eleventh and twelfth centuries, when kasab must have come within reach of a larger strata of the population, it remains relatively rare among the grave goods. What has survived can hardly represent the best and finest examples of contemporary kasab weaving.

Even though kasab and silk tapestry-woven decoration worked against a linen ground, were fairly well represented among the Fatimid finds, it is significant that hardly anything has survived from garments made of compound and striped silks. Such fabrics must have been quite common in the period. The documents of the Cairo Geniza illustrate that even the middle class wore silk. Among the correspondence of the Tustarī brothers in Cairo–Fustat, we find the following reference in a letter sent from Iran to Egypt in 1026:

> I also sent . . . a box covered with leather containing a Sahībī robe of khazz silk and a gilded Sahībī garment of khazz, first class, with ibrīsim silk.[22]

In 1010 the Tāhertī brothers of Kairwan (or Kairouan), Tunisia, wrote to the Tustari brothers in Egypt about a special order:

> I would like the robe to be deep red, as red as possible, and the white and yellow also to be of excellent colour. I did not like the colour of the yellow which arrived . . . The Sig[laton] robe is of extreme beauty, but it is not the colour which they ordered. For this is white and blue, but instead I w[ished to have] one of the blue onion colour, an open colour, according to your taste.[23]

The type of garments referred to in these documents are shown in artistic depictions of human figures, such as those on Egyptian and Persian pottery between the twelfth and the early fourteenth centuries, on Persian stucco figures of the twelfth and thirteenth centuries, and in the thirteenth-century miniatures of the Baghdad School.[24] But what we have among the grave goods are not fragments of these valuable garments, but rather the more common and cheaper linen

---

[22] Goitein, *Letters of Medieval Jewish Traders* (see n. 6), p. 37 (no. 2).

[23] Ibid., p. 77 (no. 11).

[24] There are numerous examples on Seljuq ceramics in Esin Atil, *Ceramics from the world of Islam* (Freer Gallery of Art, Smithsonian Institution, Washington, DC, 1973). Examples of the stucco figures are in the collections of the Metropolitan Museum of Art, New York, and the Detroit Institute of Art. For the miniatures, see Richard Ettinghausen, *Arab Painting* (Skira, 1962), and Esin Atil, *Art of the Arab world* (Freer Gallery of Art, Smithsonian Institution, Washington, DC, 1975).

and woollen goods, and the simple cottons from the eastern provinces of the Caliphate. There seems therefore to be little doubt that the most expensive textiles seldom if ever accompanied their owners to the grave even in Islamic times.

There is another major difficulty in basing our conclusions about medieval Mediterranean costume on the textile remains that have been discovered in Egypt. As excavators and dealers alike appear to have favoured decorated rather than plain parts of textiles that have been brought to light, it is generally speaking only the ornamental bands, squares and medallions which have been collected. The undecorated and thus 'uninteresting' sections have seldom been preserved. Complete, or at least reconstructable, garments are extremely rare.[25]

One final question may be raised regarding the interpretation of the Egyptian finds: the problem of dating. Can we separate the late antique pagan material from the early Christian; or the early Christian/Byzantine stuffs of the major centres from the contemporary production of provincial workshops; or the fabrics of the Christian era from the fabrics of Islamic times; or the garments worn by Christians and/or Jews in the Islamic period from those worn by Arabs? We must admit that at present we can neither date the Egyptian material with any great precision nor can we be certain that our assumptions are correct in separating the different groups of textiles chronologically or culturally. The most obvious exceptions are those Islamic pieces that are dated or that can be fairly closely dated through the epigraphical characteristics of their inscriptions.

There are several schools of thought about the dating of 'Coptic' textiles. Pierre du Bourguet for one believes that most of them should be dated after AD 640, and associates many groups with dates as late as the tenth to twelfth centuries.[26] While some of his suppositions, and similar ones put forward by others, may well be correct, they are based on purely stylistic distinctions and degrees of stylisation rather than on archaeological evidence. Having studied the material in some depth, I have come to the conclusion that the dating suggested by scholars of the late nineteenth and early twentieth centuries is more accurate. They were more familiar with the evidence available from

[25] For collections of complete tunics from the late antique, Byzantine, and Coptic periods of Egypt, see the Musée du Louvre, Paris; the Metropolitan Museum of Art, New York; the Royal Ontario Museum, Toronto (Figures 16.1–16.4, 16.14, 16.13); and the Victoria and Albert Museum, London (Figures 16.5, 16.6 16.8, 16.9, 16.15, 16.16). For tunics in European church treasuries, see n. 7. The Victoria and Albert Museum also has a good collection of Egyptian Mamluk shirts (Figure 16.16).

[26] Pierre du Bourguet, *Musée National du Louvre: Catalogue des étoffes coptes*, I (Paris, 1964).

the then-current archaeological excavations, and thus dated the 'Coptic' material to between the third and the eighth and ninth centuries, placing the emphasis on pre-Islamic times.[27]

Problems of garment construction

In spite of all the difficulties presented by the material, it is clear from what has been said that we have in the Egyptian finds, the documents, and the artistic depictions, rich resources for the historical interpretation of more than just textiles and costume. It is also clear that only an interdisciplinary approach will enable us to formulate legitimate conclusions from all the material.

In addition to the traditional methods of studying Mediterranean textiles, I should like to introduce another approach through the study of garment construction. As Dorothy Burnham has emphasised, the construction of traditional garments can reveal more about clothing than their cut.[28] Based on the size and width of the woven fabric, determined by the loom upon which it was woven, garment construction may suggest cultural–historical influences as well as technological changes, especially changes in the technology of the loom. In the case of our present study, the construction of Mediterranean garments could reflect the unity and diversity of this internationally closely linked world.

To illustrate the significance of garment construction in the Mediterranean, I should like to consider the most characteristic garment of late antiquity and the early Middle Ages, the tunic (Figures 16.1– 16.4).[29] Made of either linen or wool, the tunic was woven in a single piece on a wide vertical loom. The loom-width is always twice the garment's length (Figures 16.5–16.8). Both the evidence of the written sources and a closer examination of the actual garments indicate that they were woven on the two-beam vertical loom, what several authors of the first century AD refer to as the 'new loom'.[30] It came to replace the 'old loom', the vertical warp-weighted loom of classical antiquity.[31]

---

[27] For a bibliography of the early excavation reports, interpretive studies and catalogues, see Kendrick, *Catalogue of Textiles from Egypt* (see n. 7), I–III (1920–22).

[28] Dorothy K. Burnham, *Cut my cote* (Toronto, 1973).

[29] For a summary of the early references and a detailed description of various tunics, see Wilson, *The Clothing of the Ancient Romans* (see n. 14), pp. 55–71, 138–41, 152–62, 167–72. On the weaving of tunics, see Anne Marie Franzén, 'En koptisk tunica', *Rig*, XLIV (Stockholm, 1961), pp. 76–98, and Margarethe Hald, 'Ancient textile techniques in Egypt and Scandinavia', *Acta Archaeologica*, XVII (Copenhagen, 1946), pp. 49–98.

[30] From Ovid (first century BC) to Servius (fourth century AD) there are references to both the warp-weighted or 'old' loom, and the two-beam vertical or 'new' loom. For Egyptian references on the latter, see the edict of Diocletian (XIII, prices of spinning and weaving equipment) in Frank (ed.), *Economic Survey of Ancient Rome* (see n. 6), V, p. 359; see also II, pp. 276, 475; Wipszicka, *L'industrie textile dans l'Egypte romain* (see n. 2), pp. 48–54.

[31] Marta Hoffmann, *The Warp-Weighted Loom* (Oslo, 1974).

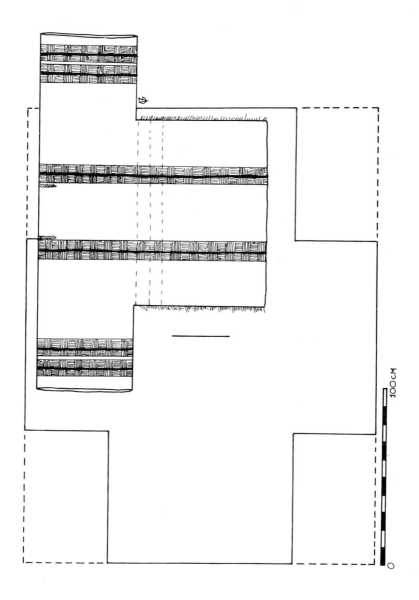

16.5   Tunic of bleached linen tabby with tapestry-woven decoration in purple wool, details in linen (loom width 259 cm). Akhmin (Panopolîs), Egypt: Byzantine period, probably fourth century AD

Although undecorated tunics could quite easily have been made on the 'old loom', and some were indeed woven on it,[32] the appearance of the tunic and of the two-beam vertical loom may not only coincide with, but directly depend on the other. It is possible that they both resulted from a new, foreign influence at the turn of Republican and Imperial times, even if we know the exact origins of neither the implement nor the tunic.[33]

Although tunics were woven in a single-loom piece from the earliest known examples up to about the ninth and tenth centuries, some must have been constructed of narrow loom-widths, and thus from several pieces, from late antiquity. The appearance of figured oriental silks and the weaving of such compound silks in the late Empire brought fabrics of narrow loom-widths, characteristic products of a horizontal shaft loom, into the Mediterranean.[34] The construction of tunics from such compound fabrics had to be based on the dimension of this new type of material. Obviously, there were several possibilities for making tunics from these silks. One of them, shown in Figure 16.9, is based on the old Mediterranean idea of using the fabric 'horizontally', that is, in a fashion that imitates the look of the tunic woven in a single loom-piece. In this case, the hem-line of the garment is characteristically formed by selvages. That such a construction was used is not simply postulated through logic and artistic depictions but is attested by surviving linen garments.[35] Unfortunately we have no silk examples among the finds. This 'horizontal' way of constructing garments has survived into the twentieth century through the medium of European ethnographical costume (Figure 16.10).[36] It can also be detected in the Middle East and north Africa in abaya'-type and other mantles (Figures 16.11–16.12). Abaya's can be traced back to at least Fatimid times as exemplified by the 'Veil of St Anne' in Apt Cathedral, France, and numerous other Egyptian fragments.[37]

[32] The coarse woollen tunic of Reepsholt (first to fifth centuries AD), found in a bog in Friesland, was made on the warp-weighted vertical loom in twill weave and with tablet-woven starting borders; Hald believes that it was of local workmanship, imitating the Mediterranean fashion – Hald, 'Ancient textile techniques' (see n. 29), pp. 95–7, Figure 37; Marta Hoffmann, *The Warp-Weighted Loom* (see n. 31); H. A. Potratz, *Das Moorgewand von Reepsholt* (Hildesheim, 1942). In the second century AD, Festus described the *tunica recta*, which belonged to the traditional bridal attire, and the *regilla tunica*, which was the characteristic initiation outfit of boys, as 'a stantibus et in altitudinem texuntur'. Most specialists interpret this as a definite reference to the warp-weighted loom: Wilson, *The Clothing of the Ancient Romans* (see n. 14), pp. 21, 57–78; Hoffmann, *op. cit.*, pp. 323–4. The reference to Christ's seamless garment in the Gospel of St John (19: 23) has also been considered as an indication of the use of the warp-weighted loom.

[33] Hoffmann, *The Warp-Weighted Loom* (see n. 31), pp. 321–33, which provides an extensive biblio-

graphy; C. H. Johl, *Altägyptische Webestühle und Brettchenweberei in Altägypten* (Leipzig, 1924); Wilson, *The Clothing of the Ancient Romans* (see n. 14), pp. 21–5. R. Pfister, 'Les débuts du vêtement copte', *Etudes d'orientalisme publiées par le Musée Guimet a la mémoire de Raymonde Linossier* (Paris, 1932), pp. 433–59, pls. 45–50; Hald, 'Ancient textile techniques' (see n. 29), pp. 94–5. Hald suggests that the tunic, woven according to an exact prearranged plan, must have had a prototype, most probably of felt, to inspire this 'sophisticated form of weaving'. She believes that the idea could not have suddenly occurred to a weaver. Hald also notes that in the tomb of Tut'ankhamun, 1350 BC, there was a sleeved tunic with elements suggesting Syrian origin or at least Syrian influence; G. M. Crowfoot and N. de G. Davies, 'The tunic of Tut'ankhamun', *Journal of Egyptian Archaeology*, **XXVII** (1941).

³⁴ Compound silks with patterning all over are frequently represented on ivory carvings from the early fifth century onwards (ivory diptych depicting Stilicho (*c.* 360–408), *c.* 400, Cathedral Treasury of Monza, reproduced in W. F. Volbach, *Early Christian Art* (New York, n.d.), Figure 63. For consular diptychs, see W. F. Volbach, *Elfenbeinarbeiten der Spätantike und des frühen Mittelalters*, 2nd edn (Römisch–Germanisches Zentralmuseum, Mainz, 1952). Compound silks are also depicted on mosaics as for example in Ravenna (San Vitale; Theodora with her court, *c.* 547), and in Salonika (Hagios Dimitrios; Saint Demetrios as patron saint of children, Saint Demetrios between Prefect Leontius and Bishop Johannes, *c.*629–43). While fragments of such silks can neither be distinguished with any certainty among the Egyptian finds, nor be precisely dated, a good number of compound woollen textiles with all-over patterning, produced on a multiple-shaft loom, are well represented among the grave goods and technically appear to relate to the silks. For a select bibliography, see G. M. Crowfoot and J. Griffiths, 'Coptic textiles in two-faced weave with patterns in reverse', *Journal of Egyptian Archaeology*, **XXV** (1939), pp. 40–5; J. F. Flanagan, 'The origin of the drawloom used in the making of early Byzantine silks', *Burlington Magazine*, **XXXV** (1919), pp. 167–72; Kendrick, *Catalogue of textiles from Egypt* (see n. 7), II (1921), pp. 71–5; C. J. Lamm and R. J. Charleston, 'Some early draw loom weavings', *Bulletin de la Société d'Archéologie Copte*, V (1939), p. 194; Deborah Thompson, *Coptic textiles in the Brooklyn Museum* (New York, 1971), pp. 22–3, no. 6. Though it is certain that this group is contemporary with the pieces in tapestry- and looped-weaves, the dating of the individual textiles is still a difficult problem. Gayet's excavations at Antinoë indicate that this type of fabrics was used as cushions under the heads of mummies attributed to the second and third centuries AD (E. Guimet, *Portraits d'Antinoé* (Paris, 1912); Kendrick, *Catalogue of Textiles from Egypt* (see n. 7), II (1921), p. 72). Through the evidence of coins, a few fragments from Karanis may be placed between the last third of the third and the fourth to mid-fifth centuries (Wilson, *Ancient Textiles from Egypt* (1933), pp. 17–18, pl. 3:16–18). Whether made of silk or wool, the garments worn by some of Theodora's ladies-in-waiting on the mosaic panel in San Vitale, Ravenna (*c.*547), suggest a very similar weaving technique with the inclusion of tapestry-woven details. For woollen fragments with such tapestry-woven ornaments, see Kendrick, II (1921), no. 537, pl. 25; and Royal Ontario Museum, Toronto, acc. no. 969.323.1. Another fragment in the Royal Ontario Museum, identified by Dr Lisa Golombek as Islamic (personal communication, 1977), indicates that this type of compound weaves for woollen fabrics survived well into the medieval Islamic period (acc. no. 970.364.1). In most cases, the literature refers to these textile fragments as products of an early type of draw-loom, but their relatively simple and small pattern repeats indicate rather a shaft loom. According to Walter Endrei, even the very intricate patterns of early Chinese silks were woven on a loom with multiple shafts, and *not* on a draw-loom. In his view, the true draw-loom was invented in the Middle East during the fourth and fifth centuries AD: 'Der Trittwebstuhl im frühmittelalterlichen Europa', *Acta Historica*, VIII, (Budapest, 1961), pp. 107–36. See also Hoffmann, *The Warp-Weighted Loom* (n. 31), pp. 333–6; and Krishna Riboud, 'A closer view of early Chinese silks' in *Studies in Textile History* (see n. 4), pp. 252–80.

³⁵ Victoria and Albert Museum, London, acc. no. 2071–1900 (Kendrick, *Catalogue of textiles from Egypt* (see n. 7), II, no. 335, pl. 14); Royal Ontario Museum, Toronto, acc. no. 910.1.5 (Burnham, *Cut my cote* (see n. 28), p. 11). While the appearance of this type of cut must be connected to the narrow loom-widths of a horizontal loom and to the cut of silk tunics, the relatively plain linen fabrics of the London and Toronto examples could easily have been woven on two-beam vertical looms. The multiple-shaft horizontal loom, used for patterned silks and intricate woollens, was more likely an implement of specialised professional workshops for at least the first 600 or 700 years AD. A simplified version of the horizontal loom, used for the weaving of plain fabrics, probably became a common loom-type only considerably later.

³⁶ Veronika Gervers, 'The historical components of regional costume in south-eastern Europe', *Textile Museum Journal*, IV (1975), pp. 65–6 and Figures 7–8 on p. 72.

³⁷ Max Tilke, *Oriental Costume, their Designs and Colours* (London, 1922), pls. 9 (Tunisia), 29 (East Arabia), 31–2 (Syria), 33 (Syria or Palestine); Golombek and Gervers, 'Tiraz fabrics in the Royal Ontario Museum' (see n. 4), pp. 82–125.

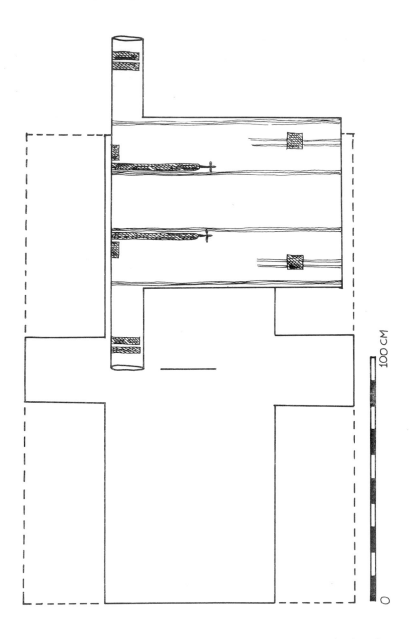

16.6   *Tunic of bleached linen tabby with tapestry-woven decoration in red wool and linen (loom width 198.9 cm). Akhmîn (Panopolis), Egypt: Byzantine period, fifth century* AD

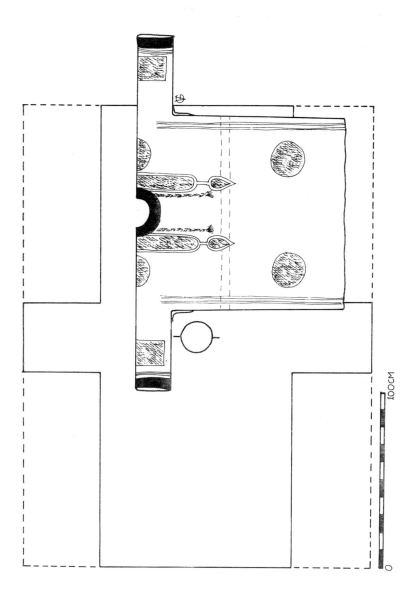

16.7   Tunic of weft-faced red woollen tabby with tapestry-woven decoration in coloured wool and linen; neckline and cuffs edged with brocaded bands (loom width c. 264 cm). Egypt: Islamic period, seventh–ninth century AD

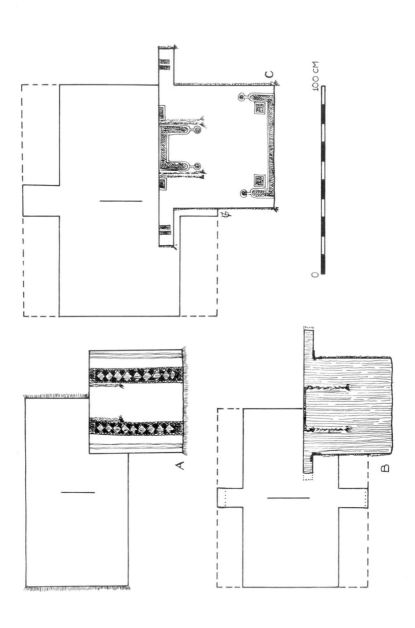

16.8   Tunics for children (loom widths: a, 103 cm; b, 95.4 cm; c, 123.4 cm). Egypt: Byzantine and Islamic periods

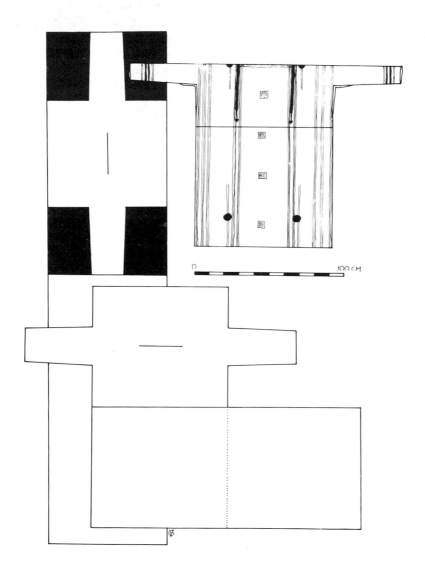

*16.9   Tunic of bleached linen tabby with tapestry-woven decoration in red
wool and linen, applied front ornaments probably added later (loom width
80 cm). Egypt: Byzantine period, fifth–sixth century* AD

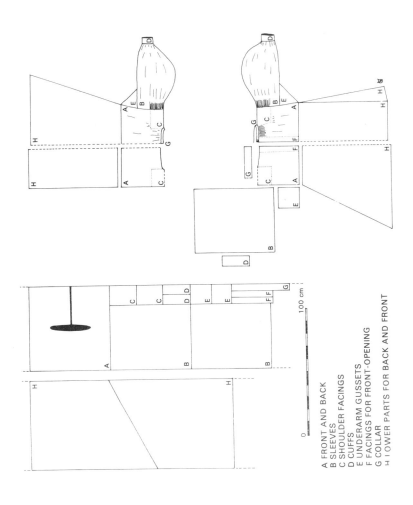

16.10   *Man's shirt of linen tabby, embroidered in black wool (loom widths 66 and 70 cm). Toledo, Spain: eighteenth century*

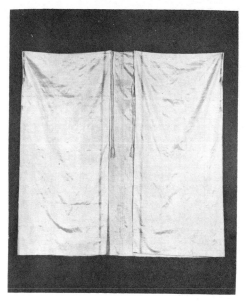

16.11 *Man's mantle* (abaya), *made of a single width of pale pink silk tabby brocaded in metallic filé.* Damascus, Syria: *late nineteenth century*

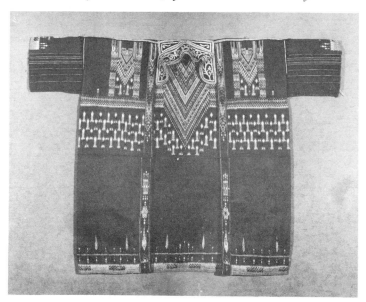

16.12 *Man's jacket* (mashla), *made of two widths of weft-faced dark red woollen tabby, decorated in tapestry weave with coloured wool, silk, and metallic filé.* Syria: *late nineteenth century*

Parallel with these developments, the now more usual 'vertical' approach to garment construction can also be seen in Egypt through the Antinoë coats and some shirts (Figures 16.13–16.14).[38] Two variations for the cut of such garments are shown in Figure 16.15. Although we cannot ascertain with any certainty when these kinds of costume first became known in Egypt and in the Mediterranean in general, one suspects that at least the Antinoë finds may be related to the Persian influences of the fifth to seventh centuries.[39] Such oriental garments, however, were worn by easterners within the Empire from a much earlier period. Tribute-bearing or captured 'barbarians', frequently depicted in monumental sculpture as well as in the minor arts, show many variants of an eastern garb.[40] According to their traditional religious iconography, such figures as Mithras, the three Hebrews of the fiery furnace, or the three Magi are, as a rule, represented wearing belted shirts, trousers and felt caps – that is to say the general mode of western Asia.[41] Palmyran tomb sculpture and the wall paintings of the Synagogue at Dura-Europos indicate that this type of outfit was commonly worn in Syria along with more classical and more Mediterranean garments.[42]

From Islamic times, 'vertically' constructed garments became more common in Egypt, and spread rapidly throughout north Africa and the Mediterranean world (Figure 16.16).[43] This originally oriental style also influenced fashion in western, northern and eastern Europe. The best known types of medieval shirts, the basic garment worn by men and women alike, was cut in this way, as is shown by costume remains and other ethnographic sources.[44]

---

[38] *Le costume en Egypte de IIIe. au XIIIe. siècle d'apres les fouilles de M. A. Gayet* (Palais du Costume, Paris, 1900); Agnes Geijer, 'An Iranian riding coat reconstructed', *Bulletin de liaison du Centre International d'Etude des Textiles Anciens*, XXVII (1968), pp. 22–5; Max Tilke, *Costume Patterns and Designs: A Survey of Costume Patterns and Designs of all Periods and Nations from Antiquity to Modern Times* (New York, 1956), pl. 4:5; Wulff and Volbach, *Spätantike und koptische Stoffe* (1926), p. 137, pl. 126 (acc. nos. 14, 231). For sleeveless shirt variants, made of woollen tabby, see Victoria and Albert Museum, London, acc. nos. T.232–1923; du Bourguet, *Catalogue des étoffes coptes* (1964), pp. 258 (F21), 318 (F191), 422–3 (G204; length 110 cm, loom-width 118 cm). For long-sleeved variants, made of fine linen tabby: see Royal Ontario Museum, Toronto, acc. nos. 910.1.8, 910.1.9 (Figures 16.14. 16.15); Burnham, *Cut my cote* (see n. 28), p. 11; Staatliche Museen, Berlin, acc. nos. 14232, 9922, 9935, each decorated with applied tablet-woven borders, long gores inserted at sides; see Wulff and Volbach, *op. cit.*, p. 136, pl. 123; Hald, 'Ancient textile techniques' (see n. 29), pp. 77–8, Figure 25. These tunics are believed to have come from Antinoë; though they are said to be 'Coptic', they are considered to betray Persian influences. There is an uncertainty about their dating, but they are generally regarded as rather early pieces. Another linen example, dated to the sixth to eighth centuries, and thought to show the influence of oriental fashion, is in the collection of the Museo Sacro Vaticano; see Volbach, *I tessuti del Museo Sacro Vaticano* (1942), p. 14, T3, pl. 2(acc. no. 1308). Other examples are in the collection of the Metropolitan Museum of Art, New York. Made of Byzantine figured silk of the ninth or tenth century, the dalmatik of Saint Ulrich in Augsburg Cathedral has the same cut as these linen shirts, see Müller-Christensen, 'Textiles in Schwaben' (see n. 7), 207, pp. 197–8, Figure 194.

[39] Agnes Geijer, 'A silk from Antinoë and the Sassanian textile art', *Orientalia Suecana*, XII (1964) pp. 3–36; Ernst Kitzinger, 'The horse and lion tapestry at Dumbarton Oaks', *Dumbarton Oaks Papers*, III (1946), pp. 1–72, with extensive bibliography on the Antinoë problem; R. Pfister, 'Le rôle de l'Iran dans les textiles d'Antinoë', *Ars Islamica*, XIII–XIV (1948), pp. 46–74.

[40] Rome, columns of Marcus Aurelius (late second century AD); battle scene of harness ornaments from Piedmont (second or third century AD; Aosta, Museo Archaeologico); Salonika, Arch of Galerius (c.300); Obelisk of Theodosius, north-west side (c.390); Barberini diptych with emperor Anastasius I (early sixth century; Paris, Musée du Louvre), etc. For reproductions, see Ranuccio Bianchi Bandinelli, *Rome, the Late Empire: Roman Art AD 200–400* (New York, 1971); André Grabar, *Early Christian Art from the Rise of Christianity to the Death of Theodosius* (New York, 1968); Volbach, *Early Christian Art* (see n. 34).

[41] Dura-Europos, wall paintings of Mithraeum, second century AD, Yale University Art Gallery; for reproductions, see Grabar, *Early Christian Art*, Figures 64–5; Pierre du Bourguet, *Early Christian Art* (New York, 1971), p. 65; numerous other illustrations in J. R. Hinnels (ed.), *Mithraic Studies*, II (Manchester, 1971). For the three Hebrews, see Rome, Catacomb of Priscilla, Chamber of the Velatio, mid-third to early fourth century; Milan, San Nazaro Maggiore, silver reliquary casket, end of fourth century; panel of an ivory diptych, sixth century (Ravenna, National Museum), etc. For reproductions, see Volbach, *Early Christian Art* (see n. 34), Figures 9, 114, 223. For artistic depictions and the iconography of the Adoration of the Magi, see Gertrud Schiller, *Iconography of Christian Art*, I (New York, 1971), pp. 100–14, Figures 245–63. For additional representations, see also Volbach, *Early Christian Art*, Figures 37, 82, 101, 103, 120, 179, 222, 254; and Grabar, *Early Christian Art*, Figure 141. The artistic prototype for the Magi paying their homage lies in those late antique compositions which depict deputations of conquered barbarians before the emperor. The oriental outfit of these foreigners also formed the source for the costume of the Magi and served as an indication of their eastern origins. Gilberte Vezin connected their particular outfit with the garments of the Mithraic priests – *L'adoration et le cycle des Mages dans l'art chrétien primitif* (Paris, 1950). This hypothesis, however, has not gained general acceptance.

[42] Henri Seyrig, 'Antiquités syriennes, no. 20, Armes et costumes iraniens de Palmyre', *Syria*, XVIII (1937), pp. 4–31. For the depiction of local oriental garments, see also the funerary mosaic of Moqimu, Edessa (Syria), third century AD (colour reproduction of copy in Grabar, *Early Christian Art* (see n. 41), Figure 49. Carl H. Kraeling, 'The synagogue' in *The excavations at Dura-Europos*, VIII (New Haven, 1956), pp. 371ff. This type of costume was known in Persia and among the nomads of the steppes since Acaemenid times. The earliest artistic representations date from the sixth and fifth centuries BC. Georgina Thompson, 'Iranian dress in the Achaemenian period. Problems concerning the *kandys* and other garments', *Iran*, III (1965), pp. 121–6; for the *kandys* in particular and for its later descendants, see also Veronika Gervers-Molnár, *The Hungarian Szür: An Archaic Mantle of Eurasian Origin* (Toronto, 1973); and Veronika Gervers, 'A nomadic mantle in Europe', *Textile History*, IX (1978). The mode continued through the Parthian and Sassanian periods. Foreigners are also depicted wearing the belted shirt and the tight trousers in Gandharan art (Edward J. Keall, 'Parthian costume portrayed on the stuccoes from Oal'eh-i Yazdigird, Iran', paper read at the Colloquium on Medieval Textiles from the Mediterranean World. It was taken by Iranian and Turkic nomads as far east as eastern Turkestan and northern China, and as far west as the Balkans and North Africa.

[43] From the medieval Islamic period, 'vertical' garment construction may be seen in the many examples of caftan-type costume depicted on ceramics and miniature painting. It was characteristic of Egyptian Mamluk shirts (Figure 16.16), and garments worn in foruteenth-century Nubia (Crowfoot, 'The clothing of a Nubian bishop' (see n. 7), pp. 43–51). Reflecting earlier traditions, this 'vertical' use of the woven cloth has survived in relatively recent ethnographical material in West and Central Asia and Islamic Africa. For examples, see Burnham, *Cut my Cote* (see n. 28); Gervers-Molnár, *The Hungarian Szür* (see n. 42); Tilke, *Oriental costume* (see n. 37), and *Costume Patterns and Designs* (see n. 38). For a different approach to 'vertical' garment construction in the Far East, see John E. Vollmer, *In the presence of the Dragon Throne: Ch'ing Dynasty costume in the Royal Ontario Museum* (Toronto, Royal Ontario Museum, 1977).

[44] The European medieval shirt is well represented in Romanesque and early Gothic miniature painting. For extant examples of medieval and renaissance shirts, and their descendants, see Burnham, *Cut my Cote* (see n. 28), Figures 4, 13, and examples from eastern Europe. For the survival of both the eastern and western medieval traditions in eastern Europe, see Gervers, 'The historical components of regional costume' (see n. 86), pp. 61–78.

16.13   Man's coat of fine fulled wool, edged with patterned silk bands.
Probably Persian, found at Antinoë, Egypt: Byzantine period, sixth–seventh
century AD

16.14   Shirt of bleached linen tabby, cut in oriental fashion, edged with
patterned silk bands. Egypt (probably Antinoë): Byzantine period, sixth–
seventh century AD

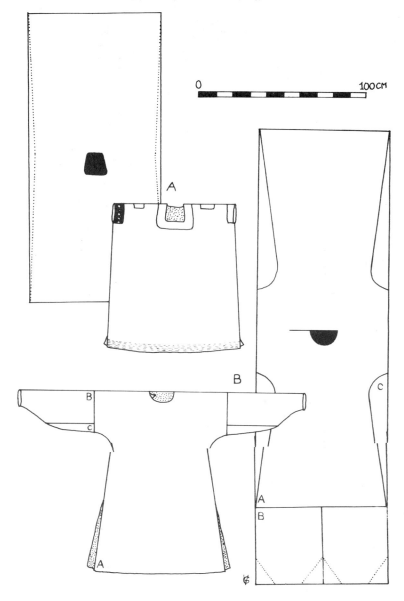

16.15a   Shirt of slightly weft-faced green-black woollen tabby, edged with brocaded bands (loom width 78 cm). Egypt: Islamic period, eighth–tenth century AD

16.15b   Linen shirt with looped pile, cut in oriental fashion (loom width c. 80 cm). Egypt (probably Antinoë): Byzantine period, sixth–seventh century AD

16.16   Shirt of bleached linen tabby, embroidered in crimson silk floss with patterned darning (loom width c. 58 cm). Egypt: Mamluk period, fourteenth century

In the light of these examples, our conclusions drawn from garment construction point much further than costume history alone. The study of this particular aspect of textiles touches upon questions of cultural, artistic and technological changes, and their possible causes. The study of costume and textiles leads as much towards understanding the complexity of the international cultural–historical background of the Mediterranean world as does any other field involved in the examination of medieval Mediterranean history.

*   *   *

The substance of this paper was delivered at the Colloquium on Medieval Textiles in the Mediterranean World, held in connection with the Annual Meeting of the Medieval Academy of America at Toronto in May 1977. I should like to express my indebtedness to many friends and colleagues who in various ways assisted me in my research: above all to Dr Lisa Golombek of the Royal Ontario Museum, Toronto, for her suggestions regarding Islamic textual sources and textiles. Special thanks are also due to Mrs Joan Allgrove of the Whitworth Art Gallery, Manchester; Miss Marilyn Jenkins of the Metropolitan Museum of Art, New York; Mr Donald King of the Victoria and Albert Museum, London; Miss Iben Kehlet of the Museum of Decorative Arts, Copenhagen, for the research facilities offered in their collections; and to Dr Marta Hoffmann of the Norsk Folkemuseum, Oslo, for her help in providing me with xerox copies of relevant Scandinavian publications. I am grateful to the Canada Council for a research grant which enabled me to work on material in English and Danish collections in the summer of 1976.

All measured drawings and tables are by the author. Unless otherwise specified, the photographs are by Mr William B. Robertson and Mr Brian Boyle, Royal Ontario Museum, Toronto.

17 Viking Women's Dress at Birka: A Reconstruction by Archaeological Methods
Inga Hägg

Parts of the vast cemeteries at the Viking town of Birka were excavated by Hjalmar Stolpe in 1873–95. What he found in the 1100 or so tombs which he opened up were the remains, burnt and unburnt, of the Vikings themselves with their women, children and horses as well as weapons, dress accessories and regular burial gifts – many of which testify to Birka's connections with distant areas, sometimes as far away as central Asia (see Figure 17.1). Of primary interest in this context and still exceptional for Swedish conditions are the remains of

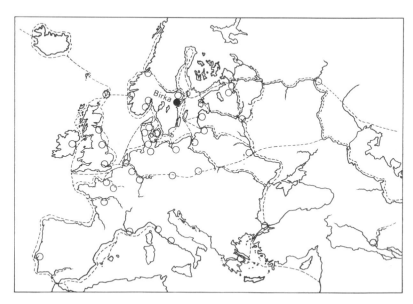

17.1   Birka, the trade centre of Sweden in the Viking Age, showing the main routes of communication

clothes, wraps and other textiles from these tombs. The abundance of preserved textiles is partly due to the large quantity of such material which seems to have been buried with the Vikings. It is also in part due to the fair number of metal objects – weapons and dress accessories – in the same graves, for metal corrosion acts as a preservative on textile fibres, most effectively on those of animal origin.

At the excavation, dress fasteners were often picked up from the tombs together with the surrounding portion of earth, which on closer examination turned out to contain plenty of organic material, principally textiles. About fifty years after the original excavation, Agnes Geijer was entrusted with the task of examining the textiles. She identified and described the different techniques used for producing the textiles.[1] Her book also includes a chapter on dress which has become the standard reference work on the subject.

Previously our conception of Viking Age costume was primarily based on contemporary illustrations of dress, and on the evidence from metal dress fasteners and their positions in tombs as compared with known dress-types among conservative ethnic groups, mostly in eastern Europe. We already assumed, therefore, that women's dress included a woollen mantle, fastened in front by a brooch, and a skirt with shoulder straps underneath it, to which belonged a set of two oval brooches.[2] The Birka textiles provided us with further evidence concerning these garments, as well as for a third one, a linen shirt worn next to the body, which was known only through Viking art but not previously revealed directly in archaeological material. As Geijer recognised that some of the linen fragments from the Birka tombs derived from this particular dress-piece, it enabled her to draw some further conclusions. Most of the fragments in question were pleated, so Geijer suggested the material in all shirts had been so treated. However, as far as the shape of the garment was concerned, nothing could be inferred which would have added to the general impression already given by representations in art (see Figures 17.2–17.3).

Since Geijer's concern was primarily with the techniques of textile production, she felt free to choose good examples for study and description instead of giving an account of every single specimen. As a result, a considerable amount of textile fragments together with surrounding lumps of earth and other material is still preserved intact or almost intact in their original find contexts; they would not have been if they had previously had to be examined and catalogued.

[1] A. Geijer, *Birka, III; Die Textilfunde aus den Gräbern* (Uppsala, 1938). About 90% of the Birka textiles remain unpublished. No purely constructive stitches as in hems, joints etc. were recorded by Gijer, as distinct from embroidery and related decorative sewing.

[2] P. G. Wistrand, *Svenska folkdräkter* (Stockholm, 1907); see also Hägg, *Herrschaftstracht und Königsmacht in Schweden* (forthcoming).

17.2a–b   Set of oval brooches, with fragments of pleated linen from the shirt on the inside

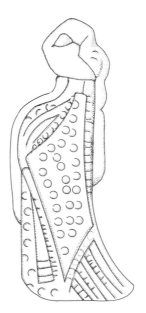

17.3   Pleated linen shirt on a female figurine of silver from Grödinge, Södermanland (Redrawn from photograph)

Over the last few years I have had the opportunity to analyse these remains – approximately 4000 fragments – in an attempt to approach the subject of Viking Age costume from a different point of view, namely the purely archaeological.[3] The conditions necessary for this were not only the favourable state of the surviving material, but also the technical equipment of a modern research laboratory where even the microcontexts could be studied.[4] This does not mean that the use of a microscope was necessary because of the sizes of the preserved fragments as such, but because of the need to trace remains of disintegrated organic materials. By this technique it was possible to carry out a study of the contexts of all the micro-stratigraphical sequences, gathering the surviving evidence in a systematic way, according to the same archaeological methods of observation and documentation as normally used in field work, including the drawing of plans and sections.

During the original excavations, plans were carefully drawn of the contents of the tombs but no sections – let alone such sections which would also show organic materials like textiles, fur, wood, etc. In fact, the dig was rather exemplary, as fragments of textiles, fur and even cist-wood were all gathered and not thrown away as at many contemporary excavations in Europe. Organic material was saved, if a little sporadically, even though they did not go so far as to record it (skeletons excepted) as archaeological finds. Out of the 4000 or so fragments of this kind which were preserved, only five instances are marked on a plan. Notes here and there in the margins of the plans, such as 'both brooches with cloth, one *cleaned*', show in an eloquent way how this category of finds was regarded: as rotted remains which covered and obscured the *real* finds, that is, the metal objects (see Figure 17.4). It is rather characteristic that when garments with decorative ribbons of gold and silver occur in these tombs, the ribbons have been plotted in on the plans but not the textile background to which they were attached (see Figure 17.5). With this in mind, it might be easily realised how important it is, for the study of the arrangements of the interior of the tombs including the personal outfit of the deceased, to reconstruct the find positions of the textile fragments as well as the original sequence of layers.

[3] I. Hägg, 'Die wikingerzeitliche Frauentracht von Birka. Einige Bemerkungen zur Hemdform', *Tor*, 13 (1969), pp. 13ff; idem, 'Mantel och kjortel i vikingatidens dräkt', *Fornvännen*, 66 (1971), pp. 414ff; idem, 'Kvinnodräkten i Birka. Livplaggens rekonstruktion på grundval av det arkeologiska materialet', *Aun*, 2 (1974). A full account also of the male costume in the Birka graves is given in *Birka. Untersuchungen und Studien herausgegeben von Kungl. Vitterhets Historie och Antikvitets Akademien. II: 1*. (Stockholm, in press).

[4] Here I want to express my gratitude to Dr Birgit Arrhenius of the Archaeological Research Laboratory, University of Stockholm.

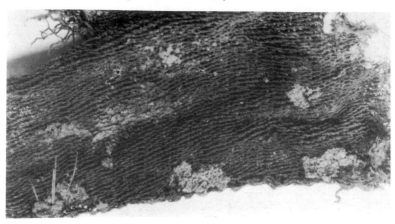

17.4a   *Frontside of woollen fragment, twill, found on top of one of the oval brooches, cf. Figures 17.8 and 17.9. Over most of the surface can be seen spots of half-disintegrated fur, especially along the folded edge to the right. Notice some preserved hairs in lower right corner*

17.4b   *Backside of the same piece. Along the folded edge a series of white woollen stitches which fastened a border of fur to the frontside (cf. Figure 17.4a) of the garment*

17.4c *Backside of fragment from same garment. Over most of the surface are remains of a silk lining which reached out to the folded edge where it was sewn together with the woollen material. All that remains of this seam are the holes from the original linen stitches along the edge*

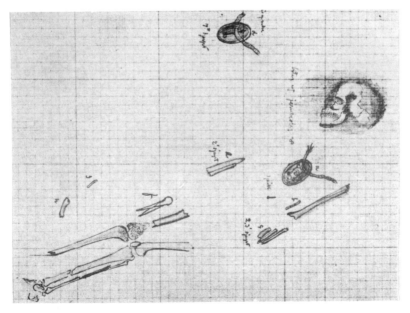

17.5a *Detail from Stolpe's plan showing find positions of skeleton, a set of two oval brooches and silver bands from the costume. The silk material onto which the bands were mounted was not plotted in*

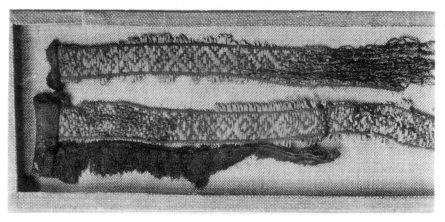

17.5b   Two fragmentary silver bands bordered with silk (the darker material). Cf. Figure 17.5a

17.6a   Imprints of round silver pendants showing on pieces of silk in oblique light

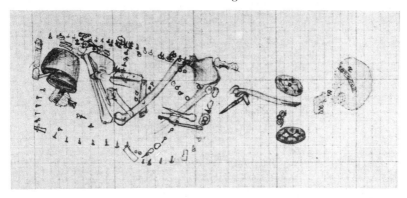

17.6b Detail from Stolpe's plan with the silver pendants plotted in between the oval brooches. Obviously the silk fragments were found on top of the chest in the same place as the silver pendants.

17.7 End-piece of silk-ribbon. On its backside an imprint of a silver coin of Sitric, King of Northumbria who died in 926. The find position of the silk fragment can be reconstructed as it is known that the coin was found close to a round brooch in the middle of the tomb

Quite often it has been possible to reconstruct the horizontal position of a fragment, whether it consisted of a single piece of cloth or of a lump with several compressed layers. The procedure is first to study the specimen in oblique light so that impressions from metal objects show in high-lighted relief (see Figure 17.6a). After this, miscolourings and patches which very frequently occur in the fragments are scrutinised through the microscope and compared to the surfaces of metal objects from the same tomb (Figure 17.7). In this way it is often possible to determine precisely which surface of a fragment or lump has been in direct contact with a certain metal object. When this is known, the first two layers in the stratification are also already known: the metal object and the textile level next to it (see Figures 17.8 and 17.9).

The sequences of layers which I have been able to reconstruct were all recorded in schematic section drawings such as the one seen in Figure 17.9, which comes from Bj. 838.[5] The fragment shown in Figure 17.10 contains several layers which were lying on top of one of the oval brooches and in Figure 17.11 are shown the several layers which occurred underneath it. Together they cover the whole sequence of preserved layers from the top to the bottom of the tomb, as shown in the sections.

The most important of all the levels in a section is that which marks out the position of the body. Textiles on top of it belong to the front of the dress and to possible covers over the body, while textiles beneath it belong to the back of the dress and to a possible bed at the bottom of the tomb. Sometimes the same textile material occurs twice in a stratification, once above and once below the body. In such cases they probably belong to the same garment. If the sides differ in the fabric of such a garment, one can often observe that the outside is turned down in the layer underneath the body and up in the layer above it. Exceptions are fragments from linings which, of course, as a rule have their outside faces turned towards the body. Not infrequently the lowest textile level has remains of feathers glued to the inside which is then also turned towards the bottom of the tomb – which obviously reveals a mattress or pillow of some kind.

It will be realised that the stratification in a tomb, even if incomplete, as often happens with organic materials, is the most reliable source we have for identification of the different dress-pieces in the tomb. In the schematic section drawing with its successive layers of textiles etc., the number of garments and the order in which they were worn on top of each other can be recognised.

---

[5] Such references are to the grave number at Birka.

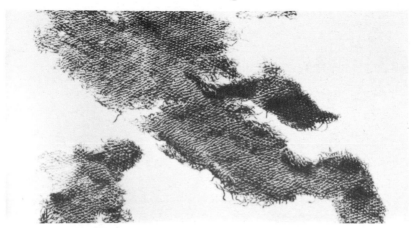

17.8 Backside of fragment of woollen tweed. The ornamented frontside of one oval brooch has left imprints and patches of bronze corrosion over the surface, which reveal the find position of the fragment

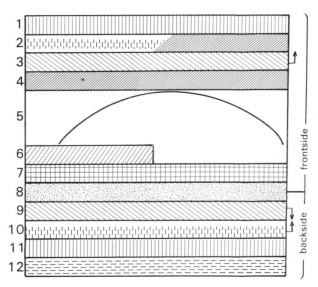

17.9 Schematic drawing of reconstructed stratification through one oval brooch. The stratum with remains of the body divides the section in one front- and one backside. To the frontside belongs a layer of woollen tweed (cf. Figures 17.8 and 17.4a–c) which has its frontside turned up (the arrow). Notice that this corresponds to a layer of the same material on the backside, obviously from the same garment. 1. tapestry 2. silk (samitum) and fur 3. tweed 4. silk 5. oval brooch 6. lozenge twill 7. linen 8. remains of body 9. tweed 10. fur 11. tapestry 12. wood (?)

17.10a   Material found on top of one oval brooch, the imprinted pattern of which is visible over the whole surface. This consists of linen and under that, tweed. Next to the tweed is wood from the cover

17.10b   Backside of the same piece

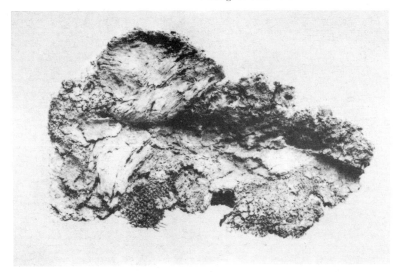

17.11 Material found under one oval brooch. Observe the slightly curved line through the middle of the piece, impressed by the edge of the brooch. Next to this is a layer with rather decayed linen together with remains from the body (ribs etc.). The linen may derive from the shirt and the tweed seen underneath it from the backside of a garment worn on top of the shirt and the skirt

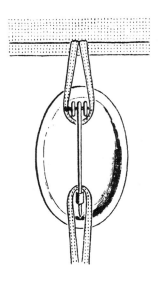

17.12 Geijer's reconstruction of the position of the shoulder-straps from the skirt in the oval brooches, as well as the way the straps were attached to the upper hem of the front piece of the skirt

Comparisons between the reconstructed sections of the Birka tombs revealed a fact of considerable importance. Viking women's dress, as we had previously known it, included three garments: a linen shirt, a skirt and a linen mantle. As reconstructed by Geijer (see Figure 17.12) the skirt would not even have been revealed in the preserved stratifications which normally consist of the portion immediately above and underneath the oval brooches. If, then, the layers containing remains of the linen shirt (when present) and the supposed mantle are identified, there still remain other textile layers which require explanation. The explanation is, quite simply, that women's dress at Birka included garments other than the three previously known. This is also clearly indicated by a number of plans.

In Figure 17.13 the contents of tomb Bj. 965 are shown with two oval brooches and a third brooch which is round, all fairly well *in situ*. Fragments of silver bands are seen in many places on the skeleton: in one unbroken line under the jaw, under the oval brooches, along the spine etc. This is one of about a dozen women's graves at Birka containing tablet-woven ribbons in positions on the skeletons where they have obviously decorated some body-garments and not, as previously held, the headgear. It is further clear that, in these find positions (under the oval brooches or across chest and shoulders) the bands cannot belong to any of the hitherto known dress-pieces. In the first find position they cannot possibly have decorated a mantle, as this was worn on top of the skirt with its oval brooches; in the second neither a skirt – which did not even cover that part of the body – nor a shirt, as this had an opening in front (see Figure 17.14). Obviously plans and sections agree on the important point that there existed garments other than the three already known ones in the Birka tombs.

Many of the preserved metal-woven band fragments were mounted on silk (Figure 17.15), which in turn appears to have been sewn on to a base of other material, such as linen or wool. Of this linen base only very scanty traces remain, sometimes a portion immediately underneath a silver band, where the oxide has preserved it. Small metal studs, discovered during the microscopical analysis, were fixed through the bands, the silk and the base material to keep the different layers of this complicated dress-piece firmly together (see Figures 17.16–17.18). In the stratification, the front of the garment is often present in a position which proves that it has been worn underneath the skirt with its oval brooches (see Figures 17.19 and 17.20b). A corresponding back is, however, seldom found. The reason is, most probably, that the basic material of the garment was usually linen which has not survived as it was separated from metal objects on the front by several layers of organic material. At the same time it becomes clear that the back of the garment lacked silk or metal-woven bands, which, if

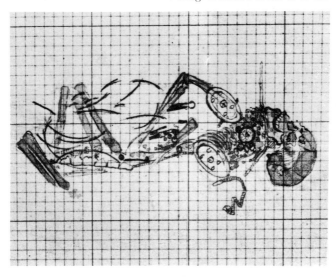

17.13   *Detail from Stolpe's plan showing positions of dress fasteners and silver bands on skeleton. One band lies in an unbroken line over the shoulders, another band is seen under one oval brooch, further pieces lie along the spine, by the arms and so on*

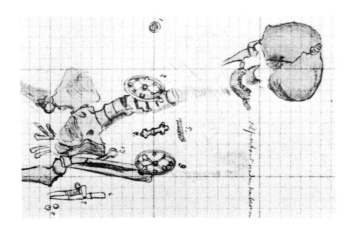

17.14   *Detail from Stolpe's plan. One horizontal silver band is seen under the jaw, another horizontal band in a position slightly above the oval brooches*

17.15   Piece of silk and silver band sewn together, the band on top of the silk

17.16   Silver band framed by two straps of silk. Mounted on a layer of linen. Notice the slightly curved imprint of the edge of an oval brooch along the edge to the right

17.17 Backside of silk fragment with silver bands: four horizontal, plainly decorative ones sewn onto the frontside of the silk; two further vertical bands and one oblique fitted in at joints between separate pieces of silk to make a larger portion of a tight-fitting garment

17.18 Backside of silk fragment and silver band joined together on the same principle as the vertical bands in the piece shown in Figure 17.17

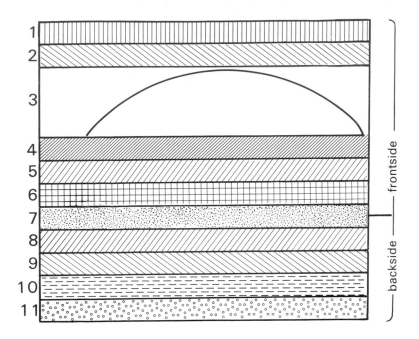

17.19   Reconstructed stratification. Over preserved wood from the bottom of the coffin remains of twill from a garment worn on top of the skirt (and oval brooches). Under the skirt, remains of another woollen garment (lozenge twill) with plain backside and with silk bands sewn onto the front side. This garment, a tunic, was worn under the skirt. Next to the body a linen shirt (i.e. the linen on top of the remains of the body). Probably a woollen wrap was spread over the body (the top stratum). 1. tapestry 2. tweed 3. oval brooch 4. silk 5. lozenge twill 6. linen 7. remains of body 8. lozenge twill 9. tweed 10. wood 11. sand

17.20a   Contents of oval brooch. Immediately underneath the brooch a band of silk from a tunic, cf. Figure 17.19. Nothing remains of the material to which the band was attached; this probably means that it was linen. Next to the band, remains of the body on top of sheepskin. Cf. section, Figure 17.20b

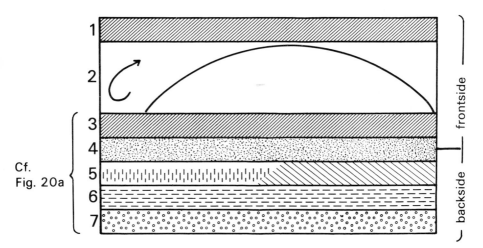

17.20b   Reconstructed section. Oval brooch over badly preserved remains of a linen (?) tunic decorated with silk bands. The body was resting on a sheepskin and underneath that, a mattress of wool stuffed with feathers. 1. silk from stratum 3 in secondary position on top of oval brooch which had tipped in the grave 2. oval brooch 3. silk 4. remains of body and linen (?) 5. wool and sheepskin 6. wood 7. sand

ever present, would have been preserved at least on occasion.

Interestingly enough, there were also in many of the women's tombs fragments of silk without attached bands: the reconstructed positions of these prove that they derive from still another garment which seems to have been worn on top of the skirt (see Figures 17.21–17.23). In a different context, I have already suggested that the two garments from which all these fragments come should be, first, a tunic, worn under the skirt and its brooches as evidenced by the silver bands on silk described above, and secondly a 'caftan' worn on top of the skirt, as proved by the positions of silk fragments like the ones in Figures 17.21–17.23. They would be the counterpieces to the oriental garments found in some of the men's graves at Birka, where they had previously been recognised by the excavator because of the characteristic rows of buttons in the front openings. The women's 'caftan' was not held together in the same way, to judge from the absence of button-rows in these tombs. Instead they may have been fastened in front by a brooch as indicated by silk fragments on the backs of some brooches (see Figure 17.24). As a rule these silk fragments (but also linen in the same position) have the shape of two small loops through which the brooch-pin has been inserted. The loops were originally sewn on to the edges of the front opening of the 'caftan'.

It has previously been assumed that this 'third' brooch in the Birka tombs was used to fasten the mantle as it was in seventh- and eighth-century contexts. It is still very likely that it fulfilled this function in some of the Birka tombs, but, on the other hand, it is a fact that textile remains, if any, on the back of these brooches very often consist of such loops around the pin – in other words, the same arrangement as seen in connection with the 'caftan' (Figure 17.24). There are only three preserved instances where a brooch-pin is stuck directly through the material – wool in all three cases – in the way the mantle was traditionally fastened (that is, in Bj. 483, Bj. 843 and Bj. 1014).

In contrast to the buttoned front of the men's caftan, the front edges of the women's were kept apart by the brooch. As should be expected with this type of garment, wedges and joints in the preserved fragments show that it must have been fitted to the body. It may also have had sleeves, as in the plan in Figure 17.25 where the skeleton has silver bands around the wristbones. The length, finally, of the 'caftan', is probably indicated by the hem decorations in tomb Bj. 905, where, however, the sex of the skeleton is not known.

It not infrequently occurs that decorative applications of silk – as a rule ribbons – or tablet-woven silver bands are sewn on to a woollen material. (Gold seems to be exclusive to men's tombs if we disregard headgear.) Interestingly enough, there are also occasions when plain woollen fragments without the decorative additions appear in a stratum where we expect the remains of the 'caftan' or the tunic to show, as in the examples given in Figures 17.26a and 17.27. The significance of this is probably that such garments were not simply purely luxurious as in the instances mentioned above, where they could just as well have been exotic additions to the costume, but that in the plainer versions such dress-pieces existed as integral parts of the costume. It would not be surprising if the long, tight-fitting jackets and robes of the Middle Ages – best exemplified in the finds from the Herjolfsnes tombs in Greenland – had traditions reaching back at least to the Viking Age.

As seen above, it very often happens that by form and stains detached fragments reveal their original positions in relation to the metal objects, the absolute positions of which, in their turn, are known from the plans of the tombs. The piece of woollen material seen in Figure 17.28 has the characteristic patches and colourings created by one of the oval brooches. A part of the hem has a hole surrounded by rust. This part has obviously been in contact with the iron pin inside the brooch. The original position for the piece is therefore under one of the brooches, (Figure 17.29, see the reconstructed section in Figure 17.30). An unusually large fragment (Figure 17.31) of the same material was, according to Geijer, found over the convex front of one of the oval brooches (observe how the plan shows the ornamentation of both brooches although at least one of them must have been hidden by textiles). At first, this seems to contradict the result just attained concerning the original position of the woollen material in the stratification. However, a look at the positions of the dress accessories on the plan (Figure 17.32) indicates that the woman had been placed in the tomb on her back, leaning slightly over to her right side with the natural consequence that, during the progress of decay, folds were created in the material of the woollen dress-piece which probably embedded also the upper side of the brooches as these successively sank towards the bottom of the tomb. When studied through the microscope, the two woollen pieces actually turned out to join each other (see Figure 17.33) along a line where they had been cut off by the edge of the oval brooch. The find position on top of the brooch was, in other words, secondary; originally both fragments belonged to the same textile level immediately underneath the brooch. Around the iron pin inside this, as is usual in these oval brooches, some fragmentary linen loops were preserved. The ends of one of these had a number of half-dissolved stitches to which a small portion of woollen fibres was attached. When the fragment is put in place under the brooch the torn part of the hem fits together with the ends of the short loop (see Figure 17.29). It therefore seems reasonable to assume that the linen straps had originally been sewn on to the hem of the woollen dress-piece.

17.21   Frontside of silk fragment made of two pieces joined together. To the left a preserved portion of the original front opening of the garment with an attached silk loop. Notice the ornamentation of the oval brooch impressed from the backside which shows that the piece was found backside down, on top of one of the brooches

17.22a   Silk fragment with holes and heavy corrosion especially on the backside which indicates that the piece was lying on top of an oval brooch in the tomb

17.22b   The silk fragment on Figure 17.22a fitted in on top of an oval brooch which is probably the original findposition. Notice the hem along one edge of the piece

17.23   Material found on top of one oval brooch. The ornamentation of the brooch is clearly visible in the surface. Immediately on top of the brooch a layer of badly decayed linen and next to that silk, which was probably sewn onto the linen material. A vertical hem is visible along the left border of the silk. In the tomb these textile layers were pressed between the oval brooch and a piece of wood from the cover of the coffin; on the photograph the latter is visible along the right edge of the fragment

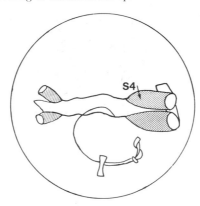

17.24   Backside of round brooch. Loops of silk around both ends of the rusty iron pin

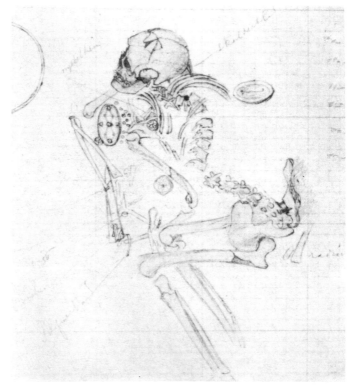

17.25   Detail from Stolpe's plan. Skeleton in crouched position with the bones of fingers and wrists in the area of the knife. Around both wrists silver bands

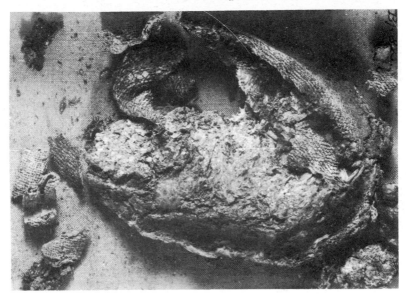

17.26a   Contents of oval brooch with fragments of lozenge twill next to the brooch; above, remains of the body, cf. section Figure 17.26b

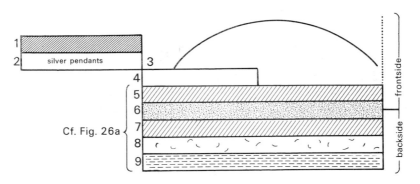

17.26b   Reconstructed stratification. Frontside of woollen tunic next to the oval brooch. Under this the remains of the body and further down, traces of the backside of the woollen tunic. Some down at the bottom of the coffin indicates the presence of a mattress or pillow in the tomb. 1. silk 2. silver pendants: cf. the imprints in silk fragment (stratum 1) in Figure 17.6a 3. oval brooch 4. front of skirt, material unknown 5. lozenge twill 6. remains of body 7. lozenge twill 8. down 9. wood

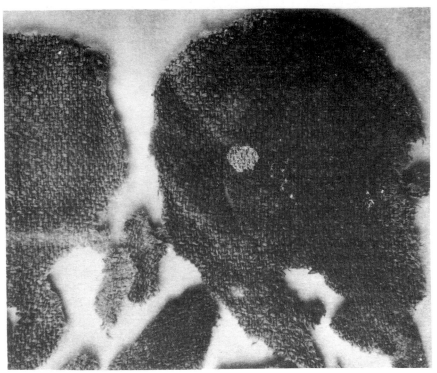

17.27 Woollen material from frontside of tunic, found underneath one of the oval brooches

17.28 Frontside of twill fragment. The upper edge is folded down and fastened by a seam towards the backside. Notice the holes and wrinkles in the material in rounded form caused by the edge of the oval brooch. Cf. Figure 17.29

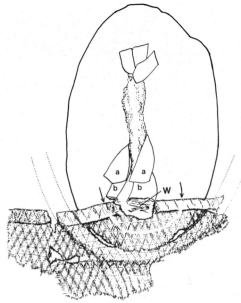

17.29   Backside of the same fragment together with oval brooch in reconstructed position. Fitted in like this, the linen loop b *in the brooch joins with the edge of the woollen fragment* w *from the upper hem of the skirt*

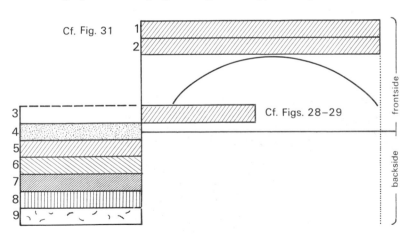

17.30   Reconstructed stratification. Next to the backside of the oval brooch an edged piece of lozenge twill, cf. Figure 17.29. A large portion of the same material (Figure 17.31) is found in a fold on top of the brooch, although it belongs to the same garment, i.e. the skirt. 1. lozenge twill (W 10e) 2. lozenge twill (W 10i) 3. oval brooch 4. lozenge twill (W 10e) 5. remains of body 6. lozenge twill 7. tweed 8. silk 9. tapestry 10. down

17.31   Lozenge twill from the frontside of the skirt, found folded over one of the oval brooches in the tomb

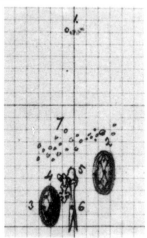

17.32   Detail from Stolpe's plan showing find positions of teeth (1), pearls (7), and metal objects (2–6). The brooches (3 and 4) have obviously successively slipped downwards towards the right in the tomb during the process of decay; as a result the right oval brooch has been embedded in textiles from the surrounding layers

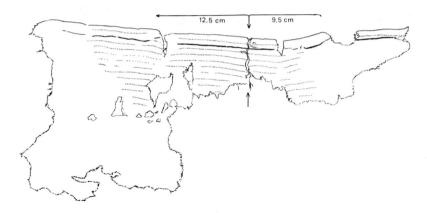

17.33   Two joining fragments from the frontside of the woollen skirt, together measuring 22 cm in length

As the straps are known to belong to the skirt, the woollen fragments must be parts of that dress-piece, which is also most probable when their original position in the stratification is considered. This is something new and quite interesting as it was previously assumed that the skirt in the Birka tombs would have been of linen material – the same material as found in most (not all) of the preserved strap- and loop-fragments inside the oval brooches. Geijer took the woollen pieces in such cases to be the remains of the mantle – not surprisingly, in view of their sometimes confusing find positions on top of the brooches. As a matter of fact, scrutiny of the find contexts has made it possible to identify remains of a woollen skirt in twenty-five instances among the *c.* 140 female inhumation tombs with preserved textiles at Birka, a comparatively high figure. This result is also interesting as we have previously counted the strap-fragments as the only preserved remains of the Birka skirt, whereas now we have quite large pieces to deal with for reconstructions of the garment as a whole. The example from tomb Bj. 597 in Figures 17.28 and 17.29 is so far the largest preserved portion of a Viking Age skirt.

The linen shirt, finally, which Geijer was able to recognise among the dress fragments, was recorded in seven tombs. In five of these the linen was pleated. However, nothing could be said about the shape of the dress-piece. The reason for this is that the easily perishable linen material is rarely preserved and the occasional remains of it are small and non-diacritical.

However, many of the metal objects from the tombs – brooches as well as scissors, knives, needlecases, etc. – have preserved portions of linen from the shirt attached to their surfaces, where they were completely incapsulated in corrosion. When the top layer of this corrosion was removed – which was done as a stage in the technical analysis by soaking the object in a weak solution of EDTA ($C_{10}H_{14}N_2Na_2O_8 . 2H_2O$) – the structure of the textile fragments appeared (see Figure 17.34). It was then possible to study and compare the textile fragments on different metal objects from one and the same tomb with the special purpose of finding out whether they derive from the same garment or not and, if so, which parts of the body were covered by this garment. By the same means one could also determine the general direction of threads or pleats in the weave which in its turn gave a general idea of the fall of the textile material over the body (see Figure 17.35). The linen remains turned out to derive from two different types of shirt – a plain one (in more than thirty cases) and a pleated one (in about twenty-five cases).

Careful comparisons between preserved portions of pleated linen, primarily on the backside of oval brooches (see Figure 17.2) have resulted in the reconstruction shown in Figures 17.36 and 17.37. In some of these cases, all that remained of the pleats inside the brooches was a striped pattern in the green corrosion which became visible after the top layer of corrosion had been dissolved in a weak solution of EDTA.

One more detail can be added to the reconstruction of the linen shirt, namely the brooch of a kind shown in Figure 17.38. At Birka such small brooches – *c.* 2.6 cm across – appear in about fifty of the female inhumation tombs. As to their function, it has previously been assumed that they might belong to the headdress. The study of their position in the tombs compared to results from the analyses of textile remains on the reverse of the brooches shows, however, that they have served as fasteners in a front opening of the shirt.

At Birka, small round brooches appear in tenth-century graves only. It is noticeable that they are more frequently found in connection with the pleated than with the plain shirt. This has obviously a chronological reason, as the pleated shirts rarely appear in tombs dating from the ninth century, whereas they are usual in the tenth-century tombs.

To the reconstruction of the shirt shown in Figure 17.37, which was based on the study of textile fragments on metal objects and the position of these in the tombs, can therefore also be added the brooch (Figure 17.38) as well as the front opening evidenced by the shape of the linen fragments and the existence of this brooch.

Our conception of dress in prehistory and early history is for the

17.34   *Iron fragments from the scissors, cf. plan in Figure 17.32. The surface completely covered by pleated linen from a shirt worn under the woollen skirt. Notice direction of pleats compared to position of scissors in tomb*

17.35   *Iron scissors covered with pleated linen from shirt*

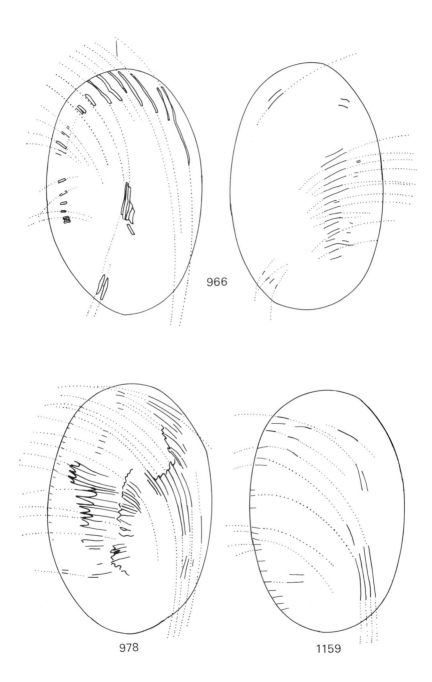

966

978

1159

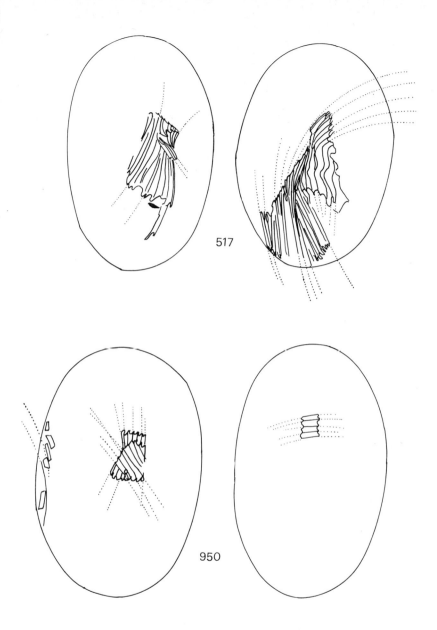

17.36 *Inside of oval brooches with remains of pleated linen. The dotted lines mark the direction of the pleats. The same general pattern can be observed in all the brooches*

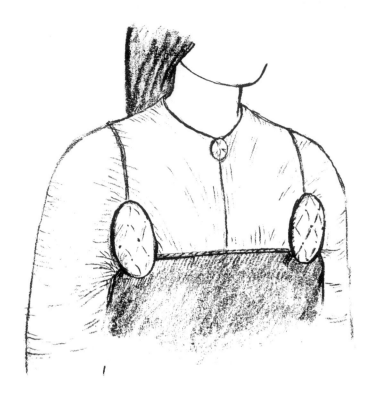

17.37　The fall of the pleated shirt reconstructed on the basis of the pleat-patterns on metal objects compared to the position of those objects in the tombs

17.38　Small round brooch with linen fragment on its backside. The pin is stuck through the material which derives from the front opening in the linen shirt

most part based on very obvious contemporary illustrations or finds of fairly well-preserved whole garments from bogs, tombs, etc. The garments are sometimes compared to descriptions by seventeenth- and eighteenth-century travellers of similar dress-pieces among conservative ethnical groups in Europe and elsewhere. In contrast to such material, that from the Birka tombs is not very substantial. However, when first studied, the evidence given by the textile fragments fitted well into the picture already available.

The archaeological approach to the subject of dress has brought forward some additional results. It is now possible to prove by the stratigraphical and other evidence exemplified here that women's dress included two further garments: one tunic worn under the skirt and one long jacket worn over it. The mantle, on the other hand, does not seem to have been in frequent use. The base material in the tunic was wool or linen, and sometimes its front had applications of silk and tablet-woven bands. There was no front opening, or, if there was, it was not symmetrically placed underneath the jaw. The long jacket was woollen, lined with linen or silk, sometimes edged with fur or lace. It was open in front, held together by one single brooch.

Furthermore, it is clear that the skirt was not always of linen but very often woollen, and that it covered a larger portion of the bosom than suggested by Geijer (see Figures 17.12 and 17.29). It is, finally, possible to recognise two different types of shirt and to suggest a reconstruction of the shape of the pleated shirt on the basis of archaeological evidence (see Figure 17.37).

The methods discussed here involve, above all, a greater possibility of recording and perhaps even saving *organic* material. This is important since there still persists among some archaeologists the same conception as pertained in the attitudes of the original excavators of the Birka material a hundred years ago, namely the traditional inconsistency in treatment of different types of material. Whereas *inorganic* finds are usually recorded immediately at the excavation, the *organic* material in general – with the obvious exception of skeletal and other bone pieces – is, at best, simply handed over to specialists for analysis. The importance of the contribution from these specialists is indisputable, but there is a danger of valuable evidence being lost if the material is handed over to them too early, before all the purely archaeological investigation is completed. The archaeological investigation is not, in fact, completed until the find contexts, *including the microcontexts*, are fully documented. It is not sufficient to regret that the recording of the micro-organic remains requires special equipment; this equipment must be in constant use if evidence of vital interest for the interpretation of a whole find complex is not to be lost. In other words, the organic material must not be excluded from the purely archaeological part of the study and the archaeologist must continue his excavation, observation and recording at the appropriate scale until all the available evidence is gathered and documented.

This aspect of the study must precede the examination by specialists for two reasons. On the one hand, museum resources do not always permit immediate treatment of the finds. On the other hand, in the case of textiles at least, the interest and purpose of the specialist is different to some degree from that of the archaeologist. The textile specialist is quite naturally concerned not to observe the find contexts, but rather to rescue the fragments for further technical studies. This specialist study must, therefore, be preceded by full examination of the material in the archaeological laboratory where the remaining context evidence is gathered systematically according to archaeological methods. Otherwise-lost evidence is thus gathered, and the subsequent specialist study may be enriched by a fuller understanding of the context.

18　Beds and Bedclothes in Medieval Norway
Marta Hoffmann

Man spends about one-third of his life asleep, and in the Western cultural area most of this time in bed. In the temperate zone and especially in the cold climate of the northern parts of Europe, he must cover himself well to keep warm during this inactive period. Neither beds nor specially made bedclothes are necessary for sleeping, and a great many people throughout the ages have done without them. They have slept on the ground or on the floor, perhaps on a layer of straw or hay brought in for the occasion, and covered themselves with their mantle. Beds and bedclothes, however, would have been used from comparatively early times among the upper classes, although very little is known in the north about the period before the Viking Age. Archaeologists have found Viking beds, but whether any of the textiles found in the graves were bedclothes used by living persons remains a difficult question. Although 'sleep is the brother of death', the funeral equipment doubtless differed from the bedclothes used in real life.

Sources
The sources available for medieval people's sleeping arrangements are of different kinds. They include surviving beds and bedclothes, which are few and incomplete, pictorial representations (including sculptures), which can be helpful, as well as written sources, which may be difficult to interpret.

In Norway beds are preserved from the ninth century onwards, but next to nothing survives of the associated textiles through the whole period of what we call the Middle Ages, that is to say, until the early part of the sixteenth century. Some late-medieval counterpanes belonging to state beds in castles and manor houses have recently been identified in Sweden and Finland, decorated with a kind of intarsia embroidery in wool with guilded leather strips.[1] They show a definite Eastern influence. As yet there is no reason to believe that such counterpanes were used in Norway, since we have no traces of this type of textile. The written sources include both official documents such as inventory lists and laws concerning inheritance, as well as literary evidence from the sagas and other contemporary writings.

There have, of course, been great differences between the bedclothes of common people and those of the upper social classes. As might be expected the latter have used bedclothes similar to their counterparts in the rest of the continent, as can be seen from the foreign terms used in the inventories. These deal mostly with the belongings of wealthy people, and there can be no doubt that there was a great deal of importation of bedclothes.

There are some pictorial representations of medieval beds in Scandinavia and Iceland. They must be used with care, as they might have been copied from manuscripts from other parts of Europe rather than drawn directly from the artist's actual experience. Moreover, the pictures may not have been made in the area where they have been found, although they may still show beds and bedclothes of the prosperous part of the population who followed European fashions. Comparison of the different sources might enable one to form an opinion about their representativeness.

Finally, another source may be used with care. In Scandinavia and Iceland, old customs and traditional handicrafts have survived among the country farmers up to this century in areas where there were few professional craftsmen. It might be worthwhile trying to compare some of the bedclothes of recent times with those mentioned in medieval sources.

The inventories, most of them dating from the fourteenth and fifteenth centuries, mention many different articles of bedclothing. They list all the bedclothes, using the phrase *alfær sæng*,[2] *en reidh seng*, or another similar expression meaning a fully equipped bed. This concept is known from the Middle Ages up to the present day in Norway and Iceland, but it is not exactly clear what it entailed. As a standard expression it was probably understood by all concerned, though it would presumably have differed both locally and according to the social setting. With all these reservations it is possible to obtain some insight into the comfort or lack of it in the sleeping habits of medieval people.

---

[1] Agnes Geijer, *A History of Textile Art* (London, 1979), p. 225; R. Pylkkänen, *The Use and Traditions of Mediaeval Rugs and Coverlets in Finland* (Helsinki, 1974), pp. 11–26.

[2] 'Sengeutstyr'. Iceland: Arnheiður Sigurðardóttir, *Kulturhistorisk leksikon for nordisk middelalder* (Oslo, 1956) (hereinafter *KLNM*), XV, col. 143. Norway: *Diplomatarium Norvegicum* (hereinafter *DN*), II, p. 313 (1368); *DN*, XII, p. 247 (1509); *DN*, XIV, p. 738 (1539).

Beds

In Norway the extant medieval beds can be divided into two distinct groups. First, there are the free-standing beds associated with the ship burials of the ninth and tenth centuries, and secondly, there are the rows of beds attached to the walls of the medieval wooden store houses, the upper floor being used for accommodating guests. In addition, in the living rooms of farms in some areas of Norway there are examples of single beds which were placed in a corner so that the walls formed two sides of the bed. These date from the seventeenth century and later, but are thought to reflect medieval practice. Free-standing beds were not common among farmers until rather later.

In the famous Oseberg barrow, remains of five beds were found, all of beech, one of them very stately with carved animal heads at the top of the head-boards.[3] This bed has now been reconstructed with great accuracy on the basis of the many pieces found at the excavation, and measurements, photographs and observations made at the time by Professor Gabriel Gustafsson (Figure 18.1). The inner length of the bed is 165 cm, the width at the head 180 cm, at the foot-board slightly less. The head-boards are 159 cm high and 45 cm wide. The bottom consists of several narrow boards inserted across the width of the bed. There were also simpler beds with bottoms of thin crossing slats. The best-preserved of this simpler type belongs to the Gokstad ship from the tenth century. Its state of preservation made it possible to assemble it completely with its four cornerposts. The only part lacking was the bottom, which could be reconstructed since all the holes for the slats were intact (Figure 18.2). This bed was exceptionally long, 227 cm, and 109 cm wide, while another bed from the Gokstad ship was only 140 cm long and 110 cm wide. In this find, too, head-boards with carved animal heads from several oak state beds were found.

One can hardly imagine that the beds from the ship burials were intended for use at sea. As persons of high rank always had to be surrounded by objects which showed their status, the beds might have been intended for use when spending the night on shore, or, more likely, they were added as part of the funeral equipment for use in the next world. Certainly, the beds in the barrows must have been those in normal use in the households of the highest social classes.

Of the sleeping accomodation referred to in the sagas, none is preserved and it is not always clear from the text what they were like. Single beds are not described. It seems that there were alcove beds

---

[3] S. Grieg, 'Kongsgården' in *Osebergfundet*, II (Oslo, 1928), pp. 81ff. It is said here that three beds were of this type, but this seems unclear. H. Stigum, 'Seng' in *KLNM*, XV, cols. 127ff.

18.1   Reconstruction of the large bed from Oseberg barrow, ninth century AD

18.2   Bed from Gokstad barrow, tenth century AD

18.3   *Beds attached to the wall from a store house in Voss, with carving in Gothic style*

18.4   *Bed, attached to the wall, from a store house in Telemark*

with doors that could be shut. Judging from Icelandic archaeological excavations, one part of a room near the wall might be raised and traces of partitions seem to indicate bedsteads.[4] Some of the raised sections were wide enough to suggest that people might have lain across them with their feet towards the middle of the room. This type of long bed attached to the walls would seem to have been more common than the free-standing beds, and also more related to the group of Norwegian extant beds attached to the walls in wooden houses.

Both types of bed continued to exist in Scandinavia beyond the Viking Age into the medieval period. The beds attached to the walls in the store houses date from between the fourteenth and sixteenth centuries, a period later than the free-standing ones from the ship burials, and they belong to a different section of society, namely well-to-do farmers. These beds stood in a continuous row, divided into two or three compartments, often decorated with carving on the side facing the room (Figure 18.3). Some beds may have had large round shield-like extensions on the vertical boards indicating the partitions, similar to the ones found on single beds in the corners of seventeenth-century houses (Figure 18.4). Up to this century the master of the house slept with his wife in such a bed, and even a child or two could find room there. They all had a solid base.

Straw or hay seems to have been the common material to sleep on, but other similar material might have been used. In the Viking beds it must have been stuffed into a sack so as not to fall through. The same type of slatted base was common in western Europe.[5] In the beds with a solid base, the straw was probably placed directly on the bed, as it has been up to our time. The sagas mention the bed-straw, and it occurs in combination with *lik*, corpse (*likstrá* – corpse-straw) meaning lying dead, or lying at death's door.[6]

Bedclothes

It is difficult to find sources which clearly reveal how a bed was made up, or which itemise all the different types of bedclothes normal in certain social groups, but an attempt has to be made to sort out which bedclothes were used under the sleeper and which were covering him.

[4] Arnheiður Sigurðardóttir, 'Seng' in *KLNM*, XV, cols. 130f. At one of the excavations in Greenland a free-standing bed has been found in a medieval house. See Aage Roussell, 'Sandnes and the neighbouring farms', *Meddelelser om Gronland*, 88, 2 (Copenhagen, 1936), pp. 69f, Figures 50, 51, 186. This bed had four cornerposts, and the excavator felt confident in his reconstruction. The bed was only 155 cm long, 95 cm wide. The bottom was lacking.
[5] M. Heyne, *Fünf Bücher deutscher Hausaltertümer* (Leipzig, 1899, 1903), I, pp. 262ff; III, p. 99.
[6] G. Vigfusson (ed.), *Eyrbyggjasaga* (Leipzig, 1864), ch. 50; F. Jonsson (ed.), *Gisle Surssons saga* (Copenhagen, 1929), p. 139; 'Magnus Lagabøters bylov' in *Norges gamle Love*, II (Oslo, 1848), 6.

On top of the straw but under the sleeper, a variety of items could be placed to make sleeping more comfortable. In a simple bed there was only a coarse woollen cloth, usually of wadmal (2/2 twill), covering the straw. A great many Norwegian and Icelandic sources testify to this. Another cloth to lie upon was called *hvítill*, which means the same as the English blanket, a white woollen piece of cloth.[7] The word is still used in some Norwegian dialects, meaning a woollen sheet, generally in 2/2 twill. Like sheets, the *hvítill* might occur in pairs, one under and one over the sleeper. In a thirteenth-century translation of old French romantic tales (*Strengleikar*), the term *hvítill* is even used for a costly coverlet with embroidery.[8] In combination with another word, like *lesnings-hvítill*, or *brothvítill*, it would seem to mean a patterned coverlet, probably of domestic production.

People slept naked in their beds. In the beds of the upper classes there might be a sheet of leather on top of the straw (*ledherlagen*), and, according to Falk, skin with the hair on may have been used on top of the straw, as we know from more recent times.[9]

The word *beðr*, seems to have been used both for a blanket to lie on and for a bolster. Among the higher social classes the latter could be filled with feather and down. This was well-known in antiquity; the well-to-do Romans filled bolsters and cushions with such material to soften hard benches or beds. It was also used among the medieval aristocracy in western Europe and must have reached Scandinavia too.[10] Domestic birds like geese were the main source for the feathers. In Scandinavia domestic birds were extremely rare, and so was the *dunbeðr* – down bolster – in the inventories.[11] It is not known when people in Scandinavia started systematically collecting the feathers and down of wild sea-birds, which was to become an important source of income. Many of the textiles in the Oseberg-ship find are stuck to layers of unidentified down, which might have been used to fill a *beðr*, providing cushions or pillows for the Oseberg queen. Bedclothes, however, have not so far been identified among the textiles in the barrow. We know from the writings of King Alfred the Great that by the ninth century the Lapps were paying taxes in

[7] M. Hoffmann, 'Kvitel' in *KLNM*, IX, cols. 579f; Hj. Falk, *Altwestnordische Kleiderkunde* (Oslo, 1919), pp. 205f.

[8] *Strengleikar* (Oslo, 1850), p. 40.

[9] *DN*, II, p. 694 (1488); *Norske Regnskaber og Jordebøger*, III (Oslo, 1905), p. 5 (1518); Hj. Falk, *Altwestnordische Kleiderkunde* (see n. 7), p. 203.

[10] M. Heyne, *Fünf Bücher* (see n. 5), III, pp. 100f.

[11] *DN*, IV, p. 351 (1366).

[12] See the reference to Othere in Alfred the Great's edition of Orosin's history; *Ottar*, III (Tromsø, 1957). P. Simonsen, 'Alfred den store og Ottar' (translation of text based on *Alfred the Great, his Life and Works* (London, 1884), and F. M. Stenton, *Anglo-Saxon England* (Oxford, 1943)).

feathers and down.[12] Later, we know that the Lapps sold cushions of reindeer-calf skin filled with feathers and down from wild birds to the settled population in their neighbourhood. In the 1430s the Venetian traveller Pietro Querini and his shipwrecked crew found skin cushions filled with feathers on the benches of every house where they stayed on their way between Lofoten and Trøndelag.[13]

Another term, *húðfat* or *húðfatz baeð* has a meaning which is not clear. It might have referred to a skin bolster or a sleeping bag, but the word seems even to have been used to signify a whole bedstead with a wooden frame.[14] The *beðr* is often referred to by naming its case, *vér*. The *skinbeðr* might have been filled with feathers and down. If these were not carefully cleansed and sorted they had to be put into a skin or leather case.

The cover could also be a woven textile, either striped or checked, made from wadmal or linen. It might be called *pýðeskt*,[15] German, which means an imported textile. A bolster might be called *dýna* (derived from *dún*, down), but *dýna* could also mean cushion or pillow. In the tenth-century poem, *Grotta sǫngr*, the two giant females sing about King Frode: 'may he sleep on down'. It is not stated how the *dúnklaeði ok fjaðrklaeði*, referred to in the Frostating law on inheritance, were used, whether as cushions, pillows or a *beðr*.[16] Despite its name, the *dýna* might be filled with wool, as can be seen from an Icelandic fifteenth-century source.[17] Finally, a linen sheet could be found in some better-furnished beds for the sleeper to lie on. Sheets appear in pairs in fourteenth- and fifteenth-century inventories, but they were hardly used among the common people until much later.

Pillows under the head seem to have been common. The surviving medieval beds are remarkably short (except for the one from Gokstad mentioned above) and so are the Norwegian country beds between the seventeenth and eighteenth centuries. This would perhaps seem to confirm the assumption that people slept half-sitting, with a great many pillows piled up at the head of the bed.[18] In the large Oseberg bed with the carved animals' heads, the board between the head planks is

---

[13] A. Helland, 'Nordlands Amt' in *Norges Land og Folk*, II, (Oslo, 1908), p. 887. Two sources from the end of the sixteenth century tell about the Lapps making cushions and bolsters from skin, filling them with feather and down and selling them or paying levies with them. (Erik Hansen Schønnebøl, 'Lofotens og Vesteraalens Beskriffuelse, 1591', p. 194; author unknown, 'Ganndske Nummedalls Leens Beskriffuelse Aar 1597', p. 166.)

[14] *DN*, IV, p. 368 (1368); Arnheiður Sigurðardóttir, 'Seng' in *KLNM*, XV, col. 131.

[15] *DN*, IV, p. 190 (1335).

[16] 'Grotta sǫngr' in G. Neckel (ed.), *Snorri Edda* (Heidelberg, 1962); 'Frostatingsloven' in *Norges Gamle Love*, I (Oslo, 1845), IX, 9.

[17] *DI*, V, p. 328 (1461).

[18] Hj. Falk, *Altwestnordische Kleiderkunde* (see n. 7), p. 207; H. Wentzel, 'Bett' in *Reallexikon der deutschen Kunstgeschichte*, II (Stuttgart, 1947), col. 384.

in a sloping position, which might also lead to the same conclusion. In fact many pictures in European medieval manuscripts do show pillows of different shapes and sizes piled up behind the sleeper who is half-sitting in bed. We might safely assume that the upper classes in Scandinavia followed the rest of Europe in this as in other respects.

In the pictorial representations a long cylindrical pillow across the bed appears common in western Europe, often as an under-pillow. This is found even today in several countries. It is not unknown in Norway in recent times and must have been used in the Middle Ages, at least among the gentry. An example is perhaps to be found in the Mammen find in Denmark (*c.* AD 1000) where a woollen pillowcase, 78 by 28 cm, with wedges, might have been of this type. There are traces of the down which filled the case.[19] It is not known with any certainty what the pillows were filled with in ordinary people's beds, although there is reason to believe that hair from animals, chaff, moss and other vegetable material as well as cut-up rags, have been used from early times.

Either besides, or instead of, the cylindrical pillow, one or more pillows, either rectangular or square, were used. Again no pillows have survived, and one has to assume that the illustrations and the examples from a later date provide a reliable indication of the shape and number of pillows in the Middle Ages. The various terms in the inventories also indicate several different types of pillows. Most of such terms in the Norwegian written sources are used indiscriminately about other pieces of bedclothing or of cushions as well. As with *dýna* mentioned above, *hoegindi* (literally 'comfort') and *koddi* may both mean a pillow as well as a cushion to sit upon or to lean against, though when used in combination with 'head', the meaning of the term is clear. *Hofðalag, hofðalaegi* is used about anything placed under the head.[20] *Koddi* always means that the case is of skin, with a textile cover in addition. *Koddi* and *hoegindi* are very often mentioned in connection with a costly case ('embroidered with silk', 'silk *koddi*', 'magnificent *koddi*', etc.).[21] The slip cover *vér* might be of linen, wool or tow.

In the illuminated manuscripts there is very often a small square pillow on top of the others, close to the head. This may have a patterned cover or it may be of white linen, open at the sides with a coloured undercover showing, with a tassel on each corner. In the Icelandic sketch book one of these small pillows is shown (Figure 18.5). In some late-fifteenth- and early-sixteenth-century sources there is a pillow

[19] M. Hald, *Olddanske Tekstiler* (Copenhagen, 1950), pp. 110f.
[20] *DN*, II, pp. 147f, (1331); p. 314 (1368); Falk, *Altwestnordische Kleiderkunde* (see n. 7), p. 207.
[21] *DN*, II, p. 141 (1328); *DN*, IV, p. 190 (1335).

18.5   Death of the Virgin. From the Icelandic sketch book AM 673, fourteenth–fifteenth century. The bed is of the same type as the one in Figure 18.7

called *eyrnagát* (which may mean, pleasant for the ear); it could have a silk cover or a linen cover.[22] This must be the little pillow in the pictures, filled with down for those who could afford it. Among the poor, pillows may not have been used at all. The sleepers may have put the clothes they took off before going to bed under their heads. This is well-known in recent times in both Norway and Iceland.

A great many types of coverlets are mentioned in the sources. Some of them were intended simply to provide warmth, while others were status symbols, made of costly imported silk or printed cotton placed on top. The simplest coverlet was a blanket of wadmal. A sheepskin, as used in our own time in some areas of Norway as well as elsewhere in Europe, was also common in the Middle Ages. Among the upper classes skin from wild animals like the otter, beaver, fox and wolf have been favoured and they all appear in fifteenth-century sources.

Blaeja was the term for a textile used for covering the body.[23] The word is related to the Middle High German *blahe*, coarse linen, but it

[22] *D.N*, V, p. 408 (1429); II, p. 694 (1488). It appears in Swedish sources more often than in the Norwegian ones. In German known as *wanküssen, orkussen* (A. Schultz, *Das höfische Leben zur Zeit der Minnesänger*, I (Leipzig, 1889), p. 88); in French as *oreiller*.

[23] *Eyrbyggjasaga*, see n. 6; *D.N*, IV, p. 190 (1335); *D.N*, II, p. 141 (1328).

might sometimes be of costly material, of silk with drawn work or sprang. It is sometimes named 'English'. In the later Middle Ages the term seems to have undergone a slight change of meaning and can still be found in some dialects in the sense of sheet. In the fourteenth century sheets are mentioned in pairs in well-to-do people's inventories. Both sheets might be of linen and one might be embroidered in silk. In European painting and illuminated manuscripts the upper sheet is folded over the coverlet and sometimes also shows underneath, falling down to the floor. In the altar frontal from Årdal in Norway, dating from about 1300 (Figure 18.6), the sheet is hanging down under the coverlet and has a decorated border along its length. This kind of

18.6 Altar frontal from the church of Årdal, c. 1300. The framework of the bed does not show, and the sheet with the decorative border is hanging beneath the coverlet

sheet was widespread throughout Europe and has remained in use up to the present day. For such decoration to show, the bed would have to be of the simple frame-like type, rather than the type attached to the walls with high side-boards, where all the bedclothes had to be tucked in (Figure 18.7).

On top of the *blaeja* or the sheet of wool or linen, or in their place, came the coverlets. *Rya* was a woollen coverlet which must have been modelled on a skin.[24] It had a long knotted pile on the side next to the body. *Rya* is especially mentioned in inventories from the fifteenth century onwards. It is very common in the castle inventories of the fifteenth century in all the Scandinavian countries, and was obviously widely used among the aristocracy. Later, it disappeared from the castles to be replaced by imported bedclothes, while it became very popular among the common people, and has been used in Norway until this century.

[24] *DN*, I, p. 253 (1350); *DN*, IV, p. 351 (1366); *DN*, II, p. 694 (1488); A. Geijer, 'Rya' in *KLNM*, XIV, cols. 513f; R. Pylkkänen, *Use and Traditions of Medieval Rugs and Coverlets* (see n. 1), pp. 45–58.

18.7   Bed in the living room of a house from Setesdal, probably seventeenth century. The bed is made up with straw, a worn skin and a woollen blanket, to lie on. On top a sheepskin and a coverlet. Pillows were not used; instead people rolled up the clothes they took off when going to bed and put them under their heads

Some coverlets with-different names like *brothvítill,* or *lesningshvítill,* are difficult to identify although the names are still used.[25] They seem to have changed their meaning, which is not uncommon with textiles. They were probably patterned. Other coverlets seem to have remained unchanged until the present day – besides *rya* – such as the Lapp *grene.*[26] *Grener* are mentioned in several sixteenth-century sources, including the inventories of the castle of Bergenhus. They were woven in a heavy woollen striped weft-faced tabby, and their production probably goes back at least to about AD 600, as can be shown by linguistic evidence. These coverlets have been made until the present day by the settled Lapps living along the coast of northern Norway who sold or bartered *grener* even outside the Lapp area.

The term *áklaeði* means a textile to put on top of something. Occasionally the sources describe such a coverlet, especially if it was of precious material. Many *áklaeðe* were evidently imported. In the 1429 inventory of bishop Aslak Bolt an *áklaeði* is mentioned made of gold-brocaded silk.[27] It was lined with red *säter,* a costly Indian printed cotton. Red and brown *sayn,* probably a fine woollen, and an 'English' *áklaeði* are mentioned in the same inventory. A *buckans áklaeði* in a 1449 inventory from Gudbrandsdal was a fine cotton cloth, sometimes called *buckram* and known in many European countries under slightly different names.[28]

Sengklaeðe is another unspecified term used for coverlets. In the possessions of a noble lady in 1328 was a *sengklaeðe* with two *balderkin,* a textile otherwise known as *baudekin* or another similar name.[29] It signifies precious silk or brocade.

'English' and 'German' *sengklaeðe* are mentioned in early-sixteenth-century sources. *Salún* seems to have been a coverlet of precious material, sometimes described as being of gold-brocaded silk; it may be specified as green or as striped, or is sometimes called 'English'.[30] The term is known in French as *chalun,* and in Middle Low German as *salun.* Another imported textile was *kult,* the French *coultre,* Latin *culcitra;* this generally means a quilted coverlet, which could also be used under the sleeper. In an early-sixteenth-century list of goods stolen from a nobleman, a *kult* 'stuffed with cotton' is recorded.[31]

[25] M. Hoffmann, 'Brotkvitel', 'Lesningskvitel' in *KLNM,* II, col. 269; X, col. 519. See also Falk, *Altwestnordische Kleiderkunde* (see n. 7), p. 205.

[26] A. Nesheim, 'Den samiske grenevevingen og dens terminologi' in *Scandinavica et Fenno-Ugrica* (Uppsala, 1954); M. Hoffmann, 'Rana' in *KLNM,* XIII, cols. 655f.

[27] *DN,* IV, p. 409.

[28] *DN,* III, p. 580 (1449).

[29] *DN,* II, p. 142 (1328).

[30] *DN,* IV, p. 191 (1335); p. 364 (1368); V, p. 64 (1323).

[31] *DN,* III, p. 148 (1331); *DN,* IX, p. 737 (1532); *Eyrbyggjasaga,* see n. 6.

Other names were used for textiles that could both be used as coverlets and for other purposes. *Täpette, täpet* is one which could mean a wall-hanging in some contexts.[32] *Kǫgurr* is another.[33] Besides being used for a coverlet, this word is often used for a cloth covering a coffin or a tomb. In modern Icelandic it has come to mean a fringe.

It is not clear whether the use of eiderdowns goes back to the Middle Ages.[34] The very name in English and French is distinctive. But does it mean that the use of this type of coverlet is connected with the exploitation of wild eiderducks and not with the traditional use of domestic birds? Or does it mean that there was an influx of such down at a certain period supplanting the goose down previously used? As no systematic studies have been carried out on this subject, our present knowledge is very limited.

In Scandinavia the down from wild sea-birds was the main source for filling the different kinds of bedclothes, and the more extensive use of down coverlets must be connected with the development of the exploitation of sea-birds. It seems likely that the idea of using down for coverlets, not only for bolsters, originated among the upper classes in more central parts of Europe and spread later to the northern temperate zone. The eiderducks were much preferred, because of the fineness of their down, and the ease with which it could be obtained while the ducks were sitting on their eggs in specially built shelters. Yet no medieval document records the commercial exploitation of the birds along the coast of Norway or of the Faeroes in respect of feathers and downs, as they do in respect of eggs, *eggvaer*. There does not seem to have been a market of any importance for wild birds' down during the Middle Ages. Whenever the down-filled coverlet came into use, it was a luxury for the upper classes. The use of down-filled coverlets seems to have spread in Denmark in the sixteenth century, and considerably later in other northern countries. The first mention of such coverlets in Iceland dates from the seventeenth century.[35]

The reason for the late exploitation of sea-birds is possibly connected with the time-consuming cleansing and sorting processes necessary to make feathers and down suitable for use inside a textile cover. Uncleansed the down would have to be put into a skin case, as with the bolsters and cushions already discussed, but this would have been very uncomfortable to sleep under.[36] It is difficult to estimate the extent

---

[32] *DN*, IV, p. 351 (1366); *Norske Regnskaber og Jordebøger*, III (Oslo, 1905), p. 5 (1518); *DN*, V, p. 409 (1429).

[33] *DN*, I, p. 253 (1350); see Falk, *Altwestnordische Kleiderkunde* (see n. 7), p. 206.

[34] Falk, ibid., p. 203; K. Kolsrud, 'Fjær og dun' in *KLNM*, IV, cols. 395ff.

[35] Sengeutstyr', Arnheiður Sigurðardóttir, Island in *KLNM*, XV, col. 143; M. Hoffmann, col. 138.

[36] K. Kolsrud, 'Dunvær in *Norveg*, XVIII (Oslo, 1975), pp. 20ff.

of the use of uncleansed feathers and down in the Middle Ages. Knut Kolsrud who has studied the *dunvaer*, down rookeries, mentions the Icelandic exploitation of down from swans and eiderducks which is attested in the common law records of the fifteenth to seventeenth centuries (*Búalög*).[37] The prices are comparatively low, which in Kolsrud's opinion reveals that the down must have been uncleansed.

As is mentioned above, the Lapps had at an early time used wild birds' feathers and down, probably mainly from sea-birds, and filled them into cases of reindeer-skin for cushions and bolsters. The down must have been uncleansed. Special tools for cleansing down are supposed to have been imported into Iceland, possibly from England, at the beginning of the seventeenth century. This development was almost certainly a response to the increased demand for down-filled coverlets among prosperous people in western Europe. There is no reason to believe that such tools were known any earlier in the other Scandinavian countries. More knowledge about 'eiderdowns', in the sense of quilts filled with down, and their spread in western and central Europe may clear up some of these questions.[38]

Finally bed curtains and valances, often of costly material, should be mentioned. In the Icelandic *Eyrbyggjasaga*, the exquisite and rare bedclothes of the strange woman from the Hebrides are listed, including both a valance (*rekkjurefill*) and a set of bed curtains (*arsalr*), as well as 'English' coverlets and one of silk. The word *arsalr* is supposed to be derived from the French *dorsal*,[39] and the same term is used in the Norwegian Frostating decree in the thirteenth century. In the fourteenth century the term was replaced by another, *sparlaken*, often described as made of silk, sometimes with a valance.[40] None has been preserved in Norway, but Iceland has some beautiful embroidered valances dating from the seventeenth and eighteenth centuries, which certainly show a medieval tradition. In illuminated manuscripts from western Europe a great many large four-poster beds complete with curtains are depicted. Such beds may have existed in castles and halls in Norway, but they must have been very rare in the Middle Ages. In a few instances the written sources mention that one of the curtains, *forfall*, *fortjald*, could be rolled up and down, as can be seen in many paintings and illuminated manuscripts in western Europe.[41]

---

[37] K. Kolsrud, 'Fjær og dun' in *KLNM*, IV, cols. 395ff.

[38] See Kolsrud, 'Lundefangst', summary. *Norveg*, XIX (Oslo, 1976), pp. 95f. Kolsrud has suggested a possible development from the foot-pillow used in Germany in recent time; but does not give any evidence for the use of this as early as the Middle Ages. The term 'eiderdown' for a coverlet does not seem to be found in England or France until much later.

[39] Falk, *Altwestnordische Kleiderkunde* (see n. 7), pp. 209f.

[40] *DN*, II, p. 142 (1328); IV, p. 351 (1366).

[41] These objects are found especially in the Icelandic sagas, for example, in *Fornmannasögur*, III (Copenhagen), p. 196. See also Falk, *Altwestnordische Kleiderkunde* (see n. 7), p. 209. In the Norwegian source *DN*, I, p. 253, curtains and a valance are mentioned.

Most of the bedclothes described in medieval Scandinavian and Icelandic sources belonged to a small group of people who enjoyed much the same type of luxury as the rich throughout western Europe. Between the rich and the poor there was a great difference in the number and the quality of bedclothes. Nevertheless, all social classes have valued bedclothes very highly throughout the ages. They were demonstrated to visitors to show the standing of the family and the skill of the women. The envy and desire to possess the magnificent bedclothes owned by the foreign woman in *Eyrbyggjasaga* certainly shows a characteristic feeling of a house-proud woman towards bed-clothes.

It can be concluded that it is difficult to obtain exact information concerning the equipment of a completely made-up bed, identifying the items which were regarded as suitable or necessary for different classes of people. There are some examples in the written sources which may perhaps give an impression of the bedclothes of well-to-do people. In Akershus castle in Oslo, the 1488 inventory of bishop Karl of Hammer enumerates the following bedclothes contained in a small room: 1 *dyne* (bolster), a pair of sheets, a leather sheet, an English coverlet and a wolfskin.[42] In 1362 Margaretha Halvardsdottir in Oslo gave away a *baeð* (bolster), a *hoeginde* (pillow), a pair of linen sheets, an *áklaede* (coverlet).[43] In Bergen in 1340 a woman and her son were granted maintenance for life and 'one bed each with *dýna*, *hoeginde*, two linen sheets and an *ábreiðsla* (coverlet).[44] These beds would seem to be complete beds, although none is specially stated to be so.

The contemporary sources do not reveal much about common people's bedclothes in the Middle Ages. We have to turn to later evidence. The majority of the population lived from farming, fishing and hunting. In many ways their daily life did not change much between the Middle Ages and the eighteenth century, and descriptions of the bedclothes of this section of the population in three different districts in Norway in the eighteenth century will probably give an approximate impression of the situation several hundred years earlier. One was made by a minister in Telemark in 1768.[45] He wrote:

Dyne or sheets are not used among the farmers. Over the straw, a woollen cloth of wadmal serves as bolster and sheet, another acts as the sheet over the sleeper, and on top a skin made of six grown sheep's skins with the woolly side towards the body.

[42] *DN*, II, p. 694.
[43] *DN*, IV, p. 332.
[44] *DN*, VI, p. 179.
[45] H. Wille, *Beskrivelse over Sillejords Præstegjeld* (Copenhagen, 1768), p. 224.

Another description was made by a minister on the western coast in 1762:[46]

> Instead of eiderdown coverlets, skins are used (even as a bolster), made of several sheep's skins with the wool on, or else *ryas*, woollen coverlets which are smooth on the upper side and on the inner side provided with a pile.

The situation in Rana, close to the Arctic Circle, was described in 1834 by another minister:[47]

> The bed in the living room is provided with the usual bedclothes of the area. A reindeer skin, some pillows of calf-skin and a new sheepskin with the wool on the inner side towards the sleeper. It is, however, not unusual to find bedclothes with down. On the islands off the coast the bedclothes are woven textiles of the kind called *rya*. Under their heads the people have pillows of calf-skin filled with feathers and as coverlets a sheepskin made from six or seven skins with the wool on and processed so that they are supple and flexible.

In 1869, bedclothes nearly identical to these were described in detail for other areas by another famous theologican and early sociologist, Eilert Sundt.[48] He noted in some households one coverlet filled with down for a bed reserved for a guest or for the master and the mistress. Among well-to-do people in the towns such coverlets were becoming more used, but in the countryside the traditional bedclothes were still common. The great changes have taken place since the publication of his book, during the last hundred years.

---

[46] H. Strøm, *Physisk og Oeconomisk Beskrivelse over Fogderiet Søndmør*, I, (Soroe, 1762), p. 561.
[47] MS University Library Bergen 315 abc. J. A. Heltzen, *Forsøg til Physisk og Oeconomisk Beskrivelse over Ranens Prestegjeld i Nordlandene.*
[48] E. Sundt, *Om Renlighedsstellet i Norge* (1869, 2nd ed. (Oslo, 1975), pp. 236–9.

19 The Diffusion of Knitting in Medieval Europe*
Irena Turnau

Most research into the textile industry of medieval Europe has concentrated on the production of fabrics made from wool. The development of this major industry has aroused most interest on account of the introduction of many new devices, such as the wide horizontal loom, the hand spinning wheel and the water-powered fulling mill. Investigations undertaken by Professor Carus-Wilson herself and other English, French, Dutch and Italian historians, have indicated the scale of production of woollen textiles and the direction of the international trade in them. The beginnings of the production of silk and to a lesser extent, linen, have also been examined. On the other hand, narrow weaving industries and a variety of other textile techniques have not yet been brought within the sphere of interest of economic historians and remain the field of archaeologists and historians of art. Yet knitting, in particular, is a technique of considerable economic significance in European textile history and deserves more attention than it has hitherto received. This article attempts to reassess its importance.

Knitting is the branch of the textile industry which most closely connects production with consumption, since what it produces forms ready-made clothing. By the use of two to five needles (and since about 1589, a knitting machine too), the production of garments to cover the hands, the feet and the head became possible and they proved to be attractive and fashionable. The early history of knitting reveals the mutual interplay between technical possibilities and demand, between technology and fashion.

Knitting and knotless netting
It used to be held that certain finds in Egypt and dated to the first centuries AD represented the earliest known samples of knitting. This

* The original translation from Polish was made by Maria Starowieyska.

view has been shaken by M. Hald, who analysed specimens of Danish textiles dating from the Bronze Age and the period up to the early Middle Ages.[1] Dorothy K. Burnham has also recently shown by technological examination that the collection of Coptic products kept in the Royal Ontario Museum of Toronto was produced by the technique of knotless netting or single-needle knitting.[2] Close examination of the few Coptic relics in the Victoria and Albert Museum in London and the Umĕlecko-Prŭmyslové Museum of Prague, has confirmed my conviction that she is correct in this judgement. However, before it can be firmly stated whether the other surviving early

---

[1] M. Hald, *Oldanske Tekstiler* (Copenhagen, 1950), pp. 291–318. C. G. Karaulašvili, *Iz istorii gruzinskoj materialnoj kultury. Narodnye sposoby vjazania i pletenia v Kacheti* (Tbilisi, 1973) gives an example of a fragment of a knitted shoe from the fourth or third century BC. I have not seen this fragment, but it is probably knotless netting.

[2] D. K. Burnham, 'Coptic knitting: An ancient technique', *Textile History*, III (1972), pp. 116–24.

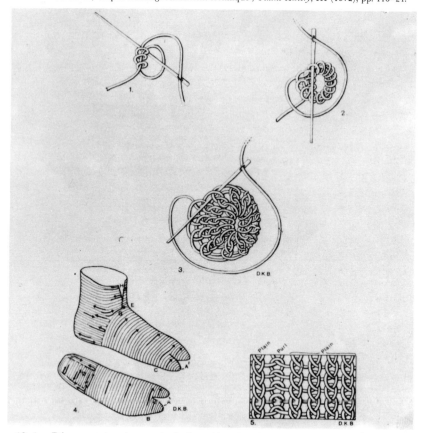

19.1   Diagram showing method of working knotless netting

relics are the product of either knitting or knotless netting, individual technological examination is necessary. Such relics are mostly kept in glass containers in museums and church treasuries, and I have not yet been able to subject them to microscopic analysis.

According to some definitions of knitting, the differentiation of items produced by two knitting needles and those produced by knotless netting would be of no great importance. Generally, knitting is understood to produce a texture composed of elastic rows of stitches made out of a thread of indefinite length by the use of two or more needles or by (more recently) a machine. Knotless netting was made with one needle and the left-hand fingers. The word for knitting in many languages correlated with 'stitch'; for example, Spanish *puntos*, Italian *maglia*, German *Strickerei* and *Wirkerei*, or *Maschen*. In English the industry is simply called 'knitting', the word derived from the very activity, and similarly with the Polish *dzianie*, the Russian *vjazanie*, the Slovakian *pleteny* and *strikovany*.[3] The term is sometimes derived from the finished product, as with the French *bonnetterie*, the Czech *puncocharstvi* or the English 'hosiery'. The technique of knotless netting has been identified and explained only recently. O. Nordland differentiated seven or more ways of twisting and threading the yarn through in the creation of the fabric. A basic compendium of textile techniques discusses not only simple knitting and crocheting, but also a number of types of stitch derived from both these techniques.[4]

Products made by knotless netting fulfilled similar functions to those produced by knitting proper, a technique which developed either later or simultaneously. They provided an elastic and close-fitting covering for the hands, the feet and the head, all particularly important in cold climates, and they also provided protection for feet that were clad in sandals only. The difference between knotless netting and knitting is well expressed by the Finnish proverb: 'He who wore knitted mittens had an unskilled wife'.[5] This distinction comes from a country where both these techniques are still in use in the villages. The apparently small difference between them is important in primitive economies. Knotless netting requires far more time than hand knitting and great skill in the fingers of the left hand, something like hand spinning on the distaff. The elaborate techniques of knotless netting have survived

[3] G. Udé, *Étude Générale de la Bonneterie. Le Vade-Mecum du Bonnetier* (Paris, n.d.), pp. 4–8; M. Brooks Picken, *The Fashion Dictionary. Fabric, Sewing and Dress as expressed in the Language of Fashion* (New York, 1957), p. 194; R. Turner Wilcox, *The Dictionary of Costume* (London, 1970), pp. 187–8; C. Willet Cunnington, P. Cunnington and C. Beard, *A Dictionary of English Costume* (London, 1960), pp. 260–1.
[4] O. Nordland, *Primitive Scandinavian Textiles in Knotless Netting* (Oslo, 1961), pp. 21–71; I. Emery, *The Primary Structures of Fabrics. An Illustrated Classification* (Washington, 1966), pp. 30–49.
[5] Nordland, *Primitive Scandinavian Textiles* (see n. 4), p. 99.

only in a few mountainous areas, particularly in Scandinavia, for the domestic production of gloves, stockings, sometimes caps, and, in Iran, slippers.[6] Both economic and technical considerations, however, tended to give less significance to the qualities of knotless netting, that is, its greater strength and its smoothness. The use of two needles instead of one long one was recognised to be a far more efficient way of producing a fabric formed of elastic stitches out of a continuous long thread.

Identifying the difference between knitting and knotless netting is important for an understanding of the origins of knitting, but it is of purely technological significance. Most publications on the subject simply describe particular collections of archaeological specimens. One eccentric work ostensibly dealing with knitting fails to distinguish between it and other types of textile product.[7] The important task is not merely drawing up lists of the relics produced by the various primitive techniques which have been found in Europe and the Mediterranean cultural area; it is necessary to attempt to identify among the mass of small and apparently insignificant products those which came to be of economic significance. Most writing on the diffusion of knitting production in medieval Europe has taken the form of describing the remaining relics or works of art, or is based on the relatively recent information derived from written sources. It must be remembered that it is one of the many textile industries that grew rapidly in scale of organisation in the Middle Ages. In this period knitting ceased to be merely a woman's pastime, such as sprang or crocheting, but also came to be undertaken by craft guilds.

Investigation into the origins of the knitting industry should indeed concentrate on analysis of all the excavation material from the territory of the Roman Empire. Although Mrs Burnham has questioned whether some Coptic specimens are produced by true knitting, several other relics found in Egypt deserve further study. It is not clear whether small socks found in Egyptian graves had been used by children, or were offerings to the dead.[8] Among the Roman textile relics recently listed by J. P. Wild is a fragment of texture found in north Holland dating from the second century AD which has been judged to be knitting. L. Bellinger has decided that the relics kept in Yale University Art Gallery dating from the period preceding the destruction of Dura, and therefore pre-256, contain knitting fragments.[9] Comparable

---

[6] Relics in Musée de l'Homme in Paris; H. E. Wulff, *The Traditional Crafts of Persia. Their Development, Technology and Influence on Eastern and Western Civilisations* (Massachusetts, 1966), pp. 228–30.
[7] H. E. Kiewe, *The Sacred History of Knitting* (Oxford, 1967).
[8] M. and A. Grass, *Stockings for a Queen. The Life of the Rev. William Lee, the Elizabethan Inventor* (London, 1967), p. 52.
[9] J. P. Wild, *Textile Manufacture in the Northern Roman Provinces* (Cambridge, 1970), pp. 59–60, 102–21, 138–9; R. Pfister and L. Bellinger, *The Excavations at Dura-Europos. Final Report, Part II, The Textiles* (New Haven, 1945), p. 54.

19.2   Brown woollen sock from the Fayûm

opinions are also frequently found in English, French and Austrian museums.[10] W. Endrei has determined that fragments of clothing found by a Hungarian expedition to Nubia and dating from the sixth–seventh centuries are knitting.[11] The Coptic striped socks from the sixth–eleventh centuries made from linen finished with woollen yarn on top, kept in the Umĕlecko-Průmyslové Museum in Prague are, in my opinion, the product of knotless netting. The second-century women's stockings found in Martre de Veyre and kept in Clermont-Ferrand, are made from cloth sewn together.[12] Some men's leggings kept in Délémont in Switzerland have provoked a lively discussion concerning not only their dating between the seventh and twelfth centuries but also the technique by which they were made.[13] The earliest Scandinavian relics have been carefully analysed and judged to be products of knotless netting.[14]

[10] A. F. Kendrick, *Catalogue of Textiles from Burying-Grounds in Egypt. II Period of Transition and of Christian Emblems* (London, 1921), pp. 88–91; J. C. Lamm, *Cotton in Mediaeval Textiles of the Near East* (Paris, 1937), pp. 157–8; R. Pfister, *Textiles de Halabiyeh (Zenobia) découverts par le Service des Antiquités de la Syrie dans la Nécropole de Halabiyeh sur l'Euphrate* (Paris, n.d.), p. 26; *Textiles de Palmyrie,* I–III (Paris, 1934–46); A. Riegl, *Die Ägyptische Textilfunde im K. K. Österreich. Museums Allgemeine Charakteristik und Katalog* (Vienna, 1889), p. 51.

[11] Nubie Abdallah-Nirgi, in the private collection of Dr Walter Endrei in Budapest. Also knitted, in my opinion, are the linen Coptic socks in the Oriental Department of the Hermitage in Leningrad.

[12] P. F. Fournier, 'Patron d'une robe de femme et d'un bas galloromains trouvés aux Martres-de-Veyre', *Bulletin Historique et Scientifique de l'Auvergne,* CXXVI (1956), pp. 202–3.

[13] F. Boucher, *Histoire du Costume en Occident de l'Antiquité à nos Jours* (Paris, 1965), p. 159; S. Müller-Christensen, *Vorbemerkung zu den Textilien in Gräber im Konigschar* (1972), p. 945; B. Schmedding, *Mitteralteriche Textilien in Kirchen und Klöstern der Schweiz* (Bern, 1978), pp. 98–9.

[14] Hald, *Oldanske Tekstiler* (see n. 1); M. Hald, 'Fra bar Fod til Strømpe' in *Om Strømper* (Valby, 1953), pp. 7–46; A. Geijer, *Birka, III Die Textilfunde aus den Gräbern* (Uppsala, 1938), pp. 128–32.

It seems clearly established that ancient Peru knew nothing about knitting before the Spanish invasion.[15] On the other hand, the discovery of two ivory knitting needles, 28 cm long (one of them damaged), speaks for the knowledge of knitting in ancient Gaul. They can be dated to the beginning of the second century AD and were found in the neighbourhood of Nîmes. They may perhaps have served for the knitting of silk.[16] All this fragmentary information deals with the relics dating from between the second and seventh centuries, and attempts to stress the need for further technological examination. It will help us to determine whether knitting had become established in certain leading centres of textile production in the Roman Empire, which would be essential for identifying the beginnings of knitting as an industry. The dating of the earliest knitting specimens in medieval Europe is not here the main question; rather, we must discuss the spread of the knowledge of the technique and its diffusion into much wider use.

Knitting relics in medieval Europe

The early knitting or knotless-netting products from the period between the second and seventh centuries were small in size and most of them were of one colour. Later specimens, determined more probably to be products of true knitting, have survived in larger fragments and contain many colours and sometimes a complicated pattern. L. Bellinger has described cotton stockings knitted in multi-coloured stripes, and has dated them to the beginning of the twelfth century.[17] They were found in Egypt, but he supposes them to have come originally from India. They were worked on two needles and involved considerable skill in the fashioning of the heel. I should rather judge them to be of Arabian origin, comparable to two fragments of a knitted fabric striped in several colours and kept at the Victoria and Albert Museum in London. Arabs are supposed to have worn woollen knitted shirts in the early Middle Ages,[18] and the surviving fragments seem to be part of such a garment. The level of Arabian knitting from the thirteenth century is evidenced in other remains surviving in Las Huelgas near Burgos in Castile. Figured knitting cushions, placed

[15] R. d'Harcourt, *Les Textiles Anciens du Pérou et leurs Techniques* (Paris, 1934), pp. 91–2, 122–3; 'Les textiles dans l'ancien Pérou', *Cahiers Ciba*, CXXVI (1960), p. 27; P. Keleman, 'Folk textiles of Latin America', *Textile Museum Journal*, I (1964), pp. 12–16.

[16] These items were found in 1906 and are now in the Musée Archéologique in Nîmes.

[17] L. Bellinger, 'Patterned stockings: possibly Indian found in Egypt', *Textile Museum Workshop Notes*, X (1954); Victoria and Albert Museum, T 87/1937, T 201/1929; there are large collections of medieval knitted stockings and socks in the Textile Museum in Washington and the Metropolitan Museum in New York.

[18] A. Mazahéri, *La Vie Quotidienne des Musulmans au Moyen Âge Xᵉ–XIIIᵉ siècle* (Paris, 1951), pp. 67, 71–4, 99, 271.

19.3   Indian or Arabic cotton patterned stockings, early twelfth century, found in Egypt

under the heads of dead Castilian kings and members of their families are the oldest and most interesting specimens of Arabian work. They have been referred to only in a general catalogue of the textile relics of Las Huelgas,[19] without any technological analysis, and are accessible only through a glass pane and are badly lit. Despite these unfavourable conditions, I judge them to be textiles produced by real knitting. A single inscription provides evidence of their Arabian origin. Those items should be considered in connection with the cushions found in many graves of that period. The majority of the cushion covers are figured silks, often threaded with gold, sometimes with coloured wools or embroidered stuffs, and mainly the products of tapestry, sprang and lace. The knitted cushions are the cheapest ones. With their ornamental style they were substituted for figured woven textiles, in the same way that later knitted carpets substituted for figured tapestries and waist-coats for whole suits sewn out of patterned cloth.[20]

The oldest cushion cover from Las Huelgas was found in the grave of Fernando de la Cerda who died in 1275. It is square, the sides being approximately 36 cm long. The pattern is composed of three colours – violet, gold and white – placed in quadrangles and octagons, presenting little houses, stars, eagles and flowers. The Arabic inscription contains the word 'blessing'. Another cushion was found in the grave of Fernando, son of Alfonso X, who died in 1283. Like the other one, it is made of woollen thread in greenish-brown, white and black, representing lions, stars, lilies and other flowers. Its dimensions are only 28 cm square. Both these specimens of Arab knitting deserve further examination. There is also a white glove, probably linen, surviving in the grave of the Infanta Mary, who died *c.* 1296. It is certainly knitted or netted, but it is not possible to analyse it further because of its bad state of preservation.

Among the knitted products of the early Middle Ages, the most frequent are liturgical gloves. Bishops and priests used them from the sixth or at the latest the seventh century. In one church inventory dating from the year 800, sixteen pairs of gloves are mentioned. Bishops' gloves were mostly knitted, while priests had gloves sewn out of woven cloth or leather. Knitted gloves were made from woollen or silk yarn, and less frequently from linen. The oldest surviving gloves are white; later they were black and violet, in accordance with the

[19] M. G. Moreno, *El Panteón Real de Las Huelgas de Burgos* (Madrid, 1946), pp. 21–3, 32–7, 85–90; J. L. y Montewerde, *Monasterio de Las Huelgas y Palacio de la Isla de Burgos y Monasterio de Santa Clara, de Tortesillas (Valladolid)* (Madrid, *c.* 1970), pp. 22–45; M. Dubuisson, 'La bonneterie au Moyen Age', *Bulletin of the Needle and Bobbin Club*, L, 1–2 (1967), pp. 40–4.

[20] I. Turnau and K. G. Ponting, 'Knitted masterpieces', *Textile History*, VII (1976), pp. 7–8. Another fragment of Arabian patterned knitting, made of twelfth–fourteenth century woollen thread, is in the Museum Kulturen in Lund, Sweden (no. KM 37716).

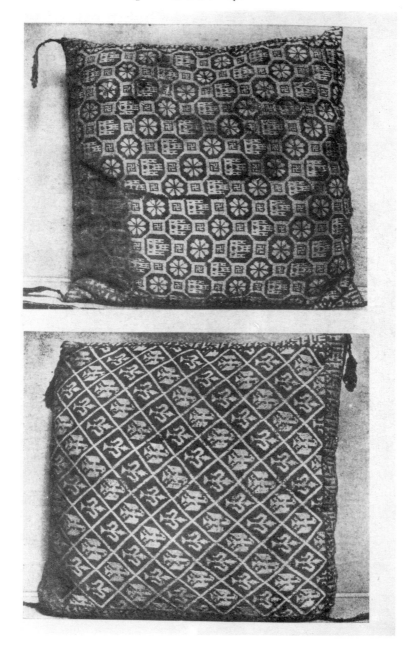

19.4   Patterned woollen knitted cushions, found in the tombs of Fernando de la Cerda, buried in 1275 (upper) and of Fernando, buried in 1283 (lower)

important liturgical colours. They have survived in church treasuries, and many of them are mentioned in the nineteenth-century literature dealing with liturgical clothes.[21]

The frequent use of knitted gloves in bishops' liturgical clothing is evidence in eleven images of seals dating from the years between 1200 and 1500. They are also shown in sculptures and illuminated manuscripts. Besides this indirect information, some thirty pairs of knitted gloves are still to be found in the keeping of church treasuries in southern or western Europe. Medieval church inventories mentioned great numbers of gloves: that of Cluny in 1382 notes twenty-two pairs of gloves; that of St Paul's Cathedral in London mentions three pairs in 1402, and one of the gloves kept in Prague is first mentioned in 1387. The general use of liturgical knitted gloves is confirmed by papal bulls of the eleventh and twelfth centuries. In form they had to fit the hand perfectly and have five elongated fingers and a long wristband (cuff) with a sacred symbol on the back of the hand. Not all of them were in fact knitted; S. Müller-Christensen has recently stated that a pair of bishop's gloves from the twelfth century in Königschar was produced by the knotless netting technique.[22] The majority of bishops' gloves were produced in women's convents.

Descriptions of Catholic liturgical clothes provide a good deal of information concerning the oldest knitted relics. The gloves kept in the treasury of the Saint-Sernin basilica of Toulouse, the so-called St Remi's gloves, can be dated from the style of the copper rosette to the thirteenth century. They are supposed to have belonged to the Joanittes Order in Jerusalem and may have followed an Arabian pattern. They seem to be of raw, uncoloured silk (though M. Dubuisson states them to be of linen), and they are rather coarsely knitted in a stocking stitch on two stout needles. A fragment of silk gloves found in the grave of an unknown bishop in the St Denis Abbey in Paris also dates from the thirteenth century.[23] A third pair of knitted gloves in red silk is kept in the abbey of St Bertrand at Comminges in the

[21] J. Braun, *Die liturgische Gewandung im Occident und Orient nach Ursprung und Entwicklung, Verwendung und Symbolik* (Freiburg im Breisgau, 1907), pp. 366–80; F. Bock, *Geschichte der liturgischen Gewändes Mittelalters oder Entstehung und Entwicklung der kirchlichen Ornate und Paramente in Rücksicht auf Stoff, Gewebe, Farbe, Zeichnung, Schnitt und rituelle Bedeutung nachgewiesen*, II (Bonn, 1866), pp. 137–47; Ch. Rohault de Fleury, *La Messe. Études archéologiques sur ses Monuments*, VIII (Paris, 1889), pp. 191–6; Ch. de Linas, *Anciens vêtements sacerdotaux et anciens tissus conservés en France* (Paris, 1860), pp. 197–236.

[22] Braun, *Die liturgische Gewandung* (see n. 21), pp. 366–80; de Linas, *Anciens vêtements sacerdotaux* (see n. 21), pp. 197–236; Hald, *Oldanske Tekstiler* (see n. 1), p. 314; Müller-Christensen, *Vorbemerkung* (see n. 13), p. 945.

[23] Dubuisson, 'La bonneterie' (see n. 19), p. 39; Braun, *Die liturgische Gewandung* (see n. 21), p. 369; de Linas, *Anciens vêtements sacerdotaux* (see n. 21), p. 197; M. T. J. Rowe, 'Fragments from the tomb of one unknown Bishop in Saint Denis, Paris', *Bulletin of the Needle and Bobbin Club*, L, 1–2 (1967), pp. 29–33.

Pyrénées and dates from the fifteenth century.[24] Other pairs of gloves mentioned in church catalogues have not survived to the present time. Such items are mentioned in Chartres, Troyes, Cambrai and Avignon; sometimes only the liturgical symbols placed on the back of the hand have survived.[25] One relic of the fourteenth century kept in the Cluny Museum in Paris is not a knitted textile, and another pair of red silk gloves is of a later period.[26]

A group of early liturgical gloves has survived in south Germany. Some of them have also been judged to be of knotless-netting work. Two pairs are kept in the cathedral treasury of Brixen; one of them is dated to about 1200, made out of bleached flaxen yarn, with rosettes sewn on top, and an embroidered cuff and rather wide fingers. Another pair, mentioned by Braun, dates probably from the fifteenth century.[27] Bock notes gloves from the abbey at Bamberg, mentioned in its 1483 inventory, but it seems that none of the seven pairs have survived.[28] Vast catalogues concerning liturgical clothes in the treasuries of German cathedrals mention medallions sewn on to the back of gloves and other relics from the sixteenth to nineteenth centuries.[29]

Knitted gloves are also found in Italy. The oldest relics are gloves from the twelfth or the beginning of the thirteenth century reproduced by Braun and kept in the St Trinity church at Florence. Similar specimens are also kept in the cathedrals of Narni and Anagni. Some Italian sculptures permit bishops' liturgical gloves to be identified, for example, the monument of Innocent IV who died in 1254.[30] Four pairs of liturgical gloves survived in England until the early twentieth century: one in St Thomas's church in Canterbury from the thirteenth century, two pairs in the treasury of St Paul's Cathedral in London and one in New College, Oxford.[31] A most interesting relic is the so-called St Adalbert's glove from Prague, dating from the

[24] *Les Trésors des églises de France, Catalogue* (Musée des Arts Décoratifs, Paris, 1965), pp. 269–72.

[25] Braun, *Die liturgische Gewandung* (see n. 21), pp. 366–80; M. Viollet Le Duc, *Dictionnaire raisonné du mobilier français de l'époque carlovingienne à la Renaissance*, III (Paris, 1873), p. 396; M. G. Houston, *Medieval Costume in England and France* (London, 1950), p. 35.

[26] E. Maillard, 'Le point à l'aiguille au XIVe siècle. Gant de l'abbé Pierre de Courpalay, + 1334', Musée de Cluny, *Hyphe*, I, 5–6 (1946), pp. 210–15. The second glove is probably from the later period according to Dubuisson, 'La bonneterie' (see n. 19), p. 39.

[27] Braun, *Die liturgische Gewandung* (see n. 21), pp. 370–2; S. Christensen-Müller, *Sakrale Gewänder des Mittelalters* (München, 1955), Abb. no. 59, catalogue no, 48; *idem, Vorbemerkung* (see n. 13), p. 945.

[28] Bock, *Geschichte* (see n. 21), p. 144; S. Christensen-Müller, *Das Grab des Pabsten Clemens II im Dom zu Bamberg* (München, 1960).

[29] Bock, *Geschichte* (see n. 21); Braun, *Die liturgische Gewandung* (see n. 21); de Linas, *Anciens vêtements sacerdotaux* (see n. 21).

[30] Bock, *Geschichte* (see n. 21), pp. 137–47; Braun, *Die liturgische Gewandung* (see n. 21); pp. 370, 377; Rohault de Fleury, *La Messe* (see n. 21), pp. 191–6; L. Hampel, 'Stricken und Wirken bis zum Jahre 1700', *Maschen. Geschichte der Mode der Strick-und Wirkwaren* (Wien, c. 1964), p. 11; A. Latour, 'Le bas en tricot', *Les cahiers Ciba*, LVI (1954), pp. 1948–9.

[31] Braun, *Die liturgische Gewandung* (see n. 21), pp. 37–47; Bock, *Geschichte* (see n. 21), pp. 140–7; de Linas, *Anciens vêtements sacerdotaux* (see n. 21), p. 217.

19.5   Flaxen liturgical glove of Bishop Otto II, buried 1192, from Brixen

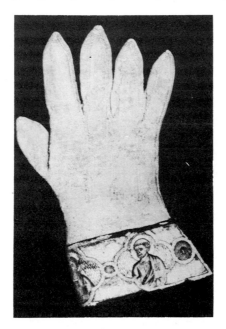

19.6   Silken liturgical glove of the late fourteenth century from a church near Prague

first half of the fourteenth century, knitted in stocking·stitch out of grey, perhaps natural, silk with three green stripes on the knitted cuff. Another knitted glove from the second half of the fourteenth century is kept in the church of St Vincelas at Staré Boleslavi, near Prague. It is knitted with fine needles out of colourless silk yarn and ornamented with coloured embroidery and golden threads on the cuff.[32] Icono-graphic evidence also shows the use of similar gloves in Silesia.[33]

The relatively large number of knitted liturgical gloves from between the twelfth and fifteenth centuries in various Catholic countries reveals the role of knitting in this period. Knitted gloves were also an element in lay attire. The working of five-fingered gloves required a highly developed technical skill in the use of silk and in fashioning. It should be remembered that in the Middle Ages gloves served not only to cover the hand, but were also a symbol of authority, dignity, grace and feeling. The giving or presenting of gloves may have expressed the concluding of a contract, and knights possessing a lady's glove were obliged to guard her honour. Flinging down a glove meant an open challenge, and the defeated party received the winner's glove as a token of victory. This custom was known in Poland from the beginning of the twelfth century.[34] The use of gloves, expensive and carefully made, had social meaning. The frequency of references to knitted gloves speaks for the diffusion of the technique of knitting.

Medieval knitted stockings and leggings have survived only in Switzerland and can be dated from the seventh to the twelfth century. The knitted leggings of Bishop Konrad von Sternberg (who was buried in Worms in 1192) have survived.[35] In the period before the fifteenth century, gloves, head covers and less frequently leggings, previously made out of cloth and sewn together, were knitted increasingly with knitting needles made out of bone or metal.

The remains of knitted garments found in northern Europe differ considerably from the objects that have been mentioned so far. They are mostly made from wool and produced by stout wooden needles. Few knitted specimens are to be found in Poland, Latvia or Russia, while the earliest Scandinavian ones are judged to be made by the knotless-netting technique. As for Poland, some six knitted fragments

[32] As in n. 31 above; M. Konopàsek, 'Nekolik poznamek k historii pletarske vyroby' [Some notes on the history of knitting], *Textilni Tvorba*, II, 9–10 (Prague, 1950), pp. 261–4; V. Rynes and B. Klosová, 'Oprava tzv. rukavice sv. Vojtěcha' [Conservation of the so-called glove of St Adalbert], *Památková Péče*, XXVI (1966), pp. 274–7; I. Turnau, 'Zabytki dziewiarskie w muzeach Pragi' [Knitting relics in the museums of Prague], *Kwartalnik Historii Kultury Materialnej*, XIII, 4 (1965), pp. 793–4.

[33] Our Lady of Klodzko (Glatz), Berlin, Deutsche Museum no. 1624 (pre-1939 reference).

[34] *Anonim tzw. Gall. Kronika polska* [Anonymous writer, called Gall. Polish Chronicle] (Wrocław, 1965), p. 124.

[35] Braun, *Die liturgische Gewandung* (see n. 21), pp. 401–2; Müller-Christensen, *Vorbemerkung* (see n. 13), p. 945.

have been found among textile relics in a twelfth- or thirteenth-century cemetery at Równina Dolna in the district of the vóivodship of Olsztyn. A. Nahlik has described these finds and suggests that these garments made of one-coloured, or light and dark striped woollen yarn were women's household work.[36] Their finishing reveals a high skill in working technique, but the lack of proper craftsman's fashioning and dressing is evident. In Latvia knitted objects dating from the fourteenth and fifteenth centuries have been found. There is a knitted cap, fastening under the chin, very like the English and German caps. Four pairs of secular gloves are made of good wool, two of them with five elongated fingers, and only the oldest thirteenth-century pair is made by the knotless-netting technique.[37] More extensive are the fragments of footwear from the eleventh and twelfth centuries, found in Bieloie Oziero, in the neighbourhood of Vologda and Novgorod. These excavation materials are kept in the Historical Museum of Moscow. Contrary to M. Dubuisson's assertion, they are made by knotless netting and not by knitting.[38]

The modest quantity of knitted relics discovered in Poland and Latvia does not permit any generalisation on the diffusion of hand knitting. That the technique was known is indisputable, and both it and crocheting were much in use.[39] The technical level of Baltic knitting in the fourteenth and fifteenth centuries seems to have been as high as in western Europe. For the production of worthwhile covers for the head, the hands and the feet, knowledge of fashioning is necessary, that is, adding or limiting the number of stitches. Practice in counting the stitches may have caused great difficulties to beginners, particularly in the making of gloves, and these are more easily made by the knotless-netting technique.[40] For caps the sprang technique was mostly used, and applied later to making belts. This is confirmed by thirteenth-century remains found in Hungary and Germany.[41] Knitting was then widely used for making shawls and other simple parts of clothing.

[36] A. Nahlik, 'Tkaniny z XII–XIV-wiecznego cmentarzyska w miejscowosci Równina Dolna, pow. Kętrzyn' [Cloth from the XII–XIVth century burial ground in the village of Równina Dolna near Kętrzyn, Poland], *Rocznik Olsztynski*, I (1958), pp. 171–91.

[37] A. Zarina, *Seno Latgalu apgērbs 7.–13. gs* (Riga, 1970), pp. 21–2 and 49 for the cap and the pair of gloves from the Historical Museum. The others are from the new excavations of the Latvian Academy of Sciences Institute of History.

[38] Dubuisson, 'La bonneterie' (see n. 19), pp. 36–8.

[39] G. Mikołajczyk, 'Początki dziewiarstwa w Polsce' [The beginnings of knitting in Poland], *Z Otchłani Wieków*, XXII (1953), pp. 157–9.

[40] For instance the glove of Gdańsk – J. Kaminska and A. Nahlik, *Włókiennictwo gdanskie* [The textiles of Gdańsk], (Łódź, 1958), p. 106.

[41] J. Höllrigl, 'A Csengödi ref. Tumplami kriptajanak leletei', [The finds in the crypt of Protestant church in Csengödi], *Archaeologiai Ertesito*, 49 (1936), pp. 49–66; Relics in Magyar Nemzeti Muzeum in Budapest; E. Heunemeyer, 'Zwei gotische Fraenhaarnetze', *Waffen und Kostumkunde*, I (1966), pp. 13–21; I. Petraschek-Heim, 'Die Goldhauben und Textilien der hochmittelalterlichen Gräben von Villach-Judendorf', *Neues aus Alt Villach*, XI, (1970), p. 118.

Development of knitting as an industry from the thirteenth century

An important advance in hand knitting was the introduction of four or five needles, instead of two. The oldest liturgical gloves show that this technique was known. It enabled the fashioning of complicated products to be more easily undertaken. The first indisputable iconographic proof dates only from the fourteenth century. The madonna from Ambrogio Lorenzetti's studio at Siena, painted in the second quarter of the fourteenth century, is shown knitting a child's ornamented frock, and she handles balls of coloured wool. The form of the frock suggests its working on four needles. This picture is, however, not so clear as a later madonna from about 1370, in which she can be seen to be making a child's frock on five needles (the picture is painted by Master Bertram from Munich, formerly in the convent of Benedictine Sisters in Buxtehude). A third madonna is shown in a sketch by Wit Stwosz, 'the Holy Family', of 1480–85.[42] It is difficult to identify this figure as knitting, since she holds a thread but no needles. R. L. Wyss, in his discussion of madonnas shown as thrifty women busy with various handworks, judges this picture to have been an image of hand knitting and supposes the artist had failed to show the needles which must have been used.[43] This view does not seem convincing, as Wit Stwosz was known to show the realities of everyday life in detail. The garment is, however, not finished, and was certainly not meant to be sewn together. Yet crocheting and sprang were not used for making larger items of clothing. The sketch had been done during the artist's stay in Poland, and he may perhaps have reproduced a female activity not remembered in detail from his home in Nürnberg. So there are some two or three iconographic documents providing evidence that the knowledge of knitting was a typical woman's occupation in Italy and south Germany in the fourteenth and fifteenth centuries. It can therefore be surmised that the discovery of knitting had occurred somewhere in the thirteenth century, at about the same time as that of the hand-spinning wheel, the wide horizontal loom and other technical devices in the textile industry discussed by W. Endrei in his book.[44]

The quantity of surviving knitting relics clearly increases in the fourteenth and fifteenth centuries, and in many works this period is

---

[42] M. Lemberg and B. Schmedding, 'Textilien' in *Abbeg-Stiftung Bern in Riggisberg, II* (Bern, 1973); date of the picture of Buxtehude (now in the Kunsthallein Humburg) from *Textile History*, III, cover; S. Sawicka, *Ryciny Wita Stwosza* [The engravings of Wit Stwosz] (Warsaw, 1957), p. 9, ill. 19b.

[43] R. L. Wyss, 'Die Handarbeiten der Maria. Eine Ikonographische Studie unter Berücksichtigung der Textilen Technique', *Artes Minores* (Bern, 1973), pp. 179–80.

[44] W. Endrei, *L'évolution des techniques du filage et du tissage du moyen âge à la révolution industrielle* (Paris, 1958).

19.7 Our Lady of Sienna, c. 1325–50

19.8   Our Lady of Buxtehude by Master Bertram of Munich, c. *1370*

19.9   *Our Lady engraved by Wit Stwosz, 1480–85*

seen as the one in which the technique was developed. But the earliest information about the craft of knitting in Paris reaches back to the year 1268 and later confirmations of their guild bear the dates 1366, 1380 and 1467. Knitters also had been working outside Paris, and there is evidence of knitters' journeymen visiting the towns of northern France.[45] Further craft guilds appear in Doornik (Tournai) in the southern Netherlands in 1429 and in Barcelona in 1496.[46] Small groups of knitters may have also been working in many other towns, and the beginning of the sixteenth century saw a number of confirmations of their guild statutes in France, Alsace and south Germany. 'Chapeliers de gants et de bonnets', mentioned by Etienne Boileau in 1292 did not, however, stand very high in the hierarchy of medieval crafts. They worked not only with woollen yarn, but are found protesting against the use of spinning wheels to process cotton. During the following two centuries their importance grew considerably and by the year 1514 they were one of the six most important Paris guilds.[47] The beginning of the craft in England has not been studied. London 'cappers', mentioned in the years 1300–11, produced felt caps rather than knitted ones. 'Hosiers' existed since at least 1328; they may have produced leggings sewn out of cloth, but knitted gaiters are mentioned from 1320.[48] Aberle states that Henry IV (1367–1413) had used knitted woollen stockings, while Henry VIII wore Spanish silk stockings, but little is known about the origins of knitted carpets, shirts, caps and stockings in England.[49] Henry VII ordered the wearing of knitted caps on feast days in 1488. This order provides evidence for falling production, of course, rather than the introduction of a new fashion. Between 1571 and 1597 it was 'obligatory for the non-gentry to wear an English-made cap of knitted wool on Sundays and holy days', an order which seems exceptional in that it attempts to assist production by means of compulsion applied to consumption. Another reference in 1461 speaks for the weak diffusion of other knitted articles in England.[50]

[45] P. Fort, *La bonneterie* (Cannes, 1951), p. 2; A. Franklin, *La vie privée d'autrefois. Arts et métiers, modes, moeurs, usages des Parisiens du XIIe au XVIIIe siècles*, IV (Paris, 1894), p. 34; XVI (Paris, 1896), pp. 272–95; B. Geremek, *Ludzie marginesu w średniowiecznym Paryżu* [Marginal people in medieval Paris], (Wrocław, 1971), pp. 257, 558.

[46] R. Leclerq, *Historique de la bonneterie dans le Tournaisis* (Hainaut, 1958), pp. 29–39; P. Molas Ribalta, *Los gremios barceleneses del siglo XVIII* (Madrid, 1970), p. 112.

[47] Endrei, *L'évolution* (see n. 44), p. 55; Udé, *Etude Générale* (see n. 3), pp. 4–5.

[48] G. Unwin, *The Guilds and Companies of London* (London, 1908), pp. 68–88, 114; W. Cunningham, *The Growth of English Industry and Commerce* (Cambridge, 1890), p. 397; Willet Cunningham, Cunnington and Beard, *Dictionary of English Costume* (see n. 3), pp. 260–1.

[49] C. Aberle, 'Geschichte der Wirkerei und Strickerei', *Geschichte der Textilindustrie* (Leipzig, 1932), p. 389; Dubuisson, 'La bonneterie' (see n. 19), p. 39.

The number of surviving knitted objects, chiefly head coverings, increases considerably in excavation materials dating from the fifteenth century. In the Museum of London and the Manchester Gallery of English Costume there are several scores of knitted caps from the late fifteenth and the sixteenth centuries. The oldest type is a head cover, fastening under the chin for wearing under a helmet in the Gothic fashion. Later round caps and berets developed, after the style of the Italian Renaissance. The products of the London knitters' workshops reveal the mass production of woollen head coverings that were fulled after they were knitted. These low-priced products of English cappers were widely used, but came to be out of fashion at the end of the fifteenth century. Excavation materials have also provided eleven fragments of stockings and knitted socks from the sixteenth century, or perhaps the end of the fifteenth, which are kept at the Museum of London. Worked on stout wooden or bone needles out of woollen yarn, they are not skilfully fashioned and did not fit the foot as well as later specimens made out of fine worsted yarn or silk. Great numbers of caps and knitted stockings of later periods have been found in various places in London and other towns in southern England. Further research might identify the situation of the workshops producing them. At present we can conclude that an extensive production of cheap woollen knitted garments had existed in England for more than a hundred years before the discovery of the knitting frame in about 1589.

Knitted head covers with earcaps, dating from the second half of the fifteenth century have been also found in excavations at Lübeck. K. Schlabow has described in detail their technique and shown how it is related to the oldest English caps. They were made in a low-quality natural wool.[51] Such knitted head covers may have been worn in many countries of northern Europe by the fifteenth century, although the surviving specimens date from the sixteenth century. A woollen beret, for instance, much like the later English relics, has been found in Trondheim in Norway.[52] The later woollen knitted caps worn in

---

[50] *Felkin's History of Machine-Wrought Hosiery and Lace Manufactures* (Newton Abbot, 1967), p. 16; N. B. Harte, 'State control of dress and social change in pre-industrial England', in D. C. Coleman and A. H. John (eds.), *Trade Government and Economy in Pre-Industrial England: Essays presented to F. J. Fisher* (London, 1976), p. 138; J. Thirsk wrote also: 'Even though no medieval archeological sites have yet yielded knitting needles or fragments of knitted fabric, it is difficult to believe that the art of knitting was unknown until the sixteenth, or, at best, the fifteenth century', see 'The fantastical folly of fashion', in N. B. Harte and K. G. Ponting (eds.), *Textile History and Economic History: Essays in Honour of Miss Julia de Lacy Mann* (Manchester, 1973), p. 53.

[51] K. Schlabow, *Spatmitteralterliche Textilfunde aus der Lübecke Altstadtgrabung* (Lübeck, 1952), p. 144; two knitted berets from the sixteenth century were found in Zadar in Yugoslavia – S. Petricioli, 'Kape i košulje' [Berets and shirts], *Vrulje*, I (Zadar, 1970), pp. 20–1, 64–6.

[52] In the Vodenskapsselskapets Oldsammling Museum in Trondheim.

Iceland are also similar.[53] We can differentiate four types of knitted head covers. The oldest are knitted nightcaps with an elongated head, which would have been easy to construct on two needles when the way of limiting the number of stitches was known. These early head covers have, however, not survived from the Middle Ages. The second type are caps made like hoods, or the modern pilot's cap, with earcaps tied sometimes under the chin. Berets, the third type, developed simultaneously at the end of the period. The fourth type is the knitted cap, but we have little information about this type, apart from the 1463 reference mentioned below.

The use of knitted textiles can also be studied on the basis of written sources. Fragments of French documents from the late Middle Ages,

[53] E. E. Gudjönsson, *Knitting in Iceland* (Reykjavik, 1979); R. Wild, *Kopfbedeckungen aus Europa* (Basel, 1964), p. 16.

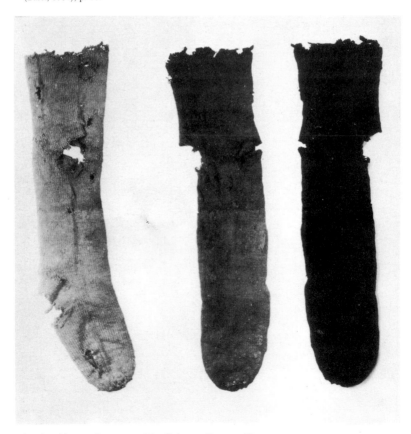

19.10   Sixteenth-century English woollen stockings

quoted in V. Gay's dictionary and by Dupont-Auberville, mention knitted gloves, leggings, stockings and head covers. Some examples are: 'Faiz à l'esguille' from 1387; 'Deux pairs de mittaines de laine faictes à l'auguille' from 1392, and finally from 1461: 'deux gants de prélat faits à l'esguille'. A reference in 1387 concerns the products of Parisian workers: '3 pairs de fine escarlete faictes à l'esguille'. The new technique was then already beginning to drive out leggings made from cloth. A 1463 reference provides evidence of the variety of knitted head covers: 'Pour deux chappeaux noirs fair à l'auguill'.[54] Further research in the archives, particularly the inventories including clothes and the study of ancient bills, might considerably increase the number of references revealing the use of the various knitted products in the different European countries. In the late Middle Ages these products were relatively cheap and – liturgical gloves excepted – destined for popular consumption. This is implied in the work of F. Piponnier on the dress of the court of the House of Anjou in the fourteenth and fifteeth centuries, though she did not find any direct reference to the use of knitted clothes.[55]

The existence of numerous knitters' guilds in west and central Europe by the beginning of the sixteenth century does not provide evidence for the start of a new branch of production, but it shows the increasing demand for knitted garments. This is connected with the growing fashion for knitted stockings, garments that became an indispensable element of Italian and Spanish Renaissance men's attire. Besides children's frocks, jackets and gloves, knitted berets become most fashionable. Fancy forms of the latter required elastic material. Thus as early as during the fourteenth and fifteenth centuries, the production of items of clothing knitted on two to five needles spread in Italy, Spain, France, the British Isles and in certain German countries. So the late medieval period had prepared the ground in western Europe for the technical revolution of the sixteenth and seventeenth centuries. The early period is therefore particularly interesting and requires further study of the material already possessed, as well as further excavation and a good deal of research into the documentary sources.

---

[54] V. Gay, *Glossaire archéologique du Moyen Âge et de la renaissance*, I (Paris, 1887), pp. 758–61; II (1928), p. 424.

[55] F. Piponnier, *Costume et la vie sociale: La cour d/Anjou XIVe–XVe siicle* (Paris, 1968); lately in the excavations at Saint-Denis a small woollen cap has been found dating from the early fourteenth century.

Index